A basic handb

A Reader's Guide concise and readable information on the characters, themes, and styles of the most important works of the European theater.

For each play:

- An annotated cast of characters
- A summary of the essential action
- A critical analysis
- An evaluation of the play in the context of the playwright's career and the development of European drama
- A biography of the playwright

Plus:

How to Read a Play

Matthew Grace was educated at Tufts College, Columbia University, and the University of Wisconsin. Professor Grace has studied and taught in France and is an assistant professor of English at Baruch College of the City University of New York. He has written on Restoration drama, Henry Fielding, Samuel Johnson, and Norman Mailer.

Abraham H. Lass is a well-known teacher, school administrator, and writer. He is the author of *How to Prepare for College, The College Student's Handbook* (with Eugene S. Wilson), *The Way to Write* (with Rudolf Flesch), and many other works.

A Reader's Guide to
50 European Plays
by Matthew Grace

with a Preface and Introductory Essay by Abraham H. Lass

WASHINGTON SQUARE PRESS

POCKET BOOKS • NEW YORK

A READER'S GUIDE TO 50 EUROPEAN PLAYS

WASHINGTON SQUARE PRESS edition published January, 1973

Published by
POCKET BOOKS, a division of Simon & Schuster, Inc.,
630 Fifth Avenue, New York, N.Y.

L

WASHINGTON SQUARE PRESS editions are distributed
in the U.S. by Simon & Schuster, Inc., 630 Fifth Avenue,
New York, N.Y. 10020 and in Canada by Simon & Schuster of Canada, Ltd., Richmond Hill, Ontario, Canada.

To Jane

Contents

Preface

> . . . ce principe certain de l'art, qu'il n'y a ni
> moralité ni intérêt au théâtre sans un secret
> rapport du sujet dramatique à nous.
>
> —Beaumarchais
>
> ([It is] . . . the unquestioned principle of art,
> that there is neither morality nor interest in
> the theater without a secret relationship be-
> tween the dramatic subject and ourselves.)

We are the protagonists of all the plays in this collection.
In every age and country, this has been the destiny of anyone who has engaged the dramatist.

To the questions, *What is drama? What is theater?* the
man of the theater has always made the same answer. The
theater, said Robert Edmond Jones, is "to be aware of
the *Now*." Said Shakespeare: "To show . . . the very age and
body of the time his form and pressure."

Every playwright lives in the world of his own day; each
one dramatizes his findings in his own fashion. Even when
he seems to be rejecting his role of interpreter, he cannot
escape it. Friedrich Dürrenmatt, speaking in an interview
of the dramatist's obligation to remain "an anarchist"—to
place himself between two stools—is just saying that he
refuses to be dogmatic; he has no simplistic solution to offer.
Eugène Ionesco, denying that he was laughing at the bourgeoisie in *The Bald Soprano,* insisted that he was trying to
evolve a free comic style like that of the Marx Brothers. But
Ionesco's comedy is as much a comment on his time as
Molière's is on his. And the reaction of the audience in each
period is a comment: how comfortably the Molière audience
laughed at his characters, and how uncomfortably we laugh

ix

at the people in the dark comedies and absurdist plays of today!

The plays in this volume, spanning years of intellectual revolution and social change, reflect the different attitudes toward man and his condition in each period, and the dramatists' different responses of styles. The "confrontation" between Corneille and Genet: where but in reading is it possible?

For the reader, indeed, many meetings of minds can be arranged: Büchner, author of *Woyzeck,* with Brecht, author of *Mother Courage and Her Children;* Racine, writing his *Phèdre,* with Anouilh, writing his *Antigone.*

The pleasure of comparison and contrast can offer the reader an opportunity to gain perspective on today's theater. He can see for himself how we have come to the content and style of the present; he can also decide for himself what is worth preserving in the repertory of the theater.

Reading a book of plays is always important because drama passes from the scene—literally and figuratively—all too soon. It is even more important when the plays are "foreign," when we have been prevented by accidents of birth, geography, or economics from seeing them in their original productions.

No editor could make a selection of fifty European plays that would satisfy every reader. The scope of such a book is too challenging. Yet we have tried to include plays that still live, not only in the memory of playgoers but in active repertory and revival.

We hope to reach a number of readers: those who have seen some of the best plays from Europe and wish to know about others; those who have still to discover any European plays earlier than last season's Broadway or off-Broadway hits; those who have seen or read many European plays and need to refresh their memory. Meeting and understanding—on the printed page—the characters, themes, and styles of these plays, the student can go on to experiencing them—in production—much more richly.

For each play, as introduction or as review, we offer the following:

1. An annotated cast of characters.
2. A summary of the action of the play.

3. A digest of contemporary critical opinion of the play, placing it in its proper context in the playwright's career and in the development of European drama.
4. A biography of the playwright.

If the plays in this collection have anything in common, despite their differences in age and quality, it is their ability to give both pleasure and insight to the reader as well as to the spectator.

What in the end differentiates one playwright from another; what is the special quality? Chekhov, always illuminating, said it is not a matter of style. In *The Sea Gull*, Trepleff, settling himself to write, and discarding one phrase after another, says:

. . . It's agonizing *(a pause)*. I come more and more to the conviction that it is not a question of new and old forms, but what matters is that a man should write without thinking about forms at all, write because it springs freely from his soul.

It may seem strange that we come down to such a word as "soul" in summing up what may be gained from studying these plays from different lands and times; yet even today, or especially today, a backward glance at these plays may help us to understand the way of the world. Each drama has been presented (as the billboards used to say) "in the principal capitals of Europe." They reveal aspects of thought and behavior so varied that in the animal world they could only be exhibited by different species. Yet they are man. They are all ourselves; nothing is alien to us.

"There are many realities," says Daisy to Bérenger in Ionesco's *Rhinoceros*. "Choose the one that's best for you. Escape into the world of imagination."

ABRAHAM H. LASS

How to Read a Play

> I am the playwright. I show what
> I have seen. In mankind's markets
> I have seen how humanity is traded. That
> I show, I, the playwright.
> —Bertolt Brecht, "The Playwright's Song"

"I am the reader," you say; "I want to know what the playwright has seen. Am I at a disadvantage, reading instead of seeing the play?"

Of course, we'd all prefer to experience these plays in performance: to know the "special alchemy composed of words, sounds, gestures, lines, movements, rhythms, and silences," as Louis Jouvet, the great French actor-manager, put it.

But in every good reader of plays, there can be a good actor-manager. *By indirections find directions out,* runs the line in *Hamlet.* From the dramatist's clues, the reader brings the play to life. As his own producer and director, he chooses the cast, designs sets and costumes, blocks out exits and entrances, determines the pace of the action, cues off-stage music and sound.

Sometimes the play-reader may even have the advantage over the play-viewer. Frank O'Connor has told the story of how, when he was directing Chekhov's *The Cherry Orchard* for an Irish community theater in Cork, he was defeated by the wonderful scene when the two sisters are chattering in the dawn with the shepherd's pipe sounding in the distance. He had no way of making a sound like a shepherd's pipe. And even if he had, how was he to get that audience to identify it as a shepherd's pipe? How could that pipe have the same unearthly effect on a Cork audience that it must have had for a Russian one? When you read the play, listen for that pipe: you will hear it well enough if there is wide-awake collaboration between you and the playwright.

"The process of reading is not a half-sleep, but, in the highest sense, a gymnast's struggle," says Benjamin DeMott in his book *Supergrow*. He continues:

"The reader is to do something for himself, must be on the alert, must himself or herself construct . . . the text furnishing the hints, the clue, the start or framework."

The reader's act of creation! And how is he to do all this? The secret lies not so much in *how* as in *when*. For the reader has one enormous advantage over the playgoer: the curtain rises and falls only when *he* wants it to. A good stage performance is like heightened living; it's over before we've realized its meaning. The reading of a play, on the other hand, is as leisurely, as deliberate as we want to make it. We have time to turn back a page or reread a scene or an act, time to make a note, time to reread the whole play.

Plays should be read at least twice. A play is like an iceberg; what's on the surface is often nothing to what's beneath it.

At first reading—a quick, light reading—we read for narrative, for plot outcome, for first impressions of character. The second time around, we know enough about these people to understand much, much more: the inner action, "the motive and the cue to passion."

When we read novels and short stories, we sometimes learn as much about the characters from the authors' comments as from the characters' speeches and actions. When we read a play, however, we have at best the fragmentary stage directions and single-line descriptions of the characters that the dramatist chooses to provide; most of the time, we understand what makes these people tick by listening to their words and looking at their actions: "listening" with the mind's ear, "looking" with the mind's eye. What makes the problem—an exciting problem to solve—is that the words on the page are only half the story. The text is deceptive. We must (on that second reading) translate the *sub*text and the *sub*plot.

In real life, we are aware that what people say and do are not necessarily what they think and feel. At any given moment, we may be saying A, doing B, thinking C, and feeling XYZ. We say (A), "It will be fun to drive out to see

...e Richie and Aunt Liz today." But (B) we take a cou-
of aspirins to assuage a slight headache that has come
at the thought of the Merritt Parkway on a Sunday; we
wonder why Ellen insists on wearing that color green;
and (XYZ) we feel a sudden desire to go upstairs and play
our latest recordings while we eat peanut brittle and read
the paper.

In many plays, we find characters making brilliant, pointed
remarks about themselves and other people; but as the play
ends, we see that the characters have done just the opposite
of what they have declared they would do. In *The Sea Gull*,
for example, Trepleff attacks the theater for its many flaws:
"We need new forms, and if we can't have them, then it's
better to have nothing at all!" Yet Trepleff's own play, when
it is produced, is very bad indeed; the disparity between what
he says about the theater and what he produces for it is part
of Trepleff's character.

If we understand the subtext of a scene, we can imagine
the tempo, rhythm, and pitch it would have in performance.
Actors indicate changes of thought through changes in voice
—inflection, tone, pitch, pause—as well as through changes
in position and through gesture and movement.

Not to understand the subtext is often to miss the point of
the characters entirely. The critic Walter Kerr has pointed
out, in "Hide-and-Seek with Chekhov" (*New York Herald
Tribune*, August 9, 1964), how easy it is to get off on the
wrong track if one believes that Chekhov's characters know
themselves: actors speak "as though no one of these folk
was in any way blind or foolish or self-deceiving. . . . Yet
Chekhov does, very frequently, make it perfectly clear that
nothing his characters say can really be taken at face value.
As a rule, what they say can almost be taken at reverse
value." (Trofimov, in *The Cherry Orchard*, for example:
how are we to take his solemn apostrophes to a better future
and his condemnations of people "who do nothing but talk"?
As complete earnestness, or, in Mr. Kerr's words, "wonderful wind, sublime and delicate fatuousness"? The difference
in our reading of the subtext will make all the difference in
tone between heaviness and comedy, between seeing Trofimov as he sees himself or seeing him as just another man
who does nothing, eternally, but talk.)

To bring to life on the stage of our mind the characters

we are reading about, we must become wholly involved them. Who is each person, where does he come from, whe is he going, whom is he expecting to meet, what is he expecting to find?

Writing about the drama, George Bernard Shaw said, "It is no mere setting up of the camera to nature: it is the presentation in parable of the conflict between Man's will and his environment: in a word, of problems."

In discovering the subplot, the reader sees the conflict and crisis in the life of the main character. The conflict may be between two sides of his own self as well as between his will and his environment. In coming to grips with the conflict, he makes an important discovery about himself or about others that changes the way he thinks or feels, and this discovery alters his direction. The reader, in suspense, asks, Which way will he go?

Strindberg, in the pre-Freudian framework of *Miss Julie*, presents the drama as a conflict of the will, but the will is extremely complex. In the conflict between mistress and valet in this play (as in the conflict between husband and wife in *The Father*), the characters reveal themselves and also expose each other as contradictory and complex.

In drama, to understand people in the context of their lives, we must pick up clues of mood, tone, and style in the dialogue; we must be alert to symbols. In *The Cherry Orchard*, we see Varya's keys at her waist and recognize that she is mistress of the house, not of herself; we see Gayeff's recital of hypothetical billiard shots, when he should have been noticing that the sky was falling in, and know him for the languid, escapist fool he is. In Ibsen's *An Enemy of the People*, we have only to hear Peter Stockmann's diatribe against hot meat for supper to understand that he is the Nay-sayer to life, as his brother Thomas is the Yea-sayer.

(E. M. Forster, in "Ibsen the Romantic," has brilliantly collected the symbols in the plays: "The symbolism never holds up the action, because it is part of the action, and because Ibsen was a poet, to whom creation and craftsmanship were one." Forster cites the white horse in *Rosmersholm*, the harps and voices that Hilda hears in *The Master Builder*, the fire of life in *Ghosts*.)

To re-create living characters, the reader does well to see them in the setting the playwright has designed for them.

In *Ghosts,* there is not only the glow of the gutted buildings of the burning orphanage in Mrs. Alving's drawing room, but the constant Norwegian rain; both are vital to comprehending the people in the drama. *Miss Julie* is something of a tour de force of psychological compression; in the preface, Strindberg says, "With regard to the scenery, I have borrowed from impressionistic painting its asymmetry, its terse and pregnant concision, and in this way I think I have increased the possibilities for creating illusion." (How Strindberg would have enjoyed such "scenery" as, for example, our contemporary Beckett has provided for *Waiting for Godot* and *Endgame!*)

Nothing in the play, not the smallest "property," is without some significance to the characters in it. The story is told of the great actor Salvini rehearsing on a stage that was empty except for one chair. At last Salvini could stand it no more and cried out, "When do I break the chair?"

Most of us are better at seeing with the mind's eye than listening with the mind's ear; yet some of the most effective clues the playwright gives us are found in music or sound effects. The most famous effect in all European drama, of course, is the slamming of the door at the end of the last act of *A Doll's House,* when Nora leaves Helmer—although a close second would be the sound of the chopping down of the cherry trees in the orchard at the close of Chekhov's play.

Reading a play involves more than imaginative looking and listening. It can be an exercise of that deeper imagination that Coleridge called the "modifying power": the ability to turn observation of the ordinary into an alchemy of insight. In reading Giraudoux's *The Madwoman of Chaillot,* for example, we must go beyond the enchanting comic portrait of the countess and her lovely zanies from the Paris *quartiers*—mad or sane in our mad times?—to see "the pimps who little by little have taken over the world" and Giraudoux's faith in man's goodness and ability to dispose of the pimps by sending them down into the bowels of the earth, as the mad countess sends the profiteers down the *oubliette* leading to the sewers.

What can drama give us? What do we want of the theater? There have always been almost as many answers as there have been play-readers and playgoers. Chekhov believed the dramatist was a sort of impartial witness. In a letter to

Suvarin, he says that Shtcheglov-Leontyev blamed him for finishing a story with the words: "There's no making out anything in this world," because he thought that a writer who is a good psychologist ought to be able to make it out—that is what he is a psychologist for. "But I don't agree with him," says Chekhov. "It is time that writers, especially those who are artists, recognized that there is no making out anything in this world, as once Socrates recognized it, and Voltaire too."

Such dramatists of our Theater of the Absurd today as Ionesco, Beckett, and Genet would find this letter to Suvarin most sympathetic. They do not try to explain either history or man's nature, giving us almost always the echoes of their personal anguish in their plays. Yet Bertolt Brecht is aware of his responsibilities to his audience, to the public born of his own time. The theater can never be the platform of any one of these dramatists; it is made of many dimensions to which they all contribute their gifts.

All dramatists, like all poets, seek a metaphor for man in his world. In these days, we are perhaps seeing the beginning of a critical (and a popular) reaction against one metaphor, man as "absurd": a reaction against the so-called Theater of the Absurd and its related theater of the sordid and the trivial. In 1964, shortly before his death, the great Irish playwright Sean O'Casey, writing in *The Atlantic* about *The Bald Primaqueera* (with only a nod to Ionesco's *The Bald Soprano*), said magnificently what many readers and audiences have felt for some time:

> The future is to have the inheritance of the theater of the ridiculous, of the absurd, of rape, of murder and sudden death, of incest, of futility, of violence, and of a basilisk pot of sexual distortions, and the land of Hope and Glory will disappear beneath the mud of a dull inferno. . . .

> Ah, to hell with the loutish lust of Primaqueera. There are still many red threads of courage, many golden threads of nobility woven into the tingling fibers of our common humanity. No one passes through life scatheless. The world has many sour noises; the body is an open target for many invisible enemies, all hurtful,

some venomous. . . . It is full of disappointments . . . a world that aches bitterly till our time here ends. Yet, even so, each of us, one time or another, can ride a white horse, can have rings on our fingers and bells on our toes, and if we keep our senses open to the scents, sounds and sights all around us, we shall have music wherever we go.

ABRAHAM H. LASS

A Reader's Guide to
50 European Plays
by Matthew Grace

Mandragola

by

NICCOLÒ MACHIAVELLI (1469–1527)

The Characters

Callimaco—a young Florentine who has spent most of his life in Paris. His return to Florence is motivated by the fame of beautiful Lucrezia. Aristocratic, brutal, and lustful, Callimaco sees women as an instrument of pleasure. He has no taste for romantic love.

Ligurio—an unscrupulous and clever parasite who lives by his wits. He exploits Callimaco's lust, Nicia's folly, and Fra Timoteo's greed.

Nicia—a rich old lawyer whose desire to have children is stronger than his regard for Lucrezia's virtue and his own honor. Foolish, overcautious, and gullible, he is an easy dupe.

Lucrezia—a pious and obedient wife, she is also human enough to realize that pleasure is more important than morality.

Sostrata—Lucrezia's mother, extremely practical and forthright, does not hesitate to compromise her daughter's virtue.

Fra Timoteo—opportunistic, scheming, and avaricious, he uses his influence as a churchman to satisfy his greed.

Siro—Callimaco's wily and loyal servant.

1

The Story

Set in Florence in 1504, *Mandragola* opens with a spoken verse prologue that describes the *dramatis personae:* "A lover wan, a lawyer, none too bright,/ And two more still:/ A wicked friar, a scheming parasite." A chorus of nymphs and shepherds announces that desire and sensuality are the only antidotes to life's pain.

In a Florentine square, Callimaco and his servant, Siro, meet to discuss the seduction of Lucrezia. Callimaco tells how he was lured back to Italy from a life of pleasure and intrigue in Paris when a fellow-countryman described the ravishing Lucrezia, wife of Nicia Calfucci. Callimaco's first glimpse of the young woman throws him into a frenzy of desire. Although Lucrezia is married to an older man, she is a paragon of virtue, modesty, and piety. Only three facts give Callimaco hope: Nicia's foolishness, his desire to have children, and the earthy worldliness of Sostrata, Lucrezia's mother.

Ligurio, a conniving former marriage broker who lives by his wits and sponges meals from Callimaco, has promised to help the young man seduce Lucrezia. Nicia is planning a trip to some mineral baths to cure himself and his wife of their childlessness. Ligurio has pledged to keep Callimaco informed of their travels so that he may insinuate himself into Lucrezia's presence. Callimaco and Siro withdraw as Nicia and Ligurio enter discussing the prospective voyage. Nicia does not like to travel. He is ludicrously cautious, distrusts everyone, and is frightened of exposing his wife to the world. When Nicia leaves to consult doctors, Callimaco and Ligurio lay plans for the older man's undoing. They decide to dissuade Nicia from going to the baths because Lucrezia might meet a richer and more handsome seducer than Callimaco. Instead, Callimaco will disguise himself as a doctor and devise some way to enter Lucrezia's company.

Ligurio finds Nicia and introduces him to Callimaco, who is dressed as a doctor and spouts Latin to impress the wealthy lawyer. Callimaco says that he will give Nicia a potion of mandrake root that has brought fertility to all the kings and princes of France. Lucrezia must drink the potion and have intercourse with a third person, for the first man who sleeps with a woman who has drunk the potion will surely die within a week. At first Nicia says, "I don't want to make my wife a whore and myself a cuckold." But he is induced to follow the plan when his two deceivers promise to find a tramp in the marketplace and throw him into bed with Lucrezia. In order to gain Lucrezia's assent to the scheme, Ligurio says that her confessor, Fra Timoteo, and her mother, Sostrata, must be engaged as accomplices.

When Ligurio and Nicia confront Sostrata with the necessity of compromising her daughter to make her fertile, she readily agrees. They go off to find Fra Timoteo, who is in the process of advising a young widow guilty of fornication. She must give money to the Church and pray. When Ligurio and Nicia, who pretend to be deaf, confront the priest, the former marriage broker says that Fra Timoteo must convince a girl to have an abortion. The priest agrees because he is offered a large sum of money. But after he has compromised his principles, news arrives that the girl has miscarried. Once in Ligurio's power, however, Fra Timoteo agrees to use his influence to persuade Lucrezia to sleep with a stranger.

When the others leave, Fra Timoteo reveals that he has understood Ligurio's motives, but that he will outfox them all and get Nicia's money for himself. Sostrata convinces her daughter to confide in the priest and to take his advice. Fra Timoteo argues that fear of evil is greater than evil itself, and "As for the act itself, it is foolish to call that a sin, for it is the will that commits a sin, not the body; the real sin is to displease your husband, and you will be pleasing him; or to take pleasure in the act, and you will not take pleasure in it." Lucrezia reluctantly consents to follow the advice of her mother and her confessor.

Callimaco, in a transport of ecstatic anticipation, is encouraged by Ligurio's news of success. Callimaco will disguise himself and allow Nicia and Ligurio to kidnap him and throw him in bed with Lucrezia. Once he has gained his object, Callimaco must explain the plot and convince Lucrezia to continue the secret liaison or be exposed as a whore. The fertility potion (really a mild sedative and aphrodisiac) is given to Lucrezia, who drinks it and goes to bed. Ligurio, Siro, Nicia, and Timoteo, who has disguised himself as the doctor, set upon Callimaco, who is dressed as a minstrel, and hustle him off to Lucrezia's bedroom.

A few hours later, they eject the disguised Callimaco from Lucrezia's house, and Nicia describes how Sostrata and he examined the "doomed" lover and put him in bed with Lucrezia. Callimaco confides to Ligurio how Lucrezia was pleased with him as a lover: "Since your cunning, the folly of my husband, my mother's lack of scruple and the wickedness of my confessor have combined to make me do what I would never have done on my own, I can only believe that some divine influence has willed this, and it is not for me to resist what Heaven decrees." The lovers arrange for future assignations and avow their love.

Everyone meets in the square and goes to church. Fra Timoteo is promised the money, Nicia invites Callimaco (who is still disguised as the doctor) to be a constant visitor in his household, and Siro and Ligurio are handsomely rewarded for their loyalty to Callimaco's plan.

Critical Opinion

In the verse prologue to *Mandragola* (c. 1518), Machiavelli declares that he is immune to the jeers, spite, and malice of the audience: "This man [the author] is malicious, too;/ Malice, indeed, his earliest art, and through/The length and limits of all Italy/He owes respect to none; though I agree/ He'll fawn and do/Service to richer, smarter folk than he." The cynicism of these lines is not merely a pose, for Machiavelli believed that men were essentially hypocritical, cowardly, and self-seeking and that normal, conventional measures of virtue and vice ignored the realities of human nature. In *The Prince* and *Discourses,* Machiavelli candidly set forth his conception of how man acts in an essentially immoral society. By expecting the worst, an individual may succeed if he is vicious, ruthless, and cynical.

Callimaco's desire for Lucrezia is totally devoid of romantic sentiment; he has left Paris solely to satisfy his curiosity about a beautiful woman whose virtue seems to be immune to the world's temptations. He does not hesitate to dissimulate, bribe, and bully his way into her bed. Once he attains his goal, he plans to resort to blackmail in order to prolong his pleasure. At one point, he loses his objectivity because of his sexual obsession, but he never fools himself into believing in romantic love. The plot to seduce Lucrezia becomes nearly as important as the gratification of Callimaco's lust. In a moment of misgiving, he is less concerned with sentiment or with sexual conquest than with his loss of self-control: "Even my legs are trembling, my stomach fluttering. My heart is pounding as though it would burst. . . ." These might very well be the words of Romeo deeply in love with Juliet; yet Callimaco is the quintessence of the Machiavellian lover, obsessed with his goal of sexual domination and uninterested in the moral and spiritual results of his actions.

Ligurio, the prime mover of the plot to compromise Lucrezia, understands the world's corruption and exploits it with consummate adroitness. Nicia's vanity, timidity, and gullibility are manipulated so that the husband is the most enthusiastic proponent of his own deception. Delighting in his own cuckoldom, the old fool examines the body of the "doomed" man to be sure of his virility and cleanliness; he literally puts Callimaco into bed with his wife to ensure the consummation of the adultery.

Sostrata entertains no qualms about her daughter's virtue and falls easy prey to Ligurio's arguments. She believes that the end always justifies the means. "If there is no other way to have children, then, conscience permitting, you must take this one." This problem of conscience will easily be overcome because Ligurio knows Fra Timoteo can rationalize any sin by twisting theology and morality to suit his needs. The prospect of wealth overcomes religious commitment, and the Bible is distorted to serve his personal ends. Fra Timoteo is not really duped by Ligurio, for he is as shrewd and self-serving as any Machiavellian. He allows himself to be used because he is sure of being rewarded by the plotters; he cleverly observes that by pretending to be fooled he will ingratiate himself with his would-be deceivers and may betray them at his discretion.

Lucrezia might very well have been the object of pity had Machiavelli not plainly indicated that her virtue and piety are aspects of feminine vanity. She is worldly enough to know that the temporal demands of her confessor, mother, and husband take precedence over the divine laws of morality. When she discovers her true situation, she readily complies with Callimaco's plan to continue the deception. Pragmatism and sensuality triumph over conjugal devotion and piety.

Machiavelli employs classic comic types to depict universal situations. He eases the audience's moral prejudices by removing the action from the arena of individual moral choice to a general context. The impetuous, violent lover, the old, foolish husband and his easily compromised young wife, the corrupt priest, the practical mother, and the scheming parasite have traditionally appeared in comedy from the Roman times.

Machiavelli's debt, in particular to Terence and Plautus, who wrote in the second century before Christ, extends from his use of stereotypes to his observance of what Renaissance critics called "the classical unities." All the action takes place in a square that is surrounded by the houses of Callimaco and Nicia and Fra Timoteo's church. The events cover less than twenty-four hours; lapses of time are nonrealistically handled by allowing action to be compressed to ignore chronological verisimilitude, as when Siro accomplishes his errands with unbelievable alacrity.

The classical nymphs and shepherds who comment upon the action at the conclusion of the prologue and first four acts are the chorus that summarizes the play's events and philosophy and establishes the playwright's moral attitude: "We know that life is brief,/With no reward but pain,/So we desert the fight and give Desire rein." Their comments are often ironic, however, for references to love and joy are quite pagan and reflect the Roman and Machiavellian view that sexual gratification is the only substantial aspect of human love. Here Machiavelli departed from the Renaissance tradition that held physical love to be a path to divine and spiritual fulfillment. Dante's adulation of Beatrice was resolved in the poet's worship of her divinity, wisdom, and beauty. Castiglione's ideal of courtly love emphasized the union of the flesh and spirit. But Callimaco's unalloyed lust cannot encompass any appreciation of Lucrezia's spiritual merit or the moral consequences of his actions.

Unlike the comedies of Shakespeare, Jonson, or Molière, *Mandragola* does not end with the unmasking of vice and the marriage of the virtuous. Christian society is ruthlessly satirized because traditional concepts of love, marriage, chastity, and order are irrelevant in Machiavelli's "real" world. Gullibility is punished when Nicia is cuckolded, but even he is delighted with the deception and does not learn any lesson from the experience. Lucrezia is converted from a virtuous wife to a lustful and deceiving adulteress who has been taught the ways of the world. Callimaco and Ligurio triumph because they are ruthless, obsessed, and devoid of any ideals.

In Machiavelli's satire, everyone is exploited by his own duplicity. Fra Timoteo quietly acknowledges that he is being used by Ligurio but skillfully takes advantage of the situation, realizing that nothing is so important to a schemer than to remain undiscovered. Callimaco, too, knows he is being exploited by Ligurio, but understands that this parasite can be useful. Nicia cruelly abuses his wife's love and virtue and is ironically duped by his own lack of respect for her.

Slapstick, *double entendre,* and burlesque of Latin add to the comedy inherent in the situation. When Nicia is told to feign deafness so that he will not bungle the interview with Fra Timoteo, he cannot resist commenting upon Ligurio's munificent offers on his behalf. The frequent references to Lucrezia's happiness mean different things to each character. Callimaco, of course, is thinking of her sexual pleasure; but her husband refers to the joy of motherhood and the spiritual gratification she will receive after she drinks the potion. When Nicia hears Callimaco's Latin, he is immediately convinced that the young man is indeed a doctor of great learning. The Latin, however, is obscene and often irreverent. The scene satirizes Latin-spouting doctors (Molière's favorite target) and their gullible patients, as well as ignorant lawyers. The frequent use of asides to the audience emphasizes the multileveled action. Machiavelli reminds the audience that *Mandragola* is indeed a play, not a slice of life.

The play's title, *The Mandrake,* is an ironic comment on man's superstitious nature. A mandrake root, shaped like a man, supposedly contained medicinal and magical qualities. In the next century, John Donne referred to it in his famous "Song": "Go and catch a falling star,/Get with child a mandrake root." But superstition, idealism, and wishful thinking play no part in Machiavelli's moral universe. Perhaps because of its hard-core cynicism, *Mandragola* has been infrequently praised in modern times.

Although Machiavelli will inevitably be remembered best for his political theorizing in *The Prince,* he has given us in *Mandragola* a wittier contribution to social criticism. If this classic Italian comedy of Renaissance intrigue remains in the repertory of the theater, it is because of both its timeless satire of human gullibility and its exposure of sixteenth-century corruption and folly. The comic invention is delightful, and in such scenes as those in which Callimaco poses as a wonder-working doctor, Machiavelli is established as a superb satiric comedian.

The Author

Born in Florence during the rule of the Medici, Machiavelli was educated in the Italian and Roman (but not Greek) classics. In 1494, after the Medicis had been ejected from Florence, Machiavelli entered government service and became secretary and second chancellor of the government before he was thirty years old. Numerous diplomatic missions allowed him to observe the conduct of wily politicians who conducted foreign policy in various parts of Europe. During his service in the government, the young man engaged in military studies and revamped Florence's militia.

After his marriage in 1502, Machiavelli did not remain faithful to his wife, but seemed nevertheless to have a close relationship with her. In 1504, he published *Annals of Italy* and a comedy, now lost, entitled *Le Maschere.* His years of government service were abruptly terminated in 1512 when his government fell to the Medicis, and he was deprived of his offices and property. Tortured, imprisoned, and humiliated, Machiavelli retired to a farm outside of Florence where he began work on *The Prince,* which he completed in 1513. This famous work derived from the longer *Discourses,* which advanced the concept of the modern state. Several other literary works, most notably *Mandragola* (c. 1518), were composed during Machiavelli's enforced retirement. *Clizia* is a comedy that, like *Mandragola,* describes intrigues, but it is also an intimate portrait of Florentine domestic life. *Belfagor,* a novel, was also completed before Machiavelli returned to public life as a military and political adviser. He died a year later, in 1527.

Le Cid

by

PIERRE CORNEILLE (1606–1684)

The Characters

Don Rodrigue—Don Diègue's handsome and brave son. Despite his attachment to Chimène, he is able to put honor before love. His heroism, dignity, and wisdom are constant. When he leads Castile to victory over the Moors, he earns the legendary title, "the Cid."

Chimène—Count Gomez' beautiful young daughter, profoundly in love with Don Rodrigue. To avenge her father's death, she struggles against her passion, but is incapable of giving Don Rodrigue up.

Don Gomez—a proud and egotistical nobleman, one of Seville's great generals. When he is not appointed the prince's tutor, Don Gomez jealously insults his friend, Don Diègue, and provokes a duel.

Don Diègue—an old and dignified aristocrat, one of Castile's glorious warriors. He relies on his son to uphold the family's honor.

The Infanta—a beautiful Castilian princess. She conceals her love for Don Rodrigue to maintain her royal dignity.

Don Fernand—the just and understanding king of Seville.

Don Sanche—passionately in love with Chimène and her champion in a duel against Don Rodrigue.

Léonor—The Infanta's governess and confidante, who advises her mistress to be prudent.

Elvire—Chimène's governess and confidante, who counsels her mistress to forget vengeance for Don Rodrigue's sake.

The Story

In an elegant Spanish villa during the eleventh century, Chimène and her governess, Elvire, discuss Chimène's future marriage. Elvire assures her mistress that Don Gomez approves of his daughter's choice of Don Rodrigue. At present, Don Gomez is at court, where he expects to be chosen as the prince's tutor. When he returns, he will probably arrange for Chimène's union with Don Rodrigue. Despite this good news, Chimène fears something will go wrong.

Meanwhile, in the palace, the Infanta and her confidante, Léonor, are also discussing Chimène and Don Rodrigue. The Infanta confesses that she has encouraged the lovers because she is in love with Don Rodrigue. If the couple should marry, then the Infanta may be cured of her imprudent passion.

The king chooses Don Diègue as his son's tutor. Infuriated, Don Gomez argues with his best friend and provokes a duel. Too old to fight, Don Diègue tells his son, Don Rodrigue, that he must avenge his father. Don Rodrigue is torn with emotion: "Father, mistress, honor, love." If he kills Don Gomez, he will arouse Chimène's hatred; if he does not act honorably, he will be unworthy of her. Whatever he does, he will lose Chimène. He decides to avenge his father and uphold his name.

Don Gomez admits to a friend that he has been too emotional, but he refuses to apologize, even at the king's request. Don Rodrigue tries to discourage his adversary, but when Don Gomez reasserts his intentions, Don Rodrigue declares he will uphold his family's honor. Don Gomez sees that this young man is indeed worthy of his daughter.

The Infanta tries in vain to calm Chimène. They are interrupted by news of the duel. When Chimène flees, the Infanta reveals that she is secretly pleased by the turn of events. Léonor reproaches her and reminds her that Don Rodrigue is not of royal descent.

Just as the king learns that Don Gomez has died in the duel, Chimène enters and demands vengeance. Don Diègue appeals to the king to preserve his son's life: Don Rodrigue acted for him. If someone must die, let the king punish Don Diègue. The king promises justice, dismissing the assembly.

Unexpectedly, Don Rodrigue enters Chimène's house and tells Elvire that he has come to ask Chimène to kill him. Elvire attempts to discourage him, but is interrupted by Don Sanche's approach. She entreats Don Rodrigue to hide in order to save Chimène's honor. Don Sanche offers to avenge Chimène. But she is reluctant to accept. Thinking she is alone with Elvire, Chimène reveals her love for Don Rodrigue. Passion conquers her resentment: although she must ask for her lover's head, her own death will follow his. Elvire advises her to moderate her desire for revenge; she has made the honorable gesture. But Chimène is adamant.

Suddenly, Don Rodrigue steps out from his hiding place. Waving his sword before Chimène's eyes, he implores her to kill him. If he killed to preserve his father's honor, the act was really for Chimène: "To erase [my] . . . shame and to be worthy of you." Chimène laments their situation. By fulfilling his duty, Don Rodrigue has only taught her what she should do. Don Rodrigue retorts that only if he is killed by Chimène's own hand will her father be avenged. She cannot have someone act in her stead. Chimène drives Don Rodrigue out, confessing that her "only wish is not to be able to do anything." If Don Rodrigue dies, she promises her death will follow.

Returning home, Don Rodrigue confronts his father and announces that now that he has completed his duty, his life is over. Don Diègue reproaches his son for his despair: "We only have one honor; there are so many mistresses!/ Love is a pleasure, honor is a duty." He tells Don Rodrigue that he must join the king's legions in order to save Castile from the Moors. By his valorous service, Don Rodrigue will replace the lost warrior, Don Gomez.

Later in Seville, Chimène and Elvire discuss the glorious victory Don Rodrigue, now known as the Cid, has achieved over the Moors. The Infanta interrupts them, seconds their praise and tells Chimène that if she insists on revenge she is offending a public hero. Let Don Rodrigue live; merely stop loving him.

Meanwhile, Don Rodrigue recounts his heroic exploits to

the king, who resolves to test Chimène's demands for vengeance. When she appears before him, he pretends that the Cid is dead. Chimène blanches. Yet when she learns he is alive, she reiterates her demand for his life: "Let him die for my father and not for our country." If the king allows Don Sanche to represent her in a duel with Don Rodrigue, Chimène promises to marry the victor.

Once again, Don Rodrigue appears before Chimène. He has come to her for encouragement. Because he is not to die by her hand, he will not repulse Don Sanche's sword. Chimène reawakens his desire to live by saying he is fighting to possess her.

Alone, the Infanta laments her fate—by his chivalry Don Rodrigue has proven worthy of her, but through her own efforts, his heart belongs to Chimène. Chimène and Elvire await the result of the duel. When Don Sanche appears, she immediately concludes that Don Rodrigue is dead, announces her love, and rejects Don Sanche. She runs to the king and asks to be sent to a nunnery. But Don Rodrigue is not dead; he has spared Don Sanche and sent him as messenger. The king calls the two lovers and unites them.

Critical Opinion

Until recently, Corneille's tragedies have been interpreted as powerful dramas in which the heroes struggle to choose between honor (duty) and love (passion). Modern criticism, however, has envisioned the four great Corneillean tragedies, *Le Cid* (1637), *Horace* (1640), *Cinna* (1640), and *Polyeucte* (1641), as more complicated depictions of man's conquest of self.

In *Le Cid,* Don Rodrigue and Chimène are not equally endowed adversaries. Their conflicts over honor and love are not parallel. From the beginning of the drama, Chimène reveals her strong commitment to Don Rodrigue, and despite the murder of her father, and her own efforts for revenge, this commitment is never altered. While Don Rodrigue can overcome his passion in order to uphold his family's honor and thus feel worthy of Chimène, Chimène never struggles on the same plane. Don Rodrigue expects Chimène to react like a man. But in the course of the play, he discovers that she is incapable of hatred and, motivated by love, will act differently.

When Don Rodrigue learns that he must fight a duel with Chimène's father, he is momentarily unsure what course of action to take. The realization that whatever he does he will lose Chimène causes him to contemplate suicide. But enraged by the idea of dishonorable death, he quickly decides upon combat in order to at least merit, if not possess, Chimène. From the moment of this decision, the play follows Chimène's point of view.

Unlike Don Rodrigue, Chimène is incapable of acting as duty instructs. She cannot be the cause of her lover's death. Repeatedly, she reaffirms this inability, at first confessing to Elvire: "I ask for his head, and I fear to possess it." Later, Chimène avows to Don Rodrigue: "My sole desire is to be unable to do anything," and at the end, Chimène publicly announces her true wish to the king by swooning, because she thinks her lover is dead, and requesting refuge in a cloister rather than marriage to the presumed victor, Don Sanche. The futility of Chimène's efforts to protect herself from love's dictates underlines her own fatality. She is incapable of fulfilling what she has sworn to do: avenge her father's death. Thus her actions are self-destructive.

After the first act, when Don Rodrigue decides to defend his honor in the duel, passion becomes the motivating force in the drama. In the extraordinary first confrontation between Don Rodrigue and Chimène, the lovers reveal their irrational thinking. When Don Rodrigue allows himself to appear before Chimène after killing her father, he does not think of himself as a murderer, but rather as someone who has acted honorably. He eavesdrops on Chimène because he is jealous of Don Sanche and fears that she will accept his offer to act as her champion. Don Rodrigue's insistence that he die by Chimène's own hand underlines his own frenzy: "To let my deplorable life end by your hands . . . I would die only too happy from such a beautiful blow." But Don Rodrigue is demanding the impossible; Chimène cannot be a torturer, and she admits her preference for the criminal: "Go, I am your countryman, not your executioner."

In the final act, once the duel between Don Sanche and Don Rodrigue has been arranged, Chimène is the victim of her passion. Because he thinks it is Chimène's desire,

Don Rodrigue expresses his willingness to die. But she begs him to fight Don Sanche not so that she may avenge her father but because she wants to be *possessed* by Don Rodrigue. Physically and morally, Chimène cannot tolerate the idea of a union with Don Sanche. "Exit victor from a combat in which Chimène is the prize," she exhorts Don Rodrigue. Chimène is far removed from Don Rodrigue's world of honor. But Don Rodrigue is not really concerned with her struggle; he worries about his own honor and doubts Chimène's love. From the first act, he is totally self-absorbed and does not change.

Don Rodrigue's singular glory and merit are reflected in the use of his warrior name, given him by the fleeing Moors. It is his undisputed glory that dominates the drama; the long interview with the king underlines his valor.

Don Rodrigue's virtuous dichotomy of honor and love is echoed by the Infanta. But in order to protect her honor, she pairs Don Rodrigue and Chimène, making her own love impossible. Later, even when Don Rodrigue as the Cid proves himself worthy of her by his conquests, the Infanta recognizes the impossibility of altering the relationships and continues to uphold her royal honor.

Critics and scholars have always admired Corneille's consummate handling of the Alexandrine poetic couplet. The drama derives its balance and energy from the lyrical and imaginative employment of this restrictive verse form. Corneille called his play a tragicomedy because the elements of fatality and human disaster are overcome, and the play concludes with marriage.

Although the first performances of *Le Cid* in Paris in 1637 were enormously successful, the play soon was violently criticized. Cardinal Richelieu disliked the drama because he had just made dueling unlawful in France. The French Academy accused Corneille of plagiarism and of breaking the rules for classical drama that dictated unity of time, place, and action. Corneille defended his conformity to the classical rules: Unity of action could be found in Don Rodrigue and Chimène's unrelenting passion. And despite the numerous settings in various apartments, Corneille asserted that Seville provided unity of place, and the entire action occurred within twenty-four hours. This famous "Quarrel of *Le Cid*," however, only increased the play's popularity. Today, *Le Cid* is still performed by the Comédie Française. The drama has been translated into many languages and is regarded as an outstanding example of the seventeenth-century classical theater.

The Author

Pierre Corneille was born in Rouen in 1606, the son of a distinguished magistrate who was later made a nobleman. He was educated by the Jesuits to be a lawyer, and through family connections received a post in the admiralty, which he held until 1650. Corneille's writing career began in 1629 with a romantic melodrama, *Mélite,* which was followed in 1632 by *Clitandre,* a full-length tragedy, and *La Veuve, La Galerie du Palais, La Suivante,* and *La Place Royal.* Cardinal Richelieu commissioned several works to embody his own opinions, but Corneille found the task uncongenial.

His first tragedy was *Médée* (1635). *L'illusion Comique* (1636), and *Le Cid* (1637) were great successes. *Le Cid,* reputedly based on a play by Guillen de Castro, raised a storm of critical controversy that nearly engulfed the French literary and political world in the late 1630s. Despite the furor, *Le Cid* heralded Corneille's enormous theatrical success, which was consolidated by *Horace, Cinna,* and *Polyeucte.* A prolific writer, Corneille composed a great many tragedies and comedies and was rivaled in serious drama only by the young Jean Racine.

Corneille became very wealthy. His fame was partially shared by his younger brother, Thomas (1625–1709), who was a playwright, critic, and historian. Corneille had been elected to the Académie Française in 1647. In 1676, Louis XIV ordered a revival of his plays at Versailles. Corneille died in 1684 and was eulogized by his great rival, Racine, at the Académie Française.

Tartuffe

by

JEAN-BAPTISTE POQUELIN (MOLIÈRE) (1622–1673)

The Characters

Tartuffe—a corpulent, somberly clad, religious fanatic who has insinuated himself into the Orgon household. Despite his outward appearance, he is avaricious, cunning, lustful, and criminal.

Orgon—a gullible, middle-class Parisian who is duped by Tartuffe's manner. He tyrannizes over his children and wants Tartuffe as his son-in-law.

Elmire—Orgon's young second wife who is sympathetic to her stepdaughter's romantic feelings for Valère and quickly recognizes the lust beneath Tartuffe's pious facade.

Mariane—Orgon's young daughter, in love with Valère. She is timid and withdrawn, except with her lover.

Damis—the bold, rash, and impudent son of Orgon; he generously returns when his father is in trouble.

Cléante—Elmire's brother, who comments upon the action.

Valère—Marianne's lover; proves himself loyal to the family when they are in need.

Dorine—impertinent, wily, resourceful, and ironic, although a servant, she chastens Orgon and Tartuffe and reunites the disputing lovers.

Madame Pernelle—Orgon's mother, as blind, stupid, and pigheaded as her son. Although she is quick to criticize others, she has no understanding of herself.

17

The Story

The Orgon family is gathered in the comfortable salon of their large bourgeois home. Madame Pernelle, in a horrible temper, criticizes everyone present: Damis is foolish; Mariane is too quiet; Dorine is impertinent; Elmire sets a bad example for the children; Cléante is meddlesome. Only Tartuffe escapes her wrath. But the family is quick to point out Tartuffe's shortcoming: He is a parasite. When Dorine remarks that Tartuffe is jealous of Elmire, Madame Pernelle, outraged, leaves. Dorine declares that Orgon gives Tartuffe everything and calls him "brother."

Just before his father enters, Damis tells his stepmother and stepuncle that Mariane loves Valère and he (Damis) loves Valère's sister. Orgon returns from the country and inquires about the health of the household. Dorine tells him that his wife has been bled because of her fever and loss of appetite, but Tartuffe eats heartily, sleeps well, and drinks quantities of wine. Orgon, who thinks only of his friend, repeatedly sighs: "The poor man."

Cléante appears and warns his brother-in-law about his ridiculous behavior. But Orgon is deaf to criticism of his beloved Tartuffe and tells how Tartuffe goes to church each day, prays, and runs to offer Orgon holy water. When the bourgeois offers a generous purse, the pious man always returns half. He has even criticized himself for having killed a flea with too much anger. Cléante retorts that his brother-in-law is foolish: "What! Don't you make any distinction/ Between hypocrisy and devotion?" But Orgon refuses to listen, and when Cléante presses for Mariane's marriage to Valère, Orgon leaves.

Later, Orgon informs his daughter that she must marry Tartuffe. She is speechless, and Dorine argues on her behalf. Even though Orgon forbids the servant to talk, she persists. Orgon leaves in a fury while Dorine lectures the timid Mariane; she should have said that she was marrying for herself, not for her father. Dorine ironically praises Tartuffe and depicts Mariane's future as his wife: a provincial matron who goes to the county fair for entertainment. When Mariane objects, Dorine replies: "You will be . . .

tartuffied!" Valère interrupts and the two lovers argue because Valère thinks Mariane will marry Tartuffe. Dorine acts as intermediary, reunites the couple, and pledges to serve their cause.

Damis reveals his anger to Dorine and says he is ready for violent opposition, but flees when Tartuffe enters. Tartuffe is thrown into a frenzy when he sees Dorine's low bodice and asks her to cover her bosom with his handkerchief. She replies: "You must indeed be very sensitive to temptation . . ./All your flesh would not tempt me."

Elmire enters and Tartuffe addresses pious salutations to her. She wants to speak to him in private so that he can bare his heart. Tartuffe reveals his feelings by squeezing Elmire's fingers, touching her knee, feeling the material of her dress, and moving his chair next to hers. He declares that he aspires to more than Mariane's favors. When Elmire pretends he is talking about his religious devotion, Tartuffe explains: "The love which attaches us to eternal beauty/Does not stifle in us love of temporal things." Elmire is his hope, domain, peace. He sighs: "Ah! As a devout believer, I am nevertheless a man. . . ." If they are discreet, they may enjoy "love without scandal and pleasure without fear." Elmire quickly replies that she will not reveal Tartuffe's infamy to her husband if he will help conclude Mariane's marriage to Valère. But suddenly Damis, who has been eavesdropping, rushes in and exposes Tartuffe to his father. Tartuffe is full of self-reproach and does not deny the charge: "Everyone takes me for a good man,/But the pure truth is that I am worthless." Surprisingly, Orgon banishes his son from the house, promises to hasten Tartuffe's marriage to his daughter, encourages his association with Elmire, and declares Tartuffe will be his sole heir.

Cléante reprimands Tartuffe for his ungenerous behavior. Instead of pleading for Damis as a truly religious person would, he has permitted an unjust banishment.

Elmire, Mariane, Dorine, and Cléante make a final attempt to change Orgon's mind. Mariane implores her father to free her from an odious marriage and at least allow her to retire to a convent. But her pleas are in vain. Even Elmire is incapable of dissuading her husband until she proposes to expose Tartuffe. Orgon must hide under the table while she encourages Tartuffe's advances. When Tartuffe declares

himself, Elmire repeatedly coughs to warn her husband. But
Orgon remains hidden, even after Tartuffe says: "Scandal is
what makes the offense/And it is not sinning if one sins
in silence." When Orgon still does not emerge, Elmire suggests that Tartuffe look for her husband outside the door.
Tartuffe retorts, why bother? He's a man "to be led by the
nose." Momentarily alone with his wife, Orgon starts to
crawl out from under the table. Elmire ironically asks:
"What! you're exiting so soon?" When Tartuffe returns,
Orgon orders the hypocrite to leave. But Tartuffe gains the
upper hand and chases the family out of their home.

Orgon is wild with rage. Not only must he leave his own
house, but he has betrayed a friend who entrusted a strongbox to his keeping. Damis rushes in, ready to kill Tartuffe
if his father wishes, but he is interrupted by the entrance
of Madame Pernelle, who still refuses to believe Tartuffe is
a hypocrite. It is not until the sergeant, Mr. Loyal, appears
with an order to vacate the house that she will face the
truth. Suddenly, Valère appears and informs Orgon that the
king has issued orders for Orgon's arrest. He must flee in the
coach Valère has ready outside. But Tartuffe arrives accompanied by a royal marshall. Tartuffe ironically says his
duty is to serve his prince. He is rudely surprised when the
officer turns to arrest him, saying: "We live under a prince
who is the enemy of fraud." Tartuffe is a traitor who has
been living under a false name. He is an infamous criminal
known to the state. Orgon starts to berate Tartuffe, but is
stopped by Cléante. He agrees to allow the marriage of
Mariane to Valère, and goes off to thank the king for his
deliverance.

Critical Opinion

Written in 1664 for Louis XIV's festivities at Versailles,
Le Tartuffe aroused a furor before it was performed. Even
at the height of his power, the French king was influenced
by his devout mistress, Madame de Maintenon. Her austere
piety encouraged religious zealots who quickly took offense
at the portrait of Tartuffe, a false religious fanatic. They
banned the play, claiming that Molière had mocked the

Roman Catholic faith. Three years later, while Louis was fighting in Holland, the playwright offered a second version under a new title, *L'Imposteur (The Impostor)*. But again it was censored and not until February of 1669 did Molière produce a revised, five-act *Tartuffe*.

In order to make sure no one misunderstood his intentions, Molière prefaced the work with a lengthy explanation. Although the nobility, fops, cuckolds, and doctors had not been oversensitive to satire, only hypocrites seemed to be incensed. Molière explained that he had used two entire acts to prepare the audience for the entrance of Tartuffe:

> The audience does not doubt for one moment, and from the beginning to the end [Tartuffe] does not commit a single action which does not paint the personality of an evil man.

When Tartuffe reveals himself as a hypocrite, Molière writes in the stage directions: "A scoundrel speaks."

Tartuffe is a classical comedy based upon the standard seventeenth-century formula: a foolish bourgeois is duped by a conniver, his wise family intervenes, and the fraud is unmasked. The younger generation, seconded by a clever servant, struggles with an uncomprehending parent who wishes to force a marriage to his own advantage. *The Imaginary Invalid, The Knowledgeable Women, The Pranks of Scapin,* and *The Miser* all employ the same devices. The ingenuity and originality of *Tartuffe* reside, however, in the vivid presentation of the characters. The play's artistry rests on its humorous situations and clever use of language.

Tartuffe, Orgon, and Dorine are clearly the most important characters. By the time Tartuffe appears in the third act, the audience, as well as the other members of his household, are aware that he is a scoundrel. He exploits the stupidity of his host and hypocritically exhibits his false piety. An egotist who cares nothing for the well-being of those around him, Tartuffe is totally self-serving. He exposes himself as a zealot and false prude when, like Arsinoé in *The Misanthrope,* he insists that people dress conservatively and cover their bodies to avoid arousing temptation in "sinful" persons.

Tartuffe is adroit only in duping Orgon; as a seducer and suitor, he is clumsy and insulting. When he insists that he is no angel and advocates "love without scandal and pleasure without fear," his lubricity is obvious.

Tartuffe never denies his guilt in the final version of the play, and one can only conjecture about Molière's depiction of the character in the earlier versions. When accused by Damis, Tartuffe readily calls himself a "wrong-doer, a guilty person, an unhappy sinner," and he confesses: "I am much less, alas, than what people think./Everyone takes me for a good man,/But the pure truth is that I am worthless." This audacious frankness elsewhere fools Orgon into thinking Tartuffe is only an oversensitive believer who reprimands himself for having killed a flea with too much anger.

When Tartuffe is unmasked so that even Orgon recognizes his hypocrisy, he reveals another facet of his vicious personality by cleverly evicting Orgon and his family. It is only Molière's *deus ex machina* that resolves the conflict between vice and honesty. Almost by divine intervention, the king's officer arrests Tartuffe, who is discovered to be a notorious criminal.

Orgon is the springboard for most of the play's comedy. He tyrannizes his family but is incapable of dominating his servant. Though quick-tempered, sentimental, and impractical, he emerges from his experience a chastened and loyal husband, father, and citizen. Dorine, a clever servant who has more common sense than her master, is quick to correct mistaken judgments, whether Orgon's or Madame Pernelle's.

Elmire, always levelheaded and good-hearted, exposes Tartuffe without usurping her husband's authority. At the end, she does not blame Orgon for their predicament, but dutifully faces their seemingly inevitable demise. Cléante is Molière's *raisonneur,* but he is clearly not the playwright's spokesman. Like the chorus in Greek tragedy, he comments upon the moral of each situation and points out the distinction between a truly religious person and a pretentious impostor. Yet Madame Pernelle correctly assesses his problem: He preaches too much.

Only Damis, Mariane, and Valère seem to be realized exclusively within the seventeenth-century theatrical convention. They are rather flat characters who reveal the problems of the younger generation. Good-hearted but sometimes quick-tempered, they might easily appear in any of Molière's comedies. Madame Pernelle is an older version of her son, and, like him, is a stock character who must be duped in order to further the action.

Molière employs comic situations as well as vivid characterizations to achieve satirical effects. The first act's exposition is remarkable for its rapid dialogue.

Tartuffe is reduced to idiocy when faced with the sound judgment and lively spirits of Dorine. He is exposed as a sneering prude by her reply to his demand that she cover her voluptuous bosom with his handkerchief:

> You are indeed sensitive to temptation . . .
> And if I saw you naked from head to toe
> All your flesh wouldn't tempt me.

But Tartuffe is most comic in his attempts to seduce Elmire. In the first, his maladroit advances turn the scene into slapstick farce. Later, the situation becomes humorous as Orgon hides under the table. Elmire's constant fits of coughing, Tartuffe's solicitous offers of licorice, and Orgon's failure to reveal himself are a satirical commentary on both men.

Molière's careful choice of language reinforces his comic portrayal of a hypocrite. In a frenzy of passion for Elmire, Tartuffe resorts to the rhetoric of religious devotion:

> In you is my hope, my domain, peace:
> On you depend my pain and blessedness:
> And finally I will be by your sole command,
> Happy if you wish, unhappy if it pleases you.

Later, he asks Elmire to "plant in my soul a constant faith" so that he may know what benefices she intends to bestow upon him. Just as Tartuffe disguises his intention in the somber habiliments of a devout believer, he masks his lasciviousness in pious phrases. Like *The Misanthrope*, *Tartuffe* is written in verse, with a trenchancy, elegance, and design that reflect the profound moral insights of its author.

Since 1669, *Tartuffe* has been part of the repertory of the Comédie Française. The role of the hypocrite has inspired

various interpretations, from that of a fat, jovial, and corrupt Benedictine monk to the mordant, sanguine portrayal
of a skinny, dry, and bitter individual made famous in the
1930s by Louis Jouvet.

The Misanthrope

by

JEAN-BAPTISTE POQUELIN (MOLIÈRE) (1622–1673)

The Characters

Alceste—an eccentric nobleman, in love with Célimène.
Philinte—a worldly and gently cynical friend of Alceste.
Oronte—a pretentious, vain courtier, in love with Célimène.
Célimène—a twenty-year-old coquette who maintains a salon.
Éliante—Célimène's cousin.
Arsinoé—an ugly prude, in love with Alceste.
Acaste and Clitandre—two fatuous noblemen.

The Story

In the elegant salon of Célimène, a young widow, Alceste rails against mankind to his friend Philinte. He distrusts all seemingly noble actions and attacks men who observe social conventions. Philinte tries to calm Alceste by urging him to recognize how unbearable life would be if people always said what they thought, but the misanthrope rejects this idea and almost gleefully anticipates his own ruin in a pending lawsuit.

Despite his harsh view of the world, Alceste concedes that he is powerless to resist the coquettish and vain Célimène. When Oronte, a conceited fop, appears and reads Alceste a sonnet, Alceste attacks it for being artificial, insincere, and shallow. He then recites an old street song that is straight-forward and simple and that he claims is superior to Oronte's courtly sonnet. As Alceste and Oronte are about to come to blows, the latter departs.

Alceste vehemently reprimands Célimène for her unfaith-fulness. She accuses him of being motivated by jealousy, not honesty. When Éliante enters, Alceste is belligerently commanding Célimène to choose between himself and her other suitors. They are interrupted by the appearance of other courtiers, who are entertained by Célimène's scathing attacks on mutual acquaintances. Alceste reprimands her, saying that true love demands ruthless sincerity and fault-finding, but Célimène rejoins that love would then be a source of pain only. The second act closes with the an-nouncement that Alceste has been summoned before a mar-shall to justify his insults to Oronte.

Clitandre and Acaste, both vain and petty marquises, pay court to Célimène. Arsinoé, an ugly prude, censures Céli-mène for vain and unchaste conduct, and Célimène attacks Arsinoé for moral hypocrisy. Arsinoé, who really is in love with Alceste, finds that her flattery of him is unavailing, and tries to alienate him from Célimène. Her rigid moraliz-ing gives Alceste a dose of his own medicine.

Philinte describes to the marshall Alceste's stubborn behavior; he only indirectly tempers his criticism of Oronte's poem. Éliante confesses to Philinte that she loves Alceste; Philinte declares his own affection for her. Alceste confronts Célimène with a love letter she has written to Oronte, but she denies it was for him and refuses to justify her conduct. But Alceste is so infatuated with Célimène that he capitulates to her will. As the act concludes, Dubois, pretending to bring secret news, tells of Alceste's impending arrest as a result of the lawsuit mentioned in Act I.

Alceste, who has lost the case, is ruined. He contemplates exile in a desert, away from base and hypocritical mankind. Despite Philinte's entreaties, Alceste refuses to reopen the case and contest the judgments. His defeat justifies his misanthropy. Philinte replies that man must learn to live as he can in an evil world, but Alceste goes off into a corner to sulk. He overhears Oronte demand that Célimène be faithful, steps forward, and asks her to choose between Oronte and himself while both are present. Célimène refuses.

Acaste reads a letter in which Célimène rejects all suitors. Alceste nevertheless forgives her, but insists they both exile themselves from mankind, in some "wild, trackless, solitary place" to "forget the human race." Célimène refuses to become a hermit, but agrees to marry Alceste if they stay in society. He refuses and leaves.

Alceste humbly apologizes to Éliante for not offering to marry her. Philinte and Éliante become engaged, and although Alceste vows to "flee this bitter world where vice is king," Philinte and Éliante undertake to change his mind.

Critical Opinion

In *The Misanthrope* (1666), Molière satirizes a corrupt world and its critic. His ridicule of society and the anti-social individual illuminates the difficulty of setting absolute moral standards in a civilized world.

Alceste, the misanthrope, is more vehement in his attitudes than the cynic who only expects the worst of human nature. Alceste finds it impossible to live with integrity in a vicious and corrupt society and proposes to exile himself to a desert. But unlike the hermit who contemplates his *own* sins, Alceste will ponder the baseness and hypocrisy of *other* men's lives.

At the beginning, Molière's portrait of aristocratic society in seventeenth-century France seems to justify Alceste's extreme position. Éliante judges that Alceste is sometimes heroic and admirable. Yet as the play proceeds, it becomes clear that Alceste is excessively inflexible and egotistical in his neurotic insistence that men should be ruthlessly honest. In Act II, he fails to live up to his own idea of proper conduct. Although many of Alceste's criticisms are justified, his manner is absurd, and he becomes a ludicrous figure.

Here Molière follows the usual formula of comedies by exposing the individual through a comparison with society's conventions.

Molière's central theme is the ridiculousness of vice. He attacks all types of insincerity. Falseness of social manners, as practiced by Philinte, is the least offensive. Next in gravity is the gossip of Célimène, Acaste, and Clitandre. Calumny (Célimène and Arsinoé), prudery (Arsinoé), and insincerity to oneself (Alceste) complete Molière's list of deadly sins. Alceste repeatedly compromises himself and his ideals (not always the same thing) when he fails to reject Célimène, whose coquetry is antithetical to his standards of moral conduct. Thus in Act II, though herself guilty of insincerity, Célimène justifiably accuses Alceste of jealousy and egotism.

The philosophical comedy of *The Misanthrope* derives its structure from elegant, civilized discourse rather than from plot manipulation. The balanced and logical verse conveys the rational and aristocratic nature of Molière's argument. Thus, Philinte, the cynical man of the world, remains unruffled by the spectacle of social duplicity and corruption. He accepts baseness and hypocrisy because he expects no better. Alceste rails against the world's abuses and berates Philinte for his participation in the "hypocritical" rituals of civilization. Philinte, in turn, rebukes Alceste for measuring human conduct by impossibly high standards. Yet, although we may agree with Philinte's temporizing, his excessive flattery of Oronte evokes sympathy for Alceste. In this episode (I, ii), the characters' disparate motives point up the play's philosophical dilemma. Oronte is a repulsive man —vain, arrogant, and artificial. But he is also one of Célimène's suitors and Alceste's rival. His sonnet written to Célimène is really a fine example of the *précieuse* love poem in vogue during Louis XIV's reign. Its demerits are not so blatant as Alceste claims, for it is well turned and carefully wrought. The verse that Alceste proposes as a model of true sentiment is different in style and genre rather than in quality. It is an old street song, masculine, vigorous, and straightforward. The lover would not take the king's gift of Paris in exchange for his mistress. This protestation of absolute and impossible love is an ironic commentary on the discrepancy between Alceste's ideal of romantic conduct and his carping and jealous behavior with Célimène.

In the following scenes, Molière advances Alceste's case against society. When Célimène and her acquaintances mercilessly attack other courtiers, Alceste is justified in abhorring a vicious and slanderous society. But each time he appears on stage, the purity of his motive is questioned and he is exposed as a simplistic, humorless killjoy.

If one of the major goals of civilized society is pleasure and companionship for the individual, then Molière's indictment of Alceste is particularly significant. The artificial and desperately clever courtiers are trying to escape the loneliness of self-knowledge. Alceste, in his overweening egotism and insistence on absolute moral standards, has also retreated into the empty world of self-love and perverted values.

Many critics have regarded *The Misanthrope* as black comedy. Nearly every one of the characters is condemned, and the audience cannot find a comfortable position from which to view the merciless exposure through ridicule. Only Éliante seems to have the inner strength to resist the extremes represented by Alceste, Philinte, and Célimène. She becomes the implicit mediator between their philosophic positions when she agrees to marry Philinte.

Marriage is the traditional end of comedy; yet this union does not resolve the issues. Alceste vows to abandon society for a solitary desert, even though the engaged couple promises to dissuade him from his purpose. Molière terminates the action of the play without giving the audience an answer to philosophical questions he has posed. The dilemma of resolving absolute honesty with social decorum can only be presented, not arbitrated.

A universal classic especially relevant to the present generation's increased social consciousness, *The Misanthrope* offers one of the wisest and most balanced critiques of a corrupt society and its fallible critics. Although it has been translated into nearly every language, the precise and elegant poetry of the original has inspired countless French-language productions throughout the world. In the 1950s, the illustrious Madeleine Renaud and Jean-Louis Barrault formed a company and, playing Célimène and Alceste, toured the United States, receiving enormous acclaim. More recently, New York's APA Repertory Company mounted a successful production of the American poet Richard Wilbur's superb English translation. But whatever the language or production facilities at hand, Molière's play has remained a durable and perennially fascinating masterpiece.

The Miser

by

JEAN-BAPTISTE POQUELIN (MOLIÈRE) (1622–1673)

The Characters

Harpagon—an old man obsessed with money. His relations with his children, servants, friends, and bride-to-be are affected by his lust for wealth and his fear of having to part with his money. He is vain, boorish, and suspicious. He is the archetypal miser with a scanty beard, rickety frame, rheumy eyes, and shabby, old-fashioned clothes.

Cléante—Harpagon's son, young, fashionable, passionate. He is forced to borrow and gamble to maintain his way of life. His love for Mariane forces him to defy his father.

Elise—Harpagon's daughter. Although victimized by her father's lust for money, she refuses to marry against her will. Her deep love for Valère is not affected by the mystery about his origin.

Valère—Elise's lover, disguises himself as a steward in the miser's household to remain close to his beloved. He believes flattery and duplicity are preferable to sincerity when dealing with Harpagon.

Mariane—the modest, beautiful, and loyal daughter of a poor neighbor who has promised her hand to Harpagon. Mariane is repelled by the old man and enamoured of his son.

Anselm—an exiled duke of Naples and wealthy Parisian merchant who is supposed to marry Elise without a dowry, but because of her love for Valère, readily renounces a forced marriage. Anselm's long-lost family is reunited when he discovers his children, Mariane and Valère.

Frosine—a shrewd, opportunistic matchmaker who lives by her wits. She is unable to get her reward from Harpagon for arranging his betrothal to Mariane.

Jacques—Harpagon's cook and coachman, a faithful, sincere man who learns the difficulty of speaking the truth in Harpagon's household.

La Flèche—Cléante's valet, defiant of Harpagon, who manages to steal the treasure buried in the garden.

The Story

In Harpagon's dark, cavernous, and sparsely furnished house, Valère and Elise lament their inability to get married. Although of noble birth, Valère does not know his parents and has taken the position of steward in the miser's household to be near Elise. Valère says that every man, even Elise's father, may be won over by flattery and duplicity. Soon he hopes to overcome all obstacles to their union. After he leaves, Cléante appears and commiserates with his sister about their father's parsimony. Cléante confides that he is in love with Mariane, a neighbor, but his duty is to follow his father's counsel and temper his passion. Elise returns her brother's confidence by disclosing her love for Valère but is interrupted by the appearance of Harpagon and La Flèche. The brother and sister leave hastily.

Harpagon violently admonishes the servant, accusing him of trying to rob him and spread rumors of his wealth. He mercilessly beats La Flèche, who curses his avarice. Harpagon is compromised, for he will not admit he is a miser, and after searching La Flèche for loot, he ejects him from the house. Alone, Harpagon reveals that he has buried a large sum of money in his garden. When his children enter, he accuses them of eavesdropping and of betraying him to his enemies. Cléante, reprimanded for his extravagant clothing, replies that he borrows money and gambles in order to keep up a decent appearance. After Harpagon advises his son to invest his money rather than spend it, he announces that he intends to marry the girl with whom his son is secretly in love. Cléante is dumbfounded and leaves, while Harpagon tells Elise that in a few hours she will marry an old merchant because he does not require a dowry. She defies him, but Valère, when asked to mediate the problem, sardonically agrees with Harpagon: Considerations of love, honor, and happiness are nothing when money is at stake. Harpagon joyfully accepts this support and rushes off to the garden to check his buried treasure. Valère assures Elise that only by indirect means will they vanquish Harpagon. She must feign illness to avoid the marriage set for that evening. When the miser returns, Valère again contends that beauty, youth, birth, honor, wisdom, and integrity must yield to monetary considerations.

Cléante is approached by La Flèche, who tells him he has made arrangements to meet a broker and borrow fifteen thousand francs. The anonymous lender will give twelve thousand francs at the exorbitant rate of 25½ percent and will force Cléante to accept worthless household junk (including "one lizard skin, 3½ feet long, stuffed with straw, a pleasant curiosity to hang from the ceiling of a room") in lieu of the other three thousand francs. Cléante is outraged but is forced to accede to the usury. Simon, the go-between, enters and is surprised that Cléante is at the lender's house. When Harpagon appears, it is discovered that he is the usurer; father and son remonstrate with each other over the profligacy of the borrower and the immorality of the lender. Harpagon rushes off to take a look at his money, and the others leave in dismay.

La Flèche and Frosine discuss Harpagon's miserliness. Frosine brags that she can outwit the miser and profit by her efforts to arrange his marriage with Mariane, but La Flèche is skeptical. When Harpagon returns, Frosine assures him that the young girl will bring twelve thousand francs a year: her simple culinary tastes will save three thousand; her indifference to clothing and jewels will save four thousand; and her abhorrence of gambling is worth five thousand. Harpagon is skeptical: "I give no receipt for something I don't actually get. I have to put my hands on something." Frosine continues to laud Mariane's virtues by revealing that the girl rejected a suitor who was only fifty-six years old because she adores older men. Harpagon strikes several poses and is flattered into believing that he is a distinguished figure, but when the matchmaker asks for money to settle a lawsuit, Harpagon rushes off.

Preparations for a banquet in Mariane's honor are supervised by the miser, who admonishes his servants not to wear out the furniture by polishing it too vigorously and tells them to hide the state of their clothing by keeping out of sight and by standing near the walls. Jacques, the coachman-cook, is instructed to prepare a feast without special provisions. Valère supports his master's demand that the servants stint on wine and food: "One should eat to live, not live to eat." But Harpagon stupidly reverses the maxim and decides that a fatty mutton stew will be cheap and filling. When Jacques, in his capacity as coachman, announces that the horses are starving and cannot draw the carriage for Mariane unless they are fed, Valère volunteers to borrow a team from the neighbor. Jacques's anger prompts him to declare candidly to Harpagon that he is the laughingstock of Paris because of his miserliness. Harpagon beats him for his impudence, and Valère finishes the job for his master. Jacques laments: "A plague on sincerity. It's a bad business. I give it up from now on, and I'll no longer tell the truth."

Mariane and Frosine are greeted by Harpagon, but the young woman can barely conceal her loathing for the decrepit old man. Cléante appears and, pretending to speak for his father, flatters Mariane, gallantly taking a diamond ring off his father's finger and placing it on hers. Harpagon is flabbergasted, but cannot reveal his lack of generosity.

Later that day, Mariane and Cléante avow their love and ask Frosine to help them. The old matchmaker says that she will find someone to masquerade as a rich noblewoman and distract Harpagon from his courtship of Mariane. Harpagon steals upon them and tricks Cléante into revealing his love for Mariane. Again, father and son exchange violent declarations when Jacques, now cured of speaking sincerely, mediates the argument by privately conferring with each party and giving the impression that each rival has renounced his claim. When the servant's joke is discovered and the argument is resumed, Harpagon disinherits his son and rushes out. La Flèche immediately appears with the treasure that he has found in the garden and flees with

Cléante. Harpagon, in a frenzy, demands a general inquisition and the immediate slaughter of all responsible for his loss.

While Harpagon makes his deposition to an officer, Jacques, seeking revenge, accuses Valère of the theft. Valère is confronted by Harpagon, but mistakenly assumes that his love for Elise is the cause of the miser's wrath. The women enter and Elise begs for her father to forgive Valère. Anselm, Elise's prospective husband, arrives and says he will not marry anyone against her will. Harpagon questions Valère's claim to noble birth, and Anselm discovers that Valère is his lost son and Mariane is his daughter. He bestows his blessings on the marriages of Mariane to Cléante and Valère to Elise and pledges to pay for the weddings. Jacques is pardoned for his calumny against Valère, and everyone is happy, including Harpagon, who goes to see his "darling money box," which had been returned to him.

Critical Opinion

The Miser (1668) is a universally admired comedy. The archetypal characters and situations continue to appeal to contemporary audiences. Molière preferred a stereotype of miserliness to a detailed psychological portrait of a specific miser. Harpagon's physical appearance, emotional constitution, and moral conduct epitomize the obsessive, tyrannical, and destructive materialism in the human personality.

Harpagon's penuriousness has undermined his physical being. He is skinny, hunched, decrepit, and diseased. His complexion is sallow, his beard sparse. His clothes are old-fashioned and threadbare. He is even too stingy to buy the wig that fashion dictates.

Paternal emotions have no meaning for Harpagon, because he sees Elise and Cléante only as financial assets or liabilities. His daughter must wed a wealthy man who will not ask for a dowry, and Cléante is merely an effeminate dandy whose profligacy is a threat to the family estate. Harpagon represents the principle of sterility. The projected union with Mariane is a means of cultivating his self-love and increasing his fortune. By ignoring the natural alliance between his son and Mariane, Harpagon violates the social order.

The miser experiences tender emotions only while lamenting the theft of his strongbox. Money has human characteristics and fulfills emotional needs: "My poor money, my poor money, my dear friend. They have deprived me of you. And with you taken away from me, I have lost my support, my consolation, my job: all is over for me, and I have nothing further to do on earth. Without you, life is impossible." Money is his total *raison d'être*, and its loss is a tragedy that will end in death. The pathos of this episode reveals that all the miser's moral and emotional values are subverted to money. He finds life in the inanimate gold coins and tries to stifle his children's emotional vitality. Yet this comedy ends with youth triumphant over old age's perversion; Harpagon is left alone with his self-love and his money. Youth (the lovers) and common sense (Anselm) vanquish moral insanity. Unlike Jonson's Volpone, Harpagon is not punished, for he is essentially a pathetic *type* and not an individual who should be subjected to suffering.

Like all comedies, *The Miser* shows how the natural social order prevails over an antisocial force. Because it is essentially a formula play, with stock characters, the story is intentionally unoriginal. But although the materials are stereotyped (two couples must overcome the disapproval of their elders in order to marry), Molière's characterizations and theatrical adroitness transcend these limitations.

The play's characters are foils for Harpagon's comic antics, exposing his vanity and miserliness. Cléante, a loyal but willful son, believes in the pleasures of the world. His fashionable dress contrasts with his father's absurdly outmoded attire. The money-lending episode reveals the miser's cruel avariciousness. Later, when Cléante removes a diamond ring from Harpagon's finger and presents it to Mariane in his father's name, the miser is exposed as a tactless man who cannot give anything of value to people he is supposed to love. Cléante's wit transforms the old man's protests into avowals of generosity, but the bitter, moral lesson lies not far beneath the comic surface.

Valère believes that flattery is the best way to deal with a monomaniac like Harpagon. The steward's exaggerated and ridiculous praise of money over love, honor, happiness, beauty, traditions of hospitality, and humane values is glee-

fully seconded by Harpagon. But the audience understands
the comic irony implicit in Valère's sardonic commentary.

Jacques's honesty elicits Harpagon's wrath and Valère's
blows. When he changes his attitude and tries to mediate
the dispute over Mariane, the scene is comic because of
Harpagon's and Cléante's vanity. Yet Jacques's attempt to
steer the middle course between sincerity and mendacity is
equally unprofitable. Only when he purges himself by accusing Valère of robbery does Jacques win the miser's ap-
probation. But if Harpagon appreciates a lie, society does
not, and Jacques's behavior ironically emphasizes the miser's
perverted values.

Unlike *The Misanthrope, The Miser* is not a comedy of the
intellect. Molière has loaded his dramaturgy with conventional *comedia dell'arte* techniques: beatings and collisions,
violent stage business and imaginative costumes, all the
components of slapstick. Harpagon's suspicious and miserly
nature is viscerally apparent to the audience when he frisks
his son's valet for stolen goods and then violently beats him
with a cane. During this scene, each character makes face-
tious asides to the audience to reconfirm the artificiality of
the drama. The miser's constant flights to the garden, his
fear of strange noises, and his hysteria when he is robbed
("I want you to arrest the whole city and the suburbs")
are comic exaggerations of normal human action, relieving
the audience of the necessity for making moral judgments.

Jacques's quick changes from coachman to cook are both
vaudevillian and profoundly satirical, for this surfeit of
costumes, like the other servants' stained and threadbare
clothing, exposes Harpagon's refusal to hire an ample staff
or clothe his servants properly.

Critics have often commented upon the structural weaknesses of *The Miser*. Frosine's plan to distract Harpagon
from his courtship of Mariane is never developed, and the
conclusion of the play is blatantly artificial. The *deus ex
machina* that allows Valère to win Elise and Cléante to
marry Mariane is a contrivance of long standing in European
theater. Yet Molière is totally justified in his refusal to
indulge in psychological drama when his intentions are different. The miser is a stock type, and any transformation
of his personality at the conclusion of the drama would
vitiate the comic effect. The artificiality of the climax leaves

Harpagon totally unchanged and unrepentant; robbed of his son and daughter, he is oblivious to the loss and glories only in the recovery of the money, his support, consolation, and joy.

The Miser is one of the most popular comedies in world literature. For over three hundred years, the Comédie Française, which Molière founded, has included it in its repertory. It has been translated into many languages, and is frequently performed the world over.

The Bourgeois Gentleman

by

JEAN-BAPTISTE POQUELIN (MOLIÈRE) (1622–1673)

The Characters

Jourdain—an extremely wealthy *nouveau riche* obsessed by the desire to become an aristocrat. He furnishes his house opulently and vulgarly, hires tutors and an elaborate entourage of servants, bedecks himself extravagantly, and pursues a young marquise. His vanity and naiveté disrupt his household, nearly deprive his daughter of her lover, and make him the laughingstock of the court.

Mrs. Jourdain—a sensible but shrewish woman who never forgets her humble origins; she mocks her husband's pretensions and trusts her daughter.

Lucile—the younger daughter of the Jourdains. In love with Cléonte, she tries to maintain decorum and obey her parents while heeding the promptings of her heart.

Nicole—the Jourdains' servant, quick to show her contempt for Jourdain's posturings. She is really closer to Jourdain by birth and temperament than he could possibly admit. Her alliance with Covielle, Mrs. Jourdain, and the young lovers ultimately brings about the downfall of her master.

Cléonte—a respectable, middle-class fellow, outspoken, honest, and loyal.

Covielle—a wily and resourceful valet who has gained Cléonte's trust. He mimics his master's attitudes when he himself courts Nicole.

Dorante—a young and indigent count, he insinuates himself into Jourdain's household and borrows vast sums of money from Jourdain on the pretense that he is embellishing Jourdain's reputation at court.

Dorimène—a beautiful, young, and wealthy marquise, the object of Mr. Jourdain's pursuit and Dorante's attentions. A true aristocrat: generous, intelligent, and courteous.

Music Master—a parasite in the household who puts on entertainments and deplores Jourdain's taste.

Dancing Master—prostituting his art to bourgeois vulgarity, he wistfully longs for a truly appreciative audience.

Fencing Master—pompous and arrogant, he belittles his colleagues and cajoles his client.

Philosophy Professor—full of cant and hypocrisy, the most vain and contentious of the tutors.

Tailor—the most despicable of Jourdain's entourage, he fobs off bizarre costumes at exorbitant prices while flattering his customer.

The Story

In the vulgar and overelaborate salon of the very wealthy Jourdain, two elegant instructors of dance and music discuss their arts and the tasteless behavior of their employer. The dancing master agrees with his colleague that although Jourdain's liberal payments are indispensable, it would be more satisfactory to have a truly appreciative public.

When Jourdain enters in a ludicrous robe and nightcap, he extorts compliments and praises his own aristocratic bearing. Both masters bestow ambiguous praise on Jourdain and prepare an entertainment that consists of a musician singing a pastoral love song. Jourdain objects to the sadness of the air and ignores the music master's comment that music should fit the words. He then sings a popular street song in a croaking voice, to the ironic approval of his teachers, who then fall into a dispute over the relative merits of music and dance.

The entertainment is presented: Two musicians perform a small oratorio in the most refined manner. The recital is followed by a dance concert. While another entertainment is being prepared, Jourdain calls his servants and dresses himself in an absurdly elaborate costume. He then clumsily

does a minuet with the dancing master and inquires how
to formally salute a marquise. His attempts to imitate the
dancing master's graceful motions are interrupted by the
entrance of the fencing master.

The fencing lesson proceeds, further revealing Jourdain's
clumsiness and incompetence. A quarrel arises among the
three tutors over their disciplines. While Jourdain is trying
to mollify the disputants, the philosophy professor enters
and extols the value of reason. But he too is drawn into
the argument when he passionately defends his profession,
and a fistfight ensues, during which the four combatants
pummel each other off the stage.

When he returns from the battle, the disheveled philosophy professor proceeds to discourse to Jourdain on Latin,
reason, logic, physics, and spelling. Jourdain is delighted to
learn the pronunciation of vowels and asks how to write
a love letter to a lady of quality. Astounded that he has
been speaking prose all his life, Jourdain curses his family
for never having taught him such wonderful facts. He wants
to write: "Beautiful Marquise, your lovely eyes make me
die of love." The philosophy professor rearranges the words
in various meaningless ways until finally the original version
is chosen.

Jourdain's tailor arrives and is admonished for his tardi-
ness. He presents a ridiculous outfit with extravagantly
plumed hat, red wig, and embroidered coat for Jourdain's
wardrobe. The tailor is scolded for having taken some
material from a former outfit for his own use, but Jourdain
is appeased when the tailor's four assistants dress him in a
ceremonial fashion and flatter him by saying: "My gentleman," "Monseigneur" (a title reserved for gentlemen of
noble birth), and "Your Highness." Jourdain rewards the
assistants generously.

Nicole enters and bursts into laughter at the sight of her
ridiculously garbed master. She answers his admonitions
by gasping that she would rather be beaten than stop laughing. But Jourdain silences her when he announces that she
must put the house in order for important guests. When
Mrs. Jourdain arrives, she joins the maid in mocking her
husband's pomposity. The two women are convulsed by
Jourdain's recitation of the stupid information he has learned
from the philosophy professor, but their mirth turns to anger

when Mrs. Jourdain warns her husband not to lend any more money to Dorante, a nobleman who has been a parasite upon the household. At that moment, Dorante appears, showers Mrs. Jourdain with compliments, and says he will pay all his debts if Jourdain will only tell him the exact figure. The sum is enormous. While Jourdain is castigating his wife for her ungenerous suspicions about Dorante, the nobleman asks for an additional loan, which is immediately granted. Jourdain is willing to sacrifice everything because Dorante tells him that he has spoken of him in the king's chambers.

After the money is paid, the two men privately discuss the impending visit of Marquise Dorimène, whom Jourdain is trying to seduce. Dorante informs the bourgeois that he has just presented a diamond ring in Jourdain's name, and now the marquise is eager to meet her admirer. In reality, of course, Dorante is courting the marquise for himself at Jourdain's expense. Nicole is discovered eavesdropping and receives a rude slap on the cheek. When she tells her mistress of Jourdain's projects, Mrs. Jourdain is unconcerned and dismisses her suspicions because she is occupied with her daughter's engagement to Cléonte. She wants the young man to declare his intentions to her husband.

Cléonte and Covielle enter and begin arguing with their sweethearts because their salutations were ignored in the street. Covielle and Nicole parody their masters' spat, but both arguments are resolved when Lucile explains that the presence of her watchful aunt prevented her from acknowledging Cléonte's greeting.

When Jourdain enters, Cléonte declares his love for Lucile and is rejected because he is not a gentleman. Jourdain rushes off and Covielle consoles his master by telling him that he will prepare a masquerade to dupe the ridiculous Jourdain.

Marquise Dorimène and her escort, Dorante, arrive and exchange compliments. Dorimène, obviously unaware that Jourdain has been courting her with lavish presents, protests that Dorante is spending far too much on her. When Jourdain appears and tries to perform the elaborate bowing ceremony he has learned from the dancing master, the results are hilarious. But Dorimène graciously accepts his homage and sits at the table as Dorante whispers to Jourdain not to be indelicate by mentioning the presents to Dorimène. A procession of sumptuous dishes is ceremoniously presented by six imaginatively costumed cooks who perform the third entr'acte ballet.

Mrs. Jourdain rushes in and disrupts the dinner, accusing the marquise of being a husband-stealer. Dorimène runs off, followed by Dorante. Alone, Jourdain is lamenting the miscarriage of his plans when he is interrupted by Covielle, disguised as a Turkish nobleman. Covielle immediately wins Jourdain's friendship by telling him he knew Jourdain's father to be a great gentleman. The son of the Great Turk is in Paris and has fallen in love with Lucile, whom he wishes to marry. But before the marriage can take place, Jourdain must be dubbed Mamamouchi, the highest Turkish title of nobility. A bevy of turbaned dignitaries begins the ceremony, chants Turkish-sounding words, dresses Jourdain in flowing robes and monstrous turban, and finally beats him. When Mrs. Jourdain finds her husband ridiculously garbed, dazed, and muttering gibberish, she fears he is mad, especially when he explains that he is now a Mamamouchi and the Son of the Great Turk shall marry Lucile.

Dorimène agrees to marry Dorante to put an end to his lavish spending. Suddenly, Cléonte and Covielle, still disguised as Turks, enter and apprise Dorante of the ruse. He agrees to go along. Lucile arrives. She protests the impending marriage until she recognizes her lover behind the disguise. Mrs. Jourdain also stops protesting when she realizes how her husband has been tricked. The play concludes with preparations for the marriages of Lucile to Cléonte, Nicole to Covielle, and Dorimène to Dorante, and the entire company takes part in a ballet.

Critical Opinion

Originally presented in 1670 as a court entertainment for Louis XIV, with Molière playing the title role, *The Bourgeois Gentleman* is a combination of different styles, influences, and techniques welded into a comedy whose satirical dissection of the *nouveau riche* is still relevant today. Jourdain is the prototype of the self-made man whose great wealth is unadorned by culture or manners. At once ridiculous and pathetic, Jourdain is a vulgar, aspiring slob whose ambition and vanity expose him to society's ridicule and duplicity.

Performed originally in a magnificent château, the play shows little sympathy for the modern ideal of the self-made man. Molière loathed the social climbers in court who contaminated the elegance of the aristocratic class. He also despised those who yielded to the temptation to exploit people like Jourdain: the characters of the dancing, music, and fencing masters, the philosophy professor, and, most pointedly, Dorante, the unscrupulous nobleman.

Molière has imaginatively expanded the ingredients of farce and the comedy of gesture into a court entertainment. The slapstick elements—battles, chases, disputes, disguises, and ludicrous costumes—theatricalize Jourdain's vanity and self-deceit. The plot allows Molière not only to explore a comedy rich in tension and laughter but to present elaborate ballets and musical entertainments in striking contrast to Jourdain, who is incapable of appreciating their refined artificiality. Like Alceste in *The Misanthrope,* who prefers a popular street song to Oronte's sonnet, Jourdain rejects the pastoral tradition and sings a ditty comparing a young girl to sheep. His childlike pleasure in things he does not understand or appreciate, his falling asleep during the musical performance, and his preoccupation with the banalities of clothing, illuminate the contrast between the world he aspires to enter and his hopeless vulgarity.

The play's opening scenes are farcical in action but subtle in verbal satire. Molière employed the language of his time —especially the technical and courtly vocabulary—to expose the futility of Jourdain's aspirations and the pretentiousness of his tutors. The philosophy professor is most cruelly satirized, for he is absorbed in the cant and jargon of his discipline without being able to relate them to life. Jourdain exposes him (and himself) when he discovers the distinction between prose and verse, pronounces the vowels, and proposes a love letter to the marquise. The audience laughs at the would-be gentleman, but sympathizes with his naiveté and goodwill. The philosophy professor, already stripped of his dignity after fighting with the other tutors, is revealed as a pompous ass. Professional jargon, distorted technical terms, the use of puns, are Molière's intellectual equivalents of the physical slapstick.

The Turkish masquerade is the play's most elaborate comic device. Jourdain, so inflamed with the desire to marry his daughter to a nobleman that he will accept the most improbable situation, becomes nearly touching when he accepts the disguised Covielle's claims that Jourdain's father was a nobleman. Of course Jourdain knows his father was a merchant, but his vanity and snobbery induce him to believe a lie.

The totally bizarre costumes, manners, and language of the masquerading Turks are patently silly—parodies of naive conceptions of the Orient shared by many noblemen of Molière's time. The vogue for the exotic, which was to develop into what the eighteenth century called *chinoiserie*, is ridiculed in Molière's exposure of the gullibility and pretentiousness of these people. When Jourdain is beaten, rolled in a blanket, and blindfolded to the accompaniment of Oriental music, chants, and rituals, the parallels between these rites and the Catholic Mass were not lost on the audience. Molière harbored an intense dislike for the religious cabals that dominated French political and cultural life. (*Tartuffe* suffered repeated attacks from the clergy and was twice banned at the insistence of powerful religious factions.)

Molière drew the portraits of his servants from the popular Italian *commedia dell'arte* tradition. Covielle is the master of ceremonies who invents and supervises the elaborate masquerades and rites that unmask Jourdain's folly. In his love scenes with Nicole, Covielle parodies his master's upper-class behavior with Lucile. Wily, ingenious, and loyal, Covielle manipulates the passions of his superiors without violating the basic relationship between servant and master.

Nicole, also in the *commedia* tradition, is an earthy young woman who does not attempt to restrain her laughter at Jourdain's posturings. She is full of common sense, a quality that only the servants and Mrs. Jourdain possess. Molière reinforces this impression by letting Nicole and her mistress speak in an unaffected peasant manner, using crude pronunciation and direct modes of expression.

The slapstick is also in the vein of *commedia dell'arte*. Jourdain is constantly exposed as a bobbling and incompetent *arriviste* who performs humiliating gestures and speeches before the marquise and endures a brutal pummeling during the Mamamouchi initiation ceremony.

Like all of Molière's comedies, *The Bourgeois Gentleman* is a social satire. The principal butts are Jourdain, a *nouveau riche* who tries to be someone he is not, and the aristocratic parasites who thrive on Jourdain's folly. The type of false aristocrat satirized in Dorante was not lost on members of the court who viewed the play. The tutors, although not aristocrats themselves, are also fiercely mocked, as is the tailor, lowest of the parasites, who unabashedly panders to Jourdain's whims and steals from his client.

The most admirable characters, Cléonte, Mrs. Jourdain, and Nicole, understand their place in a highly stratified society. The common sense and humility that Cléonte displays when he refuses to claim noble descent accentuate Jourdain's folly. And by her simple, unpretentious manners, Mrs. Jourdain exemplifies a bourgeoise who knows how to profit from her advancement but does not overstep the bounds of class. Nicole retains her refreshing honesty and, in alliance with her mistress, does not hesitate to denounce Jourdain's ridiculousness.

Molière's use of traditional comic situations is apparent in his development of the theme of youth versus age. Jourdain is foolish not only because he pursues Dorimène, who is of much higher social class, but also because she is some thirty years younger than he. His exploitation of Lucile for his own gain is a familiar comic pattern. By forcing her to renounce her lover because Cléonte is not a gentleman, Jourdain becomes a stock father character who disregards love for money and class. The natural moral order triumphs when Lucile marries Cléonte and Dorante wins the hand of Dorimène.

Music and dance are integral parts of the play. Jean-Baptiste Lully, Louis XIV's court composer, contributed the music for the first production, and the royal dancing masters devised the choreography and pantomimes. While these additions sometimes do not appeal to modern tastes, they are a vital part of the satire and contribute to the play's structure. The entr'actes consist of ballet divertissements that effectively link moods and provide a structural bond between the various scenes.

The Bourgeois Gentleman has been enormously popular

since its premiere more than three hundred years ago. One of the staples in the repertory of the Comédie Française, it has been performed in translation and recorded. Despite the many allusions to seventeenth-century life and manners, *The Bourgeois Gentleman* remains a universal and timeless indictment of affectation and pretension.

The Author

Jean-Baptiste Poquelin was born in Paris in 1622. He is best known by his pen name, Molière. Little is known of his early life except that he came from a middle-class family and that he studied in a Jesuit school. Official documents indicate that on June 30, 1643, he formed a theater group with Madeleine Béjart and eight others. Touring the provinces and presenting farces and other light fare, the company won the patronage of King Louis XIV's brother in 1658.

Molière returned to Paris, where he continued to write, direct, and stage-manage his company, which became the forerunner of the Comédie Française, the principal legitimate theater institution in modern France. Most of our information about Molière's career comes from a journal written by La Grange, an actor in his troupe. But La Grange's records are inaccurate and incomplete, and so we know little about the playwright's character or private life. He was often attacked by jealous contemporaries for his immorality. In 1662, he married Armande Béjart, who was the younger sister, not the daughter, of his mistress, Madeleine Béjart.

Molière's first major success was *Les Précieuses Ridicules* (1659). This was followed by *Tartuffe* (1664), an attack on religious hypocrisy that was banned for five years but finally gained acceptance. Molière wrote farces, masques, and court entertainments for Louis XIV. He became enormously successful.

While playing the title role in *The Imaginary Invalid* (1673), Molière was taken ill. He died in 1673 and was refused Christian burial until the king obtained special dispensation from the Archbishop of Paris.

Molière is best known for *The School for Wives* (1662), *Tartuffe* (1664), *Don Juan* (1665), *The Misanthrope* (1666), *The Miser* (1668), *The Bourgeois Gentleman* (1670), and

The Imaginary Invalid (1673). In his plays, he employs a variety of dramatic techniques: farce, slapstick, comedy of manners, and comedy of characters. Molière said that he wrote for everyone, not just the court, and that laughter was the most important moral force in his plays. He aimed to correct men's vices through laughter and ridicule. In his comedies, his pictures of society are more important than the plots, for he depicted every stratum of society, from the court to the servants' quarters, and attempted to draw a universal picture of mankind.

Phèdre

by

JEAN RACINE (1639–1699)

The Characters

Thésée—the middle-aged king of Athens whose entire life
has been devoted to adventure and heroic conquest. As a
young man, he had vanquished the Minotaur and deliberately precipitated the death of Egeus, his father. As an
adult, he is as impetuous as ever. He fears the truth,
seeks help from Neptune, who has served him once before,
and sends his son to his death. Only too late does he discover the truth.

Phèdre—a proud princess of Crete, daughter of Pasiphae
and Minos, and Thésée's second wife. After her older
sister, Ariadne, helped Thésée out of the labyrinth, Phèdre
succeeded in stealing his affections and became queen of
Athens. She is an emotional, irrational woman who, from
the beginning of the play, is dying. Her obsessive love for
her stepson drives her to an open declaration of passion,
but her conscience wins out and she commits suicide.

Hippolyte—Thésée's innocent, brave young son whose sense
of honor prevents him from telling his father the truth.
He is in love with Aricie, but fears displeasing his father.
He dies heroically, the tragic victim of the gods and his
father's blindness.

Aricie—a beautiful Athenian princess whose family is the
declared enemy of Thésée. She is a worthy companion for
Hippolyte and shares his nobility, purity, and honor.

Théramène—Hippolyte's old tutor and confidant, who encourages Hippolyte to declare his love to Aricie. He tries
to make him understand that his passion is not criminal.
He assumes the Greek role of the chorus when he recounts
his master's death.

Oenone—Phèdre's nurse and confidante, the archetype of
evil and in a sense the true author of Phèdre's crime. In
her devotion to her mistress, she accuses the innocent in
order to protect Phèdre. When Phèdre curses her, Oenone
commits suicide.

The Story

In the Peloponnesian city of Trezène, Hippolyte tells his
tutor, Théramène, that he plans to leave home in search of his
father. His motives are complex: a discomfort in his young
stepmother's presence and a need to escape from Aricie,
whom he has begun to love—against his father's wishes.

Oenone interrupts the two men with news that her mistress
is dying of some strange ailment. Hippolyte exits as Phèdre
enters, complaining that "everything afflicts me, hurts me,
conspires to harm me." Oenone exhorts Phèdre to live, if
only to keep Hippolyte from ruling and taking charge of her
son. But Phèdre confesses that she is in love with Hippolyte.
Suddenly, one of her servants announces Thésée's death.
Oenone joyfully informs Phèdre: "Live, you no longer need
reproach yourself;/Your flame becomes an ordinary flame./
By dying Thésée has just broken the bonds which caused
the crime and horror of your fire." Phèdre should unite with
Hippolyte to fight Aricie.

A little later, Aricie awaits Hippolyte. Her confidante,
Ismène, tells her that Hippolyte will pardon her family:
They are no longer state enemies. Hippolyte will be king,
and Phèdre will be powerless. Only moments before Hip-
polyte arrives, Aricie confesses to Ismène that she loves him.
Hippolyte also declares his passion for Aricie.

Just before Hippolyte is about to sail for Athens, Phèdre
appears and asks him to stay. She says she is dying and
beseeches him to take care of her son. She has pretended to
hate Hippolyte and demands pity. When Hippolyte suggests

his father might still be alive, Phèdre says: "He is not dead
because he lives in you." She loves Thésée: "charming,
young, dragging all hearts after him,/Such as our gods have
described or such as I see you." Hippolyte understands her
hidden declaration all too well, and when he tries to flee,
Phèdre confesses: "Thésée's widow dares to love Hippolyte."
She tells him that he must kill her. Oenone leads her mistress away while Théramène informs Hippolyte that there is
a rumor that Thésée lives.

Phèdre tells Oenone that she is dishonored. She has revealed her dreadful secret and has been rejected. Oenone
counsels her to suppress her passion and rule Athens alone.
But Phèdre retorts that she cannot even govern herself, let
alone a state. She blames Oenone for encouraging her immoral love. But perhaps Hippolyte has not rejected her,
perhaps he is merely unused to love. She will ask Hippolyte
to rule instead of her son. Oenone leaves to find Hippolyte,
but returns to announce that Thésée has returned. Phèdre
is dishonored and swears to die. Again, Oenone dissuades
her mistress and asks how she sees Hippolyte now. "As a
terrible monster," Phèdre replies. Oenone suggests Phèdre
accuse Hippolyte before he can accuse her. Phèdre hesitates
to "oppress and blacken innocence"; but Oenone will speak
to Thésée: "It is necessary to immolate everything, even
virtue."

Thésée arrives but Phèdre flees, declaring herself "unworthy of pleasing . . . and of approaching." Thésée asks
Hippolyte to explain her strange behavior, but he refuses
and in turn asks permission to leave in order to prove himself worthy of his father. Thésée is perplexed. His family
avoids him; he wants to know the truth. Alone with Théramène, Hippolyte wonders if Phèdre will tell Thésée the
truth.

The odious Oenone has just told Thésée that Hippolyte
loves Phèdre. Thésée calls his son and banishes him. He
exhorts Neptune to avenge him and punish this traitor.
Hippolyte is dumbfounded, denies loving Phèdre, and asks
his father to look at his life: "The day is not purer than the
depths of my heart." His only crime is loving the forbidden
Aricie. But Thésée thinks that this is a ploy, and Hippolyte
asks for pity: "What friends will plead for me, when you

abandon me?" He tells his father to speak to Phèdre and to keep her heritage of woe in mind.

Phèdre begs Thésée not to exile his son, but Thésée reveals his request for vengeance. Hippolyte even had the insolence to declare his love for Aricie. This revelation shocks Phèdre, and once alone with Oenone, she worries about her rival. She wants to destroy Aricie, but stops herself: "What am I doing? Where is my reason wandering?/ Me jealous! And it is Thésée that I implore!" Again Oenone tries to comfort her mistress and convince her that she is blameless. But Phèdre turns on her servant and chases her away.

Alone together for the last time, Aricie begs Hippolyte to denounce Phèdre and tell Thésée the truth. But Hippolyte refuses to shame his father. He asks Aricie to follow him, but she hesitates to live in exile dishonored. Hippolyte implores her to come to the city gates where they will exchange vows. He flees as Thésée enters. Aricie tells Thésée that his sentence is unjust. The king decides to speak to Oenone once more, but learns Oenone has thrown herself into the sea. While Thésée beseeches Neptune to ignore his curse, Théramène enters and recounts Hippolyte's death. A monster rose out of the water. Although Hippolyte wounded the creature, his horses suddenly ran wild in fear and dragged him to his death. Moments before Aricie arrived to join her lover, Hippolyte died, requesting that Thésée take care of Aricie in order to avenge his unwarranted death. Phèdre appears before Thésée and declares that Hippolyte was innocent. She has taken poison. As she dies, Thésée leaves to find his son and to take the unfortunate Aricie home as his daughter.

Critical Opinion

Phèdre is the best known of Racine's poetic tragedies. Unlike Corneille, who emphasized both the moral and emotional conflicts in his characters, Racine focused on the psychological order of events. Starting at the climax, the action is compressed to exclude any extraneous events. Thus, the drama's movement appears to be a logical develop-

ment of a state of mind. Writing almost forty years after
Corneille, Racine retained the fundamental classical concept
of tragedy as a depiction of universal emotions, but he
eschewed complicated plots. In the preface to *Britannicus*
(1669), Racine wrote that a great number of incidents were
unnecessary as long as the action was simple and sustained
by the force of passions and the elegance of expression. A
year later, he elaborated in *Bérénice:* "It is sufficient for the
action to be great, that the actors be heroic, and that the
passions be aroused."

The structure of *Phèdre* is based on a series of parallel
confessions: Each act opens with Hippolyte, closes with
Phèdre; the characters enact the same scenes. In Act I, Hippolyte confesses his love for Aricie to Théramène, and
Phèdre reveals her passion for Hippolyte to Oenone; Act II
opens as Hippolyte declares himself to Aricie and closes as
Phèdre reveals herself to Hippolyte. In Act III, Phèdre
accuses herself, and Hippolyte worries about guilt; Act IV
begins as Hippolyte refuses to implicate Phèdre and terminates as Phèdre accuses herself. The final act begins with
Hippolyte's farewell to Aricie and ends with Phèdre's public
confession, farewell, and death. These parallels reveal the
inexorable movement of passion. Hippolyte and Phèdre,
both victims of fate, suffer from the beginning of the
drama. Pure love and culpable passion result in the same
agonies. During the course of the drama, however, Hippolyte learns that his love is innocent, while Phèdre must
recognize that there are dark abysses of passion.

The contrasting imagery of innocence and guilt, purity
and contamination, light and dark, unifies the drama and is
a key to its psychological structure. Hippolyte is a symbol
of purity, associated with the day, light, and innocence.
Phèdre, who at the opening of the play is already descend-
ing into hell, clings to the shadows but aspires toward purity.
The last word she utters before death is "purity": "And
death, which veils light from my eyes,/Returns to the day,
which they soiled, all her purity." Death will correct her
vision; death will not act against the day: it will bring light.
The problem is to purify Phèdre's tragic vision that sees the
day (life, Hippolyte) incestuously. Thus, Racine gives special psychological significance to a banal expression: "to see
the light."

When Phèdre appears for the first time, she emerges both literally and symbolically from darkness into light. She is blinded by the daylight: after three days in bed, she is literally unable to bear the light. But psychologically and symbolically, her desire to "see the day" is a startling expression of her inner disturbance. She wishes to see the day, not a specific person, because she associates the day with Hippolyte. She has come to bid the sun farewell. Although she is the granddaughter of the sun, the source of clarity, light, and purity, she cannot live innocently. Fate looms over her entire family: her mother, enamored of Jupiter, loved him in the form of a bull and begot the Minotaur. This grotesque half-brother was slaughtered by Phèdre's future husband, Thésée, whom she stole from her sister. Phèdre's own incestuous love is but an extension of her family's curse. The thought of the sun reminds Phèdre of the shadows of the forest and of Hippolyte. She seems to plunge into an interior monologue, never directly responding to Oenone's remarks or questions. She repents having dressed with a little flair and seems to feel the need to liberate herself from constraint. Yet she suffers no matter what she does. Her seductive dress is meaningless, because Hippolyte cannot even look at her.

The image of the forest's shadows is another metaphor for Hippolyte, who in Phèdre's eyes is the wild, virginal creature of the woods. Like Phèdre, Hippolyte is doomed by heredity. His mother, Antiope, Queen of the Amazons, was the virginal protectress of the forest. Thus, Phèdre's reveries on shadow and obscurity are double torments: she can never join Hippolyte and is only reminded of her unworthiness to appear in the daylight.

Throughout the play, Phèdre condemns herself through her eyes. Her inadvertent confession to Hippolyte is prompted by her vision of him. Speaking of Thésée, she cannot prevent herself from confusing her image of the young Thésée with the youth before her. In her attempts to assure Hippolyte that she no longer hates him, Phèdre tips the scale, going from hate to love. But it is always the eye that controls and provokes the action. Hippolyte cannot bear to look upon Phèdre. Immediately after her confession, Phèdre wants him to kill her so that he will be forced to see her. From the moment of her avowal, Hippolyte also considers himself to be contaminated. He tells Théramène that he sees himself through her eyes and is horrified. Hippolyte becomes a monster to Phèdre, for each time he appears before her, he threatens her with his presence yet refuses her.

Phèdre is simultaneously moral and immoral. She is the first to condemn her illicit passion and reminds Oenone that it is contrary to all laws, but she pities herself for not having enjoyed the fruits of this criminal passion. In her rage, she considers herself affronted and even wants to call on Thésée to defend her.

The brief confrontation of Thésée with his son and wife reveals a total misunderstanding of vision. In the only scene in which all three are present, none of the characters can look at the others. Phèdre cannot bear Hippolyte's severe glance and does not understand that he will never accuse her. As a pure young man, he cannot dishonor his father. Phèdre withdraws; her desire to hide is itself a confession. But Hippolyte misunderstands her purpose. He wishes to leave before she exposes the truth, so that he may spare his father. Thésée is also unable to see correctly; he only half-listens to his son and waits for an explanation. One of the great tragedies in *Phèdre* is the difficulty of seeing correctly, the difficulty of attaining self-knowledge.

The parallel between Hippolyte and Phèdre is strengthened by the presence of Thésée, who can comprehend neither Hippolyte's innocence nor Phèdre's aspiration for purity. He commits the fatal error of calling upon the gods for help, and he suspects his crime too late. Thésée is a tragic hero whose destiny is alternately to pursue and to evade truth. When he embraces Aricie as his daughter, it is a pathetic reminder of his son's innocence. After Phèdre's death, Thésée does not understand her. He can only comment: "Such a black action," making Phèdre's position even more tragic.

Oenone is a hideous counterpart of Phèdre. A grotesque and inhuman incarnation of Phèdre's passion, Oenone encourages her mistress's blackest desires. When Thésée is presumed dead, she argues: "Your flame becomes an ordinary flame./By dying, Thésée has just broken the bonds which caused the crime and horror of your fire." But Phèdre thinks differently; her flame is never an ordinary flame, but an illusion. Her conscience confronts her with both the pain and the crime. The evil spirit Oenone can accuse Hippolyte when Phèdre cannot, but she commits suicide when she recognizes Phèdre's horror.

Hippolyte also has a counterpart. Just as Oenone is an exaggeration of Phèdre's corrupt soul, Aricie is another expression of Hippolyte's purity and innocence. Like her lover, she has been unjustly persecuted by Thésée, who has forbidden relations with any member of her family. She respects Hippolyte's sense of honor, and even though she knows the truth about Phèdre, she never tells Thésée. Also like Hippolyte, she is fated to remain a virgin; she holds her lover only when he is dying.

Racine adhered to a strict form of Catholicism known as Jansenism. If he was influenced by this rigid doctrine of sin, guilt, and salvation, it is most evident in *Phèdre* in the conception of concupiscence as the sin in which the individual commits a carnal act with his eyes. In a sense, *Phèdre* is the story of a dying woman who sinned by allowing her eyes to express desire. Her pursuit of purity is a striving for grace. Racine's pessimistic view of human passion in *Phèdre* is typically Jansenist.

A tightly knit work, *Phèdre* is an excellent example of seventeenth-century classical drama. The vivid metaphors of light and shadow, innocence and guilt, which are essential keys to the characters, make the play's structure and thematic development inseparable from the poetic form. Written in the twelve-syllable Alexandrine verse, this extremely lyrical drama compresses the action so that only the psychological development emerges. Racine's version of *Phèdre*, taken from Euripides, is recognized as one of the greatest French plays. From its first performance in January 1677 to the present, it has remained part of the repertory of the Comédie Française and has been played in translations throughout the world. In 1962, there was released in this country Jules Dassin's film *Phaedra*, a modern version of the Phèdre legend, written by Dassin and Margarita Liberaki, and starring Melina Mercouri, Raf Vallone, and Anthony Perkins.

Phèdre is one of the world's continuing challenges to a great actress. The history of the play is a chronicle of superb and diverse interpretations. In 1854, the French actress Rachel gave a performance called "apocalyptic" for the fury of its reading; twenty years later, Sarah Bernhardt eschewed Rachel's style of *"la fureur"* and emphasized *"la douleur"* in the role. She showed Phèdre as more sinned against than sinning. More recently, in 1957, at the Palace Theatre, London, the French actress Edwige Feuillère favored an even more passive reading. Like a few other great plays, *Hamlet* among them, *Phèdre* in production mirrors each age in the theater.

The Author

Born in a provincial town near Paris in 1639, Jean Racine was orphaned at an early age and grew up with his grandparents, who were devout Roman Catholics, members of the puritanical Jansenist sect. Racine's early education at Port Royal provided him with a thorough grounding in the Greek and Roman classics and instilled in him a deep religious consciousness. His devotions waned somewhat by 1660 when his theatrical career brought him into contact with La Fontaine and Parisian artistic society. Soon after, an ode on the marriage of Louis XIV having brought him royal recognition, Racine was composing poetry addressed to the king and became firmly established at court.

Racine's first significant play, *La Thébaïde,* was performed by Molière's company in 1664. Molière also produced *Alexandre le Grand* in the following year. Racine's involvement in the literary, social, and political disputes of the time earned him many enemies. The Jansenists at Port Royal turned against their protégé and mounted a bitter attack on the playwright's immorality. Savage exchanges occurred, and Boileau, the poet and esthetician, prevailed upon Racine to withdraw from the feuds and devote himself to writing plays. In 1667, *Andromaque* was acclaimed as a masterpiece. The next decade saw productions of *Britannicus* (1669), *Bérénice* (1670), and *Phèdre* (1677), all considered supreme works in this genre.

After enjoying great success, Racine withdrew from society, married a wealthy and devout Catholic, and ceased writing plays until Madame de Maintenon requested a religious play for her boarding school at Saint Cyr. *Esther* (1689) was succeeded by *Athaliah* (1691), Racine's last work. He died in 1699, a pious man who had lived a full emotional and artistic life.

Faust, Part I

by

JOHANN WOLFGANG VON GOETHE (1749–1832)

The Characters

Faust—a man of vast intellectual and spiritual powers, bored
and disenchanted with an ascetic life devoted to the pursuit of learning. He strikes a sophisticated bargain with
the Devil in which he affirms the supremacy of the human
spirit and vows never to "stretch myself on a bed of
ease," or be cast under "A spell of pleasure that can hoax
me."

Mephistopheles—an ironic and often sarcastic figure who
challenges God in a battle for Faust's soul.

Wagner—Faust's assistant, a conventional academician who
fails to see beyond his book-learning.

Gretchen—a pure young girl whose piety and innocence are
destroyed by Mephistopheles. Her humility and spiritual
strength endure.

Martha—a middle-aged widow, Gretchen's friend, who is
duped into assisting in the young girl's seduction.

Valentine—Gretchen's brother, a bold and emotional young
man whose sense of honor is outraged by his sister's fall.

The Story

The prologue is set in heaven. Raphael, Michael, Gabriel,
and a choir of angels praise the Lord. Mephistopheles asks

God's permission to attempt the seduction of a learned and good man. God expresses faith in his creatures and challenges the devil to pervert his subject.

In a vaulted Gothic study in Germany during the sixteenth century, Dr. Faust questions "the impossibility of knowledge." He has turned to magic in order to overcome the limitations of the rational mind. As he opens a book, he is confronted by mystical signs that send him to visionary heights where he attempts to comprehend the unifying force of the universe. A Spirit challenges him and is vanquished. Wagner enters and expresses a conventional belief in knowledge, but Faust retorts: "You have achieved no true refreshment/Unless you can tap your own soul first." Alone once again, Faust confesses to God: "Granted I own the power to draw thee down/I lack the power to hold thee there." As he is about to drink poison, a chorus of angels celebrating Easter morn draws him back to his childhood and the earth.

A few hours later, as Faust and Wagner stroll through the holiday crowds, the doctor receives the homage of the whole population. But rejecting their praise and Wagner's admiration, he again expresses doubts. As the evening mists descend, the two scholars observe a black poodle. Faust experiences a supernatural feeling, but takes the dog home with him. In his study once again, Faust pores over the Bible and rewrites the text to read: "In the beginning was the Deed." The dog takes on enormous proportions, spirits are heard, and suddenly the dog is transformed into Mephistopheles, who declares: "I am the Spirit which always denies." But the devil cannot leave the chamber because of a mark upon the threshold. Faust refuses to release him, but is lulled into sleep by a chorus of spirits.

When Mephistopheles returns, Faust confesses: "I am too old for mere amusement,/Too young to be without desire." The spirits sing again, and Mephistopheles tells Faust that "pleasure and action" will be a means to salvation. Faust confesses that "it is not a question of happiness./The most painful joy, enamoured hate, enlivening/Disgust—I devote myself to all excess." After further discussion, Faust signs a contract in blood, giving his soul to the devil.

In Auerbach's wine cellar in Leipzig, a besotted group of revelers are carousing. Their crude jests and antics reach a climax when Brander sings a witty parable about a poisoned rat whose death convulsions remind one of a person dying of love. Mephistopheles and Faust enter and comment on the waste and emptiness of the drinkers' lives. The new arrivals are questioned about their identity. Mephistopheles sings about a flea who lived in court and brought all his country friends and relatives to plague the courtiers. He then promises sweet wine, and bores holes in the tables that he seals with wax plugs. When the plugs are withdrawn, delicious wine flows. The merrymakers imbibe, but when they spill the wine, it leaps into flames. Mephistopheles confounds his hosts and departs with Faust.

In an infernal kitchen inhabited by grotesque witches and monkeys, Mephistopheles hands Faust a potion that will make him beautiful and young, prromising him magnificent women for his delectation. Later, in the street, Faust accosts Gretchen and is rebuffed. Mephistopheles promises Faust that he will possess the fourteen-year-old maiden. Faust and Mephistopheles place a jewel-filled casket in her cupboard; Gretchen discovers it. It touches her feminine vanity. Later, Mephistopheles and Faust humorously discuss how Gretchen's mother discovered the jewels and gave them to the priest.

In Martha's house, Gretchen sympathizes with her friend about the disappearance of Martha's husband. Mephistopheles enters, compliments Martha, and tells her that her husband has died penniless. He proposes a meeting with Faust, and the next evening, Martha with Mephistopheles, and Gretchen with Faust, promenade in the garden; there is a double seduction. After an evening of bliss in a summer house, Gretchen and Faust part.

Alone in a forest and cavern, Faust exults in the splendors of nature and asks Mephistopheles: "Do you comprehend what a new and vital power/This wandering in the wilderness has given me?" Renouncing Gretchen, Faust glories in his new-found spiritual powers. Mephistopheles describes the young girl's desolation and urges Faust to comfort her. Again in Martha's garden, the lovers declare their love for each other. Faust gives Gretchen a flask of sleeping drops to drug her mother while they make love in the next room. Valentine, Gretchen's brother, laments his sister's impurity, is fatally wounded during an argument with Faust and Mephistopheles, and curses his tearful sister with his last breath.

Gretchen is confronted by an evil spirit in a cathedral and is reprimanded for causing the deaths of her mother and brother. In a frenzy of guilt and despair, Gretchen cries: "I feel as if the organs/Were stifling me,/And the music dissolving/My heart in its depths." Meanwhile, Faust and Mephistopheles traverse a mountain range on their way to a *Walpurgisnacht* (a witch's sabbath). Nature erupts into a vast cataclysm of sound, motion, and light as voices from above and below intone various chants. Mephistopheles draws Faust into an assembly of cavorting, obscene figures. Faust sees a vision of Gretchen calling to him for help. When he discovers that his loved one is dying in prison, Faust remonstrates with Mephistopheles and rushes to save her. But on the eve of her execution, Gretchen, insane, does not recognize Faust and describes how she has murdered their infant. Finally, she acknowledges Faust's identity, but still refuses to leave the prison: "I dare not go out; for me there is no more hope." Deaf to Faust's imprecations, Gretchen prays, ignoring Mephistopheles' warning that redemption is impossible. A Voice from above proclaims: "Redeemed!" and Faust and Mephistopheles vanish, pursued by the Voice ominously calling out Faust's name.

Critical Opinion

The man who sells his soul to the devil in return for wealth and power is one of the central myths of Western literature. Apparently, Johannes Faust was an historical figure who may have attended the University of Heidelberg about the first decade of the sixteenth century and who is said to have died in 1540. A contemporary of Martin Luther, he appears in many of the great reformer's remarks and in the chronicles and governmental records of his time. In 1587, a work by Johann Spies, the *Faust-Book,* appeared in Germany and was immediately translated into English. Scenes were adapted by Christopher Marlowe in *The Tragical History of Doctor Faustus* (c. 1593). The Faustian myth has been variously adapted to signify the dangers of the intellect and the triumph of the human spirit and mind.

In 1770, Goethe was impressed by a puppet theater adaptation of the Faust legend. He was especially interested in the contrasting attitudes expressed by the conventional Christian outlook and the scientific rationalism of his own age. Keeping Marlowe's title of "tragedy" in mind, he set to work on his own tragedy and labored at it until eight months before his death in 1832. He called his epic poetic drama "the work of his life time" (*hauptgeschaeft*—his main business).

Since its first appearance, *Faust* has absorbed scholars and critics. Although seldom performed on the stage, it has been a fertile source of inspiration for such composers as Berlioz, Wagner, Gounod, Liszt, and Mahler as well as the great twentieth-century writers, Thomas Mann and Paul Valéry.

The dramatic and poetic elements of *Faust,* Part I, are a remarkable combination of conciseness and expansion. The economy and variety of the dramatic movement telescope actions and moods to create a unified effect. The prologue in heaven establishes a tone of epic grandeur. The universe and earth are connected in a picture of cosmic scope. The major theme of *Faust* is introduced in the poetry through contrasting images of heaven and earth, day and night, the movement of tides and celestial spheres, and the "storms in rivalry which are raging/From sea to land, from land to sea,/In frenzy forge the world a girdle/From which no inmost heart is free." This titanic conflict is translated into moral terms when Mephistopheles, proclaiming that man is but a grasshopper, is answered by the Lord: "Men make mistakes as long as they strive." These opposite views of man will clash, with Faust as the battleground: Mephistopheles will descend to earth and try to prove mankind's baseness. He denies; Faust strives.

The theme of contrast and conflict is extended on both the human and superhuman planes when Faust grants that he has turned to magic so that he may go beyond mere human knowledge and discover the unifying force in the universe. He has a stupendous vision and almost understands "Where all the powers of nature stand unveiled." He asks: "Am I a God? It grows so light!" As he communicates with the Earth Spirit, he sees that he has reached the limit of human power: "I who am Godhead's image." But the spell is broken when the pedantic and unimaginative Wagner dramatically reveals the gap between intellectual and spiritual knowledge. Faust, realizing that he has reached the ultimate that a human being can achieve, prepares to commit suicide. But the prologue's antithesis between earth and heaven is reenacted in Faust's spirit when the chance appearance of Easter worshippers brings him back to the world and his childhood; he stays the poisoned flask at his lips. This kind of unity informs every verse and episode of Goethe's grandiose yet finely wrought dramatic poem.

The next scene further prepares us for the entrance of Mephistopheles by depicting Faust and Wagner strolling through the tumultuous crowd of merrymakers outside the city gates. As the evening gloom descends, the black poodle appears as a supernatural creature to Faust's inflamed imagination. Once again in his study, Faust embarks upon the road to self-annihilation as he attempts to translate the Gospel according to Saint John and change "In the beginning was the Word" to "In the beginning was the Mind," and then to: "In the beginning was the Deed [or the Power]."

If Faust embodies the greatest, most Godlike aspect of humanity, the power to *strive,* the devil represents "the Spirit which always denies." Plunging beyond human feelings, Faust curses sensual pleasure, love, hope, and patience. The spirits lament the destruction of the "beautiful" world, and the bargain between Faust and the devil is struck.

But it is significant that the all-encompassing spirit of Faust allows him to reject the witches and then to approach Gretchen without Mephistopheles' prompting. The contrast between Faust's great passion and his use of Mephistopheles to achieve his desires symbolizes the gap between human aspiration and human weakness. The psychological insights and humor with which Goethe invests the affair between Gretchen and Faust is worthy of the greatest dramatist. Scenes flow into each other with remarkable impact and economy.

Goethe has dispensed with elaborate plot exposition by allowing his characters to explain events and create moods through the poetry they speak. Gretchen's character is quickly drawn; her conventional, feminine, sentimental character, her piety, beauty, and pathetic helplessness and simplicity contrast dramatically with both Faust and Mephistopheles.

When Faust renounces Gretchen while surveying the vast and tumultuous scenes of nature, Goethe allows his hero to free himself from the bonds of love, power, and necromancy and achieve a unified vision of the cosmos through his contemplation of nature. But human character is full of contradictions, and Faust returns to Gretchen, but dishonors her and destroys her family. The conventional dramatic scenes between Gretchen and Faust, Gretchen and her young sister, who gossip about a fallen woman, and Gretchen and her dying brother, establish the young girl's character and the implacable, ordained movement of events. The pathos of the prison scene, where Gretchen has been driven mad by the murder of her mother and her bastard child and the death of Valentine, is effective in both human and philosophical terms. Both Faust and Mephistopheles are vanquished by Gretchen's total submission to orthodox Christianity and the Church, which condemn murder and infanticide. Her unquestioning faith in God's redeeming spirit saves her from perdition and causes Mephistopheles and Faust to flee in terror. At this moment, the contrast between Mephistopheles' evil and Gretchen's purity becomes blindingly evident to Faust. He is triumphant over the devil because his moral perceptions explain his alliance with evil. Although tainted, his moral sense is not obliterated.

The first part of *Faust* explores man's capacity for good and evil. Often the two impulses coalesce, for the scientific and skeptical Goethe rejected the Christian idea of moral absolutes. It is the motion, the striving toward perfection and knowledge, that is most important. Faust has attained a degree of salvation in his full understanding of Mephistopheles' procedures. The most famous scene of the play, the *Walpurgisnacht,* shows Faust escorted to a witches' orgy. Mephistopheles introduces Faust to a cavorting, satanic assembly. As they push through the crowd, they encounter the evil instincts of man: avarice, mendacity, and lust. Faust engages in a wild dance with a young witch, but suddenly, when a red mouse emerges from her lips, he turns and sees a vision of Gretchen, fettered and suffering. He realizes his sin and hurls himself from the assembly. He regains enough spiritual equilibrium to overcome the mad temptation of the *Walpurgisnacht.*

Goethe's protagonist differs from the Fausts of earlier legends because his motives are not so much religious as personal. A true romantic creation, he searches for ultimate fulfillment on all levels and realizes that this quest is essentially futile, especially when the services of an impotent being, Mephistopheles, are enlisted. Mephistopheles is not Faust's ultimate antagonist. He represents a metaphysical position of total negation that can dominate the mightiest of human spirits.

Faust confronts the black depths of his own soul, symbolized by Mephistopheles in Part I. Mephistopheles embodies the ultimate in vanity and amorality, but he is not a formidable opponent for the learned doctor. Only Faust can teach Faust, and when his infatuation with Gretchen matures to love, he glimpses the limitations of self. Through his struggles, Faust recognizes the moral nature of the universe in a manner that science, philosophy, and sensual abandon could not reveal.

Part II of *Faust* is a metaphysical allegory that really does not continue the action of the preceding section. Realism, humor, and dramatic conflict are replaced by a complex poetic structure that substitutes abstract philosophy for human characterization. Although Part I has been performed, Part II is not a viable dramatic work. When the Austrian composer Gustav Mahler incorporated sections of Part II into his *Eighth Symphony,* he was attempting to express in musical terms a theme of immense and often obscure philosophical ramifications. But generally, Goethe's work has been regarded as a closet drama: a poem better understood and enjoyed when it is read.

Part I of *Faust* is still performed by German theater groups. It retains its significance for men who would ponder the outer limits of human knowledge and morality.

If the enormous scope of *Faust* makes it suitable for only a few experimental stage productions, it is a challenge to some of the world's most interesting directors. Visitors to the Schauspielhaus in Hamburg in the last twenty years have admired a new staging by Gustav Gründgens; devotees of Ingmar Bergman have gone to his Malmö Theater to see his production of the *Urfaust,* an earlier and simpler version of Part I, published after Goethe's death.

The Author

Goethe is considered to be not only the greatest German poet but the catalytic genius who inspired more than a century of romantic art. Born in Frankfurt-on-Main, he lived a long and stormy life. Youthful visits to Italy and involvement in contemporary political, intellectual, and literary controversy helped mold the fiery idealist who sought classical equilibrium in art. After extensive travels and studies, he produced his first works, dramas with a political theme. Goethe's influential novel, *Wilhelm Meister,* and his association with Schiller and other German poets of the age, brought him to the forefront of European Romanticism. It was his *Sorrows of Young Werther,* in 1774, that set off an extravagant emotional and literary revolution in Europe. It resulted in numerous suicides and many literary works inspired by the story of a young man whose self-destruction was symptomatic of the times.

As diplomat, historian, dramatist, novelist, poet, and critic, Goethe dominated European letters and became a living legend. When he revolted against the Romantic movement, which he had done so much to found, his followers continued to regard his classicism as an ultimate extension of the romantic intellect. Nearly every notable figure in the arts paid tribute to Goethe, either in person at his home in Weimar, or through correspondence and in literary or musical works. Although a great philosopher, Goethe emphasized the need to base actions on nature and experience. *Faust* was literally the work of his lifetime; he completed the great poem only shortly before his death in 1832.

Mary Stuart

by

JOHANN CHRISTOPH FRIEDRICH VON SCHILLER
(1759–1805)

The Characters

Mary Stuart—the young, beautiful Scottish queen who has
been held captive by Queen Elizabeth of England for over
a month. Dignified, proud, and idealistic, she is not afraid
to recognize passion, or to appeal to Elizabeth as a sister
queen.

Queen Elizabeth—the cold and power-conscious queen of
England who wishes to be a symbol of virginity, strength,
and leadership. In a world of pretense and steely emotions, she is alone and unloved.

Earl of Leicester—an opportunist who poses as Elizabeth's
lover while claiming to be Mary's protector.

Sir Mortimer—Paulet's young nephew, who pretends to be
Elizabeth's protector, but passionately loves Mary. Mortimer pretends to Protestantism, but is a fervent Catholic
convert.

Talbot, Earl of Shrewsbury—Mary's former prison warden,
the champion of moderation and prudence, who pleads
for Mary's salvation.

Sir Andrew Melvil—Mary's loyal friend who returns to her
before her death. He has become a priest in order to give
her the last sacraments.

Lord Burleigh—the Machiavellian Lord High Treasurer responsible for the rapid completion of Mary's death sentence.

Sir Amias Paulet—the dutiful prison guardian who refuses to betray his prisoner or to allow any illegal action against her.

Hanna, Nurse Kennedy—Mary's loyal companion, more sensitive to her mistress's suffering than is Mary herself.

The Story

In the English castle of Fotheringhay, on February 6, 1587, Nurse Kennedy finds the jailer Paulet breaking open Queen Mary's desk and taking jewelry and letters. Paulet declares that Mary is England's greatest enemy; she left Scotland as a murderess and is now conspiring against England to "bring the times of the Spanish Mary back." Kennedy's protests are interrupted by the arrival of the queen. She asks Paulet to deliver one of the confiscated letters to Queen Elizabeth in order to arrange an interview. Paulet agrees, but later refuses to allow Mary to see a priest. Mortimer enters and rudely ignores the queen.

Alone with Kennedy, Mary laments her past; she is frightened by the memory of her murdered husband, Darnley. But Kennedy assures her that Darnley had treated her cruelly and deserved his fate. Blinded by passion for Bothwell, Mary had merely acquiesced in Darnley's death; the deed was not hers: "Indiscretion is your only crime." Thoughts of her own death are interrupted by Mortimer, who, with great respect and dignity, informs Mary that he will aid her. While studying in France, he had converted to Catholicism, learned of Mary's imprisonment, and returned to England. He tells her that Parliament has found her guilty of conspiracy, but Queen Elizabeth is still delaying the sentence. Mortimer vows to save Mary, and she tells him to go to Lord Leicester, her feigned enemy, for support. Lord Burleigh arrives from Parliament to inform Mary of the verdict. She calmly denounces the decision and the unparliamentary methods, suggesting that Burleigh should not "mistake for justice what is useful to the state." When Mary leaves, Burleigh tells Paulet that the jailer is to bring about her death, but Paulet vows that he will protect the queen as long as she is in his custody.

At Westminster, Queen Elizabeth, surrounded by English lords and French ambassadors, discusses arrangements for her marriage to the king of France. The English want to be sure of an heir and the continuance of Protestant rule in England, but Elizabeth is reluctant to marry, preferring to retain her fame as the Virgin Queen. Nevertheless, as a political gesture, she sends Aubespine and Bellièvre back to the French king with a royal sash and a ring as tokens of her favor, but she cuts short Aubespine's concern for Mary's fate. When the ambassadors leave, Elizabeth questions her counselors on her future course. Burleigh asks for Mary's head; Talbot defends her and attacks the injustice of Parliament's sentence; Lord Leicester counsels moderation: Mary should be allowed to live under the threat of death. Elizabeth, who is annoyed by any sympathy for Mary, eagerly greets Paulet and his nephew. Mortimer pledges his loyalty to Elizabeth and reveals that he had acted as a spy for her cause while in France. When the counselors leave, Elizabeth asks Mortimer to assassinate Mary. He agrees and is surprised to learn that his uncle has already refused a similar request.

When Elizabeth leaves, Mortimer gives Leicester a letter from Mary in which she pledges her love and asks him to save her. Leicester, who was once in love with Mary, has given all his recent attentions to Queen Elizabeth, only to discover that she will marry the king of France. He worries that Catherine de Medici's son will easily win the queen's affection. When Mortimer announces that he intends to set Mary free, Leicester is hesitant and demands assurance that his name will not be connected with any conspiracy. Leicester refuses to risk his life and reputation. Mortimer admonishes him and sends his "vows of everlasting love" to Mary. In a jealous rage, Mortimer declares: "I volunteered to be/Her means of rescue, not your love-note bearer." When Elizabeth finds Leicester looking pale, he cleverly says that he has been lamenting her loss to the French prince. Flattering her vanity, he persuades Elizabeth to surprise Mary in the prison woods.

For the first time since her imprisonment at Fotheringhay Castle, Mary roams freely in its park. Her ecstasy is interrupted by Talbot, who warns her that Elizabeth is coming.

Moments later, Elizabeth and Leicester arrive, pretending
that they have come by chance while hunting in the nearby
woods. Mary struggles with her pride and humbly kneels
before the English monarch, declaring that her misfortunes
have been due to fate, not Elizabeth. In a jealous rage,
Elizabeth accuses Mary of trying to murder her and usurp
her kingdom. Mary humbly renounces all claims to the
throne, asking only for freedom, but when she is accused of
murdering her husband, the Scottish queen denounces Elizabeth as an illegitimate monarch and pronounces herself the
real queen. Elizabeth storms away. Mary's elation is interrupted by Mortimer's passionate declaration of love. He
cruelly denounces Leicester as a coward and declares that
he and his men will free Mary that night. Horrified by
Mortimer's ravings and his call for the death of all the jailers,
including Paulet, Mary tries to fight off his mad lust. Paulet
rushes in to announce that the queen has been murdered.
Mary flees to the tower. Mortimer learns that Elizabeth has
merely been attacked and rushes into the castle, declaring:
"I stay, in spite of all to save her head,/Or else upon her
coffin make my bed."

During the same evening, Aubespine, Kent, and Leicester
assemble in the palace. The would-be assassin is a French
Papist who has received a counterfeit passport from Aubespine. An arsenal of weapons has been discovered at the
French ambassador's home, and he must leave England
immediately; the English-French marriage alliance has been
cancelled. Burleigh accuses Leicester of having led Elizabeth
toward her death. Leicester fears that he has been discovered.
Mortimer enters and reveals that Burleigh has found a letter
from Queen Mary, addressed to Leicester, urging him to keep
his word. Mortimer encourages the weak lord to use his
influence to save himself and the Scottish queen. Suddenly,
Leicester calls the guard to arrest Mortimer. After swearing
his allegiance to God and Queen Mary, Mortimer curses
Elizabeth and stabs himself.

Meanwhile, Elizabeth and Burleigh discuss Leicester's
treachery. The queen jealously accuses her former lover, but
is reluctant to act. Leicester storms in and says his actions
were guided by his attempt to save Elizabeth. He exposes
Mortimer and, at the suggestion of Burleigh, vows to prove
his devotion to Elizabeth by carrying out the death sentence

with Burleigh's assistance. Shouts are heard; the people are demanding Mary's head. Davidson presents the death warrant for signature. Talbot again counsels prudence; Elizabeth should avoid a decision until she is calmer. She cannot satisfy the people, because they ask for Mary's head today, but will become her avengers after the execution. Alone, Elizabeth ponders her course. In a rage at having to answer to anyone but herself, Elizabeth signs and hands Davidson the warrant, saying that "a mere piece of paper does/Not make decisions, names don't kill." When Davidson presses her to discover her intentions, she is evasive and flees, leaving the secretary befuddled. Burleigh enters, sees the document, seizes it, and rushes away as Davidson screams: "You'll ruin me!"

Early in the morning, Fotheringhay Castle is filled with Mary's ladies and her royal servants, including Mervil. Everyone is dressed in black; they mournfully discuss the scaffold and the black-draped execution chamber below. Magnificent in white, with a crucifix at her throat, Mary meets her friends and tells Mervil that she has prepared her will. She bids her servants farewell and declares that now her only wish is to receive the Catholic sacraments. Mervil uncovers his head, revealing that he has become a priest. She confesses to the sin of jealous hatred against Elizabeth, repents the death of her husband at the hands of her lover, and declares that her heart is now free. When Mervil inquires why she does not ask for absolution for her part in the Parry and Babington assassination plot, Mary denies any guilt and says that her secretaries bore false witness. Mervil offers her the chalice. Moments later, Mary drinks the Host and receives absolution, and Burleigh and Leicester enter to lead Mary to the scaffold.

Mary falters as she passes Leicester, and he takes her into his arms. She says: "You once promised to lead me from/ This prison, and you lead it to me now." She reminds him of the tender love that could have been his had he not chosen the other queen. After the procession leaves, Leicester remains alone, unable to witness Mary's death and recognizing for the first time his great and tragic mistake.

In her royal apartments, Elizabeth awaits her lords and is visited by Talbot, who has just returned from a visit to Mary's secretaries, Kurl and Nau. Kurl is in a dishevelled frenzy and confesses that the conspiracy letters to Babington were not genuine; it was Nau's scheme to implicate Mary. At Talbot's suggestion, Elizabeth agrees to reopen Mary's trial and calls for Davidson to return her warrant. Dumbstruck, Davidson confesses that he has given it to Burleigh. Elizabeth denies ever ordering it, and Burleigh announces Mary's death. Elizabeth banishes Burleigh for his haste, orders Davidson to the Tower to be executed, and asks Talbot to be her sole counselor henceforth. Shrewsbury advises Elizabeth not to punish her loyal friends who have acted in her behalf and announces that he must retire from the court. The Earl of Kent informs the queen that Leicester has gone to France. Elizabeth is left alone.

Critical Opinion

The passionate struggle between Mary Stuart and Elizabeth Tudor for the throne of England is one of history's most stirring dramas. Elizabeth, the Protestant child of Henry VIII and Anne Boleyn, became queen in 1558 at the death of her hated Catholic half-sister, Mary Tudor. A blood cousin, Mary Stuart, heiress to the throne of Scotland, claimed her right to queenship as a Catholic and the legitimate granddaughter of Margaret Tudor, a sister of Henry VIII. Their twenty-nine-year battle, which ended after nineteen years of captivity and Mary's death in 1587, is the basis of Schiller's *Mary Stuart*.

A highly structured, compressed drama, *Mary Stuart* is a unified, forceful, symmetrical work. In both form and theme, the play reflects the irreconcilable antipathy of passion and intellect, idealism and realism, experience and prudery, Catholicism and Protestantism.

The five-act tragedy resembles a carefully balanced equation: the play opens and closes with Mary (despite Elizabeth's presence in the final scene, the strength of Mary's farewell overshadows the conclusion); acts two and four are totally Elizabeth's, and in the third act, the fulcrum point, the two antagonists meet. Just as the structure mathematically opposes one queen against the other, so are the queens' retinues paralleled. A woman of passion, Mary is surrounded by devotion, love, and even lustful frenzy; a cold, unfeminine

sovereign, Elizabeth must always be surrounded by imper-
sonal men. The stark privation of Mary's prison contrasts
with her queenly manner and beauty, while the opulence of
Elizabeth's palace merely accentuates her barrenness and
solitude.

Despite physical circumstance and knowledge of certain
death, Mary always maintains her dignity, nobility, and faith
in humanity. When Paulet confiscates her jewels and letters,
Mary regally reassures her companion Kennedy: "We can
be treated basely/But they cannot debase us." She distinguishes between Parliament's expedient death sentence and
real justice ("You are governed not/By your advantage but
by what is of advantage to your Sovereign and your country./Do not, therefore, my noble Lord, mistake/For justice
what is useful to the State."), just as she distinguishes between men of calculating intelligence and men of feeling.
Mary appeals to Elizabeth as a woman, sister, and queen,
refusing to acknowledge a totally masculine parliamentary
tribunal. She idealistically believes two sisters can be reconciled in peace and tries to arouse Elizabeth's sympathy and
understanding. By appealing to Elizabeth as a woman, Mary
deprives Elizabeth of a political justification for her actions
and emphasizes the highly *personal* nature of her condemnation. Elizabeth, who would like to show the strength, wisdom, and self-sufficiency attributed to men, reacts emotionally
as a jealous woman. Facing her persecutor, Mary pleads for
mercy, renounces all claims to the throne, and appeals to
Elizabeth as a goddess and sister, while Elizabeth glorifies
only power and violence.

When Elizabeth debases Mary's dignity and attacks her
purity, Mary loses control. Yet, in the face of death, her
self-possession and nobility return. To the last, Mary underlines the issue of feminism opposing male and female sensibilities when she asks for Hanna Kennedy to accompany
her to the scaffold: "It cannot be my sister's will/To see
offense done to my sex through me/And that rude hands of
men should touch me now!" She exits from life, a woman of
feeling, penitent for her sins of passion, yet proud of her
human emotions. Mary's final words, addressed to the Earl
of Leicester, reiterate the sincerity of her love and the finality of her death.

The antithesis of Mary, her Scottish cousin, Elizabeth

Tudor is a cold egocentric. While Mary reflects on her passionate life, Elizabeth glorifies her virginity. Forced by Parliament to begin arrangements for marriage with the French monarch, Elizabeth says: "My wish has always been to die unwed,/And my choice would have been to have my fame/Consist of this: that on my gravestone people/Should some day read: 'Here lies the Virgin Queen.'" In many respects, *Mary Stuart* is a part of women's liberation literature before the fact. While Mary enjoys the passive role tradition has assigned her sex, Elizabeth decries the double standard, outraged that her subjects see her as a woman instead of a king.

Elizabeth is irrationally jealous of Mary's reputation and beauty. Although Elizabeth wants male strength and courage, she is, ironically, a victim of her femininity. Subject to jealousy, she must prove her superiority to Mary. She agrees to meet Mary when Leicester flatters her vanity and can only muster the courage to sign Mary's death warrant by remembering that Mary has stolen her lover, just as she has usurped her legitimacy by questioning the validity of a Protestant marriage. Mary's death will restore the bridegroom and kill Catholicism, thereby legalizing her birth. But having signed the death sentence in an emotional frenzy, Elizabeth cannot carry out her decision with bold purposefulness. She ambiguously hands the fatal document to Davidson, leaving the execution of the edict to fate. Once the act is completed, she willfully disavows her part in the murder, justifying the sentence but condemning the execution.

Mary's two lovers, Mortimer and Leicester, and their masquerades, also reflect the contrast between Mary's world of passion and Elizabeth's cold realism. Elizabeth's world is one of pretense. She is unable to love and is, therefore, unloved. Mortimer masquerades in her court as a loyal subject ready to kill her enemy when in reality he is a traitor. Leicester, posing as her lover, secretly loves Mary, but is too much the opportunist to enjoy either passion. Even Elizabeth's most devoted friend, Talbot, Earl of Shrewsbury, resigns from her service, leaving Elizabeth totally alone at Mary's death. Her solitude stands in sharp contrast to the companionship and devotion that surround Mary to the end.

Mortimer so convincingly demonstrates his commitment

to Elizabeth that he is asked to assassinate Mary; yet he passionately loves her and gives his life in an attempt to save her. His frenetic and lustful passion, which parallels his fanatical conversion from Protestantism to Catholicism, is a manifestation of youth. The same innocence and energy that lead Mortimer to trust Leicester, despite his personal jealousy, inspire Mortimer's suicide.

In contrast to Mary's would-be lover, Mortimer, Leicester never expresses his true feeling. An opportunist, he once preferred to court the queen of England rather than the Scottish queen, and now in the face of danger he is afraid to acknowledge Mary's summons. He fears exposure in court, but is flattered by the knowledge that Mary loves him. Like Elizabeth, who is incapable of action, Leicester lets himself drift into events. Burleigh's accusation of treason and Mortimer's opportune appearance before Leicester inspire the earl's only act: a denunciation of Mortimer.

Leicester, like Elizabeth, can only think of himself. He cannot witness Mary's execution. He only pities himself for his betrayal of her love. Totally impotent, he flees to France, unable to face his complicity in the murder.

The secondary characters reveal a similar contrapuntal movement. Mervil returns to Mary despite incredible impediments and has even become a priest to serve her in her last hours. In contrast, Elizabeth's loyal servant, Shrewsbury, the first to plead for Mary's salvation, abandons the queen. Burleigh's singleminded bloodlust and eagerness to accomplish the execution are balanced by Paulet's dutiful service and humanitarian sense of morality. Elizabeth can boast of no women friends, while Mary is constantly accompanied by the faithful Hanna Kennedy, and before her death, she is consoled by her ladies-in-waiting.

Although Schiller told Goethe that *Mary Stuart* is in the "Euripidean style," and the five-act structure resembles Greek dramaturgy, the play reveals more similarities to Racine and Shakespeare than to Euripides. Like the classical seventeenth-century French dramatist, Schiller begins his play at the climax: The death warrant has been issued; Mary's sentence must merely be carried out. And like Racine who, in *Britannicus, Bérénice,* and *Phèdre,* pits two characters against each other in a highly emotional situation, Schiller uses scenes of confrontation to trigger the action. The final image of

Elizabeth, alone on the stage after having executed Mary, resembles Racine's vision of Nero after his murder of Britannicus. The blank verse, the use of English history, and the pageantry of Elizabeth's court, reflect a definite Shakespearean influence. Yet the brilliance of *Mary Stuart*—the strong portraits of the queens, the charged atmosphere, the finely structured symmetry, and the ingenious use of history —is uniquely Schiller's. The carefully structured symmetry and the constant counterpoise of the two queens' antithetical ways of life reflect Schiller's highly romantic vision. The stone and chains of prison and the comfortable palace, Mary's sensual beauty and Elizabeth's marblelike countenance, as well as the religious opposition, tend to create the sense of an arbitrary, contrasting universe. The final scene of Mary, going to the scaffold as a martyr after her absolution, implies a heavenly ascent, while Elizabeth is left alone in a self-made hell. Schiller tends to glorify Catholicism, the poetic ritual of absolution, communion, and spiritual ecstasy. He seems to see in Protestantism only privation, opportunism, and self-righteousness.

Mary Stuart, which was written in 1800 in German, is best known to English audiences in Stephen Spender's adaptation, which was premiered by the Old Vic Company with Irene Worth and Catherine Lacey in 1958. During the 1971–1972 theater season in New York, *Mary Stuart* was successfully mounted by the Lincoln Center Repertory Company.

The Author

The son of an army surgeon, Johann von Schiller was born in Germany on November 10, 1759. After studying law at a military academy, he turned to medicine. During his training, Schiller began to write lyric poetry. From 1777 to 1778 he finished his first play, *Die Räuber,* which he published in 1781 at his own expense. In 1782, the drama was successfully performed at Mannheim. Schiller subsequently completed three more dramas and began *Don Carlos,* which appeared in 1787. Now an established playwright, Schiller accepted a position as "theater poet" in Mannheim in 1883.

After completing the blank verse drama *Don Carlos,*

Schiller became interested in history and wrote a series of historical works, including a history of the Thirty Years' War. During this period, Schiller obtained a professorship at the University of Jena through Goethe's recommendation. Now married, Schiller was overwhelmed with financial worries, and his health began to fail. The hereditary prince of Holstein-Augustenburg awarded Schiller a pension, enabling the poet to study philosophy and esthetics.

By 1794, Schiller had become a good friend of Goethe and wrote a treatise on poetry in 1795–96 ("Uber naive und sentimentalische Dichtung") ("On Naive and Sentimental Poetry"). Schiller classified art as ancient, modern, classic, romantic, naive, and sentimental. Critics have interpreted his classification as an apology for his own sentimental, modern works.

At the end of his life, Schiller again turned to the theater and, using history as a source of inspiration, in 1798–99 created the Wallenstein trilogy that was based on the Thirty Years' War. The success of *Wallenstein* marked the height of Schiller's career. He moved to Weimar to live near Goethe. *Wallenstein* was followed by *Mary Stuart* (1800) and *The Maid of Orleans* (1801), as well as translations of Shakespeare's *Macbeth* (1801), Gozzi's *Turandot* (1802), and Racine's *Phèdre* (1803–04). In 1804, Schiller completed his last drama, *Wilhelm Tell,* based on the life of the Swiss hero. Schiller died at Weimar May 9, 1805, after many years of illness.

The Inspector General

by

NICOLAI V. GOGOL (1809–1852)

The Characters

Anton Skvoznik-Dmukhanovsky—the chief of police (the Russian equivalent of mayor), a powerful, aggressive, corrupt official who has risen from humble origins. He is harsh, cruel, and worldly.

Anna Andreyevna—the chief's wife, a middle-aged, vain, and flirtatious woman who tries to dominate her husband.

Marya Antonovna—the chief's daughter, a mindless and vain young girl.

Luka Lukich Hlopov—superintendent of schools: lax, stupid, corrupt.

Ammos Federovich Lyapkin-Tyapkin—a corrupt, obtuse, pompous judge, obsessed with breeding hunting dogs.

Artemy Filippovich Zemlyanika—a clever, cruel sycophant. As supervisor of charitable institutions, he ignores human suffering and practices bribery and extortion.

Ivan Kuzmich Shpekin—the fatuous postmaster who whiles away his time reading the letters sent through his office.

Peter Ivanovich Dobchinsky
Peter Ivanovich Bobchinsky } busybodies who are so alike as to cause confusion of identity even between each other.

Ivan Alexandrovich Hlestakov—a petty official from St. Petersburg who, because of his profligacy and self-indulgence, has lost all his money while traveling to his uncle's country home. He is about twenty-three years old, very skinny, and engagingly mindless in his behavior.

Osip—Hlestakov's manservant, a wily old bully.

The Story

The chief of police summons the town officials and reads them a personal letter he has received informing him that an inspector general from St. Petersburg will shortly visit the public institutions. Consternation is general, for every facet of the local government is inefficient and corrupt. Panic-stricken at the prospect of exposure, the chief orders a crash program to cover up the most blatant abuses. The charitable institution is filthy, and the patients are dying of neglect; the courthouse is used for breeding geese, and the court-room is a garbage heap of scattered records; the schools are mismanaged and staffed by idiots; the post office is in chaos.

Two citizens, Dobchinsky and Bobchinsky, bustle in with news that someone who must surely be the inspector general has been at the inn for two weeks and refuses to leave or pay his bill. The police are dispatched to clean the streets and the chief rushes to the inn. Everyone is ordered to cover up his malfeasance.

At the inn, Osip, a servant, complains of the hunger and discomforts and humiliations he has endured since leaving St. Petersburg with his master, a low-ranking clerk in an obscure government office. Hlestakov has been profligate, losing his money and pawning his valuables to pay gambling debts. When the clerk enters, Hlestakov tells Osip to order a meal from the innkeeper, but is rudely reminded that their credit has long been exhausted and that the city officials will soon prosecute them for failure to pay their bills. When a meal is finally brought up, Hlestakov criticizes it, but consumes it ravenously.

The chief of police is announced and a ludicrous scene follows. Both the chief and the clerk cower and bluster, mistaking each other's intentions. Hlestakov thinks he is about to be arrested for debt, and the chief mistakes the young man for a high government official traveling incognito, and fears punishment for his corruption and incompetence. When Hlestakov asks for a loan, the chief thinks it is his discreet way of demanding a bribe and immediately offers two hundred rubles and invites him to stay at his home. He sends a note to his wife and departs for an inspection of the charitable institution.

At the chief's house, his wife and daughter prepare for the inspector general from St. Petersburg. They bicker about their wardrobe. When Hlestakov, the chief, and other officials return from the charitable institution, the officials congratulate themselves for their efficient administration. Hlestakov greets the chief's wife and daughter with flowery compliments. Seeing that everyone is impressed, he boasts of his duties in the capital (actually, he is in the fourteenth rank of clerks—nearly the lowest). He claims he has written numerous operas and plays and is a friend of Pushkin, of counts, and even of the czar. The more preposterous his tales, the greater the awe of his gullible hearers.

When Hlestakov retires for a nap, the women fight over his affection, and Osip bullies everyone into tiptoeing around so as not to wake his master. The officials want to bribe the inspector general—a common practice—but without incurring his displeasure. When he awakes each official presents himself for an interview. When Hlestakov realizes their purpose, he helps them by asking them for a loan, which they immediately give him.

After he has bilked them of more than a thousand rubles, Hlestakov writes a letter to a St. Petersburg friend describing the episode and urging him to write a satire on provincial bureaucracy. As Osip is on his way to mail the letter, a delegation of merchants petitions Hlestakov to stop the chief's confiscation of their wares as mandatory bribes. As they express their grievances, the cruelty and corruption of the officials is further exposed. Hlestakov loses patience and dismisses them. He makes love to the chief's daughter. They are interrupted by the mother, who sends the girl out and then herself becomes the object of the young man's passionate lovemaking. When the daughter and chief enter, Hlestakov begs for the daughter's hand and threatens suicide if refused. The match is made.

Meanwhile, Osip and Hlestakov quickly order the fastest horses in preparation for a getaway. The chief and his family gloat over the good match, make plans for an opulent life in St. Petersburg, and attack the merchants and others who have questioned their authority.

The postmaster rushes in with Hlestakov's letter to St. Petersburg, which he has opened. Everyone who has been duped engages in violent recriminations. As they are shouting at one another, a policeman announces that the inspector general from St. Petersburg has arrived and demands to see them immediately. They all freeze in attitudes of shock and horror.

Critical Opinion

Gogol's play is a farcical satire on avarice, corruption, and stupidity. Without exploring the darker side of man's nature, the playwright has exposed the most blatant and ridiculous manifestations of a universal folly. In a sense, *The Inspector General* is apolitical, although it does attack the ingrained vices of the Russian bureaucracy. The broad slapstick of the play saves it from being really offensive (because, after all, it is not realistic).

The universality of the satire is underscored by the dramatist himself in prefatory remarks entitled: "Characters and Costumes: Notes for the Actors." Here, Gogol indicates that the characters are meant to be types, not specific individuals. The chief of police is the archetype of provincial officials appointed by the imperial authorities in St. Petersburg and responsible to them only. Susceptible to corruption, and subject only to a remote and indifferent bureaucracy in the capital, he is shrewd and tenacious. He devotes a considerable part of his time to intimidating his constituency. He is the natural product of an absurdly centralized and corrupt governmental system. Gogol does not intend to contribute to or precipitate the downfall of czarist Russia. He merely wants his audience to laugh at the pomposity and folly of officials.

The other characters, including Hlestakov, are all immediately recognizable types. Gogol explicitly instructed the actor playing the clerk: "The more sincerity and simplicity the actor puts into this role, the better he will play it." The minor characters are also important, but "require no special explanations: their prototypes may be found in almost any community." Each actor must get into his character just far

enough to grasp his personality, but no profound psychological revelation is intended. It is important to know that
the chief's wife "Sometimes . . . gets the upper hand of her
husband simply because he is unable to answer her, but this
power extends only to trifles and consists of curtain lectures
and nagging." None of these instructions are used in the
play's action, but they are vital for actors imagining the
characters' life off-stage as well as on.

These two elements are typical of Gogol's art. He is able
to pinpoint the ridiculousness of the characters through the
use of closely observed details and general traits familiar to
everyone. He blends the caricature with honest moral out-
rage to produce a scathing, comic portrait of a corrupt
society. Even the Russian names of the characters indicate
their tawdry natures. The chief's surname may be translated
as "Rascal-Puftup"; Hlestakov is "Whippersnapper"; the
judge is "Bungle-Steal"; and so on. This is the traditional
way of telling the audience not to expect the probing of
profound psychological mysteries. Here is pure farce. People
are like animals stripped of civilization's veneer; they react
spontaneously and foolishly. The audience laughs, recognizing itself but feeling insulated from any threat because the
characters on the stage are so grotesque. Fun is the essence
of the play.

The last scene is a tableau. With the announcement that
the real official from St. Petersburg demands their presence
at the inn, the chief and his cohorts strike stylized attitudes
that Gogol describes: "The last speech [summoning them
before the inspector general] should produce upon all a sudden electric shock. The whole group should strike its pose in
a twinkling. A cry of astonishment should be uttered by all
the women at once, as if proceeding from a single bosom."
The chief of police stands "like a post, his arms outspread
and his head tilted backwards," and he is the center of a
static whirlpool of surprise and comic fear. After giving
explicit instructions about this dumb-show, Gogol says: "For
nearly a minute and a half the group remains in this position." Like a mod-movie's stop-action, this final tableau
formally reveals the vulnerability of the figures who have
been bumbling their way through this foolish world.

Gogol wrote *The Inspector General* at the suggestion of
Pushkin, the great Russian romantic poet, who, like Hlesta-

kov, was mistaken for a government official in a provincial town. The result of this suggestion is one of the most viable stage comedies ever written.

When Gogol published *The Inspector General,* he inserted the motto, "The mirror mustn't be blamed if your face is at fault." *The Inspector General,* with its scathing picture of municipal corruption, got past the censors because the czar enjoyed it. The characters are all either scoundrels or idiots; not one fails to be human. Actors go on playing Gogol's people zestfully, and audiences continue to laugh, because Gogol was a man without malice.

The Author

Born in western Russia of Polish ancestry, Gogol spent his early years in the Ukraine. A sickly child, he was influenced by his mother's obsession with folkloric mysticism and his father's literary pretensions. When he was nineteen, Gogol moved to St. Petersburg (Leningrad) and began publishing prose sketches of Ukrainian life. Gogol's occupations as a government bureaucrat, teacher, and tutor left him unsatisfied. In 1829, at his own expense, he published an epic poem *Hans Küchlegarten,* which was such a failure that Gogol purchased all the available copies and burned them. More failures in St. Petersburg, including a disastrous audition for the Bolshoi Theater Acting Troupe, convinced the young man that his fortunes lay elsewhere. He set out for America, but never got beyond Germany and returned to the civil service in St. Petersburg.

Gogol's first successful publications were prose works that treated rural life in the Ukraine. *Evenings On a Farm near Dikanka* (1831–1832) brought him to the attention of Pushkin and other influential friends who obtained a teaching position for him at a girls' school and then a lectureship in medieval history at the University of St. Petersburg. He resigned in 1835 to devote himself to literature. In rapid succession he wrote *Taras Bulba* (1835), *Arabesques* (1835), and the two volumes of *Mirgorod* (1835) in a torrent of literary creativity.

The lukewarm reception of *The Inspector General* (1836) plunged Gogol into a severe depression. He left Russia for twelve years, living in Rome and traveling to Switzerland and France. In his self-imposed exile, he completed *Dead Souls* (1842), *The Overcoat* (1842), and a comedy entitled *The Marriage* (1842). Gogol's mental depression coincided with his increased interest in the salvation of Russian society. Defining traditional institutions, his works shocked progressives in Russia. In 1848, Gogol returned to Russia after a trip to the Holy Land and started the second part of *Dead Souls*. But during the winter of 1852, overwhelmed by melancholia, Gogol burned his manuscripts, including the continuation of *Dead Souls,* refused to eat or follow the advice of his doctors, and died in February 1852.

Woyzeck

by

GEORG BÜCHNER (1813–1837)

The Characters

Woyzeck—an army orderly in the service of the captain. In his mid-thirties, he is of low intelligence, passionate, and superstitious. Woyzeck's devotion to Marie, his mistress and the mother of his son, is deep, abject, tainted with jealousy.

Marie—an earthy townswoman who has given Woyzeck a son and accepts his support.

Captain—a bullying, loutish officer who enjoys abusing Woyzeck to show his own superiority.

Doctor—the prototype of the doctor who views the world completely "scientifically," without any moral considerations.

Drum-Major—a colorful, virile, aggressive soldier who seduces Marie.

Andres—Woyzeck's barracks-mate.

The Story

Friedrich Johann Franz Woyzeck, an infantry rifleman and captain's orderly in a German army unit, is the paid subject of a series of experiments being conducted by a heartless physician. For three months he has been slowly

85

starved on a diet consisting exclusively of peas. His constitution has been weakened, and his mind and emotions have been reduced to animalistic levels. Woyzeck lives with Marie, a prostitute who has borne him a son, Christian. His family, which he passionately loves, is his central concern in life.

When the play opens, Woyzeck is deep in the throes of a paranoid depression that is intensified by the captain's cruel taunts. He shaves the captain and is alternately chastized and praised: "Woyzeck, you're a good man, but, Woyzeck, you have no morals." He replies that Christ loves all men, the sinners as well as the virtuous, and if he were rich he could be moral and refined.

In an open field, while gathering firewood, Woyzeck and his friend Andres discuss the supernatural. Woyzeck cries that he sees the supernatural. Both men flee. Meanwhile, in the city, Marie quarrels with a neighbor after the drum-major has strutted past and flirted with her. She is singing to her child when Woyzeck enters and offers to take her to the fair. That evening, they arrive at a booth where a charlatan exhibits a monkey dressed as a soldier and a horse that supposedly can reason. Both animals are repulsive, but Woyzeck and Marie are strangely drawn to the show, and they are told that the obscene horse is a "metamorphosed human being." Also at the fair, the sergeant and drum-major make lewd comments about Marie.

Sometime later, Woyzeck surprises Marie while she is wearing a pair of earrings the drum-major has given her in return for sexual favors. At first violently jealous, Woyzeck forgives her when he is filled with tender love for his small son. Woyzeck goes to the doctor, who examines him and reprimands him for urinating in the street. The doctor sees everyone as a mechanical and chemical object. He decides that Woyzeck is mentally disturbed and raises his allowance because he is such an interesting case.

While in her room with the drum-major, Marie admits her submission to damnation. On the street, meanwhile, the captain is analyzed by the doctor and becomes outraged when told of his imminent death. When Woyzeck appears, the captain taunts him with Marie's unfaithfulness. As he becomes violently agitated, the doctor observes him in an inhuman, scientific manner, offering to raise his wages again as the orderly becomes hysterical and rushes off to confront Marie. Woyzeck upbraids her and tries to strike her. She says he is repulsive, and he leaves, consumed with jealousy and uncertainty.

Upon his return from the guardhouse, Woyzeck is told by Andres about a dance in a suburban inn. Woyzeck goes there and discovers Marie and the drum-major dancing. He delivers a tirade against sexual indulgence and carnal sin, and after an apprentice sermonizes on the world's evil, Woyzeck flees madly to a field. But he cannot drown out the sound of the dance music. Voices tell him to kill Marie. Even when he returns to the barracks, he is obsessed by the scene at the inn.

Again at the doctor's, Woyzeck is subjected to inhuman scrutiny and sterile theorizing. The doctor humiliates Woyzeck in front of medical students. At the inn once more, Woyzeck argues with a sergeant, lashing out at the world in a confused and pathetic fashion. He returns to the barracks to sort out his worldly belongings and will them to Andres, while muttering ominously about murder and his own death. Andres tells him of the drum-major's boast of possessing Marie. Woyzeck is obsessed with knives and Marie's death. When he returns to the inn, he is beaten by the drum-major.

Woyzeck goes to a Jewish pawnbroker, purchases a knife, and buries it in a field. Meanwhile, Marie talks with a fool and unburdens her guilty conscience. In a brief street scene, a grandmother tells Marie and some children a tale about a little girl who became disillusioned. The moon was a piece of rotten wood, the sun a faded sunflower, stars golden flies stuck in a spider's web, and the earth an upside-down pot. Woyzeck appears and takes Marie to a pond at the edge of the woods where, after raving about her sins and the color of the moon, he stabs her to death. As he flees, two men approach, hear a moaning sound, and run away in terror.

Woyzeck, now totally mad, returns to the inn and joins in the dancing. When the people notice blood on his hands and arms, he runs back to the pond, throws the knife into the deep water, and tries to wash the blood from his body.

The children in the street excitedly discuss the discovery of Marie's corpse. Woyzeck, still wet from his bath in the pond, terrifies his son, who is carried off by an idiot boy. The final scene of the play is set in the morgue. In a brief tableau, Woyzeck, bound and surrounded by the characters in the play, dumbly stares at the body of his Marie.

Critical Opinion

The stunning, elemental force of *Woyzeck* derives from its structure. Twenty-nine brief scenes depict the disintegration of Woyzeck, culminating in his murder of Marie. A poor, uneducated, pious, and superstitious man who is victimized by the cruel world around him, Woyzeck struggles with both his own nature and the hostile environment (human, animal, and even inanimate) that seems designed to destroy him. The staccato pace of the play, combined with the sparseness and directness of the dialogue, creates a feeling of demonic inevitability.

Woyzeck is indeed the victim of overwhelming forces: science, militarism, economics, sex, superstition, and stupidity. For the doctor and the medical students, Woyzeck is merely a specimen to be studied; his human feelings are ignored. Though possessed of formidable intelligence, the doctor is completely devoid of sympathy and conscience. He views the human world as an accumulation of physical and chemical processes that must be investigated at any cost. Woyzeck's physical and emotional disintegration are induced by the doctor in the name of science.

While the doctor destroys Woyzeck's physical being, the captain assaults his will power, self-respect, and humanity. The captain exploits his orderly to prove his own merit, continually emphasizing Woyzeck's inadequacies. When threatened by the doctor's diagnosis, the captain viciously turns on Woyzeck and tells him about Marie's unfaithfulness. By undermining the confidence of another man, the captain regains the arrogant security that depends on his superiority to others.

In order to provide for his family, Woyzeck must subject himself to the captain's indignities and the doctor's inhuman experiments. Throughout the play, Woyzeck laments his degradation and suggests that if he had more money he could be a different and better man.

Woyzeck's love for Marie is twisted into jealousy when

she gives herself to the virile drum-major. Woyzeck cannot accept Marie's promiscuity. He reacts with horrible violence; love and tenderness are perverted into cruelty and murderous energy. This parallel between man and beast is continually emphasized by the captain, the doctor, and the charlatan at the fair. Monkey and horse, whether dressed as a soldier or capable of reason, remind man that he cannot escape his bestial nature.

The primitive aspects of Woyzeck's personality are heightened by his superstitious nature. While at the beginning of his ordeal, Woyzeck can distinguish between fantasy and reality, his disintegration is marked by the gradual blurring of the two; and as he approaches madness, the voices become an extension of his innermost desires. Although his religious upbringing forbids murder, the primitive, superstitious elements in his personality overwhelm him.

Woyzeck's low intelligence makes him incapable of battling the malignant forces that surround him. He is sensitive and humane, but the world of the doctor and captain is no place for the simple, virtuous man.

Büchner's sense of irony points up the tragic plight of his character and, by extension, of all common men. The accumulated details anticipate the inexorable conclusion of this drama: the old woman's tale prefigures Woyzeck's disillusionment, and Christian's departure with the idiot suggests that the son will relive the father's experiences.

Büchner's two major dramas, *Woyzeck* and *Danton's Death,* have appealed to adventurous theater groups throughout the world. *Woyzeck* was produced recently in Paris and New York, and *Danton's Death* was mounted in New York in 1965. Many people first came to know about Büchner through an adaptation of *Woyzeck* by the twentieth-century composer Alban Berg. Perhaps the most successful and famous opera of this century, *Wozzeck* (1914–1921) is a powerful and inventive translation of the Büchner drama into music. Produced in major opera houses throughout the world, *Wozzeck* has done much to reawaken interest in Büchner's work.

Its themes of spiritual alienation and social injustice, as well as its stark and brutal style, have made *Woyzeck* one of the most deeply felt and relevant plays in today's theater.

When American filmgoers saw the East German film

Wozzeck, made after the war and released here in the 1960s, it reminded them of Brecht. A hundred years before Brecht, Georg Büchner was the true originator of Epic Theater, as Brecht and director Erwin Piscator revived it. Brecht's Berliner Ensemble productions in East Berlin after 1949 made it apparent that Büchner, who had anticipated the Naturalism of the 1880s and the Expressionism following World War I, was a seminal playwright.

The Author

Georg Büchner was born in 1813, the son of a German army doctor who conducted experiments in a grisly laboratory attached to the house. His mother came from a well-to-do family and imbued her son with a profound feeling for humanity. Büchner proved himself to be an excellent scholar. He devoured philosophy along with Shakespeare and the Greek classics. A university student during the 1830 revolution that shook Europe, he became a member of Young Germany, a radical movement that advocated reform of governments and institutions.

In 1832, Büchner was sent to Strassburg to study medicine, and he became involved in political conspiracies. Upon his return to Germany, his involvements deepened. He was hounded and pursued by the authorities. The repressive brutality of the government appalled him. In Strassburg again, he barely escaped jail. After receiving a medical lectureship in Zurich, Büchner settled there, only to die of typhus at the age of twenty-four.

Büchner's dramas were composed under great stress and were not performed during his lifetime. *Leonce and Lena,* a romantic comedy, was influenced by Shakespeare's *As You Like It.* Of the two remaining plays, *Danton's Death,* an historical play dealing with the French Revolution, embodies many of Büchner's political and philosophical ideas. *Woyzeck* again depicts man's inhumanity to man, but this time in a more universal setting. In both of these works, Büchner inveighs against exploitation, barbarism, and cruelty.

Since World War I, Büchner's plays have attained a certain popularity. *Leonce and Lena* was given in London in 1927 and received subsequent productions throughout the world. *Danton's Death* was revived in Berlin in 1927 and in New York in 1938 and 1965. *Woyzeck,* both in its original form and as the opera by Alban Berg, is the most often performed of Büchner's dramas.

A Month in the Country

by

IVAN SERGEYEVICH TURGENEV (1818–1883)

The Characters

Arkady Sergeich Islayev—a rich landowner, husband of
  Natasha; a candid, straightforward man who takes pleasure
  in administering his estate and finds somewhat annoying
  the sophisticated activities of his wife and her entourage
  of friends.

Natalya Petrovna (Natasha)—Islayev's wife and the mistress
  of a large domestic establishment. She is sentimentally,
  platonically attached to Rakitin, a friend of the family.
  Natasha is impetuous, romantic, bored, and moral.

Vera—the seventeen-year-old protégée of the family, an
  orphan who has grown to be an ardent, naive girl, full of
  vitality and happiness.

Anna Semenovna Islayev—the *grande dame* of the household, Islayev's mother, only remotely aware of the romantic passions swirling around her.

Lizaveta Bogdanovna—Anna Semenovna's companion, a
  thirty-seven-year-old spinster who sees Shpigelsky's proposal as an escape from genteel servitude.

Mikhaylo Alexandrovich Rakitin—a thirty-year-old friend
  of the family who has conducted a futile, sentimental, and
  platonic romance with Natasha. Cultured and sophisticated, he lacks the bravado to consummate his relationship
  with Natasha.

Alexey Nikolayevich Belyayev—a twenty-one-year-old student from Moscow who is spending a month in the country as tutor to the Islayev household. Naive and unassuming, he is imbued with a spontaneous love of life and youthful simplicity that endear him to everyone, including Natasha, Vera, and the female servants.

Afanasy Ivanovich Bolshintsov—a forty-eight-year-old, fat, clumsy lout who, because of his wealth and position, decides to woo young Vera, under the direction of Shpigelsky.

Igaty Ilyich Shpigelsky—a forty-year-old doctor, a scheming, cynical, and avaricious man. He thinks he has no illusions and detests everyone, including himself.

The Story

In the drawing room of an elegant estate, about 1840, a group of people are playing cards while exchanging badinage. Rakitin, reading a French novel, engages in a gentle raillery with Natasha, remarking that she has been out of sorts. She parries his remarks in a sophisticated, light-hearted manner. Her ten-year-old son, Kolya, enters with Belyayev, the Russian tutor, a student from Moscow. After they leave, Natasha seems flustered and says she would like to help the student with his education and career, and perhaps make him part of the family.

Dr. Shpigelsky arrives and tells an amusing story about a young girl who could not choose between suitors. He then takes Natasha aside and says that Bolshintsov, a wealthy neighbor, is asking for the hand of her seventeen-year-old ward, Vera. Natasha laughs and chides the doctor for being an emissary for such a ridiculous proposal, but she promises to sound out Vera's feelings.

Vera and Kolya, excited from playing with Belyayev, interrupt the interview and are told to leave. Rakitin again questions Natasha about her sudden coldness to him, but she artfully avoids revealing her true feelings and chaffs him for his foibles. She loves him, but he does not attract her sexually. He does not have the boldness to win her completely, and is enslaved in a sentimental relationship. Later, when Natasha is finally alone with Belyayev, she discovers that he is modest, self-effacing, even naive. As she babbles on about her childhood, he remains reserved and tells her simply that he lost his mother early in life and that his father ignored him. Just as Natasha is trying to reveal her love for him, they are interrupted by Vera and the doctor. Natasha suddenly sees that there is great rapport between Vera and Belyayev, and she selfishly begins to encourage the doctor's project.

The next day, Belyayev comes in, and greets Vera, who quizzes him about his life in Moscow. After he tells her about his background, she tells how she was adopted by Natasha's mother and, since her benefactress's death, has been Natasha's ward. Belyayev confesses that he, too, is an orphan. They have much in common. When Natasha and Rakitin enter, the young people rush off. Rakitin observes that Natasha is perturbed and tries to understand her motives, but she avoids his queries and attacks Rakitin for being precious and effeminate.

After this exchange, Rakitin encounters Belyayev and discovers that he has an imperfect knowledge of French, although he has translated a novel. The openness of the young man is very winning. After Rakitin leaves, he remains quite shy when Natasha again tries to sound him out about his feelings. They parry and the young woman finds it impossible to declare her true feelings for him. Her emotions become more heated; she offers to educate him. He tells her that he is afraid of her. When Rakitin reenters, Belyayev leaves and Natasha, now more bitter than ever, attacks her old friend. Rakitin begins to perceive that Natasha is in love with the tutor, but cannot accept the notion that such a callow youth could win the affections of his idol. A few moments later, Shpigelsky and Bolshintsov come upon the scene. The doctor invents the story that his client was looking for mushrooms and could not come directly to Natasha's house. In reality, the fat lout was too timid to approach without hesitation. He tells Shpigelsky of his lack of confidence, and the doctor, remembering the three horses promised him if the suit for Vera's hand is successful, goads his friend with ridicule and cynical advice.

The next day, Rakitin learns from Shpigelsky that the doctor's interest in Bolshintsov is pecuniary, not altruistic. Like two men of the world, they discuss the suit, and Rakitin reluctantly agrees to aid the doctor. When Rakitin and

Natasha again confront each other, she finally confesses her love for Belyayev, saying she is in love for the first time in her life. Rakitin is devastated, but agrees to help marry Vera to Bolshintsov.

When Vera is told that her hand is in demand, Natasha, through clever ruses, obtains her confession that she *might* be in love with Belyayev. Natasha nearly faints with jealousy and mortification. She engages in painful soul-searching, confessing to herself that she nearly tried to marry Vera off to Bolshintsov so she could have Belyayev to herself. But she regains her composure in time for a brief interview with Rakitin in which she seeks his advice. She accedes to his decision to leave, and decides to fire Belyayev. Just as she bursts into tears, Islayev, her mother-in-law, and others enter, inquiring about the disturbance. Rakitin quickly eludes their questions and promises to explain everything the next day.

Determined to fire the tutor, Natasha calls him in and indirectly inquires if he is in love with Vera. She accuses him of behaving improperly, but he disclaims any romantic attachment to Vera and is amazed by the news that she has professed her love for him. Floundering in her jealousy for Vera and her love for Belyayev, Natasha is in great conflict. Belyayev offers to leave, she asks him to stay, and he relents. But then she says she will decide if he should stay. In a transport of guilt, Natasha remonstrates with herself for her duplicity and cruelty.

The following day, in a deserted part of the house, Shpigelsky and Lizaveta Bogdanovna, the middle-aged companion to Islayev's mother, talk about their lives. He offers to marry her and discloses his philosophy of life: He is a cruel wolf, pretending to be placid and accommodating, but really he is a rapacious man, cynical, materialistic, bored, hypocritical, and misanthropic. Lizaveta promises to accept or reject his proposal the next day, and reveals herself to be a hard-headed cynic, too.

After the doctor and Lizaveta leave, Vera meets Belyayev and apologizes for compromising him in the eyes of Natasha. Belyayev confesses that Natasha said Vera was in love with him; she denies it and he replies that he loves her as he would a sister. Suddenly, Vera understands: Natasha is really in love with the tutor. He is incredulous, but Vera insists and, when Natasha suddenly enters, confronts Natasha with her revelation, bitterly accusing her of destroying her youth. After Vera leaves, Natasha breaks down and proclaims her love to Belyayev. He is thunderstruck at first, but suddenly declares his love for her. He refuses to leave. Natasha dismisses him and then implores him: "Remain! And let God pass judgment on us!" Rakitin, Islayev, and the doctor enter and then depart, bitter and confused about the passions surrounding them.

The next day, Anna Semenovna remonstrates with her son about the mysteries and emotional outpourings that have blighted the summer's carefree spirit. She suspects Rakitin of an affair with her daughter-in-law. Islayev promises to speak to his friend. In a man-to-man talk, he suggests to Rakitin that perhaps he should leave to avoid embarrassment. Rakitin agrees and futilely tries to warn his friend of Natasha's attachment to the tutor. When Belyayev arrives, Rakitin confronts him as a rival and tries to get him to withdraw from the house, bitterly inveighing against love. Belyayev coolly listens to the lecture and bids Rakitin farewell. Vera begs Natasha's forgiveness for exposing her to the tutor and then disconsolately admits that she is in love with Belyayev. Out of desperation, she tells the doctor that she will accept the repulsive Bolshintsov. When Belyayev comes to say goodbye, he tells Vera that he has caused too much misery in the household to remain.

Islayev asks Rakitin why the tutor is leaving, and is maliciously told: "Between you and me . . . Vera fell in love with him." Everyone prepares to leave: Vera to marry Bolshintsov, Lizaveta Bogdanovna to marry Shpigelsky, Rakitin to avoid Natasha, and Belyayev to return to the quiet of Moscow after a month in the country.

Critical Opinion

Turgenev subtitled his play, "A Comedy in Five Acts," but unlike the classic comedy that ends in a festival of happy marriages, *A Month in the Country* is really a bitter satire on sentimental, conventional love, with a denouement featuring two very unromantic betrothals. Vera's engagement to Bolshintsov and Lizaveta Bogdanovna's to Doctor Shpigelsky are arrangements of convenience; the parties enter into their relationships only because they have admitted defeat in their quest for love.

Vera's disillusionment with her guardian and the entire adult world is heightened by her tragically delayed realization that she loves Belyayev. She accepts the repulsive, middle-aged Bolshintsov to escape from a social position that makes her dependent upon those who have betrayed her. Natasha's jealous machinations thwarted any chance Vera might have of finding a young, romantic mate. In bitterness and defeat, she scorns Natasha and rejects the social and financial dependence she has grown to hate.

Lizaveta, already thirty-seven years old, knows that she is doomed to be the companion of an aging woman who will always treat her as a servant. Her union with Shpigelsky, though loveless, will free her from genteel servitude.

Bolshintsov admits that he has never even spoken with a woman, and at forty-eight knows that his chances for true romance have passed. Vera will be merely a pretty object; he will be unable to communicate with her on any level. Curiously, the worldly and sophisticated Shpigelsky is in a similar position. Weary of his own duplicity, he confesses his strengths and weaknesses to Lizaveta, offering her a loveless union that may give both of them the security they need to continue their twisted and stupid existences.

Comedy is supposed to end in marriage for its principal characters, but Turgenev's drama leaves Belyayev and Rakitin without mates and Natasha caught in a deadly provincial existence. Tied to a sympathetic but unromantic husband, entrapped in a household of vapid women, Natasha is deserted by everyone who might bring her adventure and love. Rakitin, her platonic lover, has escaped from the emasculating relationship that threatened to drag on for years of sterile unfulfillment. Belyayev, ardent, rational, handsome, and engaging, has left the country forever, to return to his student's life in the intellectually and emotionally rich city. Even Vera, who might have given Natasha warm affection and intelligent companionship, has flung herself out of the establishment.

The comic desertions by Rakitin, Belyayev, Vera, and

Lizaveta are cruel punishments for Natasha's pathetic and often ignoble actions. Her possible redemption (for on balance she seems to be a moral, sensitive, and emotionally resilient woman) is left in question, but it is a possibility. Rakitin's ignominious defeat in love may change his precious and effeminate idea of romance, but Turgenev's art is too subtle for so dogmatic a conclusion. Rakitin *may* return a changed man; Natasha *may* find strength and meaning in her child and husband; but the audience *may* also believe that Rakitin's return will simply be a return to the *status quo ante.*

Set in Russia, *A Month in the Country* is, despite certain details and trappings, a truly European play. Although it lacks the wit, grace, and sparkle of Alfred de Musset's French comedies or the earlier comedy of manners in England, its merit lies in Turgenev's careful delineation of character and his logical unfolding of plot line to coincide with the moral and emotional crises of his protagonists.

In Act I, Natasha, plainly upset, causes Rakitin to ponder the reasons for her distraction. When Shpigelsky asks for Vera's hand on behalf of Bolshintsov, Natasha is tempted to use her power to eliminate her ward as a rival. Rakitin senses Natasha's change in attitude as the play progresses, but it is not until the fourth act that he discovers its cause, and by then the moral ambiguity of his own relationship with her prohibits him from acting like an outraged lover. Belyayev, engagingly innocent of the passions he has inflamed, reacts quite unpredictably when he is informed of Natasha's love. He nearly returns it, but the burden of these seemingly innocent infatuations causes him to withdraw. Rakitin's influence on the young tutor adds another ironic twist to the play.

Belyayev is banished from the provincial society that he hoped would be a source of pleasure and rest. He gladly risks the physical uncertainties of a student's life in Moscow for the moral purity and intellectual substance it may offer. Not a Byronic figure, for he does not admire poetry and he prefers critical articles to *belles lettres,* Belyayev enjoys the outdoors more than he enjoys the members of the Islayev household. Although not exceptional in any way, Belyayev has no illusions about his life. He modestly jokes about the inaccuracies of his translation of a French novel and maintains a genuine respect for his employers, although they act like fools.

The minor characters in *A Month in the Country* are clumsily drawn: Schaaf, the German tutor, is given a ludicrous accent as the primary source of his humor; the servants, Matvey and Katya, are stock characters who merely move the story along until the principals appear; even Bolshintsov is not drawn with much originality, for he remains shadowy and drab rather than truly comic. Yet despite these lapses, Turgenev's perceptive creation of Natasha and her entourage grows in substance and depth as the play reaches its climax.

A Month in the Country explores problems that are still relevant. Vera's unhappy escape from the Islayevs is the result of a very real conflict between generations. Natasha, a matron of nearly thirty years, constantly remarks that her ward and Belyayev are so young. To achieve her own ends, she zealously twists the moral principles that she should be inculcating. The "generation gap" has separated Natasha from her ward and the man she loves.

The eternal conflict of principle and passion is carefully explored by Turgenev. He ironically endows the wrong people with the greatest devotion to principle. But in Belyayev he may be saying that both principle and passion can exist simultaneously. If he seems pessimistic about the survival of romantic love, he is also dramatizing the importance of acting one's age. Vera and Belyayev succeed, but are thwarted by the perverse behavior of Natasha, Rakitin, Shpigelsky, and Bolshintsov. Their attempts to achieve fulfillment in a society that is unsympathetic to true feeling is Turgenev's sad comment on some aspects of our society today.

The subtle psychological drama continues to remind us of how much Chekhov—the greater artist—owed to his predecessor. The total dramatic impression of Natalia Petrovna, the wife of a wealthy landowner, is not unworthy as a "first sketch" for *The Three Sisters* or for Madame Andreyevna in *The Cherry Orchard*. The delicate balancing of nuances and the combination of the realistic and the poetic, often attributed to Chekhov alone, should be shared by Turgenev as well.

The Author

Ivan Sergeyevich Turgenev was born in 1818 to rural nobility in Central Russia. His studies in Moscow, St. Petersburg, and Berlin, and long sojourns in France, gave him a cosmopolitan sophistication, but he always remained essentially a Russian author.

Turgenev began his literary career with imitations of English, French, and German models. When he wrote *A Month in the Country* (1848–50), he had already produced several dramas, among them *The Parasite* and *The Bachelor*, psychological dramas that were only mildly successful. When he finally published, in 1854, his last play, *A Month in the Country*, he said that it was not really intended for stage presentation. Indeed, it was not produced until 1872. The triumphant Moscow Art Theater production did not take place until 1909.

Turgenev drew upon Balzac's tragic melodrama *Stepmother* for the basic situations and characters of *A Month in the Country*. The same dramatic situations continued to appeal to Turgenev. His last novel, *Virgin Soil* (1877), contains many elements of the earlier plays.

After 1850, Turgenev abandoned the theater to write novels. He is distinguished for his subtle characterizations and urbane handling of psychological and social problems. *Fathers and Sons* (1862) remains his most famous work. As his popularity increased, Turgenev continued to diagnose the social and spiritual malaise that gripped Russia during the last third of the nineteenth century. He died in 1883.

The Power of Darkness

by

LEV NIKOLAYEVICH TOLSTOY (1828–1910)

The Characters

Petr—a forty-two-year-old rich peasant who has one child
by a former marriage and another by his present wife,
Anisya. He is in poor health and plans to leave his money
to his sister.

Anisya—ten years younger than Petr, wanton and brutal,
and concerned only with her own lust and security.

Akulina—the sixteen-year-old daughter of Petr by his first
marriage, feeble-minded and partially deaf. Her affair with
Nikita reveals her pride and vanity.

Anyutka—the ten-year-old daughter of Petr by his second
wife. After exposure to the horrors of the household, she
yearns for immediate death and salvation.

Nikita—twenty-five years old, proud, handsome, and impulsive. He believes he can control all situations with his
charm.

Akim—Nikita's father, a pious, ugly peasant whose silly
speech mannerisms do not detract from his deep sense of
morality, humanity, and propriety.

Matrena—Nikita's mother, a scheming, avaricious, and meddling woman. Her immorality is instrumental in causing
the deaths of Petr and her son's bastard child.

Marina—gentle, innocent, and stoical, she understands her
place in the world and resigns herself to a quiet life of
labor and submission.

Mitrich—a retired soldier who has become Nikita's farm-hand. He is full of worldly and spiritual wisdom.

The Story

In a nineteenth-century Russian peasant village, Petr orders Nikita to complete the farm work. Seriously ailing, the master lives with his two daughters and a young wife, Anisya. But Anisya and Nikita are secret lovers. Matrena tells her son, Nikita, that she does not care if he does not marry Marina, an orphan whom he has seduced. But Nikita's father, Akim, insists on the marriage. He is dissuaded from commanding Nikita to do the honorable thing (only after he is bullied by his wife). After learning that Anisya and Nikita are lovers, Matrena resolves to give Anisya poison that will hasten Petr's death. Although first expressing shock and hesitation, Anisya is convinced that she will achieve happiness after she has killed her husband, taken his money, and married Nikita.

Despite Akim's demands, it is agreed that Nikita will not marry Marina, but will stay in Petr's household for another year. When Nikita is left alone, he scoffs at the world's censure of his sexual libertinism. He haughtily rejects Marina, who has come to make a final plea for her love.

Petr's health has deteriorated. He has hidden his fortune and called for his sister. Anisya prevents Akulina from conveying the message, administers more poisoned tea to Petr, and consults with Matrena. The women conduct a fruitless search for the money and decide that Petr must have tied it around his neck. As Petr sinks into a coma, Anisya takes the money and gives it to Nikita to hide. Petr's death is announced to the village.

Several months later, Nikita has married Anisya, begun an affair with Akulina, and squandered nearly all the money on his new mistress or on drunken orgies. Mitrich, the old laborer Nikita has hired, comments on the sins of the world and Nikita's waywardness. A neighbor advises Anisya to go to the police to prevent Nikita from spending all the money. Akim, visiting his son, listens to Mitrich give a peasant's version of how banks use their depositors' money to exploit people and earn high interest. Nikita arrives drunk, bullies his father, and commands Akulina to show the luxurious gifts he has bestowed on her. He gives Akim ten rubles to buy a new horse and continues his drunken antics until his father, revolted by the spectacle, throws the money on the table, exhorts his son to mend his ways, and leaves. Nikita weeps.

About nine months later, a matchmaker has arrived to arrange a marriage between Akulina and a member of his own family. Matrena allays his misgivings and arrangements are concluded. Meanwhile, in the barn, Akulina is giving birth to Nikita's child. Matrena tells her son to dig a hole in the basement because the child has died. Nikita falters, but is prevailed upon by the women. The wailing infant is thrown into the basement, Nikita places a board over it, sits on it, and crushes it to death, wailing: "How it cracked underneath me! What have they done to me! And it's still alive, alive sure enough!" He continues to hear the crying child and laments the ruin of his life.

In an alternate ending to this act (IV), Tolstoy omitted the explicit murder scene and substituted a long dialogue between Mitrich and Anyutka, during which the infanticide is heard off-stage, and the old man attempts to divert the ten-year-old girl's attention from the murder. Mitrich tells how he saved a young child from soldiers and brought her up. He also inveighs against peasant women: "they are ignorant, nasty, animalistic." At the conclusion of this variant ending, Matrena scolds her son for thinking that the child is still wailing, and Mitrich comforts Anyutka: "They sure scared you, those nasty women, much good it may do them!"

Mitrich lies drunk on a stack of straw while Akulina's prewedding party is in progress. Marina approaches and asks two girls to fetch her husband, who is at the celebration. Nikita stumbles in, begs Marina's forgiveness, and declares his love. She replies that because she is now married to an old widower their romance is over. Her drunken husband staggers in, and Marina helps him back to the celebration. Anyutka calls Nikita to the party so he may bestow his blessings on the couple. He cannot bring himself to go and tries to hang himself when Matrena intercedes and scoffs at his pangs of conscience: "What's in the cellar? Cabbage, mushrooms and potatoes, I suppose. Let bygones be bygones." Anisya enters, insisting that Nikita give the blessing so the engaged couple may proceed to the church for the ceremony. After the women leave, Nikita again tries to hang himself. He is stopped by Mitrich, who suddenly rises from the straw. The old man tells of his drunken days of soldiery, the beatings, and people's attempts to bend him to their will. Mitrich claims that he is his own man, beholden to no one. Nikita suddenly throws away the rope and joins the ceremony where, in the presence of everyone, he confesses to betraying Marina, poisoning Petr, and murdering his and Akulina's child. Akim consoles him: "Repent in sight of God; do not fear men." Nikita concludes: "I did it all by myself. I planned it and did it. Lead me wherever you want to, I shall say nothing more."

Critical Opinion

Produced by the Moscow Art Theater on November 5, 1902, one month before Gorki's *The Lower Depths, The Power of Darkness* was originally considered to be a naturalistic rather than a philosophical and moral drama. After the premiere, Stanislavski realized that despite Tolstoy's detailed portrayal of peasant life, justice could not be done to this drama by merely re-creating the authentic peasant atmosphere. Like all of Tolstoy's art, *The Power of Darkness* appears to be a spontaneous and natural portrayal of events that, upon examination, have a deep and universal symbolic meaning.

The well-knit story is no more than a series of events culminating in infanticide and the agonized confession of a guilty man. But Tolstoy's genuine understanding of the peasant mind, which he believed represented the Russian spirit, goes beyond the confines of the village where this sordid drama takes place. Although each character is individualized, Tolstoy created characters that embody the wisdom and degradation, the nobility and the baseness of the peasant spirit. Avarice, lust, and pride are as much a part of peasant life as they are of the glittering world of *War and Peace*. Man is engaged in a painful search for the meaning of life and for final redemption from the forces that assault his best instincts. Nikita, a young, attractive, and virile peasant, is sexually amoral. His natural vitality and good spirits predispose him to a life of the flesh, but the world will not permit this, and so he is drawn into a series of moral dilemmas. After deserting Marina and defying his father's muddled but valid morality, he discovers that the vanity of the flesh leads to murder and damnation.

Like Ivan Ilytch, the protagonist of Tolstoy's great short story, Nikita must find truth through suffering. Torn by allegiances to himself, his parents, and the traditional codes of society, Nikita loses his spiritual independence first as he casually accepts complicity in Petr's murder and then as he destroys his bastard child. Openhearted and generous by nature, he does not really care for money or social position. Under the sway of his mother, however, Nikita marries Petr's widow, squanders her money on his half-witted stepdaughter and, taking to drink, perverts his innocence. Like the heroes of Greek drama, Nikita learns to accept his destiny.

Nikita lives blindly, letting people and events act upon him, acquiescing to murder, incest, and infanticide, until higher moral truths impinge upon his vanity and self-respect. He becomes a man when he accepts guilt for all the acts of the women around him. Like Oedipus at the conclusion of Sophocles' *Oedipus Rex,* Nikita asks to be led off to his punishment. By acknowledging guilt for all human sins, the young man triumphs over the Power of Darkness.

Akim is a devout peasant who understands the significance of his son's betrayal of Marina. Handicapped by an unprepossessing demeanor and ludicrous speech mannerisms, the old man has withdrawn from the corrupt world of Matrena and Nikita. He returns the ten rubles, refuses to drink tea with his son, and hurls himself into a winter storm, exclaiming: "Let me go; I won't stay. I'd rather spend the night under a fence than in this filth of yours." When Nikita confesses, Akim ecstatically proclaims: "God will forgive you, my beloved child! You have not spared yourself. He will spare you."

Akim and Mitrich present complementary visions. Akim admonishes his son: "Repent in the sight of God; do not fear men," and Mitrich tells Nikita: "But seeing I'm not afraid of people, it's easy for me." Like Luka in *The Lower Depths,* Mitrich is the archetypal old Russian whose suffering has brought him wisdom. Once ruined by drink, Mitrich

has become abstemious and industrious. When moral chaos
drives him back to vodka, he accepts his ruin, realizing that
he has chosen his own course. The sagacity and spiritual
independence that Mitrich embodies prompt Nikita to abandon thoughts of suicide, return to the celebration, and admit
his guilt.

In the variant ending to Act IV, Mitrich is given a central
role. He comforts Anyutka as the infant is being murdered.
Suddenly lashing out against the hopelessness of her plight,
he laments:

> How can girls like you help getting spoiled? Who
> teaches you anything? What do you ever see? What do
> you ever hear? Nothing but nastiness. I'm not very
> learned, but still I know something; not very well, but
> anyhow better than a village woman.—What's a village
> woman? Just mud. There's huge millions of your sort
> in Russia, and you're all like blind moles—don't know
> anything.

The women in this play are enslaved by superstition and
convention. The men weigh morality, the women consider
expediency only. After he has murdered his infant, Nikita
constantly emphasizes his terrible fall and the destructiveness of the women: "Oh, what have you done to me? I am
no longer a man." But Matrena and Anisya, oblivious to
moral as opposed to social consequences, devote their energies to the continuation of a corrupt society that is based
upon money, security, and respectability. If a young woman
is tyrannized over by a sick, old man, she must poison him,
steal his money, and wed her lover; she must marry off her
rival, even if an infant is murdered. Matrena's schemes drive
Anisya to these acts because, as Mitrich remarks, a peasant
woman is enslaved by fear and ignorance. These unnatural
acts are justified by a necessity that overwhelms elementary
humanity. Little better than the vain, half-witted Akulina,
these women are victims of an order that demands the
destruction of the moral spirit and the extinction of life
itself. Only Marina, reconciled to her fate as the wife of an
older man, uses her native instinct and good sense to reconcile her desires with a constructive social role.

Tolstoy might well have entitled this drama *The Power of*

Light. The light of man and God in a world of crime permeates the play's final scenes. Mitrich and Akim reaffirm the nobility of man and the transforming forgiveness of God that triumph in Nikita, giving him a heroic stature.

Tolstoy included a variant ending to Act IV because he believed that the infant's murder might be too harrowing for presentation on the stage. This ending gives more prominence to Mitrich and allows the audience to understand his role in dissuading Nikita from suicide.

The initial production of *The Power of Darkness* did not satisfy Stanislavski. Tolstoy's play was brought to international attention in a Paris production in 1888 by Antoine's Théâtre Libre. The following year the play was given in Berlin. It is widely regarded as Lev Tolstoy's dramatic masterpiece.

But despite the critical admiration for *The Power of Darkness* and its popularity in the art theaters of Europe late in the nineteenth century, the tragedy is seldom performed today. Perhaps modern directors, all too ready to agree with Tolstoy himself—who thought his plays were a sideline and was impatient with the limitations of dramatic form—shy away from the problems inherent in his mixture of peasant naturalism and quasi-mystical speculation. The modern reader, interested in Tolstoy the novelist, may find in this 1886 drama many profound revelations of the moral and religious crisis that resulted in his conversion to mystical Tolstoyan Christianity.

The Author

Born into a noble Russian family, Tolstoy was orphaned in 1837 and brought up by aunts. After studying languages and law at the University of Kazan, the twenty-one-year-old Tolstoy established a school for peasants on his estate, Yasnaya Polyana. When this scheme failed, he left for Moscow and St. Petersburg (now Leningrad), where he embarked upon an orgy of dissipation. His military service during the Crimean War included the epic defense of Sebastapol against the British, Turks, and Sardinians. The siege, which succeeded after 349 days, greatly impressed the young officer. His *Tales of Sebastapol* and *War and Peace* draw upon this experience.

Tolstoy's early publications include *Childhood* (1852), *Boyhood* (1854), *Youth* (1857), and literary criticism and essays. After leaving the army in 1855, Tolstoy returned to his school for peasants. Four years later, he devised an abortive scheme to free the serfs. Extensive travels in western Europe and a life of debauchery confirmed his pessimistic view of Western civilization and man's fallen nature. In 1862, Tolstoy married, retired to the country, raised a large family, and wrote his two great novels, *War and Peace* (1865–69) and *Anna Karenina* (1875–77).

After a profound spiritual crisis in 1876, prompted in part by the death of his brother, Tolstoy espoused the ideals of Christian love and passive resistance and developed his personal credo in a series of religious books that incurred the displeasure of the established churches and the government.

Tolstoy's first play, *The Power of Darkness* (1886), reflected his knowledge of the peasantry. Produced in Moscow by Dantchenko and Stanislavski at the Moscow Art Theater, the play met with limited success. Meanwhile, Tolstoy had written a satirical comedy, *The Fruits of Enlightenment* (1889), and two religious dramas, *Redemption* (1900) and the incomplete play *The Light that Shines in the Darkness*.

At the end of his life, Tolstoy gave up his worldly possessions, became estranged from his wife, and led a life of renunciation and idealism. He died at eighty-two, just as he was embarking upon the life of a religious pilgrim.

Peer Gynt

by

HENRIK IBSEN (1828–1906)

The Characters

Aase—Peer Gynt's widowed mother, the embodiment of maternal affection and loyalty, with a sense of humor that enables her both to criticize and to honor her son.

Peer Gynt—a stalwart, adventurous, and self-centered man who believes that destiny has singled him out for glory.

Solveig—the pure and faithful woman who loves Peer and waits for his return from his adventures.

Helga—Solveig's younger sister.

Ingrid—a wealthy farmer's daughter, who allows herself to be abducted from her wedding by Peer.

Three Cowherd Girls—wanton types of women, they entice Peer to live with them in the mountains.

The King of the Dovre (The Mountain King)—he reigns over a world of grotesque and perverted monsters (trolls) and sees the true nature of Peer's desires.

A Woman in Green—the Dovre king's daughter, who seduces Peer and brings him to her father's hall.

Troll Courtiers—hideous creatures whose motto is: "Troll, to thyself be—enough!" Similar to the Furies, they attempt to destroy Peer.

An Ugly Boy—Peer's bastard son from his union with the woman in green.

Voice in the Dark (The Boyg)—an invisible troll demon; symbolic of evil.

109

Mr. Cotton, M. Ballon, Herr von Eberkopf, and Herr Trumpeterstraale—Peer's four guests on his yacht. They represent, respectively, voracious English mercantilism, French imperialism, German militarism, and Swedish egotism.

Anitra—daughter of an Arab chief who becomes Peer's mistress and disciple, mostly because she is attracted by his jewels.

Professor Begriffenfeldt, Ph.D.—the insane director of a Cairo lunatic asylum who introduces Peer to his wards.

The Story

In a Norwegian forest at the beginning of the nineteenth century, Peer Gynt and his mother squabble about Peer's accounts of his fabulous adventures. When Aase hears Peer's tale of how he rode a buck over a mountain cliff and through the skies, she accuses him of having stolen the story from a Norse legend. She scolds him for lying and for having broken the arm of a blacksmith during a drunken brawl: "You bring me to the grave/With your madcap goings on." When Aase tells Peer that his former wealthy girl friend is going to marry, he sets off for the wedding after mischievously placing his mother on the roof so she cannot follow him.

At the wedding, Peer learns that the bride has locked herself away from the groom. When asked to coax her out, he carries Ingrid off to the mountains, enjoys her favors, and, after several weeks, deserts her. But throughout this escapade, Peer is obsessed by the memory of Solveig, an exquisite young girl who rejects his advances when she learns of his Rabelaisian reputation.

After leaving Ingrid, Peer encounters three filthy and wanton cowherd girls who, in a Bacchic frenzy, boast of their sexual appetites and invite him to live with them. He accepts, but sometime later, mad with guilt and desire, he imagines fantastic castles and other apparitions and screams: "Peer Gynt, you were born into greatness,/And great you'll become before long." He rushes toward a mirage, only to be struck unconscious on a rock.

In another episode, Peer meets a ragged woman who

claims to be a princess. He goes along with the charade and says that he is a prince; they go off to make love. Later, in the hall of the Mountain King, Peer is surrounded by grotesque monsters called trolls, who want to devour him. The king offers his daughter, with his kingdom as dowry, if Peer will become a troll and follow the motto: "Troll, to thyself be—enough." He accepts all the conditions, including the wearing of a devil's tail and giving up his Christian faith, but he resists the demand that he slit his eye lens so that he will see everything awry. At the king's signal, the courtiers attack Peer, but just as he is about to be destroyed, church bells toll, "the Trolls flee. Uproar and wild shrieks. The King's Hall collapses. Everything disappears."

On a wooded hill, Peer slashes out in a duel against a Boyg, an invisible Troll that is the embodiment of evil. Peer cannot pass and is driven mad, biting his own hands, when the Boyg says: "Rely on your fists; have faith in your strength." In the fierce battle, as he sinks to the ground, church bells again save Peer.

After alienating Solveig and her little sister, Helga, Peer goes off into the woods and vows to be an independent soul. Meanwhile, his family's farm has been foreclosed and Aase is left destitute. Peer builds a new hut in the forest, and Solveig comes to him saying she has left her family to live with him. Peer joyously welcomes her, but is terrified by the king's daughter and his demented bastard son who vow to hound him to the ends of the earth. Peer decides to leave Norway, and Solveig vows to wait for him. Before he leaves, Peer goes to Aase's deathbed, where a moving reconciliation and farewell take place.

Many years later, on a Moroccan coast, Peer and a group of businessmen sit at a table and discuss the great issues of life. Now a middle-aged millionaire, Peer has an enormous yacht that he has purchased with profits from the slave trade in America and the manufacture of religious articles for China missionaries. The Englishman, Swede, Frenchman, and German who are dining with him listen attentively as Peer recounts his fabulous adventures. He wants to become emperor of the world through the power of gold, which he will obtain by being true to his "Gyntian Self": "All that makes me live the life I live. It's all that makes me me," he proclaims. When Peer says that for profit he will join the

Turks to keep the Greeks in subjugation, the guests are scandalized and use his ruthless attitude as an excuse to steal his
yacht. Peer implores God to destroy the thieves. A moment
later, in a tremendous explosion, the yacht is sunk.

In the mountains, Peer comes upon a sumptuously bridled
horse and fabulous clothes that thieves have abandoned after
stealing them from the emperor. He is mistaken by the
peasants for a great prophet and god. After appropriating
these possessions, Anitra, an Arab girl, becomes his mistress
and disciple, but when his jewels run out, she refuses to
follow him on a pilgrimage of self-discovery. Peer strips the
emperor's clothes from his body and vows to renounce
women and travel around the world in search of reality. He
marvels at the Sphinx and the Pyramids. He encounters a
German named Begriffenfeldt who says Peer is the Messiah
and promises to take him to a place where he will be able
to practice his Revelation based on Self.

At a lunatic asylum in Cairo, Begriffenfeldt locks up the
keepers and frees the prisoners, proclaiming the death of
Absolute Reason and the founding of the Kingdom of Self.
A horrendous succession of insane men salutes Peer as
emperor. Peer's reasonable answers to their insane questions
drive them to greater madness or suicide. Peer begins to lose
his senses, and as he collapses the lunatics enthrone him and
place a crown of straw on his forehead.

Years later, now an old man, Peer is aboard a sinking
ship as it approaches the coast of Norway. Clinging to an
overturned lifeboat, Peer kills the ship's cook in order to save
his own life. Finally gaining the shore, he comes upon the
funeral of a man whom he had seen many years ago chopping off a finger to avoid military service. The pastor tells
how this man lived a virtuous and quiet life because he was
himself: "The substance of the inner man rang true." Later,
Peer meets a mourner at the funeral of Ingrid, the bride he
had abducted, and he learns that he himself has become a
legendary figure who was supposedly hanged long ago. Peer
begins to tell one of his fables and leaves his audience puzzled by an enigmatic story about the devil.

In the depths of the Norwegian forest again, Peer wonders
about the meaning of life and, peeling an onion, discovers
that there is no center, only leaves folding in, layer upon
layer. He comes upon his ancient hut. Solveig is singing.

Peer cries: "What a trickster is Fate! My Empire was here."
But Peer's journey is not ended, for he encounters spirits of
the forest and the night and finally meets Death himself in
the form of a button-molder who wants to melt Peer down
with the common mass of men. Peer begs for eternal individuality and promises to bring testimonials to the greatness he
has achieved.

The Mountain King refuses to help Peer even though
Peer has become the greatest of all trolls by following the
motto: "To thyself be—enough." Peer is aghast at this revelation and suddenly realizes that his life has indeed been
empty. Given another chance by the button-molder, Peer
meets the devil, who will not even let him be damned. Having failed to attain earth-shaking goodness or evil, Peer sets
off into the woods and hears Solveig in the hut. She welcomes him and offers salvation, "in my faith, in my hope and
in my love." He cries, "My Mother! My Wife! You holy
woman! Oh, hide me, hide me within your love!"

Critical Opinion

Peer Gynt (1867), Ibsen's ambitious drama in verse,
marked the culmination of the playwright's interest in the
fabulous, the metaphysical, and the poetic. Although the
social realism of such plays as *Ghosts* (1881) and *Hedda
Gabler* (1890) has become the trademark of Ibsenism,
for many people this free-wheeling and colorful panoramic
vision of a man's quest for greatness and identity is Ibsen's
most interesting work.

The philosophical theme of the play is revealed when the
Boyg tells Peer to go round about, and Peer later discovers
that experience is made of many layers without a central
core. Peer advances from a boasting and brawling liar to an
old man who has experienced everything and who realizes
that egotism, the pursuit of the Gyntian Self, brings hollow-
ness and waste. This final revelation in the arms of Solveig
may be too late to save him from the button-maker's melting
pot, but Ibsen reminds the audience that the journey is more
important than the destination. Peer's end in his hut in the
Norwegian mountains is more than a simple return: it is

symbolically important. Like Ulysses, who was a different man when he regained Ithaca, Peer acquired wisdom and self-knowledge in his fabulous travels.

Peer is born the hero and antihero, a Rabelaisian Faust who encounters the corrupt world and is himself sullied and purified by his experience in it. His abduction and abandonment of Ingrid, his violent defiance of convention, and his totally egotistical sensuality make him a romantic hero. Yet many critics have viewed Peer Gynt as the soulless and opportunistic modern man who is the antihero of so much modern literature. Although Peer's misinterpretations of Christianity, foggy sense of moral rectitude, and ruthless materialism make him part of the modern world, there is a vitality and moral wisdom in the character that suffuses the whole play with a humanity and energy typical of the romantic drama. Certainly a terrible irony emerges at the end of the play when the Mountain King tells Peer that by following the troll maxim, "To thyself be—enough," he has unwittingly become a monster. But this irony is not tragic or antiheroic; it is affirmative and redemptive, for Peer and all men understand the workings of a moral force that demands damnation before salvation.

Peer's adventures, beginning in the forest with his mother and progressing to the troll king's palace, lonely mountaintops, deserts, a lunatic asylum, the turbulent sea, and finally back to Norway, all lead him into encounters with the earth-spirits of wisdom and antiwisdom. Peer plunges into an ever-deeper vision of human existence as his fantasies of heroism and greatness come to fruition at the moment he senses that he is a charlatan, an exploiter, a ruthless man without sufficient self-knowledge for salvation.

In *Peer Gynt,* fantasy is mixed with reality to create a symbolic metaphor of man's spiritual state. The mythological and symbolic monsters of evil in the troll king's court are an embodiment of the corruption and moral perversion that rule the real world. Ibsen here creates a metaphysical paradigm of the total moral vision that Peer will be subjected to. The businessmen, philosophers, slaves, missionaries, and seamen are translations of man's bestial and perverted nature. Peer's guests on his yacht admire his ruthlessness and opportunism, but would censure his support of the Turks on con-

venient moral grounds. They significantly come around to
his callous view of self-gratification, and still pretending to
have moral and ethical motives, they steal his yacht and
leave him to perish in the desert.

The lunatics see the world through distorted lenses, as the
trolls, through their slit eye lenses, see "normal European
and Christian attitudes without understanding them." The
trolls instinctively recognize their new emperor, just as the
lunatics recognize Peer as their Messiah and crown him
with a wreath of straw. Three times Peer is recognized as
king of the trolls: in Norway; as a prophet in the desert; in
the Cairo lunatic asylum. At the end of the play, the Mountain King reveals that Peer has been king of the trolls nearly
all of his life—a moral monster contaminating the mad
world.

The hypocrisy of false religion is satirized often in the play.
Although he claims to be a Christian, Peer's actions are
pagan, as are his misquotations of Scripture. Perhaps Ibsen
intended an irreverent parallel to the New Testament when
he has Peer (Peter) thrice deny his identity (as Messiah).
Peter denied knowing Christ, the Messiah; but Ibsen's hero
is enough unto himself, and may embody the two biblical
persons, three times denying his *own* identity.

The settings and scenic effects in *Peer Gynt* are nearly as
important as the action itself. They propel the events and
action while commenting on them. Taxing all the resources
of the scenic director and designer, Ibsen's dramaturgy
demands vivid and convincing changes of scene to communicate the epic, picaresque, and nationalistic qualities of his
giant drama. The changes—from mountain passes to peasant
wedding to disappearing castles to pyramid-dominated desert-
scapes to asylums and shipwrecks—are integral parts of this
vast play. A Faustian drama of search, discovery, escape, and
capture, *Peer Gynt* follows its hero through a universal
odyssey.

When Peer calls Solveig wife, mother, and woman, and is
embraced by her eternal love, we see the archetypal vision
of man returning to the source of all life. Peer has made
an epic journey, from the bantering first scene with his
mother through subsequent episodes of abduction, promiscuity, escape, and treachery. Solveig's unquestioning and
pure love is the ultimate in loyalty and forbearance. Peer's

recognition of it and his submission to it may eventually redeem him from anonymity and mediocrity. He ultimately comprehends the meaning of his quest and the transcendance of love, humility, and true feeling.

Ghosts

by

HENRIK IBSEN (1828–1906)

The Characters

Mrs. Helen Alving—widow of Captain Alving and mother of Osvald. She has spent her life trying to obscure the true nature of her husband and to come to terms with her conflicting ideas about feminine duty and independence.

Osvald Alving—a young artist, sensitive and emotional, who has just come home from Paris to spend the last days of his life with his mother.

Pastor Manders—a priggish, self-righteous, and self-deceiving man tied to a false religion and to a conventional morality.

Jakob Engstrand—a scheming, hypocritical carpenter, supposedly the father of Regina, who wants to set up a "Seamen's Home" that in reality would be a brothel.

Regina Engstrand—the Alvings' maid, Osvald's half-sister, beautiful, vital, ambitious, and selfish.

The Story

On the country estate of Mrs. Alving, among the gloomy, rain-drenched fjords of western Norway, Regina, the maid, and Engstrand, an old and crippled carpenter, confront each other. Regina is contemptuous of Engstrand, who wants her to help him found a seamen's home. The carpenter chides

his daughter for her snobbishness and is reminded that her
mother, too, was vain about being in the Alvings' service.
As Engstrand lewdly suggests that Regina's physical charms
will bring success to his hostel, Pastor Manders enters and
he leaves.

Regina, very solicitous of Pastor Manders' comfort, rejects
his advice that she return to her father's house. Instead, she
indirectly asks Manders for a position in his home, but he
evades the issue, and they are interrupted by Mrs. Alving.
Manders and Mrs. Alving arrange for a ceremony to open
an orphanage dedicated to the memory of Captain Alving.
Manders says the orphanage should not be insured because
protection might imply a distrust of divine Providence and
adversely reflect on the pastor's integrity in the community.
Mrs. Alving is swayed by Manders' fears of the newspapers
and public opinion and agrees not to insure the orphanage.

While Mrs. Alving is telling Manders that Regina should
not return to Engstrand's house, young Osvald appears.
When Manders discusses the moral dangers of an artist's life
in Paris, Osvald assures the pastor that although some artists
live with their common-law wives and families, they are
really devoted men. Manders condemns these "illegal unions
—dissolute relationships," but is emphatically rebuked by
Osvald's descriptions of the debaucheries of so-called respectable citizens who leave their families to come to Paris for a
dissolute holiday. Mrs. Alving agrees with Osvald and is
rebuked by Manders for opinions that he considers not
worthy of her.

When Osvald leaves, the pastor reminds Mrs. Alving
about her desertion of the captain after one year of marriage. Manders insists that women must remember duty:
". . . It is not a wife's place to judge her husband; your duty
was to resign yourself and bear your cross with true humility." Although the captain had been unfaithful at first, says
Manders, he completely reformed upon Mrs. Alving's return.
But Mrs. Alving passionately replies that the captain remained lecherous and drunken, and seduced a young servant.
She was obliged to send Osvald away to school so he would
not be corrupted by his father. Manders is astounded to learn
that Mrs. Alving has built the orphanage with her husband's
fortune so that she may forever forget him. As they are

entering the dining room, they overhear Osvald's flirtation with Regina.

An hour later, Mrs. Alving resumes her confession to the pastor and tells him that when Alving made the servant girl pregnant, he gave her three hundred dollars and sent her off to marry Engstrand. Manders is scandalized by this compromise in morals. Mrs. Alving says that by marrying Captain Alving for his wealth and against the dictates of her heart, she too was guilty of a moral transgression. She was once in love with Manders, but her family had forced her to marry the captain. When Engstrand arrives, the pastor rebukes him for his duplicity about Regina's origins, but the carpenter replies that he married Regina's mother out of compassion and Christian charity. Manders, taken in by Engstrand's lies, promises to help the carpenter build the seamen's home, and they leave together.

Osvald, after drinking some liquor, tells his mother that he is pleased to be home but that he is very ill and afraid of what provincial life will do to him: "I'll never be able to work again! Never—never! I'll be like a living corpse! Mother—can you imagine anything more frightful—!" In Paris, Osvald tells her, he suffered a nervous collapse and was told by a doctor that he had inherited a venereal disease and that his brain would soon be destroyed. Rejecting the imputation that his father gave him this disease, Osvald blames himself. But Mrs. Alving realizes the truth. Ghosts from the past—her husband's dissolute way of life—have destroyed her son and her happiness. Osvald says that only Regina, young, sensual, and beautiful, can help him to endure his hideous doom. Mrs. Alving invites Regina to drink champagne with them, and just as she is about to reveal the truth about Regina's paternity, Manders enters. The orphanage is seen burning in the distance.

The glow of the gutted buildings still illuminates the drawing room a few hours later when Engstrand enters and tells Manders that he saw him accidentally drop a match into some wood shavings at the orphanage during a prayer meeting. Terrified of public exposure, the pastor says he will help Engstrand get money for the seamen's home. (The audience knows it will be a brothel.) Meanwhile, unaware of Manders' guilt, Mrs. Alving agrees to give the remaining orphanage money to the seamen's home, rounding out the final irony of her husband's memorial: first a home for illegitimate children, then a brothel. The pastor is totally compromised when he accepts Engstrand's offer to take the blame for the orphanage fire.

Finally, Osvald and Regina are privately told that they are half-brother and sister. Osvald is crushed by the revelation that his father was a degenerate monster. Regina is infuriated. She had hoped to go to Paris with Osvald and has been cheated out of her patrimony. She decides to live with Engstrand at the seamen's home. When Mrs. Alving implores her not to destroy herself, she defiantly and despairingly shouts: "What do I care!"

Left alone, Mrs. Alving and her son discuss his approaching end. Osvald shows his mother a lethal dose of morphine and makes her promise to give him the poison when his mind finally collapses. At first, Mrs. Alving refuses to accept her son's fate, but finally promises to abide by his wish. Moments later, she is overwhelmed by terror as Osvald sinks onto the couch, his mind destroyed.

Critical Opinion

Ghosts is Ibsen's most vehement attack on the stultifying and destructive forces of convention, hypocrisy, and self-deception. It is a profoundly moral and pessimistic play. Past and present are dovetailed with precision and logic in the inevitable, tragic conclusion. Because Ibsen dispensed with the traditionally clumsy dramatic exposition, and integrated revelations about the past into the fabric of the action, *Ghosts* has a continuity of movement that reminds one of the classical Greek drama.

As the play unfolds, each situation provokes a revelation about the past and raises truth and irony to a new level. Although the audience learns about Captain Alving decades after the man's death, his evil lives on through his wife's guilt, his illegitimate daughter's ultimate fate, and his son's hideous disease. These are the "ghosts" that dominate individuals, families, and entire societies. They are allowed to invade the present and destroy the future because cowardly men become enslaved to the dictates of convention and self-deception. These themes of guilt, expiation, and retribution unify Ibsen's drama. The skeletons in the Alving closet are universal. They haunt the entire society. In a moment of terrible illumination, Mrs. Alving grasps the fateful and destructive nature of individual life:

> You know, Manders, the longer I live the more convinced I am that we're all haunted in this world—not only by the things we inherit from our parents—but by ghosts of innumerable old prejudices and beliefs—half-forgotten cruelties and betrayals—we may not even be aware of them—but they're there just the same—and we can't get rid of them. The whole world is haunted by these ghosts of the dead past; you have only to pick up a newspaper to see them weaving in and out between the lines—Ah! if we only had the courage to sweep them all out and let in the light!

Mrs. Alving, a liberated and enlightened woman, has been cursed by her girlhood acceptance of the conventional forces that obliged her to marry Alving. Her deep and natural affection for Manders was thwarted by his refusal to acknowledge the bonds of friendship and love. Helene Alving's acceptance of life with her husband ironically gives her strength while it literally plants the seed of her destruction in the person of her diseased son. The past dominates the present and future, and her valiant efforts to exorcise the curse and agony of life with the captain are negated when the orphanage is destroyed and the benevolent picture of Alving she drew for her son is suddenly erased. Osvald, her only hope for the future, is triply destroyed by the past: He can no longer practice his art, his hallowed memory of his father proves an illusion, and his mind is rotted by a disease inherited from the captain. Regina, the captain's natural child, becomes a prostitute.

Ibsen introduces these ghosts from the past at dramatic moments throughout the play. He skillfully develops relationships between Mrs. Alving, the captain, and Manders. Manders is far more complicated than he first appears to be, for his denials of emotional involvements (his love for Mrs. Alving and his friendship for the captain) are both the cause and product of his enslavement to the dictates of public opinion. After Mrs. Alving accuses him of having deserted the family when the captain was in need, the audience learns of her love for the pastor and his rejection of her love because he feared public censure. The final irony for Manders is his destruction of the orphanage, a symbol of the guilt upon which he bases his religious and emotional visions. The orphanage symbolizes the conventional propriety that Manders is enslaved to; yet it is a fitting and ironic memorial to a dissolute man because it is a place for unwanted children. Manders' self-serving pledge to help Engstrand found the seamen's home is doubly ironic: He has compromised himself by allowing another to take on his guilt, and he has materially aided an unscrupulous man to open a brothel and to make Regina a prostitute.

If situation, character, and time are integral, symbolic aspects of this play, the setting is also an important element. The perpetual rain and claustrophobic social milieu of the Norwegian provinces are omnipresent. The burning orphanage, seen through the drawing room windows, glows like a vision of the Last Judgment and hell itself. In the final moments of the play, when Osvald's mind disintegrates, the sun appears. "The sun rises. The glaciers and peaks in the background are bathed in the bright morning light." In Osvald's reaction, Ibsen has expressed the ultimate irony—the light of truth and the birth of day bring death: "In a dull toneless voice," Osvald mutters: "Mother—give me the sun . . . the sun . . . the sun."

Ghosts created one of the greatest scandals in modern theatrical history when it appeared in European capitals. Universally condemned as an obscene and disgusting exploitation of an unsavory subject, the play was misunderstood as a sensational tract against venereal disease and the secrecy that surrounded it. The play has only recently been appreciated for the catholicity of its moral vision and the tragic power of its art. *Ghosts* condemns conventional morality, false guilt and shame, and individual and social hypocrisy. These are universal themes in man's troubled quest for a meaningful, humane, integrated existence. The timelessness and penetration of Ibsen's art is one of the landmarks of nineteenth-century drama.

Hedda Gabler

by

HENRIK IBSEN (1828–1906)

The Characters

George Tesman—a thirty-two-year-old scholar, married to beautiful, aristocratic Hedda Gabler. Uxorious, naive, unimaginative, and sentimental, Tesman is blind to Hedda's passionate needs.

Hedda Gabler Tesman—the vain, self-centered wife of George Tesman, who longs for a romantic, passionate life that she is too conventional to pursue. She is neurotically ashamed of her femininity and is driven to destroy Tesman and Lövborg, the two men who love her, and to end her own life.

Miss Juliana Tesman—Tesman's aunt and guardian during his minority, the kind of self-effacing but domineering woman who has pampered her loved ones into almost total helplessness.

Mrs. Thea Elvsted—the wife of an older man whom she married for convenience. She has left her family to devote herself sexually, spiritually, and intellectually to Eilert Lövborg. She is Ibsen's foil for Hedda.

Judge Brack—the libertine bachelor lawyer and judge who dominates Hedda and destroys Tesman and Lövborg. A scheming and heartless man, Brack sees that the lust and power within the framework of established society are his most effective instruments for mastery of others.

Eilert Lövborg—the young, passionate, Bohemian scholar

and historian who has tamed his wild and intemperate disposition and has written two monumental and imaginative books on the history of civilization. Lövborg's liaison with Mrs. Elvsted is intellectual as well as sexual. She has inspired him to regulate his life and to create philosophical and historical works. Lövborg's obsession with Hedda, however, drives him to self-destruction.

The Story

In an elegant villa, Miss Tesman prepares to greet her nephew and his bride on their return from an extensive wedding trip. George affectionately salutes his aunt, and they discuss the adventures of the trip and his immense luck in winning the beautiful, aristocratic daughter of General Gabler. When Hedda enters, she coldly acknowledges Miss Tesman's presence and maliciously insults her. When Miss Tesman leaves to attend to her invalid sister, Hedda refuses to make amends.

One of the bouquets welcoming the married couple has been presented by Mrs. Elvsted, who enters and discusses events during the Tesmans' absence. Eilert Lövborg, a great genius who nearly killed himself with alcohol and debauchery, has been the tutor of Mrs. Elvsted's stepchildren. He has completely reformed and has published a widely praised book on "the march of civilization," which contrasts with George Tesman's projected treatise on the domestic industries of the Brabant during the Middle Ages. Mrs. Elvsted is apprehensive because Lövborg has left her husband's employ and is now in town, once again prey to his old temptations. Hedda cleverly gets Mrs. Elvsted to reveal that she has left an unhappy marriage to devote her life to Lövborg. Tesman writes a note to Lövborg inviting him to their house that evening.

During Judge Brack's visit, it is revealed that Tesman has gone heavily into debt to pay for his bride's opulent villa. And now, because of Lövborg's book, Tesman may be denied the professorship he was counting on. After Brack leaves, Hedda stormily receives the news that until the professorship has been settled, she may not entertain on an extravagant scale nor have a saddle horse and men in livery. She pulls her father's pistols from their case and violently proclaims that they will now be her only entertainment.

A few hours later, Hedda playfully aims a pistol at Judge Brack as he makes his way through the garden to the villa. During their intimate conversation, Hedda says that she despises her husband and has married him only out of boredom. Brack insinuates that he would be an entertaining lover if she would accept him, but she at first rejects the idea because she fears scandal. When Brack indicates that he will be very circumspect and not expect her to get a divorce, Hedda tacitly concedes that an adulterous affair might be possible. But a moment later, when Brack ironically insinuates that Hedda may soon have Tesman's child to occupy her, she violently rejects his jibe: "I often think that there is only one thing in the world that I have any turn for, . . . boring myself to death."

Eilert Lövborg arrives in response to Tesman's invitation. He announces that he has written a monumental continuation of his book and shows everyone a parcel containing the completed manuscript. Brack invites Lövborg to a bachelor party, but the young man quickly refuses, fearing the temptations of alcohol. As Brack and Tesman retire to another room, Lövborg passionately reprimands Hedda for marrying without love. Lövborg and Hedda were once involved with each other and Lövborg is still obsessed with her. Confused and frightened by this threat to her conventional existence, Hedda spurns him.

When Mrs. Elvsted appears, Hedda viciously insinuates that earlier in the day Lövborg's mistress had doubted his power to abstain from alcohol. He furiously turns on Mrs. Elvsted, begins drinking a strong punch, and later accepts Brack's invitation to the bachelor party. In horror, Mrs. Elvsted implores her lover not to go, but enraged by Hedda's insidious jibes he leaves with the men. Mrs. Elvsted turns on Hedda: "You have some hidden motive in this, Hedda!" And Hedda cruelly replies that now *she* can mold a great man's destiny.

At dawn the next day, Lövborg has not returned. Mrs. Elvsted, exhausted and despairing, goes upstairs to rest just before Tesman enters with the news that he has read Lövborg's manuscript at Brack's party and that it is a world-shaking document. He also describes how, after Lövborg became drunk and dropped the manuscript on the road, Tesman picked it up and told no one. Hedda quickly takes the manuscript from him just as Tesman is informed that his invalid aunt is dying. He rushes off, leaving Hedda with Lövborg's manuscript.

Brack hurriedly announces himself and says that after his bachelor party Lövborg caused a riot in a brothel, accusing the owner of stealing his manuscript. This scandal makes Lövborg's social ostracism obligatory, says Brack, who also reveals that he knows about Lövborg's passion for Hedda and that he will destroy Lövborg or anyone else who comes between him and his adulterous lust. Frightened by this brutal vindictiveness, Hedda accedes to Brack's wishes and promises to shun Lövborg. Lövborg comes in just as Mrs. Elvsted, awakened by the voices, enters the drawing room. He tells her that their life together is finished because he has destroyed his manuscript and tossed it into a fjord. Mrs. Elvsted, horrified, says that Lövborg has destroyed their child, and rushes out. Lövborg confides to Hedda that he has really lost the manuscript in a brothel and that his life is now over. Hedda says nothing about her possession of the treasure and offers Lövborg a pistol so that he may kill himself "beautifully." After he leaves, Hedda burns the manuscript in the stove, saying: "I am burning your child."

Later that afternoon, Miss Tesman, in mourning for her sister, is consoled by Hedda. Tesman arrives, distraught with grief for his aunt and apprehensive that something has happened to Lövborg, whom he has not been able to find in order to tell about the manuscript. Hedda, relieved that the secret is still safe, privately tells her husband that she has burned Lövborg's masterpiece for Tesman's sake so he may secure his professorship. Tesman is at first scandalized and then overwhelmed by this sign of love. Mrs. Elvsted returns, followed by Judge Brack, who informs everyone that Lövborg has shot himself in the breast and died in the hospital. Hedda triumphantly says: "Well, well—the breast is a good place, too." Mrs. Elvsted shows Tesman the rough drafts of Lövborg's book, and together they withdraw to begin the arduous task of reconstructing the dead man's work.

Brack takes Hedda aside and tells her that Lövborg really died when the pistol was accidentally discharged during a scuffle at the local brothel, where he was trying to retrieve a piece of property he claimed had been stolen. The bullet pierced his bowels. Her romantic illusions shattered, Hedda is further broken when Brack cruelly threatens to have her dragged into court for giving Lövborg the pistol. Only he knows its ownership and now Hedda must give herself to him in order to avoid a scandal. Hedda suddenly goes into another room and plays a wild dance on the piano. Her husband tells her to stop. A shot is heard. The curtains part to reveal Hedda's lifeless body. There is a pistol wound in the temple. Brack screams: "Good God! People don't do such things."

Critical Opinion

Some critics have suggested that Hedda is, figuratively at least, the spiritual daughter of Nora, the emancipated woman who leaves her husband in *A Doll's House*. Aristocratic, beautiful, and "modern," Hedda seems emancipated from sexual and domestic slavery to men. Yet Hedda represents Ibsen's idea of the ultimate perversion of feminine modernism. Although she may drink punch and smoke cigarettes, dictate the tastes and life-style of her husband, and consider men as intellectual comrades, Hedda is ultimately reduced to reliance upon her femininity. Like all women, Hedda is subject to age, loss of beauty, and the inevitable biological result of sexual activity, children. She must rely upon her intellectual and spiritual resources in order to maintain her identity.

Hedda's tragedy is that these resources are twisted or inadequate. She is obliged to pose—both for herself and those around her—and camouflage her weaknesses. Bored and incapable of love, Hedda is not a soulful, poetic, and mysterious being cast adrift on the bourgeois society she despises; she is really a slave to its values and, as she confesses to Brack, one who would rather suffocate in her life with Tesman than cause scandal by seeking a divorce. Her "respectability" throws her into Brack's power when he threatens her with exposure. Her suicide is at least partially motivated by the desire to avoid social disgrace.

These fears of exposure are symbolically portrayed by Hedda's avoidance of light: She closes the curtains to shut out morning sun and prefers night to daylight. Hedda also fears the natural when she insidiously destroys Mrs. Elvsted's warm, feminine relationship with Lövborg, mocks her husband's love for his aunts, refuses to admit that she is pregnant, and perversely toys with her father's pistols, the phallic symbols of her revenge on both Lövborg and her feminine identity.

Like Emma Bovary, Hedda Gabler demands beauty and romance to dispel her boredom. Her conception of these is shallow and egotistical, reflecting her limited imagination and her callousness. Hedda wants Lövborg to blow his brains out "beautifully"; she is surprised when told that he has shot himself in the breast, for she had always thought of him as an intellectual, not a man of feeling.

Eilert Lövborg, the lover of Hedda and Thea Elvsted, the author of two brilliant books, and the consort of prostitutes, has fulfilled his destiny. Mrs. Elvsted realizes this as she enlists Tesman in the reconstruction of the destroyed manuscript. No longer capable of guiding or destroying anybody, and fated to be dominated by the lascivious and relentless Brack, Hedda takes her own life. The manuscript, the "child" of Lövborg and Mrs. Elvsted, will be reborn, with her despised husband acting as the stepfather.

In life, Hedda is a destructive and self-deluding woman. The play's title, using her maiden name, indicates her refusal to acknowledge her marriage to Tesman. She tampers with the life and the work of Lövborg, destroying both. She is capable of inspiring only a lustful, cold desire in Brack. Only at the end of the drama does she call her husband by his first name and perceive Brack's cruelty. But no tragic awareness is possible for this neurotic and cowardly woman whose tremendous passion and will are perverted to the use of a demonic and destructive personality.

In the play, Thea Elvsted, Lövborg's amanuensis, emerges as Ibsen's truly emancipated woman. She has the courage to leave a loveless marriage and devote herself to a creative and passionate man. The tragedy of the drama might seem to be Hedda's destruction of Lövborg, but ultimately it is the grim irony of Mrs. Elvsted's conquest of George Tesman, and the inevitability of their successful reconstruction of the manuscript that vanquishes Hedda and leaves her life meaningless.

The three men in *Hedda Gabler* represent different aspects of Hedda's amorous nature. George Tesman is a conventional, emotionally tepid, and unimaginative man who won his wife simply because he was the most convenient suitor when she was bored and insecure. Tesman's ties to his maiden aunts, his myopic attitude toward Hedda's feelings, and his limited intellectual interests contrast sharply with Lövborg's bold masculinity.

Adventurous, original, and violently passionate, Eilert Lövborg is the poetic Bohemian who must be crushed in society's Philistine embrace. Lövborg's obsession with Hedda is met by her confession that she is a coward who cannot endure his attentions. Lövborg, a great philosopher and historian, dies a gruesome death in a brothel. He is the true romantic, tormented by society, reaching for the stars, and perishing in the mud.

Standing between these two extremes is Judge Brack, a cynical libertine who would prefer a *ménage à trois* with Hedda and Tesman to the responsibility of marriage. Calculating, ruthless, and shrewd, but fundamentally conventional in his imagination, Brack is surprised when Hedda commits suicide. His plan to possess her did not take into account the tragic egotism that finally drove Hedda to shoot herself. Always safe and discreet, Brack is at once more clever than Tesman and more cowardly than Lövborg.

Like *Ghosts,* the action in *Hedda Gabler* takes place in about twenty-four hours. Ibsen's tightly-knit dramaturgy allows him to omit conventional exposition and plot development, fusing character and action in the compelling figure of Hedda herself. The four acts revolve around Hedda's attempt to escape her stultifying existence. In Act I, she is returning from a wedding trip that she confesses was excruciatingly boring. Her new journey takes her into the past, where she encounters her old lover, her father's pistols, and her premarital yearnings to guide a man's destiny. Her journey is completed at the end of the fourth act, when she has closed all avenues for self-expression: past, present, or future. Her suicide is sudden and logical, for unlike Madame Bovary, Hedda Gabler is familiar with instruments of death. The progression from honeymoon to suicide is as inexorable as any to be found in a Greek tragedy. Although some critics have questioned whether or not Ibsen should have made

Hedda kill herself, the entire play is a calculated, and artistically convincing, preparation for her final nihilism.

During the 1950s, *Hedda Gabler* received a stunning off-Broadway production in New York. Under the direction of the late David Ross, Anne Meacham's portrayal of the heroine established a standard for modern interpretations. Ibsen's compassionate yet unrelenting vision of a neurotic and destructive woman is considered to be one of his greatest plays. It demonstrates his enormous dramatic craftsmanship and his penetrating, uncompromising probing into the darknesses of the human psyche.

The Author

Henrik Ibsen was born in 1828 in southeastern Norway. When his father's business failed eight years later, the boy was forced to attend a school for poor children. His dreams of becoming an artist or physician were shattered. So in 1844, Ibsen became a pharmacist's apprentice in Grimstad, a small provincial city. He met some Norwegian patriots and wrote undistinguished political verse before moving to Christiana, where his writing earned him a job at the Bergen theater in 1851. Travels to the Continent widened his experience. During the next five years, he stage-managed and directed 145 plays and wrote five of his own.

Upon his return to Christiana in 1857, Ibsen found himself a famous national dramatist, revered for his play *The Vikings of Helgelland*. After a period of debauchery not unlike Eilert Lövborg's, Ibsen turned to patriotic historical drama and wrote *The Pretenders* (1863). Disgusted by his countrymen's failure to aid Denmark in its futile war against Prussia, Ibsen exiled himself from Norway for twenty-seven years. In Rome, he wrote *Brand* (1865) and *Peer Gynt* (1867). Both were tremendously successful.

Abandoning romantic drama, revealing how deeply he was influenced by Emile Zola's theories of Naturalism, Ibsen wrote a series of plays that have established him as one of the most important playwrights of modern times: *Pillars of Society* (1877), *A Doll's House* (1879), *Ghosts* (1881), *An Enemy of the People* (1882), *The Wild Duck* (1884), *Rosmersholm* (1886), and *Hedda Gabler* (1890) have been extremely influential dramas. Ibsen developed a technique of compressed exposition, natural dialogue, realistic setting and situations, and philosophically important themes that revolutionized dramatic writing. Many of these plays provoked violent protests and some were banned throughout Europe because of their allegedly antisocial themes and "indecent" subject matter.

When Ibsen returned to Norway in 1891, he was received as a national hero. His final works, including *The Master Builder* (1892), *John Gabriel Borkman* (1896), and *When We Dead Awaken* (1900), combined Ibsen's earlier interests in romance and symbol with his mature, realistic modes of dramatic rationalism. At his death in 1906, Ibsen was regarded as the most revolutionary and influential dramatist of modern times.

The Father

by

AUGUST STRINDBERG (1849–1912)

The Characters

The Captain—a middle-aged cavalry officer who combines
a military career with scientific work. A freethinker, ironic,
and passionate, he is surrounded by a household of domineering women whom he despises.

Laura—a vindictive and scheming woman who insists upon
having her own way in all matters, including the education of her daughter.

Bertha—their teen-age daughter who has aspired to be a
painter. She realizes the tyranny and oppression of the
household and her father's passionate wish to liberate her.

The Pastor—Laura's brother, intelligent and perceptive but
too weak to assert his will against the women who dominate his life. He admires his sister's strength, but condemns her duplicity.

The Doctor—a detached scientist who understands the conflicts around him and foresees the tragic denouement, but
refuses to become involved.

The Nurse—an old woman who dominates the captain by
reminding him that she cared for him during his childhood.

Nöjd—an orderly in the captain's house whose masculine
and earthy intelligence is admirable in a woman-dominated
world.

The Story

During December 1886, the captain and the pastor discuss the pregnancy of one of the unmarried servants. Nöjd has been accused, but he rejects the idea that any man can be sure of his paternity and refuses to be burdened with another man's child.

After the orderly leaves, the two men ponder the future of Bertha, the captain's daughter. His wife, Laura, the old nurse, the captain's mother-in-law, and the servants are trying to exert religious and personal influence. The captain has decided to send the girl away to school. Laura's determination to keep Bertha under her tutelage has produced a conflict in the marriage; the father fears that the girl is being brought up to despise men.

When Laura enters, she attacks the captain for his poor management of their finances and resumes the argument about Bertha's education. The captain reminds his wife that as master he controls his family, but Laura vows she will be victorious. When the captain explains his orderly's contention about fatherhood, Laura seems impressed. As he prepares to leave, the captain tells her to summon him when the new doctor arrives.

As soon as the doctor appears, Laura tells him that her husband is mentally unbalanced, a spendthrift with erratic habits who claims to be able to see life on other planets through a microscope. The doctor reserves judgment and warns Laura: "Don't allow anything to prey on the patient's mind. In a case of instability, ideas can sometimes take hold and grow into an obsession—or even monomania." On the entrance of her husband, Laura leaves the two men to talk about investigations of meteoric analysis through a spectroscope. The doctor observes that Laura has either mistakenly or intentionally distorted her description of the studies. The captain laments the delay in the arrival of scientific books from Paris. He is racing to publish his findings before scientists in Berlin, and he needs the books to complete his work.

The captain invites the doctor to stay at the house, then bids him goodnight. His solitude is disturbed by the nurse, who sides with Laura in the dispute over Bertha. Although the nurse has raised the captain from infancy, he accuses her of turning against him and attacks her Baptist faith, but immediately confesses: "Help me, for something is going to happen. I don't know what, but I know it's evil, this thing that's on its way."

A scream is heard from the other room. Bertha rushes in and begs her father to protect her from Laura's mother, who has been making her participate in communications with the dead. Bertha complains about the gloom and oppression in the household and rejoices when the captain promises she may live in town and pursue her studies there.

When Laura asks Bertha to decide her fate, the captain refuses to let her because he wants to make the decision for himself. The child leaves and he accuses Laura of lying to the doctor. Laura suggests that Bertha is illegitimate and, therefore, the captain has no legal or moral power over her destiny. The couple declare war, and Laura says: "It's odd, but I have never been able to look at a man without feeling myself his superior." The nurse tries to treat the captain like a child and reassures him of Bertha's legitimacy. But she is repelled by the captain's violent invective. He orders his sleigh and leaves the house.

Later that evening, the doctor observes that Laura's insinuations about the captain's mental health seem unfounded and that "one must be scrupulously accurate when bringing charges which might lead to a man's being certified." Laura suddenly conceives of a scheme to strip the captain of his civil and family powers. When she confesses that she has been intercepting his correspondence to book dealers and scientific colleagues, he warns her that her actions might lead to a persecution mania in her husband. Laura tells the doctor that her husband has doubts about Bertha's legitimacy and that six years earlier he confessed in a letter to a physician that he feared for his reason. The doctor promises to look into the matter, but when the captain enters, he detects the lie fabricated to explain the doctor's presence. The subject of infidelity is explored as the captain relates his experiences with women who were supposedly attached to other men. He knows of Laura's schemes to corrupt the doctor's judgment and dismisses him.

The captain calls Laura, whom he knows has been eavesdropping, and says he has learned she is responsible for the missing mail. She has thwarted his scientific aspirations: "You wanted . . . to stop me winning laurels of any kind, because this would stress your own inferiority." After intercepting Laura's letters, he has learned that she has been spreading rumors about his mental condition to his friends. He warns that he can function only as long as his willpower is unaffected, but insanity is now imminent, and if he should kill himself or become ill, she will be destitute. He begs Laura to free him from suspicions about Bertha's legitimacy, but she ambiguously insists upon her virtue. When he accuses her of wanting total power over the child, she replies: "Power, that's it. What's this whole life and death struggle for if not power?" The captain recalls that before their child's birth he was very ill and remembers the lawyer saying that without heirs Laura could not inherit his estate: "I recovered and we had a child. Who is the father?" Laura insists on the child's legitimacy, but the captain breaks down: "Can't you see I'm helpless as a child? Can't you hear me crying to my mother that I'm hurt? . . . I renounce every vestige of power and only beg for mercy on my life." He weeps bitterly, and after a pathetic speech, modeled after Shylock's in the *Merchant of Venice,* he explains that his parents had him against their will and therefore he was born without a will.

Laura acknowledges that the first stage of their romance contained elements of a mother-son relationship that later changed into an incestuous affair that she despised: "The mother became the mistress—horrible!" She later explains: "The mother was your friend, you see, but the woman was your enemy. Sexual love is conflict." Laura then shows the captain the letter he wrote expressing doubts about his sanity; she is going to have him committed to an asylum. He hurls a lamp at her.

The following evening preparations are being made to put the captain in a straitjacket and carry him off. The pastor asks Laura if she has no guilt in this affair, but she disingenuously describes the captain's erratic and violent behavior. The nurse is told to trick the captain into the straitjacket. The captain breaks out of the room he has been locked into, carrying a pile of books from which he quotes the history of woman's unfaithfulness. Bertha enters and innocently scolds him for speaking harshly about her mother: "You're not my father if you talk like that." The captain accuses her of being in league against him and confesses: "I am Saturn who devoured his children because it was foretold that otherwise they would devour him. To eat or to be eaten—that is the question. If I don't eat you, you will eat me—you've shown your teeth already."

After Bertha leaves, the nurse slips the straitjacket on the captain. He confronts Laura for the last time, saying that all women are his enemies, comparing himself to Hercules victimized by Omphale. The captain suffers a stroke and dies. Bertha goes to her mother's arms and Laura exclaims: "My child! My own child!" The pastor intones: "Amen."

Critical Opinion

The classical simplicity that Strindberg achieves in this startling and disquieting drama is a facet of the playwright's mastery of conventional dramaturgy. The action proceeds with unerring logic and inevitability. The seeds of the captain's destruction—planted at various times throughout his life—germinate and flower with inexorable naturalness. Strindberg here makes a clear statement of his battle-of-the-sexes thesis without resorting to the unconventional and often daring dramatic technique he later employed in *Miss Julie* and *A Dream Play*.

Emile Zola, the principal exponent of naturalism, recognized in *The Father* an extension of his essentially scientific theories that human character is exclusively influenced by heredity and environment. Zola praised Strindberg for his portrayal of the unconscious and mysterious elements in Laura's personality, those elements that escape scientific analysis. Laura is the archetypal woman figure who embodies the playwright's complex and often contradictory attitude toward the female sex. For the purposes of this play, which is one of the great documents of misogyny, Strindberg emphasized the primitive, cruel, and destructive qualities of womanhood.

A castrating female (the captain refers to himself as a capon), Laura deprives her husband of sexual fulfillment, domestic authority, and intellectual achievement. She is interested in power and domination as ends in themselves. The dispute over Bertha's education is merely a pretext to climax the couple's lifetime of strife. She has surrounded her husband with a matriarchal domestic establishment that includes her own mother, her husband's former nanny, the governess, and ignorant and superstitious servant girls. Laura intercepts the captain's correspondence, slanders his character in letters to his friends, and turns the newly arrived doctor against him. She conceives of the female role as a quest for domination. Like Hedda Gabler, Laura is conventional and externally unfeminine. (She will not look at herself in a mirror.)

For Laura, power can be maintained only through the mother-child relationship. Her first years of marriage were based on maternal love: "I loved you as if you were my little boy. But didn't you see how, when your feelings changed and you came to me as a lover, I was ashamed? . . . The mother became the mistress. Horrible!" Sexual love between men and women implies male dominance and is therefore repulsive to Laura. She explains that her submission to the captain was a means of attaining power: "Sexual love is conflict. And don't imagine I gave myself. I didn't give. I only took what I meant to take. Yet you did dominate me . . . I felt it and wanted you to feel it." Laura thus makes the conventional distinction between maternal and sexual love, deliberately eliminating the latter from their relationship. Motherhood is power, and the loss of Bertha will signal her failure to dominate both daughter and husband. When the captain asks Laura if she hates him, she replies: "Sometimes—as a man." The captain retorts: "It's like race hatred. If it's true we are descended from the apes, it must have been from two different species." The conflict is a question of power, not of moral sentiment, compassion, or love.

The portrayal of the captain is partially naturalistic. The captain traces his own misfortunes and deprivations at the hands of women when he recounts how his mother emotionally and physically rejected him, how his sister taught him submission, how his first mistress gave him venereal disease in return for the love he offered, how his daughter

has allied herself with her mother, and how his wife drove
him to his deathbed.

When he could not find emotional fulfillment and was
balked in his desire to go to war, the captain turned to
scientific investigation. But Laura intercepted his letters,
prevented the delivery of books necessary for his research,
and blasted the household's tranquility. The captain believes
that his last hope for self-esteem and moral sanity rests in
his scientific researches and his daughter's love. When Laura
robs him of the first, he laments: "And now—now when
I should be stretching out my hand to gather the fruit, you
chop off my arm. I'm robbed of my laurels; I'm finished.
A man cannot live without repute."

Laura has so thoroughly undermined her husband's physical and mental health that the captain is an easy prey to
suggestion. When Nöjd and the captain discuss the uncertainty of paternity at the very beginning of *The Father*, the
classic dramatic irony that controls the play is introduced.
Later, in conversation with Laura, the captain exposes the
fatal weakness in his will by which his wife may achieve
his destruction. The implicit parallel to Sophocles' *Oedipus
Rex* is underlined when Laura describes the incestuous conflicts between the captain and herself. In the depths of his
despair, the captain cites historical, mythical, and literary
precedents to demonstrate the hopelessness of his predicament. The Bible, Homer, and the classical myth of Omphale
and Hercules mirror the tragic significance of the captain's
agony. His intelligence is perverted into an instrument of
self-destruction.

Strindberg's title, *The Father*, ironically posits the drama's
principal dilemma. Fatherhood suggests immortality through
biological and spiritual fulfillment. Deprived of the immortality of his paternity, the captain laments:

I grafted my right arm and half my brain and spinal
cord on to another stem. I believed they would unite
and grow into a single and more perfect tree. Then
someone brought a knife and cut below the graft, so
now I am only half a tree. The other part, with my
arm and half my brain, goes on growing. But I wither
—I am dying, for it was the best part of myself I gave

away. Let me die. Do what you like with me, I am finished.

Fatherhood also means authority and domination, but these have been usurped by Laura.

The major witnesses to this conflict, the doctor and the pastor, are cravenly neutral. Cloaked in scientific impartiality and family loyalty, they deny their manhood and responsibility. The possibility that the captain might be saved by their humanity and moral strength contributes to the tension of the drama.

Although some critics have suggested that the captain's fall is unheroic, it is clear that he is a modern hero who is crushed between forces that Strindberg so plainly depicts in this play. Strindberg thought that modern man was victimized by women who dominate without realizing the consequences of their power. The imagery and structure of *The Father* repeat the thesis and expand it beyond the precincts of the bedchamber. *The Father* is Strindberg's answer to Ibsen's *A Doll's House*. Ibsen revealed the dominating male; Strindberg the dominating female.

After its first production in Copenhagen in 1887, *The Father* was severely criticized for being lugubrious and unchivalrous. The playwright defended his work in the preface to *Miss Julie* (1888), saying it demonstrated life's "strong and cruel struggle." The play achieved notoriety and success in subsequent productions. It was first performed in English in 1927. The most talented actors of the times have been attracted by the part of the captain: Michael Redgrave (1949) and Trevor Howard (1964) are among those who have given distinguished performances in the role.

Miss Julie

by

AUGUST STRINDBERG (1849–1912)

The Characters

Miss Julie—an elegant and passionate young aristocrat of twenty-five whose upbringing has taught her about the battle of the sexes. She despises men, but succumbs to her sexual desires.

Jean—a thirty-year-old valet who has worked ambitiously to improve his station in life.

Kristin—the thirty-five-year-old cook, Jean's mistress, conventional, religious, and superstitious. Her peasant pride and orthodox conception of class distinctions preserve her common sense and independence.

The Story

Jean and Kristin discuss their mistress, who has joined the servants in the Midsummer Eve festivities. As they sit in the kitchen of the count's manor house, they criticize Miss Julie's erratic conduct since the breaking of her engagement to a lawyer. Jean tells Kristin how Miss Julie made her fiancé leap over her riding whip and accept a beating after each jump. While Jean eats a fried kidney and drinks French wine stolen from the count's wine cellar, Kristin stews some food for Miss Julie's dog, Diana, who ran off with the gatekeeper's mongrel. They recall that Miss Julie's mother was more at home with the servants than with the nobility.

When Miss Julie enters, Jean compliments her elegantly, but is hesitant to join her in dancing with the servants. But she orders him, and he reluctantly leaves with her.

While they are gone, Kristin cleans up in the kitchen and curls her hair. Upon Jean's return, they resume their conversation about Miss Julie: She is about to have her menstrual period and is acting strangely. Jean embraces the cook, but they are interrupted by Miss Julie, who scolds the valet for leaving the dance without her. They banter in French and Jean tells her that although he has learned languages and manners while working in a hotel in Switzerland, his father was only a laborer on the next estate. As Kristin snores in the corner, Julie and Jean drink beer, a lower-class beverage, and Julie commands him to kiss her foot. He chivalrously complies, but tells her that their behavior will inspire malicious gossip among the servants.

Miss Julie recounts a dream in which she sees herself on top of a pillar and feels compelled to get down: "I have to get down but I haven't the courage to jump. . . . There can't be any peace at all for me until I am down, right down on the ground." Jean is then moved to tell of his recurrent dream: Lying under a tree, he wants to climb it, dominate the landscape, and rob a nest of golden eggs, but the trunk is too thick and smooth and he cannot reach the first branch. As their conversation becomes more intimate, Jean boldly kisses her and is rebuffed. He tells how as a child he crept into her garden and admired her. He fell in love and tried to kill himself in despair: "There was no hope of winning you—you were simply a symbol of the hopelessness of ever getting out of a class I was born in."

Suddenly, the revelers approach the kitchen. Fearful of being discovered together, Jean and Miss Julie retire to the valet's room after he promises to respect her chastity. The merrymakers enter the kitchen, dance, sing, and drink. After they leave, Jean and Julie emerge in an excited and disheveled state. It is clear that they have made love.

Jean tells Julie that they must run away together to Lake Como, where he will open a hotel and she will be the *grande dame* of the establishment. Julie wants affection and

romance, but her lover is busy formulating plans and refuses
to make love to her again in the shadow of the manor: "As
long as we're in this house, there *are* barriers between us.
There's the past and there's the count. I've never been so
servile to anyone as I am to him." When Julie insists upon
a declaration of love, Jean replies: "No sentimentality now
or everything will be lost." Julie despairingly cries: "I'm
falling, I'm falling." Jean offers her a glass of the count's
wine and they exchange insults, calling each other thief and
whore. The valet admits that his fine speeches to her were
fabrications, and Julie is broken: "Go on. Hit me, trample
on me—it's all I deserve. I'm rotten. But help me! If
there's any way out at all, help me!"

Jean pities her and explains that he was disenchanted
to discover that aristocrats are as base and animalistic as
their servants. He becomes passionate again, but Julie pulls
away, drinks more wine, and relates how her mother believed in equality of the sexes and brought her up to be a
man. She was taught horse-breaking, hunting, and plowing
and was forbidden to engage in feminine pursuits. The men
on the estate were given women's jobs. When the system
failed, her mother became mentally deranged and set fire
to the estate on the day the insurance lapsed. After a period
of destitution, the count borrowed money from a neighbor
who was her mother's lover. The money belonged to Julie's
mother, who thus avenged herself on the count for asserting
his masculine prerogatives. Julie learned to hate all men and
swore to her mother never to become the slave of any man.

Julie laments her fall and confesses that although she
hates men, she yields to sudden transports of sexual desire.
When she confesses her wish to die on the romantically
beautiful shores of Como, Jean retorts: "Como is a rainy
hole and I didn't see any oranges outside the shops." Julie
wants them to run away and die together and is surprised
to learn Jean believes in God and considers suicide a sin.
He also says that Julie is now below him; he does not
understand her aristocratic sensibility, which is obsessed
with guilt, honor, and self-esteem. Julie capitulates to Jean's
mastery: "Give me orders. Set me going. I can't think any
more, can't. . . ." He commands her to dress for the journey
and rob her father. When she is gone, Kristin emerges from
her room and invites Jean to hear a church sermon on the

beheading of John the Baptist. Not angry when she learns of Jean's conquest, the cook decides to leave the count's employ: "But you don't want to stay in the service of people who are not respectable, do you? I wouldn't demean myself."

After Kristin leaves, Julie enters dressed for a journey, carrying a birdcage. The journey without Jean would be intolerable because the train "would stop at every station while I yearned for wings." Jean refuses to let her take her pet bird that, Julie says, is "the only living creature who cares for me since Diana went off like that." As Jean is about to decapitate the bird, Julie screams: "Kill me too! Kill me!" Drawn to the chopping block, she watches Jean and hysterically screams:

> Oh, how I should like to see your blood and your brains on a chopping-block! I'd like to see the whole of your sex swimming like that in a sea of blood. I think I could drink out of your skull, bathe my feet in your broken breast and eat your heart roasted whole.

The count's carriage is heard in the drive and Julie approaches Kristin, who has returned, and pleads with her, woman-to-woman, to join them at the hotel in Switzerland. She hysterically repeats Jean's former description of their life together in order to induce Kristin to be their cook in the hotel. But her frenzied recitation exhausts itself. Kristin retorts: "I've always had enough self-respect . . . not to go below my own station." She exposes Jean's thefts from the count's estate and leaves.

Shame, remorse, and indecision overcome Julie: "Help me. Order me, and I'll obey like a dog. Do me this last service—save my honor, save [the count's] name." Jean proffers his razor and tells Julie to go to the barn. The bell rings, summoning Jean to the count's service. He exclaims: "It's horrible. But there's no other way to end it. . . . Go!" Holding the razor, Julie walks firmly through the door.

Critical Opinion

In the foreword to *Miss Julie*, Strindberg explains the play's universality. Taken from a true story, the play elicits terror and pity from the audience. Strindberg posits that "it is tragic to see one favored by fortune go under, and still more to see a family heritage die out. . . . The fact my heroine rouses pity is solely due to weakness; we cannot resist fear of the same fate overtaking us."

Miss Julie is a naturalistic tragedy centering on the class problem. Yet the orientation is both naturalistic and psychological in its exploration of an individual character's spiritual torment: "My treatment of theme is neither exclusively physiological nor psychological." Strindberg rejects the conventional idea of two-dimensional stage "characters" and reminds his reader that the human soul is complex and multifaceted.

The man-hating Laura reemerges in the beautiful figure of Miss Julie. Strindberg comments that "the type implies degeneration; it is not a good type and it does not endure. . . . The type is tragic, revealing a desperate fight against nature." A true aristocrat, Miss Julie is obsessed with a sense of honor that mystifies the worldly and pragmatic Jean. When she ponders on how to expiate her fall and degradation, he consults train schedules and calculates the amount of money he will need to make his fortune in Switzerland. Puzzled by Julie's agonies, Jean tells her to come down to his level so he may raise her up again. The problem is not so simple for the complex Miss Julie. Strindberg does not simplify the problem and reminds us that:

> It is not because Jean is now rising that he has the upper hand of Miss Julie, but because he is a man. Sexually he is the aristocrat because of his virility, his keener senses, and his capacity for taking the initiative. His inferiority is mainly due to the social environment in which he lives, and he can probably shed it with his valet's livery.

Thus we are still in the world of *The Father,* although in this play the primeval battles for mastery rage on different levels.

Unlike Laura, Miss Julie is vanquished because she is an aristocrat with tainted heredity and environment. A man-hater, she has tried to deny her womanhood and has sought mastery over the opposite sex. Her pathetic attempts to enlist the aid of Kristin reveal the futility of her notion that the women must unite against the men. More feminine than Laura, Miss Julie is sexually passionate. Ultimately, her natural instincts cause her to yield to Jean. She destroys herself not because of her puritanical or moral scruples but because her intellectual and emotional history militate against the survival of a woman who has fallen below her social class and admitted male superiority. Like her mother, who went insane after the failure of her plan to turn women into men, Miss Julie resorts to violence and destruction.

Miss Julie, more complex than *The Father,* is built upon a highly organized scheme of symbols. In the opening scene, Kristin is making a stew for Julie's dog, Diana (named after the virgin goddess of the hunt), who has run off with the gatekeeper's mongrel, anticipating her mistress's fall. This recurrent symbol stresses the essential bestiality of the human personality. Animals reappear when Julie attempts to escape with her bird. She identifies with it and says it is the only creature, since Diana's defection, that cares for her. Capable of flight (escape), the bird is caged and domesticated, like its mistress. Jean's brutal slaughter of the small animal precipitates Julie's final loss of will.

The lovers' dreams are opposed: Julie, on top of a pillar (which is both aristocratic and phallic), feels compelled to jump down, but not only to reach the ground: "And if I did get to the ground, I'd want to be under the ground." Total degradation and death are her destiny. In his dream, Jean sees himself lying under a great tree in a dark wood, much as he lay in the shadowy thistle patch in his youth. He wants to climb to the top: "but the trunk is so thick and smooth and it's so far to the first branch." The sunlight and golden eggs at the top of the tree are the wealth and leisure he desires. The sexual connotations of his dream include his wish to advance by way of the phallic tree, his search for a branch (the conquest of Miss Julie is the first rung up the social ladder), and finally his obsession with robbing a nest of golden eggs—a symbol of both masculine domination of a woman and social and financial security. While Miss Julie must achieve her act by violent movement (jumping or falling), Jean envisions a gradual ascent toward his goal.

Kristin wants Jean to hear a sermon about John the

Baptist, a saint who was decapitated because of Salome's lust and hate. He had rejected her. Strindberg underlines the parallel between Julie and Salome (both sexually inflamed but rejected women) when Julie sees the little bird's blood. Raging with desire and hate, she conjures up gory images: "I think I could drink out of your skull, bathe my feet in your broken breast, and eat your heart roasted whole."

A dominant symbol of the play is the Midsummer Eve bacchanale, a Swedish festival that takes place on the longest day of the year. A pagan festival of renewal, it is a traditional time for drinking and lovemaking under the light of the midnight sun. The release from convention is contagious, and Miss Julie succumbs to temptation. Flowers, dances, songs, and drink are aphrodisiacs for both Jean and Miss Julie.

Strindberg indicates that *Miss Julie* should be performed without an intermission: "Meanwhile, in order to provide respite for the audience and the players, without allowing the audience to escape from the illusion, I have introduced three art forms: monologue, mime and ballet. These are all part of drama, having their origins in classic tragedy, monody having become monologue and the chorus, ballet." The playwright asks his actors to *ad lib* and perform in a natural manner. Kristin and Jean, each alone, perform monologues and mime, and the chorus of carousing and singing servants comments on the off-stage action while Jean and Miss Julie make love. This ballet is not the usual crowd scene; it must be choreographed in a meaningful and suggestive manner.

Strindberg instructs the set designer to copy "impressionist painting [and] its asymmetry and its economy." Yet the copper pots and other kitchen utensils must be real, not cardboard replicas, and the physical details of the setting must enhance the psychological realism of the action.

Miss Julie was first performed in Copenhagen in 1889. Antoine's Théâtre Libre production (Paris, 1893) was a milestone of naturalistic drama. Not produced in Sweden until 1906, the play has since become one of the most popular classics of modern drama and is performed in translation all over the world. First given in London in 1927 and then subsequently in 1960 and 1965, the play has enjoyed revivals in the United States. It was made into a

film in 1950 by the great Swedish director Alf Sjöberg—
a film acclaimed as "the finest product of Swedish cinema"
in a poll among national critics in the magazine *Chaplin*
in 1964.

The Author

The son of an unsuccessful Stockholm shipping agent and
a dissolute barmaid, Johan August Strindberg was brought
up in squalor amidst constant domestic strife. The fourth
of a dozen children, August resented his mother, who had
borne three illegitimate children to his father and had
married him only three months before his own birth. The
domestic situation deteriorated even further in Strindberg's
thirteenth year, when his mother died and his father married
a woman who was a cruel stepmother.

Finally free from family oppression, at the University of
Uppsala, in 1867, the young Strindberg led a stormy career,
often quarreling with his professors. He transferred to the
University of Stockholm, where he began to write plays
and won a scholarship from King Charles V of Sweden.
Strindberg then embarked on a literary career with a full-
length historical play, *Master Olaf* (c. 1873).

After a passionate and unconventional love affair, Strindberg married the Baroness Siri von Essen in 1877 and had
three children by her. His family situation proved no better
than his parents'. The young author gave full vent to his
resentment in a provocative collection of short stories,
Married (1884), in which the misogyny that characterized
his later dramas became apparent. *Married* was immediately
banned.

The battle of the sexes soon became a major theme in
Strindberg's work. *The Comrades* (1886), *The Father*
(1887), *Miss Julie* (1888), *The Link* (1893), and *The
Dance of Death* (1901) contain many autobiographical elements. But Strindberg seemed to have learned little from
his stormy marital experiences, and after divorcing the
baroness in 1891 he married two more times, thus constantly renewing his hatred for women. He continued to write
while traveling widely through Europe and especially Germany. Recurrent fits of insanity and persecution mania de-

stroyed his life's tranquillity but provided the material for his dramas.

Greatly influenced by Zola's Naturalism, Strindberg wrote an "Essay on Modern Drama and Modern Theatre" in 1889 in which he explained that "the great naturalism delights in struggle between natural forces, whether these forces are called love and hate, rebellious or social instincts. . . ." But he differed from pure French Naturalist tradition in adding psychological strife to the forces of heredity and environment.

Strindberg's early Naturalistic plays were followed by a series of experimental "dream plays" of which *A Dream Play* (1902) is the most famous. Strindberg's varied theatrical styles include historical plays, *Gustav Vasa* (1899) and *Erik XIV* (1899), a symbolist play, *Swanwhite* (1901), and semi-supernaturalist plays *The Bridal Crown* (1901) and *Easter* (1901). At the end of his life, Strindberg had written over twenty-nine plays, as well as numerous poems, critical essays and other volumes. His interest in the practical aspects of the theater led him to found the Intimate Theatre in Stockholm in 1907 for the performance of his own works.

The Sea Gull

by

ANTON CHEKHOV (1860–1904)

The Characters

Irina Nikolaevna Arkadina—an aging actress, mother of twenty-five-year-old Trepleff and mistress of Trigorin, a fashionable writer several years younger than she. Although enormously successful on the stage, Arkadina is tightfisted with her relatives, insecure with her lover, and jealous of her son's youth and talent.

Konstantine Gavrilovich Trepleff (Kostya)—Arkadina's son, trapped in her brother's provincial home without an independent income. Adoring his mother, he is a violent, moody, and sensitive young man who wants to become a great writer and who is desperately in love with Nina.

Peter Nikolayevich Sorin—Arkadina's brother, a bitter and disappointed old man who has never fulfilled his two desires: to marry and to be a writer. Sorin's bitterness is tempered by his humanity and sense of humor.

Nina Mikhailovna Zaryechny—a nineteen-year-old whose wealthy father's affections are alienated by her step-mother. She is beautiful, conventional, romantic, and gullible.

Ilya Afanasevich Shamreyeff—Sorin's steward. Vulgar, loud, and importunate, Shamreyeff is the embodiment of insensitivity.

Pauline Andreevna—Shamreyeff's wife and the frustrated pursuer of Dr. Dorn.

Masha (Maria Ilyinishna)—the somber, repressed, and passionate daughter of Shamreyeff and Pauline. She is desperately and secretly in love with Trepleff.

Boris Alexeevich Trigorin—a successful writer, lover of
Arkadina. He is neurotically obsessed with his creations;
yet his facility and glibness fail to mask a spineless,
destructively romantic personality.

Eugene Sergeevich Dorn—a forty-five-year-old retired physician who has apparently experienced the intellectual and
sensual pleasures of the world. He is sympathetic, mildly
cynical, but humane.

Seymon Semyonovich Medvedenko—a whining, obtuse, and
self-pitying schoolteacher, given to inane philosophical
discourses and obsessive concern with money and position.
Masha marries him on the rebound from Trepleff.

The Story

In the closing years of the nineteenth century, a
group of Russian writers, actors, and their families gather
at a country estate on the shores of a lake. Trepleff, an
aspiring playwright, is about to present a play he has written,
which will be recited by Nina. While the stage is being
prepared, Medvedenko, a poor schoolteacher, quarrels with
Masha. Smoking cigars and taking snuff, Masha rejects
Medvedenko's advances. They are interrupted by Sorin and
the others who assemble because the audience must be
seated at eight-thirty precisely, when the moon will rise
over the lake. This tableau will form the backdrop for the
improvised stage constructed by Trepleff, who plans to
introduce a new kind of theater that will reject conventional
melodrama in favor of profound and poetic statements. Just
before the performance, Nina appears and tells Trepleff that
although her father and stepmother think he and his family
are too Bohemian, she has managed to escape for a few
minutes for the play.

Immediately before the curtain rises, Pauline and Dr.
Dorn appear. Obviously in love with Dr. Dorn, Pauline has
become a nagging shrew in her attempts to attract him.
Meanwhile, Trepleff exchanges vicious barbs with his mother,
Arkadina, as they quote and paraphrase the famous closet

scene from *Hamlet*. After their encounter, the play, which is set 200,000 years in the future, begins. But Nina's long soliloquy is irreverently interrupted by members of the audience. When sulphur is burned for the entrance of the devil, Trepleff impetuously stops the play as a protest against the audience's discourtesy. A few minutes later, Nina steps off the stage and confides to Arkadina that she wants to become an actress. Dr. Dorn is genuinely moved and intrigued by Trepleff's play, but Trepleff ignores his compliments and leaves in search of Nina. When Masha is left alone with Dr. Dorn, she confesses that she is miserably and futilely in love with Trepleff.

Later, Arkadina tells Dr. Dorn that she defies time and death by refusing to let herself age. Sorin, her brother, laments his bad health, but justifies his penchant for sherry and cigars by telling Dr. Dorn that they are the consolations for an unfulfilled life. Arkadina and Shamreyeff, the steward, argue about the availability of carriage horses for a trip into town. Shamreyeff resigns as steward and Arkadina resolves to leave.

Nina enters and innocently gives Pauline and Dr. Dorn some flowers, but Pauline jealously destroys them. Trepleff then encounters Nina and lays a dead sea gull at her feet. He has killed it out of boredom, he says. They quarrel about Nina's failure to appreciate the play, and Trepleff leaves. Moments later, Nina meets Trigorin and reveals her deep feeling and respect for him as a man and as an artist. Trigorin explains that his creativity is a compulsive need; yet Nina, herself aspiring to be an actress, romantically insists upon the magic and mystery of the artistic life. They deplore Trigorin's imminent departure with Arkadina and take leave of each other, visibly in love. But their separation is deferred as Arkadina decides to remain at her brother's estate.

Several weeks later, amidst preparations for the guests' departure, Masha confides to Trigorin that she is going to marry Medvedenko only to forget her true passion for Trepleff, who has recently attempted suicide. Nina and Trigorin exchange farewells, and Nina gives him a medal with a reference to one of his books. Sorin decides to go to town with his sister and her entourage because provincial life is too boring, but he suffers a dizzy spell and retires

after futilely pleading with Arkadina to understand her son
and give him some money.

Attempting to follow her brother's counsel, Arkadina
bandages the wounds Trepleff inflicted in his attempted
suicide. They vow to try to understand each other. Trigorin,
having discovered the allusion on the medal Nina gave him
("If you ever, ever need my life, come and take it"), confides his passion for Nina to Arkadina. She hurls herself
at Trigorin's feet and madly reasserts her possessive and
desperate love for him. Arkadina praises him extravagantly
and fiercely reminds him that he is totally dependent on
her. He capitulates, exclaiming: "I have no will of my
own. . . . I have never had a will of my own. Flabby,
weak, always submitting!" Moments later, in a whispered
and rushed farewell, Nina tells Trigorin she is going to
Moscow, and they plan a rendezvous.

Two years pass, and the same group is reunited at Sorin's
estate. Masha, now married to Medvedenko and the mother
of a child, expresses disgust with her domestic situation.
Sorin, in declining health, still laments his unfulfilled ambition, and Dr. Dorn tells of his recent trip to Genoa.
Trepleff confides to Dr. Dorn that Nina had a child by
Trigorin, was abandoned by him, and became a third-rate
actress in the provinces after the child died. Although
Trepleff followed her around Russia, she refused to see
him. Medvedenko adds that he has seen her in town.

Trigorin then compliments Trepleff on his published
stories, but later, during a card game, Trigorin admits to
the others that Trepleff "still can't discover how to write
a style of his own. There is something strange, vague, at
times even like delirious raving. Not a single character that
is alive." Arkadina confesses that she has not read her
son's writing, and the party retires to the dining room.

Trepleff and Nina meet in the drawing room and exchange passionate and wild declarations of love, regret,
and despair. They long for the past and agonize about what
time has wrought. Nina is disoriented, refers to herself as
a sea gull, and declares that she now loves Trigorin more
than ever before. She goes away despite Trepleff's pleadings,
and when the rest of the party reenters the drawing room
after dinner, Trepleff rushes out. Shamreyeff presents the
stuffed sea gull shot by Trepleff two years earlier. An ex-

plosion interrupts the conversation; Dr. Dorn goes to investigate and returns to inform Trigorin that Trepleff has killed himself.

Critical Opinion

Because Chekhov's mature dramas largely consist of conversation, the essence of his plays has often eluded audiences and critics. A dramatic technique that avoids bold, overt action must center on the inner conflicts of the characters. Soliloquies, fragmented dialogues, and seemingly trivial social banter create the illusion of life as it happens, not as observed by a playwright with a theme. But Chekhov's meticulous artistry has provided dialogue and action to convey the essential comedy and tragedy of existence.

The symbol (as well as the title) of the play is a sea gull. Like Coleridge's albatross and Ibsen's wild duck, this bird represents the purity and vitality of nature and stands as a link between man and the universe. Its gratuitous destruction by Trepleff emphasizes man's blindness to goodness, innocence, and beauty. When Nina confesses: "I am drawn here to this lake like a sea gull," Chekhov establishes the parallel between the two. Trigorin understands this identification when he predicts Nina's destruction: "A young girl, one like you, has lived all her life beside a lake; she loves the lake like a sea gull and is happy and free like a sea gull. But by chance, a man comes, sees her, and out of nothing better to do destroys her, like this sea gull here." Two years later, after her innocence has been destroyed by Trigorin, Nina writes letters to Trepleff in which she refers to herself as a sea gull. And in her final meeting with Trepleff, nearly mad, again she insists upon the identification. The actual bird that Trepleff shot reappears the day of that meeting, stuffed. Trepleff ignores it, and Trigorin has forgotten it. But its appearance, coincidental with Nina's return, emphasizes the transformation of a vital, free, beautiful creature into a pathetic and loathsome object.

Trepleff and Trigorin are destroyers of the sea gull. Both act out of boredom, frustration, and weakness: Trepleff, because his play has failed; Trigorin, in order to escape the ennui of his affair with Arkadina. Although they are different kinds of writers, the two men are tragically similar. They exploit Nina for the sake of their art and are castrated by the relentless tyranny and jealousy of an older woman, Arkadina. Their crime against Nina—and against truth, innocence, and beauty—takes different forms. Trepleff, obsessed with his pursuit of the ideal, uses Nina to recite lines that depict an inhuman, dead universe. His insensitivity permits him to use a beautiful young woman, a rising moon, and a magnificent lake as vehicles for an empty and heartless artistic vision. Trigorin, on the other hand, uses Nina merely as a character in one of his fashionable and superficial books. To him, she is an idea for a literary notebook rather than a woman. Like Trepleff, who cannot create living characters in his writings, Trigorin admits that the people in his novels are merely figures in a landscape. Life is fiction for both Trepleff and Trigorin, and when they encounter truth and reality (the sea gull—Nina), they can only use and destroy them.

As part of his rejection of the natural and conventional in art and life, Trepleff's new sensibility and revolutionary esthetic blind him to the natural and vital aspects of humanity. He believes in absolutes, and when disappointed by his mother, his play, and Nina, he cannot go on. After Nina tells him that her love for Trigorin has increased despite her injuries, Trepleff understands that his pursuit of the absolute, in the person of Nina, is in vain. Ignoring the self-knowledge she has gained, Nina remains infatuated with Trigorin. In this scene, Trepleff discovers the central, tragic reality that informs Chekhov's major dramas: Although truth may be revealed, it does not alter human existence. The implication is fatal for Trepleff. Art, the revealer of truth, is futile. Suicide is his only escape.

The figure of Arkadina dominates the whole play. A beautiful, dynamic, and successful woman, she is so egotistical and insecure that her life off the stage elicits no more humanity from her than her theatrical roles. Her hate and jealousy are barely controllable. She treats her lover, Trigorin, like a son, possessing and controlling him. And he confesses his love for Nina and submits totally to the older woman's will, as a son would to his mother. With her son, Trepleff, Arkadina behaves as if she were on stage.

Her recitation of Gertrude's confession to Hamlet indicates that she can understand her life only through play-acting.

Chekhov's allusion to *Hamlet* points up the deep Oedipal relationship between Arkadina and Trepleff. Sexual and artistic jealousy dominate their lives. In Shakespeare's play, Hamlet reprimands his mother for her sexual commerce with the king. Ironically, Arkadina and Trepleff understand the roles of lust and jealousy as they pertain to themselves and to Trigorin, a King Claudius who possesses the mother. Trigorin is a successful artist (King Claudius) and destroys Nina (Ophelia) to the dismay of Trepleff (Hamlet).

Time is an enemy of all the characters in this play. Arkadina, terrified of old age and death, clings to a younger man and attempts to destroy the young people in the drama, Trepleff and Nina. She tells Dr. Dorn: "I make it a rule never to look ahead into the future. I let myself think neither of old age nor of death." In response, Dr. Dorn ironically sings a fragment from Gounod's *Faust*, an opera about man's quest for absolute wisdom and power. Arkadina employs all the artifices at her command to maintain her youthfulness: makeup, coiffeur, stylish clothing, and sumptuous costumes on the stage. Yet she feels her mortality when Trigorin tries to leave her: "My beautiful, my marvel . . . you are the last chapter of my life."

Unlike his mother, Trepleff is concerned with the future only. He wants to destroy the past by creating a new art, and he sets his play 200,000 years in the future. His inability to cope with the present drives him to suicide.

Trepleff's Uncle Sorin is full of regrets for his unfulfilled past, and Dr. Dorn, a man who has lived fully, is preoccupied with the Faustian idea of having seen, done, and known everything. Time is also a cruel and ironic force for the lovers and would-be lovers in *The Sea Gull*. Masha, in love with Trepleff, marries Medvedenko, repeating her mother's error: marrying one man (Shamreyeff) and loving another (Dr. Dorn). Characters act hastily and desperately out of fear of having time pass them by; yet they foil their own deepest passions.

Chekhov subtitled his play, "A Comedy in Four Acts"; yet a drama that ends with a major character's suicide does not fit the conventional definition of comedy. Comedy is traditionally concerned with love, and, indeed, *The Sea Gull* does treat love in many of its aspects: sexual, parental, and literary. The frustration that each character experiences in his pursuit of love is comic because it parodies truly tragic and earth-shaking aspirations. A group of provincial and self-deluding people are enmeshed in situations that range from the ludicrous to the pathetic, but their responses seldom rise above banality because of their fear of understanding themselves and their inability to act upon their limited self-knowledge.

The Sea Gull, the first of Chekhov's four masterpieces (the others are *Uncle Vanya, The Three Sisters,* and *The Cherry Orchard*), is an extremely difficult play to perform. The acting and staging must be delicately adjusted to avoid melodrama, broad comedy, or stark tragedy. Nevertheless, this play is frequently presented throughout the world and has been presented in two recent screen versions. Its many-faceted relevance undoubtedly makes it an appealing choice for directors and actors. Few dramas touch upon the problems of identity, creativity, love, and time as penetratingly as *The Sea Gull.*

The Three Sisters

by

ANTON CHEKHOV (1860–1904)

The Characters

Andrey Sergeyevitch Prozorov—the only son of a deceased army officer, he lives in a provincial town with his three sisters. Once hopeful of becoming a professor at Moscow University, Andrey marries a shrewish, unfaithful woman, becomes fat and withdrawn, and gambles, losing his sisters' property, and his self-respect.

Olga—a high school teacher who yearns to leave provincial life and return to Moscow. The most conventional of the three sisters, Olga is also the most optimistic. She becomes headmistress, dooming herself to a life in a provincial school system; yet she still desperately entertains illusions of attaining freedom.

Masha—the wife of a loving but unimaginative teacher, she is the only one of the sisters to have married, but is now disillusioned and bitter. She later falls in love with Vershinin.

Irina—the youngest of the sisters, she dreams of finding true love in Moscow, but finally accepts Tusenbach as a compromise.

Natasha—Andrey's wife; she is a domineering, aggressive, heartless woman, unfaithful to Andrey.

Fyodor Ilyitch Kuligin—Masha's husband; pompous, conventional, and dull. Always quoting Latin and exclaiming about his happy marriage, Kuligin is unaware of Masha's loneliness.

Lieutenant-Colonel Alexander Ignatyevitch Vershinin—the battery commander in the provincial town, he maintains a philosophical optimism despite his neurotic wife's periodic attempts at suicide. A good-natured and sympathetic man, he falls in love with Masha.

Baron Nikolay Lvovitch Tusenbach—an earnest, loquacious nobleman who vows to leave the army to engage in manual labor. He believes Russia's ills will be cured by work. Passionately devoted to Irina, he finally wins her consent to marry him, but is killed in a duel on the eve of his marriage.

Ivan Romanitch Tchebutykin—an elderly army doctor who lives in the Prozorov household. Once in love with the sisters' mother, he is a defeated, withdrawn man who drowns his sensibility in drinking and reading newspapers. He believes that nothing really matters.

The Story

In a provincial town during the last years of the nineteenth century, Olga reminisces about her childhood in Moscow before her father took her away. Olga has one desire: to give up her job at the high school and return to Moscow. Irina, her sister, also wants "To sell the house, to make an end of everything here, and off to Moscow." Meanwhile, Tchebutykin, Tusenbach, and Solyony gossip and bicker. Tusenbach, an aristocrat, plans to resign from the army and go to work to save his soul. Russia's salvation, he says, could be achieved if everyone worked. Solyony bitterly taunts the baron, and Tchebutykin gloomily admits that he hasn't "done a stroke of work since I left the University, I have never read a book, I read nothing but newspapers."

It is Irina's name day, and a celebration is planned. Masha joins the party, and Tchebutykin presents Irina with a silver samovar, saying that he was in love with her mother and she and her sisters are all he has in the world. Vershinin is announced and is warmly greeted when it is discovered that he has come from Moscow and knew the sisters' father. He is even dimly remembered by the girls. The officers engage in philosophical discussions about the future of Russian society, but are interrupted by Andrey, who is introduced to Vershinin. Andrey, who hopes to become a professor in Moscow, is in love with Natasha, a crass young woman. He is teased about her coarseness but defends her. Kuligin, a boorish and complacent teacher, declaims mindlessly on the goodness of the world but is interrupted by Natasha. She is criticized by Olga for wearing tasteless colors. When everyone is seated at the table, Natasha suddenly leaves the room followed by Andrey, who comforts her and vows his undying love.

A few years later, Natasha, now head of the household, orders henpecked Andrey to keep the Mardi Gras revelers away so their child can sleep. She also wants to move Irina to a smaller room to make way for the child. Andrey makes no objection and withdraws to receive a deaf porter from the rural board. He unleashes a tirade against the passage of time and loss of opportunity and his entrapment in a disgusting domestic situation.

Masha and Vershinin talk about their unhappy lives: Vershinin has a neurotic wife and two daughters and hates provincial life, and Masha is bored with her husband and longs to go to Moscow. He declares his love. She is confused but flattered. Tusenbach encounters Irina and tells her that he loves her, but she rejects his overtures. They are interrupted when Masha tells Irina about Andrey's huge gambling losses. Irina vaguely replies: "Well, it can't be helped now."

The men return to a philosophical conversation about happiness, society, time, and change. Tusenbach believes that man will always find life difficult and death awful; Vershinin believes that "In two or three hundred, perhaps a thousand years—the time does not matter—a new, happy life will come," and that the purpose of their existence now is to work and suffer. The conversation becomes desultory. Tusenbach asks Solyony why he hates him. Solyony is offended, strikes a romantic pose, and replies: "When I am *tête-à-tête* with somebody I am all right, just like anyone else, but in company I am depressed, ill at ease and . . . say all sorts of idiotic things, but at the same time am more conscientious and straightforward than many."

The guests are sent home because Natasha's baby needs

quiet. Tchebutykin, who has a room in the house, exclaims to Masha: "I never had time to get married, because life has flashed by like lightning and because I was passionately in love with your mother, who was married." Andrey replies: "One shouldn't get married. One shouldn't, because it's boring." They go out and Solyony apologizes to Irina for his tactless behavior and proclaims his love for her. He melodramatically concludes when she rejects him: "But there must be no happy rivals. . . . There must not . . . I swear by all that is sacred I will kill any rival." Natasha intrudes, tells Irina that she must give up her room for Andrey's child, and dashes off for a sleigh ride with Protopopov, the head of the Rural Board. Irina and Olga, depressed and tearful, bemoan their dreary fates, and Irina sobs: "Oh, to go to Moscow, to Moscow!"

A few years later, during a great fire in the town, the household is, alternately, in states of excitement and lassitude. Andrey has locked himself in his library, Natasha will not let strangers into the house because her new child might get influenza, and Olga gives away all her clothing to refugees of the disaster. Natasha tells Olga to dismiss the old maidservant, and Olga bursts into tears. Tchebutykin, totally drunk, morosely soliloquizes: "They think I am a doctor, that I can treat all sorts of complaints, and I really know nothing about it, I have forgotten all I did know, I remember nothing, absolutely nothing. . . . Last Wednesday I treated a woman at Zasyp—she died, and it's my fault she died. Yes . . . I did know something twenty-five years ago, but now I remember nothing, nothing."

Vershinin, begrimed and exhausted from fighting the fire, announces that his regiment may be transferred to some faraway place. Tchebutykin accidentally smashes a clock and philosophizes on existence, while Vershinin again talks about the perfection of future civilization. It is revealed that Andrey has mortgaged the family home to pay his gambling debts and that Natasha is having an affair with Protopopov. Irina confides to Olga that she is so disgusted with her life that she cannot go on. Olga advises her to marry Tusenbach even if she doesn't love him.

When Masha confesses to her sisters that she is in love with Vershinin, Olga is horrified. Andrey, oblivious of everything, delivers a self-justifying tirade against his sisters, defending his wife and his high position on the rural board. But he breaks down into incoherent, pathetic ranting. Irina tells Olga that she will consent to marry Tusenbach.

Some months afterward, members of the regiment pass by the garden to say farewell. Tchebutykin, who will leave the next day, promises to return in a year when he retires from the army; but the young soldiers wistfully remark that their departure is permanent. Kuligin, now clean-shaven because his headmaster wears no beard, seems unaware of the melancholy around him. Everyone is sad despite Irina's imminent marriage to Tusenbach, who has finally resigned his commission and taken a job in a brickyard. Olga, who has reluctantly become headmistress of the high school, is now trapped forever.

Tchebutykin alludes to a bitter encounter during which Solyony challenged Tusenbach to a duel to take place that afternoon. The sisters vaguely understand the danger but do not act. Tchebutykin, totally dispirited, keeps repeating: "We are not real, nothing in the world is real, we don't exist, but only seem to exist. . . . Nothing matters!" When Andrey admits that Natasha is vulgar, stupid, and unfaithful, Tchebutykin invites him to leave everything and join him on the road: ". . . walk off and just go, go without looking back."

Solyony, on his way to the duel with Tusenbach, calls for the doctor and vows to shoot the baron "like a snipe." He sprinkles scent on his hands: "I've used a whole bottle today, and still they smell. My hands smell like a corpse." Tusenbach promises Irina that he will soon return. Vershinin bids farewell to Masha; and Natasha, bullying everyone in sight, tells Irina that her clothing is in poor taste and that she, Natasha, will chop down the trees surrounding the house when she gets complete control.

Tchebutykin enters with the news that the baron has been killed by Solyony: "But it doesn't matter." Olga comforts Irina, exclaiming: "Our life is not ended yet. We shall live! The music is so gay, so joyful, and it seems as though a little more and we shall know what we are living for, why we are suffering. . . . If we only knew—if we only knew!" Tchebutykin reads his newspaper and mumbles: "It doesn't matter, it doesn't matter."

Critical Opinion

In *The Three Sisters* (1901), Masha, Olga, Irina, and
their brother Andrey are incapable of movement toward
freedom. They suffer from physical and moral paralysis.
Although Masha attempted to escape from the ennui of
provincial life by marrying Kuligin at eighteen, she discovered that her husband was a complacent lout. The
others yearn to go to Moscow, symbol of youth, romance, intellectual attainment, and cosmopolitan adventure. But each
member of the Prozorov family becomes trapped. Olga is
advanced to headmistress and cannot leave her post; Irina
accepts a job and a fiancé, both promising no fulfillment;
Masha settles for an ephemeral affair with Vershinin; and
Andrey, encumbered by two children and an adulterous
wife, buries his frustrations in gambling and a petty government post.

The physical environment of *The Three Sisters* contributes
to the lethargic atmosphere. The small provincial town is
plagued by abominable weather and can offer only a
limited, temporary social life. The impermanence of this
milieu is made tragically graphic in the final act, when
the sisters and Andrey are left behind by the departing
army. Nothing changes in the town, a symbol of their lives,
except what passes through and acts on them externally.

Jobs with the local school, the telegraph office, the bureaucracy, and the rural board enervate the most vital forces of
youth, hope, and talent. All hope for change is subtly frustrated by the passage of time, perhaps the most destructive
physical force in Chekhov's drama. By carefully joining
his acts, which are separated in time by months and years,
the playwright achieves a continuity that is at once realistic
and symbolic. The characters lament that life has passed
them in a flash and that their youth and freedom have
slipped away without their knowing it. The structure of the
play symbolically reiterates this theme. At the conclusion of
Act I, Andrey romantically commits himself to Natasha.
Act II begins, several years later, as he suffers under the
full burden of life with the virago and their first child. The
second act terminates with the sisters repeating the play's

opening lines, lamenting their inability to go to Moscow, while Act III finds them totally enmeshed in their provincial existence and slowly succumbing to the unromantic reality of life's defeats. The end of the drama is a recapitulation of the beginning, as the sisters mourn their failure to get to Moscow and promise themselves an ultimate escape.

The paralysis that dominates the Prozorovs and their friends has its most shattering effect on their loves. Tchebutykin's life has been ruined by his passion for the sisters' mother; Tusenbach is killed because of his love for Irina; Solyony becomes embittered by Irina's rejection; Masha's life is ruined because she married too young; Vershinin is saddled with a woman who tries to kill herself; and Olga remains unloved.

Love requires commitment and energy. But the characters in *The Three Sisters* cannot fuse their intellectual passions with vitality. Inertia overcomes their rational and intellectual powers. The Prozorovs relinquish their hopes in a series of self-defeating gestures that render them impotent. Andrey's great potential is wasted on petty politics as he withdraws from the world in order to escape from his virago wife. The sisters seem to let things happen to them and continually lament the course of events without grappling with opportunities or dangers. They overlook Andrey's gambling and ignore the imminent duel between Tusenbach and Solyony. Even after disaster befalls them, they seem only partly aware of the reasons for their defeat.

Chekhov's mastery of dramatic irony is seen at its peak in *The Three Sisters*. The men's vacuous philosophical musings and the sisters' futile battle with destiny are presented in satirical counterpoint. The characters are incapable of achieving a meaningful relationship between their personal lives and the abstract ideas they profess. In Tchebutykin's preparation to attend the duel in which Solyony will kill Tusenbach, Chekhov graphically dramatized the pathetic futility of existence.

When Masha tells the doctor that he should try to prevent the duel, he replies: "The baron is a very good fellow, but one baron more or less in the world, what does it matter. Let them! It doesn't matter." Andrey reprimands Tchebutykin for taking part in an immoral activity, but is told: "That only seems so. . . . We are not real, nothing in the world is real, we don't exist, but only seem to exist. . . . Nothing matters!" These characters fail to communicate with each other in this most crucial scene, for Masha's direct response to Tchebutykin ignores the issue, which is literally one of life and death: "How they keep on talking, talking all day long. To live in such a climate, it may snow any minute, and then all this talk on top of it." Solyony and the baron are forgotten as "time" and "events" move them inexorably toward their fatal confrontation.

In his subtle portrayal of the insensitivity of sensitive human beings, Chekhov reveals the wellspring of his special kind of tragedy: the tragedy of ennui, waste, lassitude, impotence, and frustration. With the exception of Natasha, all of the characters are humane, sensitive beings. But they accidentally destroy their lives—and each other—by their pathological incapacity to understand the nature of their dilemma: "If we only knew, if we only knew!" says Olga in the last line of the play.

The Three Sisters is considered by some critics to be Chekhov's finest drama, although *The Cherry Orchard,* performed four years later, is undoubtedly more popular. *The Cherry Orchard* carefully and richly blends comedy, pathos, and tragedy. More classical in structure and theme, *The Three Sisters* is a dark play in which the comedy is touched with ironic bitterness filled with tragic implications. In *The Cherry Orchard,* Madame Ranevskaya may leave Russia and return to a futile but emotionally rich life with her lover in France. But Andrey and his sisters are hopelessly entombed in the provincial town, the symbol of the impotence and ennui that possess their souls.

In a recent Broadway production, starring Luther Adler as Tchebutykin and Kim Stanley as Olga, *The Three Sisters* provided a startling reminder that, skillfully mounted, Chekhov's drama is vibrant with the tragedy of contemporary man.

The Cherry Orchard

by

ANTON CHEKHOV (1860–1904)

The Characters

Ranevskaya (Lyuboff Andreevna)—an aging aristocrat who has just returned to Russia from residence abroad. A passionate, kind woman but an impractical landowner, she lives by intuition and refuses to face "things as they are."

Anya—Lyuboff's romantic seventeen-year-old daughter.

Varya—Lyuboff's twenty-four-year-old adopted daughter, mistress of the house. The keys at her waist remind us of her flight from self-confrontation into the stronghold of household duties. She is supposedly engaged to Lopahin.

Leonid Andreevich Gayeff—Lyuboff's brother. He is a garrulous, sentimental, unrealistic man who is carried away with his own rhetoric.

Yermolay Alexeevich Lopahin—the son of a serf, he has become a very rich merchant. Though obsessed by the desire to avenge the degradation of his ancestors, he is good-natured and honest.

Pyotr Sergeevich Trofimoff—a thirty-year-old perennial student. Once the tutor of Lyuboff's son, he has become an idealistic revolutionary. His romance with Anya has little importance for him.

Boris Borisovich Semyonoff-Pishtchik—a debt-ridden landowner and neighbor of Lyuboff, he is always trying to borrow money to pay the interest on his mortgage. Voluble and good-natured, he often falls asleep in the middle of his own speeches and is usually in a fever pitch of excitement.

Charlotta Ivanova—the governess. Although from the lower classes, she has become "educated" and can perform magic tricks and other frivolous entertainments. Her private thoughts are essentially pessimistic and cynical. Pishtchik woos her, but she spurns him.

Semyon Panteleevich Epihodoff—a clerk who has somehow attached himself to Lyuboff's household. He is totally inept and clumsy and becomes the butt of everyone's jokes, including his own.

Avdotya Feodorovna Dunyasha—the maid, courted by Epihodoff.

Fiers—the eighty-seven-year-old valet of Gayeff. He represents the fidelity and devotion of the old serf class. Although he was emancipated more than forty years ago, his dedication to the idea of service causes him to continue as before.

Yasha—a young, arrogant servant who has been to Paris in Lyuboff's service and considers all things Russian to be detestable.

The Story

It is near dawn of a spring day in 1901. In the drawing room of Lyuboff's house, Dunyasha and Lopahin banter as they await Lyuboff's return from abroad. Through the windows we see the myriad blossoms of a cherry orchard outside. Lyuboff enters with her entourage and is greeted jubilantly, but she is tearful because the drawing room, still called the nursery, evokes sad memories of her past. The present weighs heavily, too, for the mortgage on the estate has not been paid. Anya reveals the events that caused her mother's self-imposed exile from Russia: "Six years ago our father died, a month later our brother Grisha was drowned in the river. . . . Mama couldn't bear it, she went away, went away without ever looking back."

Fiers, the valet, serves coffee while the others talk about old times and the joy of their reunion.

The estate and the cherry orchard will be put up for auction on August 22, a date that seems impossibly remote to Lyuboff and Gayeff. Nevertheless, Lopahin asks Lyuboff to trust him as she did when his father was a serf on her estate. He proposes that the property should be divided into plots, the buildings and orchard razed, and the land leased to summer residents. But it is unthinkable to Lyuboff and Gayeff that the orchard should be felled, and they ignore Lopahin's counsel. Impatient with their nostalgia and impracticality, Lopahin implores them to recognize the march of progress. But he is ignored and the conversation digresses to a hundred-year-old bookcase in the nursery.

Pishtchik asks for a loan for his property's mortgage, but Varya announces that there is no money at all. The various skeins of conversation follow seemingly independent courses, but comment upon each other in a subtle counterpoint; Lyuboff and Gayeff reminisce about the past and the others pursue their own concerns. Trofimoff's entry provokes bitter memories of Lyuboff's drowned boy, and in a transport of emotion, she agrees to give her last money to Pishtchik.

The next day, in a field, the servants discuss their lives. Charlotta, the daughter of circus performers, pensively admits that she does not know where she came from or where she is going. Epihodoff muses about his unrequited love for Dunyasha, who is attracted to Yasha. When Lopahin, Gayeff, and Lyuboff enter, they discuss the family's money problems and extravagance. Lyuboff tells the story of her life: "I married a man who accumulated nothing but debts. My husband died from champagne—he drank fearfully—and to my misfortune I fell in love with another man. I lived with him, and just at that time . . . right here in the river my boy was drowned and I went abroad. . . ." Lyuboff followed her lover and purchased a villa in southern France. There she nursed him through his illness. When he recovered, he took her money and went off with another woman. "I tried to poison myself—so stupid, so shameful—and suddenly I was seized with a longing for Russia, for my own country, for my little girl—."

Fiers, pursuing Gayeff into the field to give him an overcoat, tells how at the time of the emancipation of the serfs (1861) chaos threatened Russia. Trofimoff and Lopahin argue, and the student delivers a tirade on the weaknesses of Russia's intelligentsia: "It is only that one must work and help with all one's might those that seek the truth. With us in Russia only a very few work. The great majority of the intelligentsia that I know are looking for nothing, doing nothing, and as yet have no capacity for work." Lopahin misunderstands Trofimoff but unknowingly demolishes his empty rhetoric when he insists that he gets up at five every morning. After more conversation, there is a pause and the characters hear a distant, unidentifiable sound, "like the sound of a snapped string, dying away, mournful."

A stranger appears and begs for money. Lyuboff, finding no silver in her purse, gives him a gold piece. Dismayed at her extravagance, Varya and Lopahin go off with her, leaving Anya and Trofimoff to enact a ludicrous love scene in which Trofimoff preaches about upper-class guilt and the duty of the aristocracy to make reparations to the lower classes. Anya ignores his speeches and admires the rising moon.

On the evening of August 22, a party is being held on the estate. The conflicts among the characters become inflamed with the merrymaking. Pishtchik and Trofimoff quarrel, Charlotta performs tricks and cruelly rejects Pishtchik's advances. Gayeff is in town attending the auction of the estate. He hopes to purchase it with money from a great-aunt. The tension mounts and Lyuboff argues with Trofimoff, who says: "Whether the estate is sold today, or is not sold—is it not the same? There is no turning back, the path is all grown over. . . . One mustn't deceive oneself; one must for once at least in one's life, look truth straight in the eye." Lyuboff retorts that she understands love, that her ancestors have lived near the cherry orchard for generations, and that her son drowned on the estate. She is fatally tied to the cherry orchard by her past. She tells Trofimoff that in a telegram from Paris her lover has begged her to return and to nurse him to health again. When the young man is unsympathetic, Lyuboff turns and attacks him for not knowing about love. Terrified, he runs off and attempts to escape upstairs. But he trips and falls in a clatter, and they laugh in derision.

Suddenly, Lopahin and Gayeff enter, drunk and exhausted. The cherry orchard has been sold to Lopahin, who exults over how he has risen from the "beaten, half-illiterate Yermolay, who used to run around barefoot in winter." He gleefully shouts: "I bought the estate where my grandfather and father were slaves, where you wouldn't even let me in the kitchen." The loan from the great-aunt was insufficient to save the estate for the family. Everybody withdraws, leaving Anya and Lyuboff weeping bitterly.

Several months later, the household prepares to leave the house, which has been stripped of all its furnishings. The various strands of conversation recapitulate and elaborate upon the characters' relationships. Lopahin has purchased champagne, Lyuboff has given away her purse to the servants, and Trofimoff continues his idealistic speeches. As the time for departure approaches, Epihodoff reassures everyone that Fiers, who is ill, has been sent to the hospital. Pishtchik announces that he has received money from Englishmen who have discovered valuable minerals on his land. He repays part of his loan to Lyuboff and rushes off in comic confusion. Lyuboff's attempt to bring Lopahin to propose to Varya is inconclusive. As the party departs, we hear the sound of axes felling the cherry trees: Lopahin could not wait for the family to leave before destroying the estate.

After a few moments, Fiers, who has been left behind after all, stumbles across the empty stage muttering: "Life has gone by, as if I hadn't lived at all—I'll lie down awhile —you haven't got any strength, nothing is left, nothing—." For the second time, according to Chekhov's explicit stage directions: "there is a far-off sound as if out of the sky, the sound of a snapped string, dying away, sad."

Critical Opinion

The Cherry Orchard (1904) effectively conveys the moods of loss, premonition, and hope that obsessed the Russian intelligentsia in the decades before the 1917 revolution. Although not forecasting the overthrow of czarist Russia, Chekhov dramatizes the universal awareness that the old order was dying. Throughout the play, these auguries of radical change are worked out in human rather than political terms.

The major characters in *The Cherry Orchard* embody certain forces in Russian society, but they are also unique persons with feelings of their own. Lopahin is more than a boorish, avaricious man. Essentially generous, honest, and humble, his motivations are rooted in an understandable

desire to rise above his background of servitude. Although
he is involved in the crass pursuit of money, he is not the
stereotyped nineteenth-century villain who uses his wealth
as revenge against the world. Lyuboff may be regarded as a
representative of the frivolous and decadent aristocracy. But
she is an intelligent, passionate, humane woman with genuine feelings for her family, lover, and country. And Trofimoff, the student who spouts doctrinaire slogans about the
progress of humanity, is at the same time a vulnerable young
man whose intelligence exceeds his sensibility.

The characters in this play, although immobilized by their
inability to face reality, still possess more self-awareness than
the people in *The Sea Gull* and *The Three Sisters*. The moral
blindness in *The Sea Gull* and the spiritual paralysis in *The
Three Sisters* have been transformed into what almost approaches a fatal acceptance of life on its own terms.

Lyuboff continually ignores Lopahin's warnings that the
estate will be lost but seems to acknowledge that things have
indeed come to an end for her in Russia. She extravagantly
gives a dance on the night of the auction and bestows her
entire purse upon the servants when she leaves, but she is
not completely mindless. She senses that her return to Russia
is less of a homecoming than a farewell. After having
attempted suicide in Paris, she longed to see her children
and country again. Lyuboff's arrival is attended by bitter
memories of her alcoholic husband and drowned son, but the
thought of her lover in Paris is never very far from her mind.
His telegrams, which she at first destroys and then discusses
with Trofimoff, are constant reassurances to her that life and
love will not end with the destruction of the cherry orchard.

Lyuboff's brother, Gayeff, has so obliterated his feelings
and consciousness with his escapist recital of billiard strategy
that the loss of his family estate evokes momentary regret
rather than despair. His new job at the bank will at least
enable him to endure old age without the cherry orchard.
He has, in his mind and new profession, escaped the desolation of his spirit that the end of the old order might have
wrought. It is the children, ironically, who will suffer most
from the destruction of the past. Anya is left behind by
Trofimoff, who goes to Moscow, and Varya, Lopahin's supposed fiancée, is deserted when he goes to the city for the
winter.

As they approach a stoical acceptance of their destinies, the other characters seem to know *what* they are, without desperately searching for knowledge of *who* they are; their identities elude them, but they do not despair. Charlotta tells her friend that she is the daughter of circus performers. She knows she is a governess, but then adds: "But where I came from and who I am I don't know—Who my parents were, perhaps they weren't even married—I don't know. I don't know a thing." Trofimoff, also, knows he is a student in the vanguard of a new order. His personal life, however, is exposed as shoddy and inconsequential by Lyuboff's attack and by his romance with Anya. Trofimoff is an insensitive, boorish, and clumsy lover.

Even Lopahin, the man who seems to know where he is going, is spiritually lost. When he falls asleep while reading and when he must be told by a servant that his champagne is inferior because it is not French, he laughs at his failures and pretensions. But although Lopahin is his own man, he is unable to bring himself to propose to Varya. We feel that, paradoxically, the more he changes the less different he will be from what he was.

The cherry orchard, like the lake and the bird in *The Sea Gull,* is a dominant symbolic character. It blossoms spectacularly on a frosty spring morning to greet Lyuboff on her return to Russia, and it stands refulgent and majestic in the autumn frost during her departure at the play's end. For each principal character, the orchard is a metaphor for the past and future. Lyuboff and Gayeff associate it with the golden memories of childhood, the paradise of the old order, and the continuity of life. Fiers remembers the harvesting of the cherries and the succulent dried fruits that were marketed long ago. But the secret of drying cherries has been lost, he thinks, and nothing is the same anymore. For Trofimoff, the cherry orchard is a symbol of aristocratic exploitation of the lower classes: "All your ancestors were slave owners, in possession of living souls, and can you doubt that from every cherry in the orchard, from every leaf, from every trunk, human beings are looking at you." And for Lopahin, the trees are merely inconvenient impediments to the land's exploitation.

Chekhov seems to feel that the orchard is a symbol of the beauty and graciousness of a way of life that has seen its

time. The snapping string, "dying away, mournful," is a
subsidiary symbol to the orchard itself. A broken heart
string, a lamentation, or the breaking of links with the past,
this sound at first anticipates the cherry orchard's destruction and then, at the very end of the play, comments on the
axes' attack on the beauty of the trees.

The Author

Anton Chekhov was born in a Black Sea port in Russia in
1860. His father was a shopkeeper who fled from bankruptcy
and left his son for three years to study at a preparatory
school. Chekhov's mother apparently was an understanding
and sensitive person, and we may surmise that he learned
much of his respect for human feeling from her.

In 1879, Chekhov joined his family in Moscow, where he
began his medical studies while earning a meager living by
writing for magazines. Before he was twenty-five he had
gained a reputation as a short-story writer, and in the next
two years he published scores of stories. His writing for
the theater during his early years (1881–1895) consisted
mainly of short pieces, principally farces and satires.

Until 1896, Chekhov devoted himself to medicine and
travel. He ministered to the sick in various parts of Russia,
including Siberia. He was only thirty-six when he retired to
a country estate near Moscow to live the life of a provincial
doctor. His declining health necessitated his moving to southern Russia, near Yalta, where he wrote his full-length dramatic masterpieces: *The Sea Gull, Uncle Vanya, The Three
Sisters,* and *The Cherry Orchard.* After nearly twenty years
of intense suffering from tuberculosis, Chekhov died in 1904
at the age of forty-four.

Chekhov's short and active career was marked by his
association with some of the greatest names in Russian
theater and letters. Stanislavski, the founder of the Moscow
Art Theater, devised a completely new technique of acting
in order to produce Chekhov's last plays. His Method System is probably the most influential school of acting even
today. Through long and arduous study and concentration,
the actor is supposed to immerse himself totally in every
aspect of the character's being. Stanislavski's successful appli-

cation of this technique to Chekhov's plays during the first decade of this century resulted in some of the greatest theatrical triumphs of all times. Even today, the Moscow Art Theater is devoted to the perpetuation of Stanislavski's complex and revolutionary ideas for the acting of plays by Chekhov and other great playwrights.

Chekhov's correspondence with other luminaries, such as Gorki and Dachenko, reveal him as an artist seriously involved in the technical and moral aspects of his craft. His humility and humanity left an indelible impression on all his associates. In the face of the most cruel suffering and disappointment, Chekhov maintained a deep and humane feeling for the human condition.

"Chekhov is an incomparable artist," said Tolstoy. "An artist of life. And the worth of his creation consists of this— he is understood and accepted not only by every Russian, but by all humanity." English and American companies have come to understand the plays not as elegies of exquisite Slavic gloom, but as counterpoints of the tragic and the absurd and as orchestrations of human action and reaction. *"My holy of holies,"* Chekhov wrote in a letter to a friend, *"are the human body, health, intelligence, talent, inspiration, love, and the most absolute freedom—freedom from violence and falsehood in whatever form these may be expressed. This is the program I would hold to if I were a great artist."* It is his appreciation of humanity that makes Chekhov a great artist; this infinite compassion lets us understand the weaknesses of the characters without condemning them.

La Ronde

by

ARTHUR SCHNITZLER (1862–1931)

The Characters

The Girl of the Streets (Leocadia)—a twenty-year-old prostitute whose beauty has not yet been destroyed by her profession. Practical and coarse, she still shows affection for some men.

The Soldier—cigar-smoking, swaggering, and brutally sensual, he vigorously pursues women for immediate sexual gratification.

The Maid (Marie)—loyal to the soldier even while sleeping with her master's son, Marie enjoys sex for its own sake.

The Young Gentleman (Alfred)—sexually inexperienced but eager to be initiated, he gains confidence after his seduction of the maid and acquires the young wife for a mistress. Sentimental, romantic, and naive, he is attracted by the literary aspect of his affair rather than its sensual pleasure.

The Young Wife (Emma)—despite her professions of chastity, she is sensual and promiscuous. Her coy behavior with Alfred quickly gives way to unalloyed desire.

The Husband (Karl)—given to lectures on middle-class morality, Karl believes that one's sexual life may be regulated according to an emotional calendar. But his blind hypocrisy is revealed when he engages in extramarital relations with a girl he has picked up in the streets.

The Sweet Young Miss—she accepts a liaison with Karl and

sleeps with the poet without really caring for either one
or understanding her own emotions.

The Poet (Robert Beibitz)—extravagant, romantic, yet
worldly, he heightens his sexual life with fanciful poetic
musings.

The Actress—a melodramatic, witty, and capricious woman,
she ruthlessly gets her way with men.

The Count—susceptible to tenderness and sentiment, with
an aristocratic, cynical questioning of the meaning of life.

The Story

Subtitled "Ten Dialogues," *La Ronde* consists of ten seemingly unrelated scenes. There is no story in the conventional
sense.

I. "THE GIRL OF THE STREETS AND THE SOLDIER"

On a bridge in the center of Vienna, a prostitute solicits
a soldier on his way to the barracks. When he tells her he
has no money, she offers her services free because he is a
soldier. After discussing the lateness of the hour and the distance to the girl's flat, the couple walk to a quay alongside
the Danube. She shows real affection for him and half-
whimsically says that he would be a good sweetheart. They
make love quickly. Before the soldier hurries off to the barracks, the girl asks for a small token of money. He coarsely
refuses and she bitterly calls after him: "Tightwad . . .
pimp!"

II. "THE SOLDIER AND THE MAID"

In an amusement park on the banks of the Danube, a
maid and a soldier walk on a dark, tree-lined path. The
sound of dance music drifts through the air. He smokes his
cigar, making it glow suggestively in the dark. The couple
banter about the soldier's penchant for dancing with many
girls. They embrace and the maid succumbs to the soldier's
caresses. A few moments later, the soldier roughly helps the
girl to her feet and they make their way back toward the

dance hall. She asks if he cares for her, but he ignores her plaintive reaching out for affection and says he cannot walk her home because he wants to dance with other girls and take them to the woods before his midnight pass expires. She promises to wait outside the dance hall. He enters and asks another girl to dance.

III. "THE MAID AND THE YOUNG GENTLEMAN"

At a country estate, a servant girl is writing to her soldier sweetheart when the young master rings. She goes to him, adjusts the window blinds, and leaves. He rings for her again and asks for cognac. She tells him it has been locked away. He settles for water. The maid returns to the kitchen, arranges her hair and clothes, returns with the water, and is embraced by the young master. He unbuttons her blouse, kisses her bosom, and confesses that he has seen her naked through the open door of her bedroom. After they have made love, the doorbell rings, the young man rises, coldly announcing that he will be at the café if anyone calls. The maid takes a cigar (for her soldier lover) from a box and returns to her letter in the kitchen.

IV. "THE YOUNG GENTLEMAN AND THE YOUNG WIFE"

In a tastelessly luxurious apartment, the young man from the previous scene makes elaborate preparations for the seduction of a visitor: sweetmeats, cognac, perfumed air. When the doorbell rings, he ushers in a heavily veiled young woman who is faint with excitement and apprehension: she is a married woman who has come for an assignation. The man induces her to discard her veil and cape and then fawns on her, heaping compliment upon compliment. Emma, the wife, professes moral revulsion at her own behavior, but consents to stay.

The couple reminisces about their first meeting and then embrace. She asks if he has ever entertained other women in this fashion, and he reavows his devotion to her. They eat sweetmeats and coyly banter. The man suddenly overwhelms the woman and carries her into the bedroom. She is compliant enough as he unfastens her boots, but she insists upon disrobing in privacy. He undresses in another room and climbs into bed with her. A few minutes later, the man and woman discuss what has occurred. Apparently unable to make love to her, the young man cites Stendhal, who in *The Psychology of Love* states that infatuated men are often impotent with the object of their passion. The woman coldly dissembles sympathy. They embrace again, this time passionately.

Afterward, the wife hurries to her suspicious husband. The young man, ecstatic, begs for a rendezvous in two days. The woman dresses (using a buttonhook she has conveniently put into her purse), they eat pastry, and she leaves the young man, who sighs: "At last, a real woman."

V. "THE YOUNG WIFE AND THE HUSBAND"

Late one evening while Emma is reading in bed, her husband enters and says he desires her. She asks why this sudden amorousness. He replies that their marriage consists of periodic "affairs" with each other. If he constantly loved her, their marriage would be a tepid, habit-ridden arrangement. This way, "friendship alternates with passionate honeymoons." When Emma seems puzzled, the husband explains that pure women of good family have no conception of love; only men of the world understand sexual relationships. Before he was married, he consorted with "disgusting creatures." Emma shows a lively curiosity about women of easy virtue and despite her husband's puritanical objections, inquires about them: "Obviously they seem to enjoy sinking [into moral degradation]!" Emma overcomes her husband's reluctance to talk when she implies she will withhold her sexual favors if he doesn't tell her about his past affair with a married woman. Karl is outraged when he learns that one of Emma's married acquaintances may have compromised herself, and he demands that his wife renounce such immoral company. He says that the married woman he once slept with was a deceiver and died young; only sexual passion—not moral attraction—drew him to her. Karl cuts short the conversation by taking Emma in his arms and making love to her.

Later, Emma dreamily wishes those ecstatic moments of pleasure could last forever—like their honeymoon night in

Venice. Karl coldly replies: "One cannot always be a lover . . . everything has its time in marriage." She ironically agrees and they go to sleep.

VI. "THE HUSBAND AND THE SWEET GIRL"

In the private dining room of an elegant Viennese restaurant, the husband, Karl, and a young girl whom he has followed in the street and invited to dinner, finish their meal. Karl compliments and fondles the girl and she half-heartedly resists his embraces. He reminds her of a man she was in love with; even his name is the same. A little drunk, the girl tells Karl that she had to spank her youngest sister for dating a boy. They joke about the number of men she has kissed. As they talk, Karl fondles the girl until, quite aroused, she succumbs after he assures her of their privacy: "No waiter will ever . . . come in here . . . not in . . . your lifetime."

After they have made love, Karl seems withdrawn, and the girl wonders why she gave herself to him so readily. She was not drugged by the wine, but maybe Karl's resemblance to her former lover weakened her resistance. Suddenly, upon discovering that it is nearly midnight, Karl suggests they part. His haste convinces her that he is married, but she doesn't mind. Although he is irritated when she implies that his wife, too, has extramarital affairs, he arranges a liaison with the girl, promising to make more suitable arrangements for their assignation. He calls the waiter for the bill.

VII. "THE SWEET YOUNG MISS AND THE YOUNG POET"

As they enter a darkened studio, the poet and the girl from the preceding scene discuss their long walk in the woods. The poet induces the girl to remove her hat and cloak and lie on a divan. When he pours cognac and begins to play the piano, the girl naively asks if he is a composer and a doctor. The poet talks about beauty and enchantment as the girl prepares herself to be seduced. She is, of course, terrified of being discovered by Karl, who apparently is keeping her now. The conversation follows the same pattern as in earlier scenes: jealous inquiries about past affairs, petty lies, and false declarations of virtue and passion. The girl ignores most of the poet's sentimentality, removes her corset, and prepares to make love. She is not even interested in her lover's identity. She is content to call him Robert.

The poet returns later to the subject of his identity. Beibitz is his name, he says, and he is the most popular playwright in Vienna. But the girl is unimpressed and only wants to get dressed. He drops candle wax on her while admiring her nude body: "You are Sacred Simplicity!" The ludicrous gulf between the earthy woman and the garrulous poet is momentarily closed as they agree to meet the next Sunday.

VIII. "THE POET AND THE ACTRESS"

In the bedroom of a country inn two hours from Vienna, the poet and the star of one of his plays admire the moonlight. She kneels to pray and he fondles her, calling her "Sacred Simplicity." He jealously asks about her former lovers. Badinage about the religiosity of peasants and the poetic muse gives way, a few minutes later, to the friendly banter of lovers in bed. They ask each other about those who are being deceived and gossip about the sexual tastes of colleagues and friends.

After making love, the actress compliments the poet on his plays. When he asks why she canceled a performance, she retorts: "For love of the poet," and they argue about whether the night sounds are crickets or frogs. When the conversation returns to Fritz, the actress' former lover, she admits her love for the poet and exclaims, "Fritz! Don't talk to me about that galley slave!"

IX. "THE ACTRESS AND THE COUNT"

One day the actress receives the count, who has entered her luxurious bedroom at noon in full military regalia. They exchange formal greetings, and she thanks him for the flowers he sent to her dressing room at the theater. The count's Epicurean philosophy allows him to enjoy life in the provinces as well as in Vienna. Happiness doesn't exist, the count cynically muses, nor does love; pleasure and passion are the only realities. The actress warmly agrees, draws the count to her, and kisses him. He resists, however, and proposes they

meet and make love after the theater: "Women, like you—
I haven't the heart to take before breakfast." But the
woman's sexual passion overwhelms him and he succumbs.

When the lovemaking is over, the count prepares to leave.
The actress reminds him of their appointment that evening,
but he tries to postpone it. She commands him to be at her
apartment after the evening's performance. He agrees, and
buckling on his sword, takes formal leave of his new
mistress.

X. "THE COUNT AND THE GIRL IN THE STREETS"

The count, fully dressed, rises from a divan and surveys
the tawdry room of a prostitute who is asleep in the bed.
Confused and uncertain, he recalls how when drunk he came
to this horrible place at the invitation of a prostitute whom
he met in a café. The sleeping girl looks innocent, and he is
touched by her beauty. "It is incredible how sometimes all
women look alike."

When the girl awakes, he inquires about her life. Almost
twenty years old, she has been a prostitute for a year. The
count is touched and disturbed by the girl's beauty and her
degrading life, and he asks if she finds pleasure or happiness
in her existence. But his remarks are beyond her. She is
coarse, earthy, and practical. He kisses her eyes and sentimentally implies that she reminds him of someone he once
loved. As he leaves, he remarks: "Actually I am annoyed at
myself. I *know* these women are after only money . . . at
least it's nice that she doesn't pretend; that should make me
glad."

Critical Opinion

The title of Schnitzler's play is a key to both its meaning
and technique. This round of love is like a game where the
participants form a circle by holding hands. The sexual drive
links them all. A count and a common soldier are symbolically joined through their involvement with a prostitute, and
the women, no less disparate, are brought together through
an elaborate but credible series of relationships. The maid

sleeps with the young gentleman, who seduces the young wife. She in turn connects the maid with the actress because her husband, Karl, has chosen the sweet young thing, who later becomes the poet's mistress. When the actress sleeps with the poet and the count, she links five women who would seem to have no connection in Viennese society.

Schnitzler has dramatized a whole world of sexual intrigue that he believes is a valid portrayal of all society. By avoiding the use of given names and emphasizing generic labels (the soldier, the sweet young thing, the husband, and so on), he has made his characters not individual case histories but figures in a larger perspective. The play is more than a portrait of decadent Vienna at the turn of the century. The psychological realism, derived from the playwright's serious and intensive investigation of psychiatric materials concerning man's most profound and consuming desires, is rooted in professional and scientific insights and experiences. Schnitzler's publications in medical journals augmented and anticipated Freud's most revolutionary conclusions about man's sexual drives. His individual experiences tempered and enriched the clinical perceptions with which he probed his artistic creations.

The lovemaking ritual is nearly identical in the first nine scenes of *La Ronde*. The man is bold and assertive, the woman, coy. Each couple discusses former sexual experiences and the man is invariably jealous. The woman's reluctance yields to the man's supposed bravado. Both the place and atmosphere of the sexual union are important. The couples consider the precise setting (riverbank, amusement park, drawing room, private dining room, bachelor flat, bedroom) and are obsessed with privacy. The upper-class women are reluctant to disrobe in front of their lovers and must prepare themselves unseen. The removal of clothing is a ritual that precedes copulation, for once the woman has consented to lift her veil, remove her hat, or discard her cloak, the rest inevitably follows.

Like a round in which different voices overlap, *La Ronde* employs themes and symbols musically. Seduction itself is the *leitmotif,* but visual and verbal connections between the scenes create an organic bond throughout the work. The cigars that the soldier smokes in the first scene will be replenished by the maid's gift, which is stolen from the young master's household. The poet's exclamation, "Sweet Simplicity!" is repeated with the actress. The intricate lies and alibis with which the women dupe their lovers are reiterated, with telltale discrepancies, from scene to scene.

Schnitzler's interest in the individual's development is adroitly displayed in these sketches. The young gentleman's preliminary experience with the maid is only a prelude to his affair with a married woman. The haughtiness he shows the maid dissolves into violent, adolescent passion that first renders him impotent and then, with the stimulus of a sexually aroused woman, allows him to experience on different levels emotional, social, and sexual adventures. Emma's departure signals his initiation into emotional decadence: "At last, a real woman."

After her illicit love affair with the young gentleman, Emma, no Madame Bovary, entertains few illusions about the nature of the social order or the potentials of her emotional life. Karl, her husband, is a ludicrous, conventional figure who lectures his wife on the differences between sexual passion and spiritual love. He prudishly reminds her that she is a mother whose upper-class background could not permit her to understand the demimonde of sexual intrigue. His final "Good night, *my child*" is a bitterly ironic exposure of a man whose vulgarity, insecurity, and lack of imagination allow him to talk about morals and his wife's chastity one night and pursue a young woman in the streets the next. During his encounter with the sweet young miss, he is oblivious of anything but blind lust. The girl's domestic predicament is not sentimentalized in the play, for although she is trapped at home, she is conventionally prudish (she beats her younger sister for dating a boy), but willing enough for a liaison with a married man. Her understanding of sexual politics is comprehensive, for she satisfies her sensual and economic needs with Karl and indulges her restlessness in the poet's atelier. While the poet baffles her, she is so certain of herself that she can lie to him and Karl with the same indiscriminate lack of scruple. The poet, like the young gentleman, experiences the varieties of sexual pleasure when he seduces the sweet young miss and creates a fictional, romantic image of her to suit his imagination. When he enjoys a rather worldly episode with the actress, he can call her "Sacred Simplicity" with the same ardor as in the preceding tableau. His conception of women is formed in his imagination, not in his experience.

The actress, of course, is more formidable than her predecessor. A lioness who dominates all men—the poet, a former lover named Fritz, and the count—she is willful and selfish, a worldly woman who has overcome sexual vassalage to tyrannize over men. The count unwillingly submits to her and is bullied into a rendezvous. Yet her absolute control of her lovers is tempered by her awareness that her fame and beauty are ephemeral.

The count, sexually cruel like the soldier, is sentimental and vulnerable like the young gentleman, the husband, and the poet. He is different in his philosophical and emotional sophistication, which is in conflict with the natural instincts aroused in a virile man who seeks pleasure in a woman-dominated society. His confusion in the prostitute's room is both touching and deplorable. He yearns for some idyllic dream of pure womanhood while he is chained to the treadmill of pleasure and male egotism.

Post coitus tristus is a syndrome common to the men in this play. After intercourse, they feel trapped and depressed. Their attempts to escape are resisted by the feminine possessive instinct. Schnitzler apparently believes that women accept their role as sexual objects and do not try overtly to usurp the masculine prerogatives of independence, aggression, and mastery. They permit men illusions of superiority and dominance; yet each woman knows precisely when and where she will be possessed.

Written during the winter of 1896–1897 and privately published in a limited edition in 1900, *La Ronde* immediately became the subject of controversy. When a public edition appeared in 1902, it was attacked as obscene and scandalous. The police banned an unauthorized Budapest production in 1912, and nine years later, members of the German People's Party, the forerunner of the Nazi Party, wrecked the Vienna theater in which it was produced. The issues of obscenity, anti-Semitism, and censorship plagued the drama during Schnitzler's life. Like all Schnitzler's works, *La Ronde* was banned until Hitler's fall.

When the Max Ophuls film *La Ronde* (France, 1950, with Simone Signoret, Jean-Louis Barrault, Anton Walbrook,

Gerard Philipe, and others) was released, it seemed to many that Schnitzler would have applauded it as the perfect modern translation of his play. Its comments on the futility of transitory relationships, in which the deceivers are themselves deceived, were made with such sophistication that a curious influence has been evident in later presentations of the play. Little theater and art group productions of *La Ronde* often seem to owe as much to Ophuls' tone and emphasis as to Schnitzler's dialogue. It is not surprising; Ophuls and Schnitzler were cynical blood-brothers, equally unimpassioned, objective, and clinical satirists of sex.

The Author

Like many Central European playwrights, Arthur Schnitzler led a double life as a professional man and as a literary celebrity. Born into an upper-class Jewish family, he followed in his father's footsteps, studied medicine, and received a degree at the University of Vienna when he was twenty-three years old. His researches in psychiatry aided Freud and earned Schnitzler a reputation as one of the pioneers of modern psychiatry.

Schnitzler moved in some of the most glamorous Viennese social circles. His early writings reveal a worldliness that he was to satirize in his later plays. His first drama, *Anatol* or *The Affairs of Anatol* (1893), centered on sexual love in *fin de siècle* Vienna. The involved psychological portraiture of the play's hero anticipates *La Ronde*. In *Liebelei* (1895), Schnitzler turned to naturalistic melodrama and told the story of a lower-class girl who discovers that her idealized lover is a philanderer. The scandalous appearance of *La Ronde* was followed by *The Green Cockatoo* (1898), *The Lonely Way* (1903), *The Vast Domain* (1911), and *Professor Bernhardi* (1912). These plays showed the playwright's wide range of moral concerns. The degeneracy of Viennese aristocrats and the emptiness of their hedonism, as well as anti-Semitism and religious fanaticism treated in a style reminiscent of Ibsen *(Professor Bernhardi)*, occupied Schnitzler's sophisticated intellect. His prose works were no less controversial. His novel, *Leutnant Gustl* (1900), which experimented with stream-of-consciousness techniques, resulted in his court martial in 1901. Schnitzler died in 1931 when Hitler was coming into power. He is now regarded as one of the pioneers of the psychological drama rather than as a revolutionary theatrical innovator.

The Weavers

by

GERHART HAUPTMANN (1862–1946)

The Characters

Dreissiger—a cotton manufacturer who gives out cotton yarn on consignment. He is a very wealthy and self-righteous man; yet he is aware of the misery and horror he is inflicting upon his workers.

Mrs. Dreissiger—Dreissiger's wife, the daughter of an innkeeper. Like many women who have married above their station, she is extremely snobbish and reactionary.

Pfeifer—Dreissiger's manager. Once a weaver himself, he is now haughty and unfeeling when confronted with the hardships of his people. He cares for nothing but his own advancement in Dreissiger's firm.

Weinhold—a tutor for Dreissiger's sons. He is a young, idealistic theology student whose sympathy for the weavers prompts him to give up his position in the Dreissiger household.

Pastor Kittlehaus—a smooth-talking sycophant who uses the word of God as an instrument of social oppression.

Kutsche—a cowardly policeman.

Welzel—an innkeeper who is more interested in keeping his trade than in showing sympathy for justice.

A Salesman—materialistic, coarse, and stupid, he is friendly only to "respectable" people.

Baecker—a young weaver who leads the revolt. He is forthright, loyal, unselfish, and honest.

186

Moritz Jaeger—a former weaver who succeeded in the army and learned that his people's condition could be improved. He joins Baecker in fomenting the revolt.

Old Baumert—a weaver who suddenly realizes that the young men's revolt is the only escape from perpetual bondage.

Old Hilse—a patriarchal weaver in another town. His patriotism and religion blind him to the reality of his situation. He refuses to join the revolt and is accidentally shot to death by the militia.

The Story

On a spring morning in 1844, a group of emaciated and bedraggled weavers gathers at Dreissiger's place to turn in cloth woven from material received on consignment. As they present their goods to Pfeifer, the manager, he inspects the web and calls out the price to be paid for the work. Each weaver seems exhausted as he receives his pitifully small payment. One woman's request for an advance to stave off her children's starvation is sneeringly denied by the cashier; another's work is judged poor and payment is reduced. The desperate requests for more money or advances have no effect on Pfeifer or the cashier.

Baecker, a vigorous young man, discusses the weavers' plight with decrepit Old Baumert. Baecker loudly inveighs against the low wages and miserable conditions: starving children, lack of firewood, sick relatives. Old Baumert even had to roast his pet dog to avert starvation in his household.

When Baecker castigates Pfeifer for the meager wages, Dreissiger, the manufacturer, is called in. Baecker assails him for his greed and inhumanity when a boy faints from starvation. Dreissiger carries the boy to the back room and later returns to scold the weavers and tell them of his misfortunes: rising costs, diminishing markets, foreign competition, hostile press, and misguided public condemnation of free enterprise. The weavers, cowed by his rhetoric, are amazed when he announces a cut in wages.

In a pathetic cottage, a group of hideously ragged and undernourished weavers labor in half-light. The children cry for food and are told to be patient. A neighbor, Mrs. Heinrich, begs for food. Everyone is destitute. Moritz Jaeger, a

young former weaver who has succeeded as a captain's
orderly in the army, enters with a bottle of whiskey and a
roast. He boasts about his new life and chides the weavers
for their abject acceptance of poverty. Ansorge, a giant of
a man, enters to hear Jaeger, and Old Baumert returns to
partake of the feast. But he vomits his food because he has
not eaten for so long. When Jaeger sings a song attacking
Dreissiger, the weavers become defiant and vow action.

A few days later, in a well-kept tavern run by Welzel, a
group of middle-class citizens, including a salesman and
Weigand, a prosperous carpenter, discusses the weavers. A
funeral in the town provokes an attack upon the extravagance and irresponsibility of the poor. Hornig, a ragpicker,
chastises Weigand for profiteering from the weavers' deaths
by making coffins. A farmer, a forester, and some weavers,
including Ansorge and Old Baumert, come in for drinks. The
forester catches weavers who scavenge firewood from the
count's forest, and the farmer gouges weavers for the cot-
tages he rents. Old Baumert complains: "We're just like an
old apple that everyone takes a bite out of."

Baecker, Jaeger, and a group of young weavers enter,
drive the salesman off, and excitedly discuss their discontent
and determination to change their lot. Kutsche, the policeman, wants them to stop singing the Dreissiger song, but
Wittig, an embittered and truculent blacksmith, throws him
out of the tavern as Baecker leads the men in a chorus of
the song. When Welzel asks Old Baumert if he will join such
a revolution, Baumert says: "A young man sometimes may,
and an old man must. . . ."

Meanwhile, in the opulent and tasteless living room of the
cotton manufacturer, Dreissiger, his wife, Pastor Kittelhaus,
and Weinhold, a theology student who is the Dreissiger family tutor, are being entertained. Kittelhaus tells Weinhold
that ideals are for young men only. A game of whist is interrupted by a disturbance downstairs. Dreissiger investigates
and reports that the weavers, just come from the tavern,
have gathered outside the house. Kittelhaus bemoans the
breakdown of law, order, tradition, and piety. Weinhold
defends the weavers and is rebuked. He resigns his post. The
police chief arrives and promises to put down the disturbance, but he is interrupted by Jaeger, who has been captured by Dreissiger's dyers. Jaeger defiantly taunts the group

and is led away to jail. Another commotion outside is re-
ported by Pfeifer, who tells how the mob has freed Jaeger
and beaten the police chief. The pastor offers to speak to
the mob, but the whole party flees when the disturbance
increases. The weavers enter Dreissiger's house, stare in
amazement at the rich furnishings, and begin to destroy
everything.

At Old Hilse's cottage in a nearby town, the family hears
of the weavers' revolt. Old Hilse and his wife are scandalized, but the younger people are thrilled by the account of
the destruction of Dreissiger's mansion and factory.

The family, like all the weavers, is starving to death, but
Old Hilse delivers a patriotic harangue about his religious
devotion and loyalty to the Fatherland. The crowd, led by
Baecker and Jaeger and Old Baumart, enter and try to get
Old Hilse to join them. He refuses, out of his traditional
respect for institutions. However, Luisa, his daughter-in-law,
leaves to join the rebels.

The men depart and encounter the militia. Several volleys
of shots are fired and Old Hilse, placidly weaving at his
loom in front of the window, is struck dead by a stray bullet.

Critical Opinion

The Weavers is one of the great classics of Naturalism in
the theater. As practiced by Zola, Tolstoy, Strindberg, and
Gorki, Naturalism became a vital force in late nineteenth-
century drama. This vision of humanity, first propounded by
Emile Zola, holds that heredity and environment are practically the sole determining forces in man's life. Chance, free
will, and spiritual illumination play no part in this rather
scientific and mechanistic universe. Naturalism quickly became a tool for social and economic reform. Zola attacked
the exploitation of miners and city workers in his powerful
novels and plays, and Tolstoy and Gorki revealed the terrible
life of the Russian peasant and social outcast in *The Power
of Darkness* and *The Lower Depths.* In *Miss Julie,* Strindberg later invested Naturalism with a poetic quality that
revealed psychological truths.

The major character in *The Weavers* is the people. Although they are individualized to some extent, the masses of

weavers and all oppressed people make the strongest impression on the audience. Applying the tenets of Naturalism to the weavers' uprising of 1844, Hauptmann forged an historically accurate document of extraordinary power.

Although in 1891, the year *The Weavers* was written, workers' conditions had hardly improved, Hauptmann subtitled his drama "A Play of the Eighteen-Forties." The sense of historical reality and accuracy that distinguishes this drama is deepened by its contemporary implications for an audience of the 1890s, who at once recognized the social message and the universality of the theme of suffering.

In *The Weavers,* Hauptmann stripped poverty of its hitherto sentimental romantic aspects. He gave his audiences no opportunity to salve their consciences. Although he did not aim for revolutionary reform, he treated economic exploitation in humanistic terms by vividly juxtaposing the absolute wretchedness of the weavers with the vulgar affluence of Dreissiger. Every detail of the setting is minutely specified at the beginning of each act. There is a clear intention here to create a poetic vision with visceral impact. The reader is told that the walls of the weavers' shack "are partly pasted over with paper and partly filled up with straw," and that the weavers themselves have "a stark, irresolute look—gnawing, brooding faces." Dreissiger's house is minutely described, even to the "pictures reflecting poor taste (that) hang in gilt frames from the walls."

The weavers' spirit of revolt is motivated by need more than by ideology. Hunger and other physical miseries blindly drive the weavers to destroy their enslavers' houses and factories. As the anatomy of this rebellion is carefully limned by Hauptmann, the audience understands why Old Hilse, though desperately poor, is a symbol of the conservative and patriotic man who clings to the only status he can be sure of. Although patriotism and religion, two powerful reactionary forces in this play, prevent Old Hilse from joining the revolt, Old Baumart, his contemporary, is drawn in because the young men have dramatized for him the impossibility of escaping from enslavement. He is an idealist who believes that youth can remake the world and that the old must help correct the deplorable conditions that their generation has created.

Baecker and Jaeger embody the visionary and adventur-

ous spirit of youth. Unselfishly and decisively, they sacrifice
security for justice. Baecker says that he would rather starve
outside of Dreissiger's employ than languish as a contributor
to his wealth, and Jaeger returns to his people after attaining
success in the army and becoming independent of Dreissiger.
The fervor and loyalty of these men stand in sharp contrast
to the selfishness of the middle-class people in the tavern.
Welzel, the salesman, and Weigand, the carpenter, are not
really satisfied with the *status quo,* but they fear any change
as a threat to their security. They will accept injustice and
suffering and even profit from them as long as they can be
sure of their own petty comforts.

The forces of reaction, embodied in religion and the state,
aid Dreissiger in his battle with the weavers. Pastor Kittelhaus and the police chief resort to pietistic nonsense and
brutal force to assuage the weavers. Dreissiger sounds re-
markably contemporary when he blames *outsiders* for the
disturbances: "I assure you . . . if blameless people . . . such
as me and my family . . . in a law-abiding community . . .
can be openly and continuously insulted . . . without proper
punishment, really . . . then I regret that I have different
ideas of law and order." Conscious only of the manifestations of discontent and blind to its roots, Dreissiger falls
back upon middle-class slogans and brutality in order to save
himself.

The importance of Hauptmann as an innovator can hardly
be overestimated; his position as a landmark in the history
of drama is forgotten now that his popularity has dwindled
and Ibsen and Strindberg have superseded him in the art
theaters. But Hauptmann was the first to use a crowd as his
hero. Büchner and Schiller had suggested it; Hauptmann was
first to introduce the proletariat as protagonist and to treat
a revolutionary theme realistically, not poetically. Parallels
with the contemporary issues of economic exploitation, racial
injustice, international imperialism, and the issue of law and
order are evident. Hauptmann's dissection of various attitudes toward violent social change is still universally and
startlingly valid.

To this extent, he is one of the true patriarchs of contemporary social drama. Although he was not to repeat the
artistic success of *The Weavers* in his lifetime, the play was
an important model for others to imitate.

The Author

Born into a middle-class German family, Gerhart Hauptmann (1862–1946) derived his social conscience from his father, who was a hotel keeper, and his sense of religious devotion from his mother. He studied art and dabbled in philosophical and scientific disciplines, with little academic success. Under the influence of Darwin, Zola, and other "social scientists," Hauptmann began writing historical and naturalistic plays. He joined the intellectual society of Zurich in the late 1880s, and in 1889 wrote *Before Dawn,* a drama about alcoholism among miners.

A succession of plays established Hauptmann's reputation. By the turn of the century, he became one of the most highly respected German authors. His three most famous plays, *The Weavers* (1892), *Drayman Henschel* (1898), and *Rose Bernd* (1903), were the foremost examples of German Naturalism. Hauptmann's enormous versatility produced comedy, fantasy, history, and symbolic dramas about classical and Germanic myths.

Hauptmann's works have remained relatively unknown to non-German audiences because of his use of dialect, his regionalisms, and his frequent references to uniquely German subjects. His refusal to denounce the Third Reich has further harmed his international reputation. But an increasing number of readers outside Germany are becoming acquainted with his deep humanism and the potency of his artistic creations.

Earth Spirit

by

FRANK WEDEKIND (1864–1918)

The Characters

Dr. Goll—Lulu's first husband, who is old and jealous.

Dr. Schoen—the influential editor of a newspaper who vainly struggles to free himself from Lulu's spell. He enters into an engagement contract with a respectable woman and forces Lulu to marry first Dr. Goll and then, after the old man's death, the painter Schwarz.

Alva—Dr. Schoen's son, an impresario who advances from an observer of Lulu's seductiveness to her promoter in a dance act, and finally becomes a slave to her charms.

Schwarz—his portraits of Lulu bring him fame. He sees in her the quintessence of womanhood. After Dr. Goll's death, he marries her, believing that she is the ideal woman.

Prince Escerny—an African explorer, he is overwhelmed by Lulu's charms and bitterly acknowledges that his disciplined life in Africa was ill-spent; he wants Lulu to master him.

Lulu—sometimes called Eve, Mignon, or Nelly; the incarnation of the Earth Spirit. Sensuous, beautiful, capricious, and enigmatic, Lulu suffers humiliation because she feels that the essential part of her being is linked to Dr. Schoen.

Countess Geschwitz—an artist, passionately in love with Lulu.

Schigolch—an old and decrepit beggar, a mysterious and evil presence who alternately appears to be Lulu's father, former lover, and manager.

The Story

The prologue opens in front of a circus tent. An animal trainer announces the coming spectacle. Man and beast will fight in a narrow cage: Although times are bad and the public attends "farces, melodramas, operas, Ibsen," the trainer promises that "only through me alone/May the wild and true and beautiful beast be shown." He commands an attendant to bring on a snake, played by the actress who will be Lulu. After displaying the voluptuous specimen, he fondles her and promises that he will soon place his head between the tiger's jaws.

In Schwarz's studio, the artist and Dr. Schoen discuss the portrait of a magnificent woman dressed as a clown. Schwarz offers to introduce his friend to the model just as Lulu and her husband enter. Dr. Goll, jealously guarding his beautiful wife, supervises her change into costume, and the men watch as Schwarz paints.

Alva invites the men to attend a rehearsal for a variety show he is staging. Dr. Goll reluctantly leaves Lulu with the painter. After a few minutes, Schwarz makes violent love to her; Lulu evades him coquettishly, and just as she is about to be seduced, Dr. Goll breaks through the door, staggers in, and dies of a heart attack. Schwarz and Lulu try to calm each other. The artist is shocked by her callous attitude and her statements that she does not know if she believes in God, has a soul, or if she has ever been in love. Completely trapped by Lulu's charms, Schwarz becomes her slave.

In a sumptuous and elegant salon, Schwarz and Lulu (whom he calls Eve) discuss his sudden success as a painter. They receive an announcement of Dr. Schoen's engagement to the daughter of a nobleman. After Schwarz leaves, Schigolch, an old beggar, enters and praises Lulu for the grand style of living she has attained. Apparently the two know each other very well, and, as they talk and drink, it is uncertain whether the old man is her lover, father, or manager. He strokes her knee and speaks endearingly, asking: "What are you now?" "An animal," she replies. She gives Schigolch money and he leaves.

Dr. Schoen enters and warns Lulu that he is making "superhuman efforts" to elevate her in society. "You can be ten times prouder of your name than of your intimacy with me. . . ." Dr. Schoen has been Lulu's protector and lover; he has married her to Dr. Goll and Schwarz and arranged for the painter's success. He now wants Lulu to free him so that he may marry his fiancée and consolidate his social position. Lulu replies: "If I belong to anyone in the world, I belong to you." When Schwarz returns, Dr. Schoen tells him that he found Lulu as an impoverished flower girl, rescued her from the streets, took her as his mistress, and promoted her worldly interests. The painter is crushed by this revelation, withdraws to another room, and cuts his throat. Dr. Schoen avoids a scandal by dictating a misleading story to a reporter who appears on the scene.

In a theater dressing room, Lulu is preparing to go on stage. Dr. Schoen enters and resumes his attempts to free himself from her. After he leaves, Alva discusses her dancing and personal life, and Lulu replies: "No one knows anything about anyone else. Everyone thinks himself the only unhappy victim."

Prince Escerny compliments Lulu on her dancing and asks for her hand, confessing that he wants to deliver himself unconditionally into the power of a woman. She rejects him and goes on stage. As Alva and the prince discuss Lulu's beauty, she staggers into the dressing room, unable to dance anymore because she has seen Dr. Schoen and his fiancée in the audience. Dr. Schoen enters and calls her shameless. She replies: "I couldn't begin to care what you think. Why should I want to be better than I am? I'm satisfied." Lulu declares that she has broken Dr. Schoen's self-control by allowing him to humiliate her. She then reveals her animal nature and brutally compels him to write a letter at her dictation. He writes, breaking his engagement, and collapses, gasping: "Now—for—the—execution. . . ."

Now Dr. Schoen's wife, Lulu is established in a splendid residence. The Countess Geschwitz, a Lesbian, invites Lulu to an artist's ball for female transvestites. Dr. Schoen, exasperated and broken, rebukes his wife. Schigolch, Rodrigo (a servant), and Hugenberg (a schoolboy) are staying in

Dr. Schoen's house, hoping to seduce his wife. When Alva
enters, everyone except Lulu hides. He begins to make passionate love to her. Dr. Schoen emerges onto a gallery and
sees them. He disappears, and all the hidden lovers panic
and try to escape. Dr. Schoen reappears and hands Lulu a
revolver, demanding that she destroy herself. She takes the
gun and mortally wounds him. The lovers gather around the
dying man, who turns to his son and says: "Don't let her
escape. You're the next one. . . ."

Critical Opinion

The animal trainer's image of man and beast fighting in a
narrow cage sets the tone for Wedekind's play about bourgeois morality and sexual drive. Except for Lulu and the
countess, each character in *Earth Spirit* is tormented by
unattainable desires for middle-class respectability and sexual
bliss. Dr. Schoen, the central male figure, lives a double
existence and is unable to resolve his craving for worldly
power and his lust for Lulu and all she represents. As the
play unfolds, the audience learns that Dr. Schoen acquired
Lulu from Schigolch when she was about twelve years old,
brought her into his household as a daughter, but soon
became her lover. Upon the death of his wife, Dr. Schoen
understood that an alliance with this vital and luxurious
creature would deprive him of the high social position he
was seeking. He married her off twice while secretly enjoying her favors. But Dr. Schoen cannot endure this double
life and is compelled to break off with Lulu in order to marry
his socially acceptable fiancée. Schoen futilely attempts to
escape from Lulu, declaring:

> I'm through with you. I know where the angel in you
> leaves off and the devil begins. If I accept the world as
> it is, then it's God who must answer for it, not I. Life
> is no amusement for me.

Dr. Schoen imposes his own standards on Lulu, viewing
her according to his own image of woman. Lulu castigates
him for this: "Your faith in my integrity knows no bounds!

You don't believe I'm merely an enchanting creature; you also believe I'm one with a heart. I'm neither one nor the other. Your misfortune is that you think I am." It is also the misfortune of Lulu's other admirers and—by extension—of all mankind.

In the play's last act, Dr. Schoen is married to Lulu and is surrounded by her lovers and would-be lovers—male and female, his servant, and son—and is at last driven back upon the morality that he has been fighting against all of his life. But Lulu is amoral. A true animal, she refuses to give in to social convention or commit suicide; she ignores Dr. Schoen's demand that she kill herself. Instead, she kills her oppressor. Alva, his son, will be her next victim.

To Dr. Goll, Lulu is a young wife who must be jealously watched. His desire to have Lulu immortalized on canvas is the ironic, futile gesture of an old man trying to halt time. When he leaves Lulu unguarded to attend the rehearsal of a risqué revue and returns, he dies from the shock of his betrayal, just as his successors, Schwarz and Dr. Schoen, will succumb.

If Lulu is a depraved creature to Dr. Schoen, she is the essence of immorality for Dr. Goll and a paragon of chastity to Schwarz. The painter has so idealized her that he fails to see her as a woman; she despises him for it. When he learns of his betrayal, his entire imaginary world, symbolized by his paintings of Lulu, disintegrates, and he cuts his throat. Lulu has become a symbol of corruption too ugly to live with.

Schigolch's relationship to Lulu is clarified in the sequel to *Earth Spirit*, *Pandora's Box* (1903), in which Wedekind reveals that the former lovers Lulu and Schigolch are now bound to each other by an incestuous passion compounded of lust and paternal affection.

Many things to all men, Lulu at least may present a coherent image to the modern audience: Beautiful, wanton, and mysterious, she admires men who will master her, is sexually excited by whips and beatings, and seeks out the strongest and most virile men to test her ability to dominate the opposite sex. Her triumph over Dr. Schoen comes when she tells him: "You conquer half the world, you do whatever you like—and you know as well as I that . . . you are too weak—to tear yourself free of me." After Dr. Schoen's capitulation, Lulu remarks: "You will please go now. You mean nothing to me anymore." Lulu wants only strong men so she can exert her primal force and destroy them by her will and body. Although neither a castrating female nor a liberated one (she will, in *Pandora's Box,* be forced into a life of common prostitution), she annihilates men because they are full of illusions and lack the sexual power to fulfill her.

Earth Spirit shows Lulu triumphing over each curtailment of her freedom. She is an animal who knows its habitat, powers, and appetites. When she kills Dr. Schoen, she destroys the middle-class values that have oppressed her, but she ironically delivers herself over to a sexual demimonde that will enslave her.

Wedekind emphasizes the elusive quality of Lulu's identity by placing her in artistic settings, evoking the archetypal dichotomy between reality and illusion. As an artist's model and music hall performer, she inspires visions that have little to do with her quintessential reality; but the subjective vision of each artist or member of the audience (men-lovers) makes Lulu fascinating. Rapidly changing costumes, she represents every aspect of sexual desire. She poses as Pierrot, the archetypal tragicomic figure; she wears ballerina costumes (Alva thinks the white one brings out her childlike quality, but the prince thinks it makes her look bodiless. He prefers the pink costume because in it she looks womanly. But Alva feels that pink makes her look too animalistic). Lulu masquerades as the Queen of the Night, Ariel, Lascaris, an Arab dancing girl, and as a sexually provocative bareback rider. Proud of her ability to change clothes rapidly, she boasts that she can effect a transmogrification without the assistance of a female dresser, but asks the nearest man to help her fasten a hook or adjust her bodice.

Wedekind rejected the literalness and monotony of Naturalism. *Earth Spirit* is a forerunner of the Expressionist mode in drama. Laconic, disconnected dialogue, abrupt changes in mood, atmosphere, tempo, and language, garish sets and costumes, and violent action are part of the arsenal with which the playwright attacked the sentimental melodrama of the French romantics and the rigidity he saw in Ibsen's plays. His characters are projected with violent directness; they externalize their inner passions and conflicts.

Wedekind's views on sexuality changed throughout his dramatic career. In *Spring's Awakening,* he posited the view that sexual passion was a source of truth, beauty, and vitality. But in *Earth Spirit* and *Pandora's Box,* he traced the corruption of pure sexuality by its own impulses as well as by the philistine forces of bourgeois society. Lulu is essentially a passive, immobile, amoral force who functions independently of the passions raging around her. By killing Dr. Schoen, however, she becomes subject to the imperious demands of a society that cannot tolerate an Earth Spirit. In *Pandora's Box,* Lulu emerges from prison and, like Zola's Nana, is destroyed by men. After betraying her sexual instincts and becoming a prostitute, she is disemboweled by a sex maniac, Jack the Ripper. Wedekind's darkening vision culminated in *Death and the Devil,* in which he questioned his own thesis that eroticism had its own soul and was its own reward.

Earth Spirit and *Pandora's Box* might well be considered documents in the history of women's liberation. Wedekind understood that love and freedom are impossible if a woman is merely an object of men. Lulu's tragedy is precipitated by her exploitation by men who will not permit her to exist in a natural state. Dr. Goll's possessive jealousy, Schwarz's stupid idolatry, Alva's fatuous romanticism, and above all, Dr. Schoen's schizophrenic obsession with keeping Lulu but not accounting for her are aspects of man's domination over women. In *Pandora's Box,* when myriad lovers attempt to possess Lulu's spirit, these assaults reduce her to prostitution and death.

Up until fairly recent times, Wedekind's plays have been neglected, at least partly because of their extraordinary sexual candor and their uncompromising hostility toward the artistically, sexually, and socially coventional. The Austrian composer Alban Berg (1885–1935) is largely responsible for the renewed interest in Wedekind's work. His opera *Lulu* (1934), based on *Earth Spirit* and *Pandora's Box,* is widely regarded as one of the greatest twentieth-century operas. Berg's masterpiece compresses the shocking events of Wedekind's bizarre plays with musically daring forms. Berg's use of twelve-tone compositional techniques intensifies the eerie, expressionistic elements in Wedekind's tragedies.

Wedekind's erratic style is not easy to translate to the modern stage without verging on the ludicrous. For the reader, he is relevant. In his haunted dramas, which inhabit the realm of sexual nightmare, from the most luridly realistic to the most profoundly allegoric, one may still learn of the "varieties of sexual experience."

The Author

Benjamin Franklin Wedekind was born in Hanover, Germany, in 1864, the child of German parents who had met in San Francisco. Wedekind's father was a physician who had been involved in European revolutionary movements and had lived in the capitals of Europe and North Africa, as well as the United States. After Frank's birth, political and emotional problems obliged the family to move to Switzerland, where the young boy and his brother grew up. After studying at the University of Lausanne, Wedekind moved to Munich in 1884.

In 1886, after a quarrel with his father over his choice of literature as a profession, Wedekind took a position as a publicity agent for a soup company and also worked as a journalist. He founded a satirical review that attracted young authors, including Thomas Mann. Wedekind was jailed for insulting the emperor and found himself, like his father, enmeshed in political affairs.

Wedekind's friendship with Gerhart Hauptmann, the author of *The Weavers,* was broken off when Hauptmann used incidents from Wedekind's personal life in a play he had written. Wedekind countered by caricaturing Hauptmann as a young man who took notes while making love. Some critics hold that Wedekind's growing disenchantment with Naturalism was hastened by his feud with Hauptmann, who had popularized Naturalism in Germany. Ultimately, Wedekind found that Naturalism led to an artistic dead end.

Between 1891 and 1893 Wedekind lived in Paris, where, under the influence of the English and French decadent movement, he sank deeply into dissipation and perversion. These experiences provided the young playwright with an insight into the demonic sexual forces that drive men. The characters in his plays act upon principles that are sometimes unrecognizable to the bourgeois audience that has not glimpsed the tortured world of rampant sexuality.

Wedekind's break from Naturalism came when he was discovering Georg Büchner, whose plays exerted a strong influence on the budding dramatist. Wedekind's first important play, *Spring's Awakening* (1891), was revolutionary not only in its theme of newly discovered sexuality in young people but also in its dramatic technique. It bypassed conventional, logical development to reveal the characters' innermost thoughts through episodic scenes, disconnected dialogue, and violent action. Drawing his dramatic ideas from Goethe's *Faust* and Büchner's plays, Wedekind forged an arresting series of works. *Earth Spirit* (1894), *The Tenor* (1897), *The Marquis of Keith* (1900), *Death and the Devil* and *King Nicolo* (1905), as well as *Franziska* (1911) and *Herakles* (1917), established Wedekind as one of the most controversial dramatists of his time. It was not until 1906, however, that he achieved public recognition with Max Reinhardt's Berlin production of *Spring's Awakening*.

Wedekind acted the male leads in his dramas because he felt that the acting techniques of his day were too antiquated for his plays. He delivered many salvos against hostile critics, exclaiming: "I challenge you today, on the honor of your profession, to show at least how the roles . . . can be acted more artfully and with greater effect than they have been by me." He later praised Josef Kainz and Josef Jarno, declaring: "There is not a single leading male role which I did not write for either one or the other of those two incomparably great actors."

The theme of sexual dominance in man's life and the revolutionary nature of his dramaturgy relegated Wedekind to an obscure corner of the German theatrical scene despite his later comedies and verse drama.

Wedekind died in 1918, during the war that was to shatter the artistic and moral world that he had so fiercely battled during his life. The thematic and, above all, the dramaturgical innovations that Wedekind forged still influence contemporary European and American drama and poetry.

Some critics believe that Wedekind's contribution may be seen in the works of Brecht and Ionesco. Among the antecedents of the Theater of the Absurd, he figures in the line of development from Büchner to the Dadaists, German Expression, and the early Brecht.

Wedekind's theme of the effects of sex in life is still considered unusually frank; as recently as 1963, *Spring's Awakening* was banned in London by the Lord Chamberlain.

Six Characters in Search of an Author

by

LUIGI PIRANDELLO (1867–1936)

The Characters

The Father—a man of about fifty, stout and mustachioed, alternately eloquent and violent. A thinker and a moralist, he discovers that evil can spring from good when he benevolently allows his wife, with whom he is bored, to run off with a man who is her soul mate. But years later, when he is driven to seek a prostitute, he discovers his wife's bastard daughter and allows the family to return to his home.

The Mother—a timid and emotional woman who passively succumbs to events.

The Stepdaughter—strikingly beautiful and dynamic, she is passionate, articulate, and aggressive in her treatment of the manager and father.

The Son—about twenty-two years old. Contemptuous and supercilious, he seeks to reject both his father and his mother's bastard family.

The Boy—about fourteen years old.

The Child—a girl of about six.

   Although they have no speaking parts, the boy represents the malignant fruit of the corrupt domestic situation; the child, his sister, the innocent victim.

The Manager—officious, practical, and sometimes belligerent, he is a foil for the philosophical and emotional father.

The Actors—they mock the characters and try to take their
parts. At the end, like a Greek chorus, they alternately
express horror and disbelief.

The Story

On a bare stage, a group of actors prepares to rehearse a
Pirandello play, *Mixing It Up.* They are interrupted by the
entrance of six people, surrounded by "tenuous light . . .
almost as if irradiated by them—the faint breath of their
fantastic reality." The stepdaughter tells the manager: "We
can be your new play," and the father adds: "We bring you
a drama, sir." The manager and actors become irate, but the
father and stepdaughter, speaking for all the characters, insist
upon their reality and explain that "the author who created
us alive no longer wished, or was no longer able, materially
to put us into a work of art."

Despite the hostility of the manager, the stepdaughter and
father try to explain their presence. A horrible tragedy has
taken place in their lives, and they must be freed by acting
out these episodes: "I am dying to live that scene," says the
stepdaughter. Apparently, the father allowed his wife to go
off with another man; many years later, he was recognized
by his wife's daughter in a brothel as he was about to have
intercourse with her. The reunion of the family and the jealousy of the only legitimate son of the father and mother
have brought horrendous consequences that are only hinted
at.

The actors mock the characters' urgent pleas for a chance
to come alive. The father explains how years ago he decided
that he could no longer live with his wife because boredom
and pity replaced passion and affection in their relationship.
He replies to the son's contemptuous characterization of the
situation as merely literature: "Literature indeed! This is
life, this is passion!"

The intricate exposition of the family's drama is continuously interrupted by the manager's skepticism and quarrels
between the stepdaughter and father. She contends that the
father's denial of the mother and their penury forced her to
become a prostitute, but he insists that he was searching for
a sane, moral solution to the domestic problems that con-

fronted him. Finally, the father induces the manager to stage a play "without an author," and they withdraw into the office to devise a scenario.

Twenty minutes later, the actors and characters reassemble on the stage, and the stepdaughter comforts the child and berates the boy, who has a revolver in his pocket. The mother laments her disgrace and torment, and the son explains his resentment of his mother's bastard children. The manager instructs prop men and machinists to assemble some sets and the prompter prepares to record the dialogue in shorthand. Despite the objections of the leading actors of the company, the characters themselves begin the scene in the brothel. The manager interrupts them several times to correct their acting style. Suddenly, Madame Pace, the owner of the brothel, speaking in half-Italian and half-English jargon, appears. Following the manager's objections, Madame Pace tries to take her place in the scene, but then departs furiously. The stepdaughter, in mourning for her natural father, receives the father in the brothel setting and begins to undress, but the scene is interrupted when the manager insists that his own actors must reenact the drama. The stepdaughter laughs at their wooden and artificial behavior, while the manager insists that acting is for professionals, not characters. He explains that in a play, characters cannot reveal all their inner psychological complexity. If they did, each character "could tell the public all his troubles in a nice monologue or a regular one-hour lecture. You must restrain yourselves." The characters reluctantly accede to his wishes as the mother laments her plight and ominously alludes to a tragedy. The stepdaughter tries to comfort her, but the manager thinks they are play-acting and calls: "Curtain!" to the prompter. The stagehands mistakenly lower the curtain in front of the scene.

When the curtain is raised a few minutes later, the set contains trees and a fountain. The manager claims that the setting and actors will create the illusion of reality, but the father objects that this *is* reality. The characters' reality is fixed, but the actors' reality is subject to flux because they are merely playing roles outside their personal lives. The playwright has created characters who come alive and attain dimensions and possibilities that their creator never anticipated. Although the playwright abandoned the characters for his own personal reasons, they have nevertheless been born and are compelled to enact a drama.

The son tries to flee from the scene but is compelled to stay. Suddenly, while the characters and manager are wrangling and trying to explain themselves, the child is discovered drowned in the fountain. The son says: "I ran over to her; I was jumping in to drag her out when I saw something that froze my blood . . . the boy there, standing stock still with eyes like a madman's, watching his little drowned sister in the fountain!"

A pistol shot is heard behind the trees where the boy is hidden, and the mother rushes to the back of the stage crying for help. The manager pushes the actors aside and carries the boy's body from behind the stage props, asking: "Is he really wounded?" Some of the actors scream in terror that he is dead, and others insist that it is only make-believe and pretense. The father cries: "Pretense? Reality, sir, reality!" The manager throws up his hands in disgust and complains that he has lost a whole day of rehearsal over "these people."

Critical Opinion

In *Six Characters in Search of an Author,* Pirandello explores the dilemma of the artist and his creations. Every playwright is faced with the multiple existences of his characters: as he conceives them in his mind, as they appear in the play, and as they assume an inner logic and life of their own apart from the work. Although the play and its characters are born of his imagination, the artist's original conception is successively elaborated upon and transmuted by the director, actors, stagehands, and finally the audience. This last change is perhaps the ultimate catalyst in the crucial reaction between appearance and reality.

Pirandello recognized that characters could be independent of author and play. For example, in the past three hundred and fifty years, the character of Hamlet has become part of the consciousness of an entire civilization, apart from his existence in Shakespeare's mind, in the play *Hamlet,* and in the interpretations of various directors and actors. Subjected to voluminous analyses and reincarnated in plays on Shakespeare's theme, Hamlet has been treated as if he were a living person. Audiences and critics concede that the figure of Hamlet is a reality that transcends Shakespeare's drama. Pirandello thus posits that characters have lives of their own that may be more real than the limited expression they are permitted in the restrictive framework of a piece written for the stage.

When the family arrives on the rehearsal stage, they are bathed in a dim light that the author indicates is "the faint breath of their fantastic reality." The word *fantastic* suggests imagination and invention. The father considers himself a living being "more alive than those who breathe and wear clothes: being less real, perhaps, but truer." The six characters have been born into a play that does not exist. They want to be like Hamlet or Sancho Panza; characters who "had the fortune to find a fecundating matrix, a fantasy which could raise and nourish them." The father's inner passion drives him on to find a play.

As in Pirandello's *Henry IV,* individuals must attain freedom and fulfillment by formalizing their inner lives. They want the tragic seeds of their passion to germinate and flower in the eternal form of a play or history, in which they will be materialized; they will be released from the purgatory of being without acting. Henry IV transmutes the agony of his experience into the formal confines of history. The life of Henry IV of Germany, as recorded by chroniclers and scholars, is parallel to the book that the manager insists is necessary for the existence of a play. At the end of the first act of *Six Characters in Search of an Author,* the characters adjourn to the manager's office to construct the book that will be the beginning of their liberation. It will permit the manager and actors to realize their turbulent existences; it will objectify the subjective. But the transformation will not be easy, for the internal reality of a character demands each actor's interpretation of the role. The father, like everyone in the world, must portray a role dictated by his inner life and the image he wishes to project. He confesses: "It will be difficult to act me as I really am." The actor will achieve an effect "according . . . to how he supposes I am, as he senses me—if he does sense me—and not as I inside of myself feel myself to be." When the professional actors try to repeat the brothel scene in which the father begins his amatory encounter with the stepdaughter, the stepdaughter laughs at their ludicrously artificial performance.

The actors' reality changes from one day to the other, but the characters' is fixed forever: "Ours is an immutable reality which should make you shudder when you approach us, if you are really conscious of the fact that your reality is a mere transitory and fleeting illusion." The actor changes from day to day because like all human beings he seems to control his destiny. It is this everyday existence that is illusion while the unreal existence of the fictional character is fixed by art in time and space.

Pirandello's humanistic belief in man and in the truth of his illusion is a central theme in all his plays. The father's attempt to achieve a moral sanity is thwarted by the failure of his illusions, when he succumbs to both sexual lust and human sympathy in the brothel, and when he rescues his wife and her bastard children from starvation. Pirandello knows that although man's life consists of multiple acts, he is judged according to one misdeed. The father, the *raisonneur* for the playwright in this case, exclaims: "We believe this conscience to be a single thing, but it is many-sided. There is one for this person and another for that. Diverse consciences." Even actions can never be clear and complete expressions of the individual: "Then we perceive that all of us was not in that act, and that it would be an atrocious injustice to judge us by that action alone, as if all our existence were summed up in that one deed."

Pirandello developed a theory that in order to make life bearable man must create an illusion, a mask that he maintains for himself and the world. In both *Six Characters in Search of an Author* and in *Henry IV,* this theory, which he called *costruirsi,* is the dominating motive of the father and of Henry IV. When the father is recognized by the stepdaughter in the brothel, he explains how the shock affected him: "But every man knows what unconfessable things pass within the secrecy of his own heart. One gives way to the temptation only to rise from it again, afterward, with great eagerness to reestablish one's dignity as if it were a tombstone to place on the grave of one's shame, and a monument to hide and shine the memory of our weaknesses." The moral relativism of this antibourgeois statement typifies Pirandello's intellectual attitude toward the shams of society. These views were prompted by his personal experiences and his bitterly earned compassion for the human condition.

Suffering is the human condition, and inquiry into the causes of that suffering is the human destiny. The guilt that is expiated in the final moments of the drama is suggested throughout the play. The father's misguided desire to give his wife and her lover fulfillment is punished by his loneliness, by the prostitution of his stepdaughter, and by the death of his stepchildren. The son's hatred of the father is an additional cross he must bear for sending his wife away. Without a woman to mediate the hostility between father and son, the father was obliged to send his boy away and incur his dislike. When attempting to repent, the father received the mother and her family and intensified the hatred of his only legitimate child. The unpredictable result of man's attempt to achieve moral sanity in his life thus becomes tragically evident. There is no absolute, objective reality or moral truth, especially in the realm of artistic creation or personal conduct.

The fragmentary nature of the tragic drama prevents the audience from passing final judgment on its characters. Life cannot be organized into a conventional, realistic play with exposition, development, and denouement. "Realism" is here challenged by Pirandello's tantalizingly ambiguous presentation of the family's problem. The audience is invited to hold its judgments in abeyance because, as the father insists, the *whole* story has not been told; indeed, it can never be told, for human events are too complex to be judged by rigid moral standards. Only the distorted perspectives of the father and stepdaughter are presented. The mother, her dead lover, the son, and, of course, the child and the boy (who have no lines to speak) do not present their sides of the story.

The first two acts of this drama contain an extended exposition of Pirandello's position and the characters' tragedy. The philosophical themes are introduced and elaborated upon as the father and manager debate the feasibility of realizing an imaginary but true situation within the context of conventional drama. *Six Characters in Search of an Author* and *Henry IV* are most strikingly similar in Pirandello's adroit, fragmentary presentation of dramatic and philosophic views that coalesce into a unified vision at the conclusion of each play. Both dramas end with abrupt and violent acts. The drowning of the child and the boy's suicide come with the same sudden brutality, as does Henry's murder of Belcredi. The acts seem almost accidental; yet the playwright's ingenious preparation for each denouement justifies the long exposition.

Pirandello has been criticized for his simplistic ideas disguised as philosophical inquiry. His success as a thinker is less notable than his ability to unify the ambitious intellectual and dramatic elements of his drama. His skill at characterization and the humanity of his moral position are compelling achievements. The stories of *Six Characters in Search of an Author* and *Henry IV* are united organically with the theses they demonstrate. By his apt choice of materials and a clever manipulation of dialogue, Pirandello has attained one of the most successful fusions of drama and philosophy in modern times.

Six Characters in Search of an Author, first performed in 1921 and radically revised in 1925, was a technical and philosophical refutation of the premise in realistic drama that theater is an imitation of reality. The play-within-a-play shows that reality is an illusion, valid for some but false for others. The most popular of Pirandello's plays, *Six Characters in Search of an Author* was considered revolutionary in its own day and is now held to be one of the foundation stones of contemporary drama.

Henry IV

by

LUIGI PIRANDELLO (1867–1936)

The Characters

Henry IV—a wealthy Italian about fifty who has constructed a replica of a medieval German court in his villa. After having been thrown from his horse during a masquerade pageant twenty years earlier, he went mad and believed he was indeed Henry IV of Germany. His natural capacity for histrionics and self-pity fits perfectly into the historical role he has chosen. Once in love with Matilda and now torn by his lucid apprehension of his betrayal, he is a violent figure.

Marchioness Matilda Spina—a proud and vain woman of about forty, brutal to her lover, Belcredi, and torn between her true feelings, which she doesn't understand, and her sense of guilt and duty.

Frida—the marchioness' beautiful nineteen-year-old daughter, induced to take part in the plot to rescue Henry from insanity, but her fear and sensitivity torment her.

Baron Tito Belcredi—a slim, prematurely gray man with a nervous laugh and a rather detached and offensive attitude, the marchioness' much-abused lover.

Dr. Dionysius Genoni—an elegant, corpulent man, pompous and domineering. He is proud of his medical knowledge and rhetorical ability.

Landolph, Berthold, Ordulph, and *Harold*—four of the king's

private counselors. They are confused and frightened by
their roles and do not understand the costume drama.
Charles Di Nolli—an elegant, vain young man who is Frida's
fiancé.

The Story

The salon of a present-day Italian villa is a reconstruction
of the throne room of Henry IV, who lived about eight
hundred years ago. King Henry's three private counselors
Harold, Landolph, and Ordulph are briefing their newest
recruit, Berthold, on the history of the king he will serve.
Berthold mistakenly believed that his master would be Henry
IV of France, but is told that it is Henry of Germany and
that the date is "somewhere between 1000 and 1100." Apparently, the private counselors feel they are puppets who
are acting in a madman's masquerade. Two modern oil
paintings of Henry IV and the Marchioness Matilda seem
anachronistic in the old throne room. But Berthold is not
told of their meaning because the counselors are interrupted
by the entrance of John, an old servant dressed in a modern
tuxedo, who announces the visit of the marchioness, her
daughter, and several other people.

The visitors enter and discuss the portraits and other
mysterious matters. Frida, the marchioness' daughter, looks
exactly like the woman in one painting, although it is in
fact the portrait of her mother twenty years ago. Di Nolli,
the doctor, and Belcredi discuss the origin of the masquerade. Belcredi claims to have invented the idea of a pageant
of Henry IV and his entourage. Donna Matilda tells how
she once rejected Henry's love out of fear. During the
pageant, the man who was playing Henry was thrown from
his horse and kicked in the head, and since then he has
believed that he is the king.

The party is interrupted by the counselors, who lament
Berthold's lack of historical knowledge; he has enraged
Henry IV. The king's animosity toward Pope George VII
and Donna Matilda is recalled as the visitors don their
monks' and duchesses' costumes. Henry IV enters, with
dyed hair and rouged cheeks, and receives his visitors with
a strange hostility, accusing them of being spies of the

pope. He seems to talk nonsense about self-conception and identities and thoroughly baffles the party by his erratic behavior. He acknowledges that he is living an illusion, but implies that everyone else exists in an unreal world. After some hostile remarks about the pope, Henry asks Donna Matilda to arrange an audience for him so that his excommunication may be rescinded. After he leaves, the marchioness breaks down.

In another room of the villa later that same day, the visitors discuss King Henry's case. They hope to free him from his madness by profoundly shocking his sensibilities. But other currents run through the conversation; jealousy, hate, remorse, and intrigue have entangled the four visitors in a web of distrust and fear.

The doctor notes that there is a certain lucidity in Henry's actions that indicates that he is deliberately continuing his masquerade. ("He has lost the equilibrium of his second personality and sudden recollections drag him . . . from a morbid inclination to reflected melancholy.") Frida enters in the clothes her mother wore when she sat for the portrait in the throne room. They plan to shock the king back to present reality and show him "that the eight hundred years . . . are only twenty." The king will receive two shocks. One will bring him from his medieval role to the time of the accident during the pageant, and another to the actual present.

Henry IV comes forward and declares his love for Frida. When Donna Matilda expresses her reservations, the king launches into a frantic diatribe against all his enemies; then, alone with his counselors, Henry confides that he is not insane at all and that he understands the situation completely: "We're having a joke on those that think I am mad." He poses the traditional paradox that the mad are sane and the sane are mad, and reflects on the role of time and history in man's self-conception. (History fixes man's agonies and struggles and gives them order, while those who think they are living in the reality of the present are plunged into chaos and disappointment.) The servant John, disguised as a monk, enters to record the good deeds of King Henry IV.

Later that night, Henry, crossing his darkened throne room, is startled by the appearance of Frida dressed as her mother, Donna Matilda, twenty years ago. The painting has been removed from the frame and Frida becomes a living portrait. But she cannot carry out the plan and collapses in fear. The others rush in and declare that the whole plan was unnecessary anyway, because the king's counselors have betrayed Henry's confession of sanity. Henry violently turns upon everybody and recounts how he has triumphed over those who thought they were living in the present. Of course, he would now prefer the younger version of Matilda to the real Matilda: "I prefer to remain mad—since I found everything ready and at my disposal for this new exquisite fantasy." The others live in the confusion and flux of uncharted events and passions. Although Henry has been robbed of Donna Matilda by Belcredi, who probably caused Henry's horse to rear in the pageant twenty years ago, he has triumphed over time through history. He clutches Frida and fatally stabs Belcredi as they rush upon him to free the girl.

Critical Opinion

Henry IV is essentially a drama that questions the validity of conventional ideas about history, time, space, and identity. Pirandello successfully fuses the philosophical and psychological elements of this tragedy into a compelling investigation into the relativity of illusion and reality.

When Berthold, Henry's new counselor, asks: "Which Henry IV is it? I don't quite get it," he points to one of the central problems of the drama: Who is Henry IV? By escaping into the world of Henry IV of Germany, by studying the historical and political chronicles of the time, and by surrounding himself with costumed people who represent personages in the historical Henry's life, Pirandello's protagonist has discovered an identity that he can structure through his knowledge of history.

The play's tragedy is not that Henry IV lives in a world of illusion and fantasy but that he is capable of differentiating between the imaginary existence he has constructed for himself and the insidious events of his past, which originally inspired and necessitated his fantasy. When the other characters, who believe they are firmly rooted in reality, begin to discover the relativity of so-called absolute truths, they are drawn into a maelstrom of doubt. They discover, to their horror, that the fantastic charade of Henry IV has its roots in real, personal, and psychological needs that they share. When they accept the character and gestures of the mad king, they descend into the abyss of self-knowledge and guilt that provoked his retreat; the monstrous significance of Henry's betrayal—in love, ambition, and person—becomes startlingly clear to them. Henry's cruel reversal of their expectations and the failure of their attempt to cure him of his delusions bring tragedy and remorse to the marchioness, the doctor, and Belcredi.

Henry and his court relive and remake history by creating an illusion of reality and establishing the essential artistic paradox of the truth in fiction. Landolph exclaims: "We don't any of us know who we are really—but who are we? Names of the period!" The counselors *must* play a part: "We're like so many puppets hung on the wall, waiting for someone to come and move us or make us talk." This, of course, is the human condition as Pirandello sees it. Man is destined to play roles that often are of his choosing. In *Henry IV* and *Six Characters in Search of an Author,* role-playing and fantasies are necessary for the continuation of life. No individual ever escapes role-playing, and sometimes these roles are crucial to a person's existence. The destruction of roles in *Henry IV* results in the protagonist's murder of his rival and his leap into true insanity.

The two oil portraits of the young Henry and Marchioness Matilda in masquerade are mirrors reflecting both the falseness and reality of man's compulsion to play a role. Pirandello has constructed a double or even triple mirror image: the young Henry and Matilda are an historical illusion to their older selves, for they are no longer the same as they were over two decades ago. At the same time, the present pair are quite obviously in a masquerade that, when the portraits were painted, was completely false. When Henry appears with dyed hair and rouged cheeks and makes overtures to Frida, Matilda's daughter, he seems to be trying to re-create the mirror image of the portraits. Yet once again the portraits are proved to be both prophetic and false, for the masquerades have become real and the young people who are wearing costumes in the portraits have been

replaced by a real king and marchioness. Both Henry and
Frida are aware of their masquerade in the present; yet the
old man parodies youth with his obviously dyed hair and
rouged cheeks. Meanwhile, Frida seems to be trying to
destroy time by reliving her mother's youth. The interaction
and breakdown of these illusions result in Henry's revolt
from his loss of freedom within the masquerade. He has
become chained by the passage of real time and the end of
dissembling. The loss of his play-acting identity precipitates
a truly mad act by a suddenly sane person: the murder of
his old rival, Belcredi. The others are confronted by the
falseness of their illusions about Henry's madness and the
desirability of "reality" when they see the malignancy in
their own lives.

Henry, of course, is no madder than most people. His
channeling of personal and psychological experience into
an historical role that is in many ways mythic fulfills a universal human need. This mythical situation becomes clear
toward the end of the play: Henry is deeply in love with
Matilda, who does not return his affection. He believes she
loathes him and has rejected him in favor of Belcredi. In
history, therefore, she becomes his enemy in alliance with
the pope, who represents rival authority (religion) that he
cannot tolerate.

Belcredi is responsible for causing the masquerading
Henry's horse to rear and throw him. After years of true
insanity, the injured man decides to maintain his masquerade
and avenge himself on his rival. But the exigencies of his
new role require him to sublimate personal animosities toward Belcredi and Matilda by placing these people in historical roles, too. Thus Matilda the woman, and Matilda
the historical personage, have merged in his mind and have
allowed him to control his violent passion. They, in turn,
accede to his delusions and fulfill his desires. The breaking
of the masks brings the uncontrolled expression of Henry's
vengeful passion. The masquerades, both personal and his-
toric, are no longer viable and become the ultimate absurdity of the human condition.

The doctor stumbles upon a half-true hypothesis to explain Henry's condition: "Evidently . . . that immediate
lucidity that comes from acting, assuming a part, at once
put him out of key with his own feelings, which seemed to

him not exactly false, but like something he was obliged to give the value there and then of . . . of an act of intelligence, to make up for that sincere, cordial warmth he felt lacking." At first, the doctor does not perceive the fatal truth that Henry's illusions are flawed by intrusions of present reality. Henry misleads the doctor when he says: "Not one of us can lie or pretend. We're all fixed in good faith in a certain concept of ourselves." Later, in a fit of seeming madness, Henry reminds everyone: "But woe to him who doesn't know how to wear his mask, be he king or pope."

The security of illusions—here, historical illusions— brings a sense of order and safety. History is past and fixed, but human life is plagued by flux and uncertainty. Henry confesses at the end of the play: "I preferred to remain mad—since I found everything ready and at my disposal for this new exquisite fantasy."

Pirandello's interest in metaphysics is often frivolous, irrelevant, or confusing. But in *Henry IV*, he has successfully communicated some very intriguing ideas about the necessity of illusion and the significance of time and space. Pirandello's consciousness of the relationship between time and space is most clearly stated when the doctor exclaims:

This—our life—will at once become real also to him; and will pull him up directly, wresting from him suddenly the illusion, and showing him that the eight hundred years, as you say, are only twenty! It will be like one of those tricks, such as the leap into space, for instance, of the Masonic rite, which appears to be heaven knows how far, and is only a step down the stairs.

Both time and distance can be illusions to a rational mind. But madness provides the important life-giving connection between the two and the ultimate reality of the correct perspective.

The absurdity of Henry's plight plays itself out on several levels. Before he was thrown from the horse, Henry was a tormented and frustrated man. Hypersensitive to the persecution he endured from Matilda and her friends, he sought to divert himself by a masquerade pageant. The accident made him truly mad for a dozen years. Upon recovering, he chose to continue in his madness and dupe his enemies. Illusion ultimately fails to mask the primitive forces of sexual jealousy and desire for revenge. The intellect and its artifices are brushed aside in a spontaneous and elemental physical act: Belcredi's murder. Man's plight is absurd because he cannot construct an intellectual alternative to annihilation despite his absolute and continuing need to do so. This view anticipates the existential dramas of Sartre and Camus.

The dramatic structure of *Henry IV* has provoked some criticism. The first and longest act is essentially an exposition in which the characters present themselves and hint at the dramatic events to come. Their incomplete sentences, cryptic statements, and confusing dialogue reveal their own perturbed state of mind, and raise several questions that become resolved only in the final act. The second act develops the mysteries and hints at some of the situations that precipitated the present state of affairs. The complexity of Henry's character and the idea that there is only a thin line between madness and sanity are dramatically demonstrated. The short concluding act brings the denouement of the tensions that were established earlier. The audience discovers that Henry was thrown from his horse during the masquerade pageant and, after a period of madness, recovered his lucidity only voluntarily to continue the masquerade. His insatiable passion for Matilda (transferred to Frida) and his violent hatred for Belcredi are resolved when he stabs his rival, who screams as he is borne out: "No, no, you're not mad! You're not mad. He's not mad!"

Henry IV and *Six Characters in Search of an Author* are considered Pirandello's dramatic masterpieces. Productions of both plays are often mounted in Europe. The dramatic interest in *Henry IV* makes it an especially popular drama in college and university theaters in the United States. The adroit combination of intellectual play and dramatic action, augmented by the great scenic possibilities of the drama's setting, account in large measure for the success and popularity of *Henry IV*.

The Author

Luigi Pirandello was born into a prosperous Sicilian family that hoped he would become a businessman. After Pirandello discovered his distaste for business, his family sent him to the University of Rome and Bonn. In Germany, he earned a doctorate in philosophy and distinguished himself by his mastery of the Hegelian dialectical form. Despite his upper-class background, Pirandello remained sympathetic to the down-trodden Sicilian peasants who were being exploited by the landowners and the government. He expressed his sympathies in one of his earliest plays, a realistic drama about his native region, *Sicilian Limes* (1910). Pirandello's liberal sympathies brought him into contact with the Roman political and literary intelligentsia, and he supported the peasant land seizures in the early years of the century.

Pirandello acquiesced to the Sicilian tradition of marrying someone chosen by his family. His personal life became a nightmare. His wife became mentally deranged after the birth of their third child, and her condition gradually deteriorated. She made public scenes, accused him of infidelity, and deserted him for a time. His life was further blighted by the flooding of the mines that his family owned, causing the cessation of his private income. Unable to support himself on the earnings from his poems, essays, stories, and plays, Pirandello was forced to take a position at a girls' college in Rome. Meanwhile, his wife nearly drove their daughter to suicide. Because a private asylum was too costly, Pirandello resigned himself to keeping his wife at home. He turned to literature and became associated with the Roman theater, organizing his own theatrical company (The Odescalchi Theater) and directing his own plays. A liaison with one of the most famous actresses of the day, Maria Abba, inspired him to write brilliant pieces for her. Pirandello became disillusioned with liberal causes and then with all government. As the political situation in Europe and Italy degenerated, he donned the mask of a disillusioned cynic.

When he was thirty-seven years old, Pirandello published a novel, *The Late Mattia Pascal,* in which for the first time he examined the problem of mask and identity. After 1913,

Pirandello's concern with illusion and reality and the uncertainty of identity dominated his dramatic work. *Think of It, Giacomino* and *The Pleasure of Honesty* (1917) were followed by *Cap and Bells* (1915) and *Right You Are—If You Think You Are* (1917). But although he wrote over forty plays, Pirandello is best known for *Six Characters in Search of an Author* (1921) and *Henry IV* (1922). In these plays, he consolidated his already substantial reputation and brought to its peak a special style that became known as "Pirandellismo." He was awarded the Nobel Prize for Literature in 1934.

The influence of Pirandello's philosophical training and tragic domestic life is evident in nearly all his dramas. Infidelity, madness, guilt, and the necessity of illusions are recurrent themes. His humanism rejected rigid moral standards and evoked sympathy for the tortured individual.

The Lower Depths

by

MAXIM GORKI (1868–1936)

The Characters

The Baron—a thirty-three-year-old ruined nobleman who says that he has "always felt a sort of fog" in his head. He lived in an unthinking dream, was educated at a college for the nobility, married, dissipated his fortune, and was sent to prison for embezzling government funds.

Kostylyov—an avaricious and malignant religious hypocrite who despises everyone, including his wife.

Vassilissa—Kostylyov's wife, twenty-six, who takes a lover in place of her fifty-four-year-old husband. She tries to dominate Peppel, is insanely jealous of Natasha, her sister, and would like to have Kostylyov murdered.

Peppel ("*Ashes*" *in Russian*)—who has been associated with thievery for all of his twenty-eight years. He rejects Vassilissa, and under Luka's influence, decides to marry Natasha and go to Siberia to make a new life.

Natasha—Vassilissa's twenty-year-old sister, victimized and beaten by Kostylyov. So downtrodden that she can no longer understand her own feelings, she rejects Peppel and accuses herself of her brother-in-law's death.

Medvedev—the uncle of Vassilissa and Natasha, an officious bully who uses his power as a law officer to abuse everyone. After being dismissed from the force, he strikes an alliance with Kvashnya and becomes a drunkard.

Kvashnya—a street peddler who flaunts her common sense about men, but becomes entrapped in a relationship with Medvedev.

Kleston—a forty-year-old locksmith, one of the few inhabitants of the tenement who works.

Anna—although only thirty, she is literally worn out by her marriage to Klestch.

Luka—a sixty-year-old religious pilgrim who likes to philosophize and dispense advice about the meaning of life.

Nastya—a twenty-four-year-old prostitute who fantasizes that she has lived the adventures depicted in cheap romantic novels.

The Actor—self-pitying and self-dramatizing, he has ruined his career and health with vodka.

Satin—like the baron and Peppel, he has been in prison. Of high birth, he killed a man to defend his sister's honor, and because of his weakness and cynicism, has been unable to halt his total degradation. Despite the bleakness of his life, he believes in the future of humanity and the sanctity of the individual.

Bubnov—a cap-maker whose humorous yet biting irony provides a counterpoint to the other characters' laments.

The Story

In a basement tenement in provincial Russia around the turn of the century, a group of social outcasts argue about various topics ranging from petty debts to medical definitions. Satin declares that he is "tired of all human words . . . I've heard every one of them a thousand times if I've heard them once." In disconnected monologues the characters discuss their past.

Anna complains that she cannot breathe. Kostylyov, the landlord, enters, berates his tenants, and threatens to raise the rent so that he can pay for his offerings to the Church. He is searching for his wife, who is sleeping with Peppel. After he leaves, the group resumes its malicious gossip and philosophical meanderings. Peppel asks: "What good are honor and conscience? You can't put them on your feet instead of boots. Honor and conscience are only good to those who have power—force."

Boredom, degradation, and indifference to each other's suffering dominate the dialogues and monologues. Natasha and Luka enter. The old man observes that he sees men "getting cleverer and more interesting. They all live worse, it's true, but they all want something better." Luka is a religious pilgrim who makes philosophical comments on everyone's plight. When Nastya complains that she is not needed anymore, Bubnov retorts: "You're not needed anywhere. For that matter all human beings on this earth are not needed." Medvedev, a policeman, bullies the group by threatening everyone with arrest; yet he is indifferent to Peppel's adultery with the landlord's wife, his niece. After praising law and order, he rushes out at the sound of a brawl, commenting: "I wish when people started to fight, other people would leave them alone. They'd stop fighting themselves—when they got tired." The landlord is beating Natasha, his young sister-in-law, and everyone rushes out to watch, leaving Anna and Luka to comfort each other.

Card and checker games are in progress as Anna, now gravely ill, is dying. As the others bicker over the stakes, Luka explains to Anna that she will achieve eternal rest after life. The counterpoint of the philosophical and the profane continues as Luka advises the actor to find a hospital for alcoholics, but the actor goes out to drink.

Klestch, Anna's husband, is indifferent to her sufferings; as her life ebbs, she tells Luka that she lost her health because her husband beat her. When she expresses hope for recovery, Luka asks: "What for? For more suffering?" The policeman threatens to arrest Peppel, and they exchange taunts. Luka advises Peppel to go to Siberia because man must have faith in himself and in God: "Whatever you believe in exists."

Peppel tells Vassilissa that he no longer cares for her, and she proposes to let him marry her younger sister if he will murder Kostylyov. They are interrupted by the landlord, who is attacked by Peppel. Luka advises Peppel to free himself from his mistress because she is a vicious woman. Suddenly, they discover that Anna is dead, and the others express relief that her coughing and suffering will not disturb them anymore. Natasha is grief-stricken, but Luka asks: "How can we feel sorry for the dead? . . . We don't feel sorry for the living—even ourselves." The actor recites some lines, and as they are about to retire for the night, Satin exclaims: "Corpses don't hear! Corpses don't feel! Shout— yell—corpses don't hear!"

The characters stretch out in a littered plot of ground outside the tenement. Nastya, a whore, recites a tale she has picked up from a romance. She is savagely mocked because she identifies herself with the heroine. Luka tells a story about a man's futile search for a true and just land and advises Peppel to "look for something—want something with all your heart. You'll find it."

Peppel decides to give up thievery and take Natasha to Siberia, where he can gain self-respect; strangely enervated, she cannot respond to his offer. Vassilissa interrupts them and orders her sister home. The landlord threatens Luka and goes to beat Natasha, who, burned and dazed, flees to Peppel. A scuffle ensues; Kostylyov is found dead of a heart attack, but his wife accuses Peppel of murder; Natasha, confused and in shock, exclaims that her sister and Peppel were the murderers but that she (Natasha) should be taken to jail.

Later, the dispirited group discusses Luka's disappearance. They repeat that their existence is futile, but Satin reaffirms the dignity of the individual and the regenerating spirit of Luka's ideas. Faith in a better future supports man in his misery. Sinking back into their self-pity and nihilism, the group gossips, argues, and gets drunk on vodka. As they are singing, the baron discovers that the actor has hanged himself. Satin whispers: "Ah, spoiled the song—the fool!"

Critical Opinion

The Lower Depths is universally regarded as Gorki's best play. Its departure from Zola's Naturalism and the plays of Ibsen, Strindberg, and Tolstoy created a new kind of social consciousness in the drama. Gorki believed that man, even when most degraded, was inherently noble. His plays, like those of his predecessor Chekhov, at first consist of a series of seemingly unconnected monologues within the matrix of a loosely organized framework. The formal structure of Henrik Ibsen's plays did not appeal to Gorki's deep intellectual and moral passion. He was intent upon depicting the ultimate breakdown of a social and moral structure that denied the necessity for individualism. Thirteen years before his death, Gorki commented that his plays were, in his judgment, unsatisfactory, because "I first construct their ideological framework, and combine beforehand the course and connection of the various comical and tragical events." But although Soviet critics have been quick to appropriate the ideological position apparent in this 1902 work, *The Lower Depths* is certainly neither merely a rambling paean to the common man's integrity nor a didactic apology for individual failure in a repressive, exploitive society.

The play's structure derives from a subtle counterpoint of dialogue and the careful mixture of ironic comedy and deep tragedy. It opens in the middle of a story by Kvashnya, a forty-year-old street peddler, who says that she will never marry again, and it closes with her complaints about her enslavement to Medvedev, who has become a drunkard after having been fired from the police force. Although this is low-life domestic comedy, the defeat of Kvashnya's intentions and her failure to overcome her humane and loving instincts despite bitter experience give the drama symmetry and thematic unity. Between these events lie a welter of occurrences, insignificant and tragic, that unfold piecemeal and are ornamented by a number of naturalistic character portraits.

Klestch and Anna are tragically and selfishly indifferent to each other. Anna thinks of her salvation, and he laments his inability to pay for her funeral. Only Natasha is moved by Anna's death, but she is more affected by the others' indifference than by the death of a human being. The pathetic actor, still enamored of language and rhetoric, asserts that his "organism is completely poisoned with alcohol," forgets lines from *Hamlet* and other plays, and can recall pathetic moments from *King Lear*. He is able to escape his wretched life through drink or suicide—not through poetry and imagination. Nastya reads *Fatal Love* and doggedly insists that this foolish romance happened to her. The baron refuses to allow her this fantasy, perhaps because he himself has been destroyed by illusion.

But not only unconscious self-deception cripples the people who dwell in the lower depths. Kostylyov, a totally malignant, unredeemed man, *consciously* uses his devotion to the Church to excuse his rapacity; his adulterous wife will sacrifice sexual gratification and morality to attain freedom from her husband. Peppel, a thief, is fired with a moral purpose which is overcome by circumstance (Natasha's indecisiveness), the landlord's death, and Vassilissa's violent revenge.

The two most intriguing characters are Luka and Satin. The old man is one of the many religious pilgrims who lived a nomadic life, traveling around the countryside in quest of spiritual wisdom. His age and prophetic demeanor give the impression of sagacity and prescience. He reminds the inmates of the tenement that, whatever they do to destroy their humanity, they will die human beings and that this humanity is the ultimate truth of existence. His speech is larded with aphorisms and predictions, and he seems to be the archetype of the aged wise man who, uninvolved in worldly strife, purveys both practical advice and arcane prophecies to the uncomprehending multitudes. Luka acknowledges that "there is no order in life—nor rectitude," but submits that reason must be adhered to in spiritual as well as worldly matters. At times a poser of Socratic questions and at others a dispenser of homely advice, Luka seems to possess a gentle personality, tempered by a satirical tendency; he asks unanswerable riddles and offers solace. His sayings are compounded of idealism and hard fact: "It can't be good if you've forgotten something you loved best. All our soul is in what we love," he tells the actor who cannot remember his lines; but later, when Vassilissa wants Peppel to kill her husband, he advises: "You've got to cut yourself off from that woman!"

Critics have debated what Gorki intended in the character of Luka. Some believe that he is modeled after Tolstoy's ideal of religious devotion and pacifism; others, that Luka is a fraud, canting in vague generalities and leading the characters astray. In Luka, Gorki has created a paradoxical character, for Luka is certainly a man of the world, despite his spiritual aspirations. At the conclusion of Act I, "he laughs with a crackled senile laugh." Gorki himself, thirty years after the play's creation, rejected the validity of Luka's ideas. But whatever philosophical or political orientation the reader may bring to his interpretation of Luka, the old man is a central force in the drama. He advises and comforts the characters and presents alternatives to the horrible, fatalistic events in the play. Significantly, none of the characters (except possibly Anna, who dies quietly, if not peacefully) finds it possible to act upon Luka's advice. Peppel is crushed by the weight of circumstances; Natasha succumbs to her neurotic dependency on the rotten order that is destroying her; the actor hangs himself. Luka disappears as suddenly and mysteriously as he arrived, and the grinding events pursue their implacable course.

Satin may be the playwright's *raisonneur*. For more than two decades, Stanislavsky, the brilliant producer-director-actor and esthetician of the Moscow Art Theater, played this part. The character's prominence in the last act has led many commentators to assign great importance to his role. Although Nastya is a whore, Peppel a thief, and most of the other characters live in the underworld to which society relegates its unskilled and uneducated, Satin is "At the Bottom" (the literal translation of Gorki's work) because he killed a man to defend his sister's honor. His sister was ultimately unworthy of his horrible sacrifice, but Satin was true to himself and his ideals. He avenged himself and his conception of honor, as well as his sister, and suffered a calamitous fall for a variety of moral, psychological, and social reasons.

Typically Russian in his paradoxical cynicism and idealism, Satin believes that wisdom comes through suffering. Like the baron and Luka, he interested Gorki enough to elaborate on his past life for a 1932 filmscript of the play. In addition to the background provided in the 1902 play, we learn that Satin was a dissipated, well-educated member of the nobility who was involved in a question of honor that superseded legal and social imperatives. He probably adheres, in Gorki's words written in another context, to the "theory of purifying the soul through suffering." Satin defends Luka when he exclaims: "The old man is not a faker. What's truth? Man—that is the truth!" He ruefully acknowledges that men like himself are: "People weak in spirit." But he prophetically adds: "There are lies that soothe, that reconcile one to his lot. There are lies that justify the load that crushed a worker's arm—and hold a man to blame for dying of starvation—I know lies! People weak in spirit—and those who live on the sweat of others—

these need lies and the weak find support in them, the exploiters use them as a screen . . . Lies are the religion of slaves and bosses. Truth is the god of the free man."

Satin's humane social and moral intelligence informs his final pronouncements on the downtrodden, suicidal, doomed companions who suffer their private hells in the squalid cave he too will perish in: "In all this are all the beginnings and all the ends. Everything is man, everything for man. Only man exists, the rest is the work of his brain." These prophetic words of Gorki, uttered in an era that laid claim to renewed idealism and humanism, were accepted as Gorki's credo. They became one of the seminal ideas of twentieth-century literature.

The theme of illusion and reality, most clearly delineated in Nastya's reading of romances and Luka's proclamations about the inviolability of the human soul, lends an ambiguous strain to this powerful drama. Gorki departed from Zola, and later, Tolstoy and Hauptmann, when he stated that man was capable of anything if he would endure the physical, spiritual, and moral cataclysm of an unjust society. This note of optimism is offset by a powerful expression of cynicism and economic determinism.

Political and social preconceptions no doubt influence interpretations of a play that critics still disagree about. However, readers and viewers have always acknowledged Gorki's genuine feeling for his characters, although they have expressed reservations about the dramatic structure and ambiguity in the drama. The universality of this play is attested to by the famous Japanese film adaptation in 1957, directed by Akira Kurosawa and starring Toshiro Mifune. Eugene O'Neill, in *The Iceman Cometh,* and Arthur Miller, in *Death of a Salesman,* are two illustrious American playwrights, among many of the world's dramatists, who have taken their cue from Gorki's ability to perceive man's failures objectively and yet insist upon his dignity.

After several radical revisions, *The Lower Depths* was first presented in 1902 by the Moscow Art Theater. The play caused a political and artistic furor. The czar's spies infiltrated the theater, and the players themselves were so confused by the characters in the play that Stanislavski took them on field trips to the working quarters so they would understand their actions and psychology. With Stanislavski playing Satin, *The Lower Depths* became a staple in the company's repertory. It received a New York production in 1903 and has been widely translated and performed in many countries. In addition to the Japanese film version, there have been notable screen adaptations in French, English, and Russian. A Moscow Art Theater film in 1947 featured the eminent actor Kachalov as the baron.

The Author

Maxim Gorki (whose real name was Alexei Maximovich Pyeshkov) was born in a provincial Russian city, Nizhni-Novgorod, in 1868. Orphaned at an early age, he was brought up in the household of his grandfather, the owner of a small dye factory, in unspeakably brutal surroundings. Serfdom, abolished in 1861, was still fresh in everyone's memory. After running away from his grandfather, Gorki almost starved. He lived among peasants and workers, supporting himself by various small jobs. He was self-educated; living near the University of Kazan, he read voraciously and managed to become a copy clerk to a lawyer. Leaving this "respectable" job, he made a grand tour of Russia; for two years he shared his life with the derelicts of society. When he returned to civilization, he became a reporter for provincial papers. There was an abortive suicide attempt in 1897. He was in and out of jail for revolutionary activity. Plagued not only by the czar's police but by his own ill health, Gorki began to write short stories about the social derelicts and outcasts he knew so well. The publication of two volumes of stories brought him success and popularity; his romanticized pictures of the Russian counterpart of the American tramp—for to Gorki the derelicts were superior beings, rising above their surroundings, a rebuke to the existing social world—struck the Russian popular imagination. Young people idolized Gorki.

From Chekhov, whom Gorki admired intensely, he received copious advice about his writing. In his first play, *The Smug Citizens* (produced by the Moscow Art Theater in 1902; its original title was *Scenes in the House of Bessemenov*), Gorki painted the workers as superior to the intellectuals. This glorification of the ancestor of the "proletarian hero" won him added acclaim in the new Marxist circles.

Gorki did not like his first play, however; he was more pleased with his next play, *The Lower Depths* (also produced by the Moscow Art Theater, where Stanislavski's naturalistic production in 1902 scored a triumph). His next four plays were *The Vacationists* (or *Summer Folk*), rejected by the Moscow Art Theater in 1904; *The Children of the Sun*, 1905; *Barbarians,* 1906; and *Enemies,* 1906. Several of his plays, including *Enemies* and *The Last Ones* (1909) were banned from the Russian stage until after the Revolution.

A political exile in America, Finland, and France, Gorki met Lenin in Italy. After the 1917 Revolution, he was canonized as the first great Soviet writer. Gorki's stories, memoirs, and plays continued to celebrate the common man. In the 1930s, he projected a sequence of dramas on the fall of the czarist regime, only two of which, *Yegor Bulychev and the Others,* and *Dostigayev and the Others,* were completed; they were produced at the Vakhtangov Theater in 1932.

During the Stalinist purges of the 1930s, Gorki left Russia, ostensibly for his health. He was still highly regarded in his own country. He died, of mysterious causes, in 1936.

Cyrano de Bergerac

by

EDMOND ROSTAND (1868–1918)

The Characters

Cyrano de Bergerac—an idealistic swordsman and poet with an enormous nose. His sensitive spirit, behind a facade of blustering heroism and intellectual wit, makes him shrink under the handicap of his grotesque physical appearance.

Roxane—a young and beautiful girl, passionately romantic, who enjoys the charade of love as much as its reality. Her purity of heart and spirit inspires the admiration of all men.

Christian de Neuvillette—a young, handsome cadet who attracts Roxane. Because he is innocent and straightforward, he cannot court her in the elegant manner she desires.

Ragueneau—a pastry chef who fancies himself a poet. He loses his wife and his shop because of his obsession with poetry.

Le Bret—a nobleman, Cyrano's faithful companion and loyal friend.

Comte de Guiche—a powerful nobleman who wants Roxane to marry one of his friends so that he may take her as a mistress. Later, during the siege of Arras, he shows his true bravery and nobility, and in the final act emerges as an elegant, benevolent but sad man whose great worldly success has failed to bring him happiness.

The Story

At the Hotel de Bourgogne, a lavish theater and palace in seventeenth-century Paris, a crowd of servants, cutpurses, and guardsmen assembles. Noblemen enter, exchange gossip, and discuss the remarkable beauty of Roxane, whom the unscrupulous Comte de Guiche would like to have as a mistress. Ragueneau and Lignière, two of Cyrano's friends, comment on his absence. Cyrano has forbidden the actor Montfleury to appear on the stage.

A few minutes after the performance has begun, Cyrano arrives and interrupts Montfleury, challenging anyone who would allow the play to continue. The actor retires and Cyrano gives the manager a purse of gold to compensate for the loss of revenue. When someone reprimands him and imprudently glances at his enormous nose, Cyrano delivers an elaborate and inventive rant about its marvelous properties. Valvert, a friend of de Guiche, insults the nose and is forced into a duel during which Cyrano composes a brilliant ballade. Having vanquished Valvert, Cyrano confides that style is all he cares about and that he is in despair because he is too ugly to win Roxane.

Roxane's duenna proposes a rendezvous with Cyrano the next day. When Lignière reveals that he fears that he will be ambushed and killed by one hundred men, Cyrano promises to protect him single-handedly. The crowd marches out in a procession to witness Cyrano's martial prowess.

The next morning, in his bustling shop, the poet and pastry chef, Ragueneau, writes verse while assistants prepare the day's fare. He confuses poetry and cooking as fellow poets enter and hungrily devour the food. Cyrano arrives for his meeting with Roxane, composes a love letter to her, and ignores everyone's conjectures about the horrible monster who defeated one hundred men a few hours earlier. Roxane confides that she loves a man but lacks the courage to avow her passion. Cyrano's wild excitement is crushed when she tells him that the young man is in Cyrano's regiment. She begs Cyrano's protection for Christian.

A bustling mob salutes Cyrano's bravery, but he rejects their homage by rude retorts to the nobles' offers of patronage and friendship. De Guiche admits that his mercenaries were put to route by Cyrano and withdraws after exchanging barbed insults with Cyrano. When Le Bret admonishes Cyrano for his fecklessness, the latter exclaims that he is a free spirit and will keep his personal and artistic independence.

When Cyrano's regiment of Gascon cavaliers assembles, Christian is goaded by the others into insulting Cyrano's nose. But instead of challenging the young man to fight, Cyrano informs him of Roxane's love and proposes to write love letters to Roxane that Christian will claim. They embrace. The soldiers enter and are astonished by the scene. But their imprudent assumption that Cyrano will tolerate insults to his nose is quickly dispelled when Cyrano beats the first man to challenge him.

Ragueneau stands in front of Roxane's house and tells the duenna that his wife has run off with a musketeer and that his shop has failed. Cyrano appears with two minstrels and demonstrates his knowledge of music; then Roxane and he discuss the letters and poems, supposedly composed by Christian, that have won her heart. De Guiche announces that his regiment, including Christian and Cyrano, will be off to war. Roxane rejects his proposition that she meet him in a convent and gives the impression that she is in love with Cyrano, implying that de Guiche's most effective revenge would be to deprive Cyrano of a chance to win glory on the battlefield. De Guiche is tricked into leaving Cyrano's (and Christian's) regiment at home.

Christian arrives and refuses Cyrano's further assistance in wooing Roxane. After he stammers and fails to move her, he allows Cyrano to prompt him underneath her balcony. Finally, Cyrano pushes the young man aside and utters beautiful declarations of love in Christian's voice, sending Roxane into a swoon of passion. This is Cyrano's supreme moment, for he is finally speaking for himself. But he does not reveal his identity and Christian mounts the balcony to embrace Roxane. A monk appears with a letter from de Guiche, arranging a tryst, but Roxane invents a message commanding the monk to marry her and Christian. While the ceremony is taking place, Cyrano delays de Guiche by a fantastic account of his voyage to the moon. When de Guiche finally recognizes Cyrano, the newly married couple

appear and de Guiche angrily orders Christian to the battlefield while Cyrano ironically promises Roxane to protect
him.

The starving soldiers at the siege of Arras are on the
brink of despair. Cyrano exhorts them to have courage. He
has just returned from his nightly trip through the enemy
lines to deliver a love letter to Roxane (supposedly from
Christian). De Guiche explains the various ruses he has
employed to maintain their position, but Cyrano scoffs. He
despises expediency and recognizes only the grand gesture,
the "panache."

Christian notices a teardrop on a letter that Cyrano has
composed for him to sign, and suddenly he understands
Cyrano's true feelings. Just then a coach arrives and Roxane
emerges. Using her charm and wit, she has come through
the enemy lines. Ragueneau is her coachman, and almost the
entire coach is filled with pastries, wines, and delicacies
cleverly concealed. The feast is interrupted when de Guiche
appears and is refused a portion of the food. Alone with
Christian, Roxane says that his love letters are the sole
basis for her love, and even if he were ugly, she would still
be devoted to him. Cyrano is devastated when Christian
describes their meeting, and Christian offers to have Roxane
choose between them. At that moment, the enemy charges
and Christian falls. During Christian's last moments, Roxane
finds one of Cyrano's letters with Cyrano's tears and Christian's blood. Cyrano whispers to Christian that Roxane has
chosen her husband as her true lover, and Christian dies.
The enemy attacks and Cyrano boldly leads the counterattack.

Fifteen years later, in the park of a convent, Roxane,
dressed in mourning, awaits the arrival of Cyrano, who is a
weekly visitor. The nuns gently chide each other, and de
Guiche, "magnificently grown old," again reaffirms his love
for Roxane and confesses that he admires Cyrano. The
autumn leaves are falling. Ragueneau enters to say that a
hired murderer has treacherously dropped a log on Cyrano's
head. Roxane does not hear the news and contentedly awaits
Cyrano as the others rush out. The clock strikes; Cyrano is
late, but he suddenly appears, pale and bandaged. Roxane
has her back to him while she sews, and Cyrano is able
to carry on his usual badinage with the nuns and Roxane.

His speeches are full of references to death. Roxane shows Cyrano the letter that she has kept by her heart and Cyrano pretends to read it aloud. It grows dark and Roxane, knowing that Cyrano could not be reading, realizes suddenly that it is his letter and cries, "It was you." He refuses to acknowledge his long devotion, and as his friends rush in and twilight falls, he dies in Roxane's arms. His last magnificent speech closes with the declaration that his white plume, not Roxane's love, has given him strength in these years.

Critical Opinion

A contemporary of Ibsen and Strindberg, Edmond Rostand showed little interest in the realism or the innovations of modern drama. A typical man of *La Belle Époque* —the late nineteenth century in Paris when opulence, prosperity, and elegance were keys to social and artistic success—Rostand the Romantic turned his back on modern Europe and devoted himself to depicting the romantic and sentimental aspects of the French spirit.

Cyrano de Bergerac, subtitled a "Heroic Comedy," is an historical play. Heroic comedy contrasts with the seventeenth-century type of drama that the English called Heroic Tragedy. It posited the conflict between love and honor. Rostand's departure from Corneille, Racine, Dryden, and eighteenth-century playwrights consists of his emphasis upon the comic and pathetic aspects of the dramatic situation. Man encounters society and is faced with unresolvable dilemmas when his sense of honor conflicts with his emotions. But the drama of Rostand, unlike the Greek classical parallels that Racine and Corneille chose to exploit, presents Cyrano as a hero on a different plane. He is not destroyed by his conflicts. He emerges fully confirmed in his lifestyle.

Cyrano de Bergerac is an historical personality—a seventeenth-century wit, swordsman, and poet who wrote a fanciful work on a voyage to the moon, *L'Autre Monde*. He lived from 1619–1655. Molière, Corneille, and other historical figures are mentioned or appear in Rostand's drama, but intoxicated by France's romantic past, Rostand, like any historical *romancier,* liberally interpreted and rearranged past events to suit his poetic fancy.

Writing at the end of the romantic era, Rostand interpolated his own simple and emotional conception of the world into a colorful spectacular theatrical pageant full of violence, emotion, and, above all, blazing rhetoric. One must look to the operas of Verdi and Puccini, and to a lesser degree, to the works of Gounod, to find an equal to this flamboyant and picturesque creation. In fact, the play is unabashedly operatic in its emphasis on grand scenes, lyricism, dramatically effective scenes, and vividly drawn characters.

The great pageantry of the first act sets the scene for Cyrano's spectacular entrance. As the lackeys, citizens, nobility, and demimonde of mid-seventeenth-century France are vividly introduced, the dramatic interest gradually focuses on the character of Cyrano before he appears. Following the examples of Ben Jonson, Molière, and lesser classical playwrights, Rostand has his characters describe Cyrano to establish his personality and appearance. When he finally enters and banishes Montfleury (a famous actor in a troop that rivaled Molière's) the audience is totally prepared for his extravagant and comic behavior.

Cyrano is, in his own words, "Philosopher and scientist,/ Poet, musician, duelist." But he is horribly deformed by an enormous, discolored nose that, in the true romantic tradition, is an outward sign of his inner vulnerability. He despises society and the success and rewards of conformity. The outward gesture, the flashing sword, the renunciation of privilege, and above all, the rhetorical flourish are his hallmarks. When courting Roxane, he confesses to his friend Le Bret: "She might laugh at me;/That is the one thing in this world that I fear!" When his idol falls in love with a handsome young man, Cyrano suppresses his grief and magnanimously offers to write the poems, love letters, and speeches with which Christian woos her. In his reaction to royal patronage and universal popularity, Cyrano maintains his integrity. Even the great sacrifices he must endure —poverty and the loss of his beloved—contribute to the romantic image of himself that sustains him through a life of loneliness, pain, and disappointment. He confides to Le Bret: "My friend, I have my bitter days,/Knowing myself so ugly, so alone." But self-pity is not Cyrano's style, for he is a witty man, and crying "would be too grotesque—tears trickling down all the long way along this nose of mine./I will not so profane the dignity/of sorrow." At the end of the drama, mortally wounded, Cyrano refuses to confess his love for Roxane. His final speech is the most pathetic and sentimental tribute to his self-conception. Delirious with pain, a moment away from death, he addresses Death in this magnificent monologue:

> Yes, all my laurels you have riven away
> And all my roses; yet in spite of you,
> There is one crown I bear away with me,
> And to-night when I enter before God,
> My salute shall sweep all the stars away
> From the blue threshold! One thing without stain,
> Unspotted from the world, in spite of doom
> Mine own!—
>
>   And that is
>   —That is . . .
>   My white plume. . . .

Instead of confessing his love, which is his greatest accomplishment, he wittily and ironically vanquishes vanity and maintains his dignity by extolling the white plume that is the symbol of his honor and the mark of "panache."

The other characters in the drama, even Roxane, are stereotyped figures who add color and emotion to the superb pageant whose principal virtue is movement. Roxane does not really change in the modern psychological sense. Her vanity and innocence are suddenly replaced by wisdom and compassion. Christian is an empty and charming character and de Guiche, at first ominous and vicious, becomes generous and benign in the play's final act.

If the modern student looks for social significance in this drama, he perhaps will find a paean to the talented personality who revolts against the conventions of society and relies upon his own enormous personal force and genius to sustain his spiritual freedom. Cyrano is a lonely character whose credo is extravagantly summed up in this eloquent passage:

> So, when I win some triumph, by some chance
> Render no share to Caesar—in a word,
> I am too proud to be a parasite,
> And if my nature wants the germ that grows
> Towering to heaven like the mountain pine,
> Or like the oak, sheltering multitudes—
> I stand, not high it may be—but alone!

But Cyrano is not only admirable and pathetic, he is funny. His grand gestures and exaggerated sentiments are burlesques of the very real and touching human need for self-assertion and dignity. Rostand's drama is effective because it presents Cyrano in a comic light; the hero is a very funny man.

Rostand is obliquely critical of the late nineteenth century's worship of external form and beauty. But basically he is more interested in creating a vast and colorful drama. The stage directions envision an elaborate and stylized production. The visual spectacle demands sumptuous costumes, stage architecture, and scenic backdrops. Scenes in a palace, a pastry shop, on an elegant French street, on the battlefield, and in a convent tax the scenic designer's ability to present a splendid and romantic backdrop for the action.

After its enormously successful Paris premiere in 1897, *Cyrano de Bergerac* was produced in New York a year later. Walter Hampden converted it into a spectacular and long-running vehicle for himself and played throughout the United States in the twenties and thirties. José Ferrer made the role of Cyrano his during the next decade, won an Oscar for his portrayal of the long-nosed gallant in 1950, and subsequently appeared on television in Rostand's play.

Brian Hooker's translation, commissioned by Walter Hampden, has generally been regarded as the best adaptation of Rostand's Alexandrine verse. The Alexandrine in twelve-syllable rhyming lines was used by Molière, Corneille, and Racine and has a distinguished tradition in French poetry. Hooker's blank verse adaptation conveys much of the elegance and flamboyance of the original while appearing vernacular enough to appeal to American audiences. The English novelist Anthony Burgess devised a new translation for a 1971 production at the Gutherie Theater in Minneapolis.

The Author

Edmond Rostand's mother came from a long-established family that had won distinction during the Napoleonic period. His wealthy father encouraged him to cultivate his literary talents. When Rostand left his native Marseilles to live in Paris, he was already an accomplished writer. After marrying a poetess in 1890, he turned from his own verse to the theater and produced a series of lyrical romantic dramas, beginning with the light comedy *The Romantics* (1894) and the lyrical *The Faraway Princess* (1895), and continuing with his lasting success *Cyrano de Bergerac* (1897), and *L'Aiglon* (1900). *Chantecleer* (1910) was an ambitious and powerful allegory. A biblical drama, *The Woman of Samaria* (1897), and the plays Rostand wrote while exiled from Paris because of ill health, *The Last Night of Don Juan,* published three years after his death, and the unfinished *Sacred Wood,* did not have popular success. During the height of his career, Rostand was idolized by Parisian society and his plays provided celebrated roles for such famous actors as Constant Coquelin (who played Cyrano) and Sarah Bernhardt (L'Aiglon).

He Who Gets Slapped

by

LEONID ANDREYEV (1871–1919)

The Characters

Consuela—a circus bareback rider, ward of Count Mancini, affianced to the baron, and loved by Bezano and HE. A symbol of innocence, beauty, and grace, Consuela is gentle and yielding, but quite indifferent to her suitors.

Count Mancini—reputedly Consuela's father, but neither a count nor a father. He hopes to become rich by marrying Consuela to a wealthy nobleman.

HE—a clown in Briquet's circus who develops an act that features his humiliation when he is slapped by other clowns. A former nobleman with a mysterious past, HE is tormented by an unattainable vision of beauty and innocence.

Briquet—the fatherly manager of the circus who would like to protect his performers from the corruption of the outside world.

Zinaida—Briquet's common-law wife, a lion tamer. Jealous of Bezano's love for Consuela, she is obsessed with her lion, Sultan, whom she wants to master.

Alfred Bezano—Consuela's partner, handsome, masculine, and gentle; the Adam to Consuela's Eve.

A Gentleman—a well-dressed, mysterious caller who confronts HE with cryptic remarks about his former life and begs the clown's forgiveness.

Jackson—the head clown who instructs HE in the ways of

the circus: "Everybody here thinks out his own line of business." Jackson slaps HE and censors him for going too far.

Baron Regnard—a wealthy nobleman who wishes to marry Consuela. Regnard surprises HE when he commits suicide out of love for Consuela.

The Story

A circus has set up tent in a small provincial French town. Papa Briquet, the circus manager, chides the decadent Count Mancini for begging the clowns for money. Mancini wants to find a tutor for his daughter, the bareback rider, but Briquet argues that his circus artists are happier and safer without worldly knowledge. The two are interrupted by the arrival of a mysterious gentleman who asks to join the circus as a clown. The clowns carefully examine the new arrival and ponder what to do with him. Jackson, the head clown, informs the stranger that "Everyone here thinks out his own line of business." The new clown decides to call himself "HE": "I'll be He Who Gets Slapped . . . the funnyman Who Gets Knocked About." Briquet agrees to take him on. Consuela, the bareback rider, and her partner, Bezano, enter and discuss their new act. Consuela refuses to join her father for lunch with Baron Regnard. The performers exit and Briquet asks HE to reveal his true name for the police record. HE shyly offers his card to Zinaida, Briquet's common-law wife, but asks the couple to keep his identity secret.

HE observes that Bezano is in love with Consuela and Zinaida adds that HE must also see her love for Briquet. But when HE and Briquet leave, Zinaida calls Bezano and asks him if he loves her. Bezano declares that he is afraid of her because she orders him around as she does her lions.

The baron and Consuela are alone in Briquet's office. "Everyone is in love with you," the baron tells Consuela, and he confesses his own passion for her. She retorts that the baron must speak to her father, but the baron, calling Mancini a charlatan, declares he cannot marry Consuela. Laughter is heard from the circus ring, followed by loud applause. Everyone talks about HE's success: HE was slapped one hundred times. Jackson tells HE that the act went well, but HE must be careful not to philosophize. When the artists return to the ring, HE and Mancini are left alone to discuss the marriage plans for Consuela and the baron. Mancini hopes to be rich soon, but fears that Consuela, once she is a baroness, may shun him. He starts to talk about her humble origins but stops himself. The bouncer interrupts their interview with a letter from the baron for Mancini. Briquet enters, lamenting Zinaida's dangerous act. He is afraid the lions will hurt her. Zinaida rushes in, extremely distraught, "Like a mad victory." She mutters: "Oh, Bezano, Bezano . . . Alfred! Did you see/My lions *do* love me?" When Bezano leaves without answering, Zinaida nearly swoons. Mancini declares he will see her home.

HE and Consuela are left alone. They discuss Zinaida, and Consuela comments that her hands are "always cold, as though she was dead, actually." HE says Zinaida is in love with Bezano, and Consuela asks: "HE, what is *love?*" He takes Consuela's hand and dramatically starts to read her palm. He tells her she is a goddess who cannot marry. Alfred is also a lost god "who will never find his way to happiness again." HE prophesies that if Consuela marries the baron, she will die. HE declares that he is an old god in disguise and asks her to love him. Consuela angrily slaps HE. He pretends to be only acting, and Consuela apologizes, pats HE affectionately, and leaves. An elegant gentleman enters, recognizes HE, and asks forgiveness. The gentleman, who has a son by HE's wife, asks to talk to HE, who dismisses him.

Early the next morning, the gentleman finds HE in Briquet's office. The gentleman is shocked to see HE a clown and keeps asking to be forgiven. HE asks if the gentleman's son looks like himself: "Women often have children by a new husband who looks like the old one." HE ironically comments on the success of the gentleman's new book, in which he has vulgarized HE's ideas. The gentleman confesses that although he has a wife and a son, he is unhappy. His wife still loves HE; even in bed they discuss his brilliance. The gentleman begs HE never to return: "Of course I daren't ask you to die, but you won't ever come back, will you?" When the gentleman asks: "Are you mad?" HE replies: "I'm afraid you were never so right in your life. I am mad."

The circus is planning a benefit for Consuela, who is leaving to marry the baron. Consuela tells her father she is unhappy because Bezano yelled at her. Mancini leaves, telling Consuela not to trust HE, who again warns Consuela not to marry the baron or she will die. Consuela asks about the beautiful world of the gods. But HE tells her they are sleeping. He implores her not to marry the baron, but is again rebuked for being He Who Gets Slapped. When Bezano appears, HE privately beseeches him to prevent Consuela's marriage. Consuela loves Bezano, and the rider must save her even if it means killing Consuela or the baron. HE calls Bezano a god, but Bezano angrily storms out. Mancini returns with the baron, whom HE greets hostilely.

The evening of the farewell performance everyone in the circus is excited and nervous. The baron has bought all the reserved seats and has had the circus ring decorated with a bed of beautiful roses. Briquet confesses that everything has changed since barons started coming around. HE and Zinaida talk quietly about Consuela's marriage. Zinaida says that Consuela is not Mancini's daughter but a young Corsican he adopted. She says HE is out of place in the circus, but once Consuela leaves, HE will discover how lovely the circus really is. Like HE, Zinaida, too, used to long for security and caged herself up with her love for Bezano and her obsession for the lion Sultan.

Zinaida advises HE to forget Consuela, but HE retorts: "That comes funnily from you, Zinaida, when you want to be loved by a lion! When you're ready to risk your life for a moment's illusion of power . . . illusion of love, if you like." Mancini enters and notices HE's new costume. It is black: "Rather funereal for a funnyman."

The entr'acte begins and all the circus performers gather to toast Consuela and the baron. Consuela is moved by Briquet's sincere, loving speech. It is as if she were dying. HE approaches and Consuela asks him not to love her. She laments: "Why do they all love me?" HE gives Consuela a glass of wine to drink for a farewell toast. HE tells her to give herself up to a magic sleep. Just as the curtain goes up for the second act, Consuela complains she is tired. Her heart hurts, but HE comfortingly says: "This is death, my little Princess, I've killed you." As Consuela dies, HE tells her that she is flying to the sun. Briquet goes to get the police just as someone rushes in to announce that the baron has shot himself. HE, who has been standing quietly, gathers all his remaining strength and declares: "So you really loved her, baron. You loved my Consuela. And you wanted to get her first. No . . . I'm coming, Consuela, don't listen to him, I'm coming, I'm coming."

Critical Opinion

Leonid Andreyev's tragedy depicts the futility of trying to escape into the world of illusion. Recurrent images of illusion and reality, innocence and corruption, gods and mortals, men and beasts imbue the drama with allegorical significance.

The circus people, isolated from the world, act instinctively and are not corrupted by outside influences. Papa Briquet guards his little family, lamenting any change in his illusory universe. When Mancini suggests giving his daughter a tutor, Briquet attacks learning: "Consuela is a fine artist—now, but as soon as you teach her . . . mythology . . . and she begins to read, she'll be good for nothing, she'll get moody, morbid, it'll make her miserable, and she'll go and poison herself. . . . Oh, I know these books. . . . All they teach is immoralities and how to kill yourself." Briquet correctly foresees the cause of Consuela's death, for HE's arrival introduces a sense of mythology to the circus.

HE is even more a threat than books, for as an artist, HE embodies the corrupting spirit. Through his eyes the artists are transformed into gods; their little universe of the circus is no longer sufficient; they must attain the heavens. HE is announced as "a gentleman from another world," and his intrusion as a god unsettles the world of illusion that the circus represents. The stranger is described by others as a drunk, a ghost, and a serpent: irrational, elusive, and malignant. To Consuela, he says: "I am an old god in disguise. I've come down to earth to love you, just to love you." Later, Consuela replies: "You're He Who Gets Slapped . . . a god who gets slapped . . . perhaps they slapped you out of heaven." In the circus, HE is a malevolent force, a fallen angel like Satan, who is ejected from Heaven and invades Adam and Eve's paradise. Recognizing that gods cannot survive in the material world, HE describes Consuela as a goddess of innocence and love, merging images of Eve and Venus rising from the sea. After having poisoned her, HE implores Consuela: "Awake, Goddess, and remember the time when you rose from the sea . . . remember the sky and the quiet breeze from the east and the murmur of foam at your marble feet." HE sees himself as an omnipotent god who can direct the circus. Like Briquet, HE thinks Consuela will perish outside the world of art and illusion. If she marries the baron, HE must murder Consuela to save her divine soul. Ironically, Consuela, whose name denotes consolation, consoles no one, but torments all the men around her. As the incarnation of beauty, she is unattainable, the innocent source of frustration.

But HE is only mortal, eternally frustrated by his impotence. As an author, HE was unable to attain immortality through his art: his best friend stole his ideas and his wife and fathered HE's son. As a clown, HE is successful when he panders to the public's sadism, but when he tries to communicate a lesson about corruption, Jackson slaps him back into subservience. Finally, HE is a failure because beautiful images from mythology only torment Consuela. Unlike an all-knowing god, he fails to experience true emotion and does not recognize the baron's genuine love for Consuela. Even in eternity, HE is "slapped," for the baron dies before HE can reach Consuela in Heaven. HE's failure underlines the impossibility of transforming the real world into the world of artistic illusion. While the circus is a reality apart from mundane society, it is nevertheless inhabited by vulnerable people.

Though the people of the circus are not gods, they are caught between the world of beast and man. Briquet would like to set up bars and protect the circus from invaders: "We're the decent people—they're the animals." Zinaida, the lion tamer, is enamoured of her lion, Sultan. She, too, feels the need for achieving security through bondage: "How good for body and soul! Oh, I know how you feel. . . . I used to be the same, for ages I longed for security. . . . I wanted to cage myself up . . . chain myself to something." When Zinaida counsels HE to forget Consuela, HE bitterly retorts: "That comes funnily from you, Zinaida, when you want to be loved by a lion! When you're ready to risk your life for a moment's illusion of power . . . illusion of love, if you like. . . ." Like HE, Zinaida is obsessed with illusion and death. Consuela observes that her hands are "always cold, as though she was dead, actually." Like HE who tries to transform people into mythology, Zinaida strives for an impossible union with her own creation, the lion. The world of illusion, whether the illusion of art, deification, love, or power, is ultimately futile.

The mysterious gentleman is HE's alter-ego. He confesses to having searched for HE and now that he has found him, he begs forgiveness. Apparently, the gentleman has taken HE's wife, had a child by her, appropriated his ideas, and vulgarized them with enormous success. The gentleman can hardly recognize the clown who has divested himself of worldly conventions and lives in the circus, devoted to imaginative reality. HE exclaims: "You are a distorted image of me, your ideas are distortions of mine." The gentleman himself has been humiliated. His wife is obsessed by HE's genius and his son is the image of HE. Andreyev implies that dignity and happiness are attainable neither inside nor outside of conventional society. Maxim Gorki observed: "To Andreyev, man appeared poor in spirit, a creature interwoven of irreconcilable contradictions of instinct and intellect, forever deprived of the possibility of attaining inner harmony."

The color and vitality of circus life is a perfect setting for Andreyev's ambitious tale of illusion and reality. Like Picasso's circus people, created only a few years before, the harlequins, jesters, and other performers in Briquet's circus are ineffably fragile and vulnerable. The hothouse atmosphere of backstage is a romantic paradigm of everyman's unconscious knowledge of the creative possibilities of life. Andreyev's manipulation of dialogue and situation evokes an ironic, bittersweet mood.

He Who Gets Slapped was first produced by the Moscow Art Theater in 1915. Although Andreyev is principally known as a short story writer, his symbolic drama has attracted great interest. The late Tyrone Guthrie, playing the part of HE, revived the play in 1946, and his wife

Judith has brought the drama to the reading public through her modern adaptation. In 1971, *He Who Gets Slapped* was performed in New York.

The Author

The friend of Gorki, whose work was enormously popular in pre-Revolutionary Russia because it reflected the prevailing pessimism of the times, Andreyev was the son of poor parents. He attended school in central Russia and studied law in St. Petersburg. Extreme poverty and his natural morbidity led him to attempt suicide twice when he was a young man. After moving to Moscow, he took up portrait-painting to support himself. He received a law degree in 1897. While a court reporter for a Moscow paper, he contributed satirical sketches that were published on the front page. He married in 1902; two years later, his play *Anathema* brought him fame.

The Red Laugh (1904), an antiwar story, and *The Governor* (1905), a political protest, increased Andreyev's prestige, but in 1906, after his wife's death, he tried to kill himself again. His symbolic *The Life of Man* (1906) brought him new theatrical success, and he remarried the following year.

With the story *Seven Who Were Hanged* (1908), Andreyev was established as one of Russia's major writers, but he became increasingly disenchanted with Russian society and with humanity itself. Withdrawing from literary circles, he moved to Finland, where he fell into a profound depression and produced very little. However, the production of his most famous play, *He Who Gets Slapped* (1915), brought him new acclaim. Political upheavals in his native land revived his energies, and he attempted to rally the traditional elements in Russian society, as well as Russia's wartime allies, to defeat the Bolsheviks.

Andreyev was planning to lecture in the United States when he died in 1919.

During the years of the Soviet regime that followed the first experimentation in theater arts, Andreyev's work was in eclipse for the same reasons that had made him so popular in the pre-Soviet era; however, *He Who Gets Slapped*

was a favorite European and American choice for production
in the 1920s. Recently, because of the fact that his view
of life is not alien to that expressed by the dramatists of
the Theater of the Absurd, Andreyev has enjoyed renewed
popularity in experimental drama circles here and abroad.

King Ubu

by

ALFRED JARRY (1873–1907)

The Characters

Father Ubu—truculent, cowardly, stupid, and obscene, he wears outlandish getups that are indicative of his pretensions: a suit of mail, a Charlie Chaplin bowler hat, a ridiculous crown, a phallic cane.

Mother Ubu—grotesquely ugly, wily, disloyal, and avaricious, dressed like a French concierge, vulgar and mindless.

Captain Bordure—wearing the costume of a Hungarian cabaret musician, he is mercenary, vain, and sycophantic. His name suggests ordure.

King Vencelas—pompous, toadlike, and fatuous, the only possible victim for a man like Ubu.

Queen Rosemonde—a parody of Calpurnia in Julius Caesar, who foresees her husband's demise.

Bougrelas—a latter-day Macduff and Hamlet, he appears dressed as a baby, wearing a little gown and bonnet.

The Story

In Poland, Mother and Father Ubu exchange obscene epithets. Mother Ubu urges her husband to overthrow the king. At a banquet, the Ubus entertain Captain Bordure. Father Ubu objects to the sumptuousness of the feast and hurls a toilet brush at the company. A messenger summons Ubu to the king's palace, where the drunken company rants, and a decorated flute, presented by Ubu to the king, is passed on to the son, Bougrelas, who insults Ubu. Later, the conspiracy is organized; Ubu plans to step on the king's toe as a signal for the assassination. Mother Ubu is the priest who administers the oath of allegiance to the conspirators. At the king's palace, Queen Rosemonde counsels her husband not to appear on the parade ground because of a dream she has had. She fears Ubu's treachery.

On the parade ground, the king is assassinated according to plan. Back at the palace, Bougrelas and the queen narrowly escape. Bougrelas swears vengeance. He meets the ghost of the founder of the royal household, who admonishes him to seek revenge. Now in the king's palace, Ubu and his consort are advised by Bordure to distribute money and food to the populace so they will pay taxes. As these gifts are dispensed, there is general rejoicing. Later, Ubu decides to retract his promise of a dukedom to Bordure and rejects Mother Ubu's suggestion that Bougrelas should be bought off. When Mother Ubu warns of the consequences, Ubu threatens her. Next, Ubu abolishes all the nobles' titles and after a mock trial condemns them to death.

Ubu decides to go from village to village and collect taxes himself, but now the peasantry is in revolt against the excessive levies. Bordure, in chains, manages to escape and vows to overthrow Ubu. In Moscow, the czar and Bordure seal a pact of war. Meanwhile, in his council chamber, Ubu describes the subjugation of his people. A messenger brings news that Bordure and the czar are invading Poland. In a frenzy of fear, Ubu refuses to mobilize an army because it is too expensive, but he agrees to wage war.

At a camp outside Warsaw, soldiers prepare for battle. Ubu reviews the motley troops, mounts his starving horse, and flees to the mountains, leaving Mother Ubu to organize the defense. Later, in the crypt of the king of Poland in Warsaw Cathedral, Mother Ubu is looting the royal treasury when a mysterious voice frightens her away, gold in hand. Bougrelas, having entered Warsaw, rallies his troops, slaughtering his enemies and pursuing Mother Ubu.

Father Ubu, marching through the Ukraine, is routed by the Russians. Bordure and the czar attack, and Ubu nearly kills the Russian monarch. The Russians counterattack, wipe out Ubu's army, and force him to flee to a cave in Lithuania. A bear enters and attacks Ubu's ministers, while Ubu hides, reciting the Pater Noster in Latin. The bear is killed by an explosion of divine origin and Ubu prepares to roast it, but he falls asleep and is deserted by his ministers. He dreams of vanquishing his enemies.

Mother Ubu, having escaped from Bougrelas, finds her husband in the cave. The couple exchange obscene insults, accuse each other of cheating and stealing, and begin to fight. Ubu throws the bear on his wife and proceeds to beat her when Bougrelas arrives with his soldiers and beats Ubu. But Ubu's men arrive and rescue their king. He flees with his consort. Ubu boards a ship for Paris, where he hopes for a ministerial post.

Critical Opinion

During his short life, Alfred Jarry developed his Ubu plays from a juvenile concoction of satirical episodes into a comprehensive attack upon literature, politics, sexual mores, religion, and, perhaps above all, the false logic and apprehensions of "normal" existence. When Jarry was fifteen, he met the Morin brothers and helped them develop a lampoon against their physics teacher, a Monsieur Hébert. The Polish elements and the scatological character of the work appealed to Jarry's iconoclastic imagination, and he fashioned a play for marionettes from this first crude comedy. In subesquent revisions, Jarry developed a whole mystique around Father and Mother Ubu as he extended the possibilities of the lycée sketch.

King Ubu is a burlesque on Shakespeare filtered through a Rabelaisian vision. Adopting the scatological, distorted, and inventive language of the sixteenth-century author of *Gargantua and Pantagruel*, Jarry employed puns and nonsense and distorted words to convey the absurdity of life. Father Ubu apparently follows the same course as Macbeth: he is encouraged by his wife to assassinate the king, is assaulted by visions and ghosts, and loses his kingdom through mismanagement of the conspiracy. *Julius Caesar*,

Hamlet, Richard III, and *Oedipus Rex* are also burlesqued. The queen and young Bougrelas warn the king of impending doom. Bougrelas is accosted by the ghost of his father's ancestors and spurred to revenge, and Ubu is obsessed by his horse, which he starves to death out of sheer penuriousness. The play's dedication contains punning allusions to Shakespeare's tragedies. The orchestra (as indicated in the manuscript) is an absurd ensemble of real and imaginary Elizabethan instruments.

The political satire of *King Ubu* is, perhaps, not as crude as the action. Lust, avarice, opportunism, and misuse of power seem to be universal among the world's rulers. Jarry's exaggerations are only slightly more ridiculous than the actions of rulers past and present. Ubu conducts mock trials of the nobles and executes them to obtain their power and wealth. He appropriates his kingdom's fortune for his private use; he bribes the peasantry with circuses and gold; he betrays his fellow-conspirators; he starves the horse that he needs to conduct military operations; and he behaves with a forthright brutality that is shocking but not unusual. Ubu revels in his brazen misrule, boasting:

> A considerable number of our hirelings wearing wool stockings prowl the streets every morning and the sons of whores are doing fine. In all directions you can only see burning houses and the sight of our peoples groaning under the weight of our phynance [administration].

Ubu refuses to mobilize an army because it is too costly. He betrays his closest allies and, engaging in battlefield histrionics, reveals his cowardice. Exhorting his troops to slay the enemy, he hastily retreats and spends most of his time fleeing from the invading army of Russians.

The geographical designations in the play reflect a peculiarly Gallic sense of humor. To the French, the countries of Poland, Russia, and Lithuania evoke images of coarse, violent, oppressive boors who are insensitive to the refinements of civilization. At the Théâtre de l'Oeuvre premiere (December 10, 1896) Jarry also explained that the comedy "takes place in the legendary country of Poland or No-Where":

NoWhere is everywhere. And first of all, the country you are in. It's for this reason that Ubu speaks French. But his diverse faults are not exclusively French vices, which also favor Captain Bordure, who speaks English, the Queen Rosemonde, who chatters in Cantal [French dialect], and the Polish hordes, who talk nasally, dressed in grey. If diverse satires can be seen, the place setting makes the actors irreproachable.

Ubu's behavior is gross and obscene. Mother Ubu is a scabby, vengeful woman who takes Ubu's throne after his exile and loots the treasury, thus betraying even her husband. The counselors are stupid lackeys, and everyone in the play is confused, brutal, and selfish.

Following the example of Rabelais, Jarry employed Latin and profanity to mock religion and piety. Frequent references to God's genitals and excretory functions, and profane oaths, provide shock value and underline the iconoclasm that informs the entire drama. Obscenity, when applied to revered institutions such as (in the nineteenth century at least) kingship and religion, provides the humor of shock. Distorting, misquoting, and misusing theological materials, Jarry mocks institutions and people whose emphasis on decorum masks nonsense or perfidy.

When a bear attacks Ubu's men, the dethroned king crawls onto a rock (a pulpit) and in Latin intones the Pater Noster. But his prayer, punctuated by the cries of battle, is a sacrilegious perversion of the ritual. At its end, an explosion brings about the death of the bear and an amen from Ubu. Later, when Mother Ubu masquerades as an apparition and reveals that she has taken some of her husband's treasure, Ubu is gratified to know that the divine revelation has been confirmed. Quoting a Latin phrase: "Omnis a Deo scientia" (All wisdom comes from God), he mistranslates Latin words, demonstrating that he has learned his Latin by rote and that he considers *himself* a divine creature.

A source of both comedy and satire, sexual innuendo in *King Ubu* is both direct and subtle. The opening word of the drama is a comic distortion of the word *shit* ("merde" is transmogrified into "merdre"), and although not sexual, the reference to bodily functions soon gives way to other epithets. The transformation of a suggestive word into a nonsense word has a more obscene effect than the word itself. Ubu swears by a green candle (his penis) and continually insults Mother Ubu with scurrilous epithets: "salopin" (slut), "bourrique" (she-ass). He praises her ugliness and makes insulting anatomical references, often changing off-color words so they are more gross through their mispronunciation or the false squeamishness implied.

This manipulation of language goes beyond the sexual level and is, at times, purely farcical. Puns are used to extend meanings of words such as the battle of the Voracious and Niggardly *(les Voraces contre les Coriaces.)*

But language is not an end in itself. The entire argument of the play reflects Jarry's rejection of conventional drama and his espousal of exaggerated and illogical modes of expression. When Ubu announces: "I want to be rich. After that, I'll kill everyone and go away," he is expressing the quintessence of a political mentality that, unfortunately, dates from the beginning of civilization. Ubu's success is absurd and shocking. He is the embodiment of secret desires and nightmares.

Jarry's use of short, disconnected scenes, slapstick, and cruelty jarred conventional audiences. The violent action and language, the bloody battles, and the energy of the irrepressible protagonist give the drama a demonic thrust. Jarry's vision influenced the surrealist poets in France and may be seen in the works of contemporary avant-garde playwrights.

King Ubu, opened in 1896, was greeted by a riot in the theater and an hysterical critical battle that raged from the cafés to the newspapers. Modern productions have been frequent. One of the most notable was Jean Vilar's 1958 Paris presentation of a two-act condensed version of *King Ubu* and *Ubu sur la Butte.* The nature of this comedy has made it popular with amateur and semiprofessional performers, and *King Ubu* has often been given in informal theaters, such as café-nightclubs.

Jarry's wild farce, which savagely attacks bourgeois complacency in the activities of the monstrous tyrant Ubu, heralds the mad world of the Theater of the Absurd. Eugène Ionesco, for example, is a direct descendant of Alfred Jarry. The inventive language, grotesque characterization, and social satire of *King Ubu* anticipated Ionesco's *The Bald Soprano, The Chairs,* and *Jack, or The Submission.* Creating a *succès de scandale,* but having only two performances during its first run, *King Ubu* is now hailed as a landmark. Jarry is regarded as one of the originators of the concepts and techniques found in much of our contemporary drama.

The Author

Alfred Jarry was born in Rennes, the major city of the French province of Brittany, on September 8, 1873. He started writing at an early age, creating his first poems when he was twelve. In 1888, the young Jarry encountered Henri and Charles Morin in the *lycée* and helped them expand their satire, *The Poles.* As a schoolboy of fifteen, Jarry wrote and performed a puppet play about Père Hébé, later Père Ubu—one of the teachers at his *lycée* who was the butt of his friends' ridicule. From this beginning came the mythical figure of "King Ubu," his grotesque, Rabelaisian caricature of man's greed and cruelty.

Jarry moved to Paris in 1891 and encountered many of the influential literary figures of the day. His first book, *The Minutes of Memorial Sand,* met with little success. After six months in the army, he published *Caesar Anti-Christ.* In 1896, he founded and sponsored a lavish art review that bankrupted him. But Lugué-Poë, the avant-garde producer and director, gave him a job. *King Ubu* was published in December 1896 and performed at Lugué-Poë's Théâtre de l'Oeuvre, with artistic creations by Toulouse-Lautrec, Bonnard, and Vuillard. Two years later, the play was produced with marionettes.

From the first performance of *King Ubu,* Jarry became identified with his character and even began to employ Ubu's coarse language and mannerisms. He continued to expand the Ubu theme during the succeeding years, adding *Ubu Cuckolded* and, in 1899, *Ubu in Chains,* performed in 1937. Because of the scurrilous nature of these comedies, Jarry was unable to get either play published or performed during his lifetime. He continued, however, to incorporate his protagonist into other short works, wrote a series of songs, and presented a rewritten *King Ubu* (again for marionettes) in 1901, under the title *Ubu sur la Butte*. In his novel about Dr. Faustroll (1911), he elaborated the "science" of "Pataphysics," which is at the root of many plays of the Theater of the Absurd.

Jarry lived the life of Ubu, embarking upon a wildly extravagant existence of eating and drinking. He quickly squandered his small inheritance. His health declined. He nearly died from total physical collapse in 1906, but recovered briefly. In 1907, Alfred Jarry succumbed in a charity hospital in Paris, a disappointed young man whose violently ludicrous vision of society was too unconventional for popular tastes—although, in the light of World War II, it was prophetic of man's brutality.

Liliom

by

FERENC MOLNÁR (1878–1952)

The Characters

Liliom—a handsome, energetic young man whose vanity and
boldness make him attractive to all women. Liliom is a
basically sensitive and passionate man who is torn by
forces he does not understand. He is true to himself and
unbroken by convention.

Julie—a pretty and naive girl with a profoundly loving
nature. Her utter devotion to Liliom, both as a man and
a memory, gives her beauty and strength.

Mrs. Muskat—the middle-aged owner of the carousel who
jealously demands that Liliom abandon Julie. Essentially
good-natured and shrewd, she does not allow her strong
attraction to Liliom to conquer her pride.

Marie—Julie's companion and confidante. Although unthinking and conventional, she is generous and loyal to
Julie. Her marriage to Wolf and their subsequent affluence
do not change her naiveté.

Wolf Beifeld—Marie's Jewish husband who industriously
advances from a porter to the owner of a luxurious café.
He is simple, warm-hearted, complacent, and generous.

Mrs. Hollander—a scrappy, cynical woman, who allows
Liliom and her niece Julie to live in her photographic studio
She dislikes Liliom because he refuses to work.

Ficsur—a malignant, hyenalike man who persuades Liliom

to attempt robbery. Totally without loyalty or conscience, he cheats and deserts Liliom.

Linzman—the wily and resourceful factory cashier who Liliom and Ficsur plan to rob. He is proficient in defending himself and has a sardonic sense of humor.

The Magistrate—in the heavenly courtroom, he presides over suicide cases, giving each person a chance to return to earth and do a good deed.

Louise—Julie and Liliom's sixteen-year-old daughter. Like her mother, she is gentle, trusting, and loving, and when Liliom strikes her, she too is astonished that the blow does not hurt.

The Story

In a Budapest amusement park at the turn of the century, Liliom, a virile, handsome young man, presides as a barker on Mrs. Muskat's carousel. Amid a tumult of noise, movement, and color, he delivers a harangue to prospective riders, flirts with the girls on the carousel, and intimidates their escorts. The prologue suddenly ends, and in a remote corner of the amusement park, Marie and Julie, two young servant girls, enter, arguing about whether or not they should run from Mrs. Muskat who is pursuing them. The formidable Mrs. Muskat arrives and berates Julie for letting Liliom take liberties with her on the carousel. She says Julie will be thrown off the carousel if she ever rides again, but Liliom comes in and turns on his employer, defending his right to flirt with anyone. During an argument with Mrs. Muskat, Liliom defiantly asserts his prerogatives. He does not relent when he is reluctantly discharged by Mrs. Muskat.

Liliom promises to take Julie and Marie to the Hungarian Beer Garden after he collects his things from the carousel. Waiting for him, the girls naively banter about their romantic attachments. Marie thinks that she has lost her heart to a soldier who, it turns out, is merely a porter in uniform. Liliom returns and tells one of the girls to stay and the other to go home. Marie reminds Julie that if she does not return she will lose her job, but Julie stays with Liliom, who coarsely insinuates that she could have only one reason for staying in the park with him.

Two policemen enter, check Liliom's identity, and bluntly warn Julie of her escort's bad reputation. Julie reaffirms her desire to remain in the park with Liliom. The policemen leave, and as the lights dim, music from the amusement park drifts in, and a white acacia blossom falls. Liliom picks it up and savors its fragrance.

Two months later, Liliom and Julie are living together in her aunt's photographic studio on the edge of the amusement park. Marie is told that Liliom beat up his replacement on the carousel, and Mrs. Hollander complains that Liliom is a good-for-nothing. Marie then recounts in an amusingly naive fashion her Passionate Love and Ideal Love with Wolf, the porter. But Julie's life is darkened by more worldly cares, for Liliom will not find a job, has fallen in with a bad crowd, and has beaten her. The music from the carousel robs him of his gentleness and turns him into a manic, violent being.

Mrs. Muskat arrives, announcing that she will rehire Liliom. He enters with Ficsur after an all-night bout of card-playing and drinking. Liliom considers Mrs. Muskat's offer, but broods about her jealous demand that he desert Julie. Mrs. Muskat calls Liliom an artist and summons him back to his art. He nearly decides to return to the carousel when Julie confides to him that she is pregnant. Liliom rejects Mrs. Muskat's offer and asks Ficsur how to get money. As the distant sounds from the amusement park filter in, Ficsur mentions a scheme to rob the cashier of a leather factory. The music increases in intensity; Liliom shouts: "I'm going to be a father!" and then throws himself despairingly on the sofa.

Later that afternoon, Ficsur is teaching Liliom a sardonic thieves' song about "the damn police [who'll] get you every time." They formulate a plan to rob the cashier. Ficsur is determined to murder the man despite Liliom's squeamishness. Suddenly, a policeman comes into the studio to have his portrait taken. Liliom and Ficsur ironically hum their song. Ficsur taunts the policeman while Liliom steals Mrs. Hollander's kitchen knife. When Julie pleads with Liliom to spend the afternoon with Marie and Wolf, her fiancé, Liliom ignores her and leaves, just as Mrs. Hollander discovers the theft of the knife. Julie is horrified, for she realizes that Liliom has taken it. She suppresses her panic, however, when Marie brings Wolf in to be introduced. The young couple make a striking contrast with Julie and Liliom. As they are having their engagement photograph taken, the bitter refrain of the thieves' song floats into the studio, throwing Julie into despair.

Ficsur entices Liliom into a card game while they are waiting to ambush the cashier. Liliom is cheated out of his share of the loot. Just as Liliom is about to attack Ficsur, the cashier appears. When Liliom asks him for the time, Ficsur sneaks up and is about to stab him, but the cashier is alert, disarms Ficsur, and holds the two criminals with a revolver he has quickly drawn from his pocket. Two policemen approach on horseback, and Ficsur wrenches free of the cashier's restraining grip and flees. Liliom, trapped between the gun-bearing cashier and the police, draws the knife from his jacket and plunges it into his breast. The cashier rushes to telephone for a doctor while the two policemen stand over Liliom's bleeding body and complain about their low pay.

Half an hour later, Liliom is brought into the studio. Alone with Julie, he confesses that he beat her "not because I was mad at you—no—only because I can't bear to see anyone crying. You always cried on my account." He wanted to take Julie away to America, but now he has lost everything and will not see his child. He tells Julie to marry the widowed carpenter who has shown interest in her. Julie stonily agrees, and Liliom reiterates: "When I beat you— I was right—You must not always think—you mustn't always be right." His head sinks to the pillow. The doctor enters and pronounces him dead. Everyone says that Liliom was not a good man and Julie is fortunate he is dead. She quietly seems to agree with them, but when she is alone with his body, she proclaims her love for Liliom. The widowed carpenter enters to pay court to Julie, but is gently sent away.

After Julie leaves, a "graver, more exalted" form of the carousel music is heard, and two dark-clad men enter, arouse Liliom, and bid him follow them. They are the celestial police who bring Liliom before a tribunal, for although he is dead, his business on earth will not be ended while he is still remembered.

In a whitewashed courtroom, Liliom awaits his turn at

the bar. Two other prisoners, also suicides, plead before the magistrate. One, a richly dressed man, is given permission to return to earth so that he can kiss his little son goodbye. When Liliom's case is heard, he surlily refuses to return to earth; he regrets nothing and has no pangs about Julie and his unborn child. He admits that he beat Julie because he could not bear to see her weep. Suddenly, it is revealed that Liliom is on trial for his cruelty to Julie, not for the attempted robbery or his suicide. The magistrate asks Liliom if he would return to earth as a caretaker and live in domestic comfort with Julie, and he refuses: "Because— because that's just why I died." The magistrate retorts: "You died because you loved your little Julie and the child she is bearing under her heart." Liliom is temporarily dismissed and a poorly dressed man who committed suicide thirteen years earlier tells how on his return to earth he patched a leaky roof over his orphans' heads. The man is permitted to go to eternal rest, but Liliom must remain in purgatory for sixteen years, until his child is grown and his pride and stubbornness are burned from him.

Sixteen years later, Julie and Louise, her daughter, are entertaining a prosperous, middle-aged Marie and Wolf, who has had great success as a café owner. After they leave, mother and daughter sit down to dinner. Liliom appears and begins to talk with Louise. Julie, who has her back to Liliom, tries to send him away, but Liliom begins speaking of old times and Julie is intrigued. They talk of Julie's husband, and Liliom shares their meal. But when Liliom talks disrespectfully about his earthbound self, Julie dismisses him. Louise leads him to the gate and refuses Liliom's offer of a star plucked from heaven. She points the way out of the yard, and Liliom impulsively slaps her hand. The sound of the blow is loud, but Louise is unhurt. Liliom contritely faces Julie and admits striking the girl, but Louise exclaims that it felt like a kiss or a caress, and she asks her mother if she ever was struck without being hurt. Julie replies: "It is possible, dear—that someone may beat you and beat you—and not hurt you at all."

Critical Opinion

Liliom, a curious mixture of several dramatic styles, has charmed audiences since its first production in Budapest in 1909. The play is puzzling because of its philosophical and intellectual pretenses and the strange juxtaposition of romantic fantasy, expressionism, and naturalism. The opening evokes a poetic and fanciful world of lights, music, and carnival gaiety, but subsequent scenes develop a sordid naturalistic tale that could very well have appealed to Emile Zola. The seduction of a servant girl by a coarse and egotistical braggart, her pregnancy, the shiftlessness of the man and his suicide during a foiled robbery attempt are the materials of depressing and moralistic melodrama. But Molnár's daring insertion of blatantly sentimental and artfully poetic elements relieves this oppression.

Liliom is the modern antihero, shiftless, arrogant, vain, stupid, and cruel. But there is a touch of the lover and poet in his proud, contradictory personality. He beats Julie on the face, arms, and breast and refuses to go to work. Yet he is fiercely loyal to her and will not return to Mrs. Muskat's employ if he must desert her. He is a bully and a criminal; yet the sounds of the amusement park—with their suggestion of imaginative fantasy, gaiety, gentle fun, art, and artifice— provide a *leitmotif* that enthralls him. He refuses to settle into a mundane domestic existence and accept the stifling job of caretaker in order to support Julie and his new child. This pride and independence are both laudable and selfish, for every man abhors the compromises he must make with his soul's deepest instincts to survive in this world. Liliom's suicide is a defiant gesture against materialism. Death is preferable to imprisonment, either in a caretaker's job or a prison.

After the imaginative, evocative prologue, the play develops a lyrical and humane portrait of love, jealousy, sin, and redemption. Mrs. Muskat's infatuation with Liliom is thinly disguised when she berates Julie for enticing Liliom, whose attraction to Julie is part bravado and part lust. But to assert his independence from Mrs. Muskat, Liliom quits his job and takes up with the young girl. Only toward the end of the first scene, while sitting on a bench with Julie, does he express tenderness or affection. As twilight descends, Liliom picks up a blossom that has fallen from a tree and exclaims with childlike rapture: "White acacias!" His responsiveness to its beauty and fragrance is a symbol of the poetic and creative instinct beneath his arrogance. Julie, the embodiment of the long-suffering, loyal, and pure woman, recognizes this hidden sensitivity and remains devoted to it. Julie also understands Liliom's tenderness and forgives his later cruelty: "Afterwards he got wild—sometimes. But that night on the bench . . . he was gentle. He's gentle now, sometimes, very gentle. After supper, when he stands there and listens to the music of the carousel, something comes over him and he is gentle."

The carousel's music provokes violent emotions in Liliom. A *leitmotif* that symbolizes his attraction to libidinous freedom, it is also a reminder of his art—the art of the circus barker who can lure crowds into a world of fantasy. Mrs. Muskat tries to summon Liliom back to the carousel by appealing to his deeper nature: "Out there is your *art*, the only thing you're fit for. You are an artist, not a respectable married man."

The recurrence of the carnival music underlines the contradictory forces that tear at Liliom's soul. At the close of Scene II, he is elated to learn that Julie is pregnant, but the sound of the carousel organ causes him to "throw himself on the sofa and bury his face in the cushion." His natural instincts about fatherhood are those of pride, tenderness, and hope; yet he realizes that he will become irrevocably tied to a materialistic, conventional, and demanding world. He insists that he will never become a caretaker and settle down in domestic squalor, but his desperate need to avoid the confinements of society turn him into an outlaw. On his deathbed, Liliom is unrepentant: "I'm not asking—forgiveness—I don't do that—I don't. Tell the baby—if you like."

In the heavenly court, Liliom remains unrepentant and asks only for eternal rest. When forced to return to earth sixteen years later, after a term in purgatory, he is purified but not changed. He strikes Louise when she refuses to accept a star he has stolen from heaven, but the blow is a caress, and Molnár reveals the key to Liliom's tortured personality with poetic simplicity. Julie says: "It is possible, dear—that someone may beat you and beat you—and not hurt you at all."

Molnár's dramatic technique in *Liliom* changes abruptly from naturalism to expressionism when the hero dies. An almost scientific attention to details about the characters' heredity and environment creates a realism that at first appears to be inconsistent with the sudden appearance of heavenly policemen and the stark, other-worldly courtroom scenes. But Molnár carefully inserted nonnaturalistic elements into the first scenes in order to effect a subtle modulation from realism to lyricism.

The play opens on a stylized and fantastical note. The carousel, a symbol of freedom, sensuality, and art, becomes a central image in the play. Although the audience does not see this symbol again, its music constantly recalls these elements. Lighting effects, especially in the park and robbery episodes, convey a lyrical feeling. The expressionism of the courtroom scene, with its stark properties (a whitewashed room, green-topped table, bench, door, bell, and window through which can be seen a vista of rose-tinted clouds) is a jarring contrast to the gratingly real world of hostile policemen, economic hardship, lust, jealousy, and suicide. The coordination of these seemingly disparate elements reveals the unity of purpose and technique underlying Molnàr's dramaturgy.

To fully portray the contradictory nature of the human personality, Molnár presents contrasting perspectives: Liliom had to appear as both a real, earthbound human being and as an abstract figure who is the spiritual and moral quintessence of his earthly self. Molnár's naturalism effectively allows Liliom's spiritual beauty to be seen in the context of his flesh and blood existence. The playwright's expressionistic technique complements the naturalistic portrait of Liliom. The juxtaposition and blending of these two styles unify this sentimental drama.

Liliom puzzled Budapest audiences in 1909. Its unconventional dramaturgy and dense philosophizing caused some critics to reject it as obscure or pretentious. The autobiographical elements of the fantasy may also have accounted for the initial critical reactions. Literary gossips knew that when Molnár was divorcing his first wife, she testified that he had struck his young daughter. The curious admixture of autobiography, sentimentality, naturalism, and expressionism vitiated the play's initial reception. After World War I, however, when Central Europeans understood more about expressionism, the play was widely accepted. It was produced in London and Paris, and for the first time in New York in 1920. Revived again twenty years later, starring Ingrid Bergman and Burgess Meredith, the play was less enthusiastically received. American audiences are most familiar with *Liliom* through Rodgers and Hammerstein's musical adaptation, *Carousel* (1945).

The Author

Ferenc Molnár abandoned the legal profession to devote his life to literature. His first pieces were nondramatic, and although he realized some success with the novel *The Paul Street Boys* (1907), his plays were to bring him his greatest fame. Beginning with *The Devil* (1907) and continuing with *Liliom* (1909), *The Guardsman* (1910), *The Swan* (1920), and *The Glass Slipper* (1924), Molnár established himself as one of the most entertaining creators of the comedy of manners. Most of his plays reflect the author's sophisticated experience as a celebrated and lionized young man in prewar Budapest, which, next to Vienna, was the greatest center of European worldliness and intrigue. The charm and facility of Molnár's rather superficial dramas appealed to international audiences; they still attract film and stage stars as popular vehicles.

Before World War II, Molnár settled in the United States, where his new plays were coldly received. Though he was unfortunate in his new ventures, glamor and wealth came to him through recognition of his earlier triumphs. *The Play's the Thing* (1924), and *Carousel* (1945), the Rodgers and Hammerstein adaptation of *Liliom,* were audience favorites. Molnár died in America in 1952.

The Trojan War Will Not Take Place (Tiger at the Gates)

by

JEAN GIRAUDOUX (1882–1944)

The Characters

Andromaque—a gentle, noble, kind young woman whose love for her husband, Hector, and concern for humanity move her to fight against the inevitability of war.

Helen—beautiful and vain, she has willingly fled from her Greek husband, Menelaus, and eloped to Troy with Paris. She is totally indifferent to the war that her presence in Troy provokes, and she betrays Paris even before the war begins. Helen has the ability to foresee the future; anything that will happen is seen in bright colors. The impossible appears in dull tones.

Hecuba—Priam's cynical, strong-willed wife.

Cassandra—endowed with the ability to predict future events, she prophesies the Trojan War.

Hector—a brave, humane, and noble young general who is tired of war and contends against incredible odds to prevent a war with Greece.

Ulysses—the Greek war hero who has been sent to Troy as an ambassador of war. Despite his conviction that war is inevitable, he tries to escape destiny.

Priam—the elderly Trojan ruler who, like his subjects, is infatuated with Helen. Reluctantly, he agrees to permit Helen's return to Greece if she and Paris consent.

Paris—Hector's vain and impulsive younger brother, an incurable Don Juan.

Oiax—a drunken Greek sailor.

Demokes—a Trojan poet who sees Helen as the incarnation of beauty and poetic inspiration.

The Story

On the ramparts of Troy, Andromaque and Cassandra discuss the impending war between Troy and Greece. Andromaque poignantly insists that the war will not take place. The soldiers, led by her husband, Hector, are returning victorious from battle; she is pregnant, and the world is beautiful. Cassandra, however, is convinced that there will be a war. Paris has run away with the Greek Helen, and everyone is willing to fight to keep her. War is their destiny. Cassandra conjures up the image of a tiger sleeping at the gates of Troy. As Hector approaches the palace, the tiger opens his eyes, stretches, and begins to move.

Hector and Andromaque joyfully embrace. They speak of how men are attracted to war. Hector denies any love of battle, insisting that this last war "rings false." Hector questions Paris about Helen and learns that all the men of Troy are in love with her. She is beauty incarnate. In the distance, the old men are heard shouting salutations to Helen.

Hector confronts Priam and demands that he close the war gates. He argues that Helen must be returned to the Greeks in order to avoid war. The poet Demokes protests that Helen is the symbol of beauty, the principle of courage and energy. The mathematician calls her "our barometer" and Andromaque and Hecuba make snide comments about the old men's stupidity. In the name of all women, Andromaque begs Priam to avoid war. "Let the animals die in men's places." Paris and Priam agree to return Helen to Menelaus if she is willing.

Paris introduces his prize, but before leaving her, he asks Helen to swear that she loves him and that she will never return to Greece. Hector quickly perceives that Helen is easily influenced. She confesses that she has an unusual gift of vision: what will occur, she sees in vivid colors; what is impossible, she sees as dull gray. The war seems inevitable, but Helen agrees to go back to Greece with Ulysses. Hector tells Cassandra: "Everyone gives in to me. . . . And on the contrary I feel that in each one of these apparent victories, I've lost." Cassandra calls for Peace to appear, but in Helen's vision Peace is pale and sick.

Near the palace, in view of the war gates, Paris finds Helen flirting with fifteen-year-old Troilus. Everyone gathers for the gate-closing ceremony. While they wait, the mathematician suggests that they must think of some insults for the Greeks. Busiris, a legal expert, arrives to advise the senators about whether or not they should declare war on Greece. Hector says: "The war will not take place," while Busiris proceeds to discuss three ridiculous reasons why they must declare war. In each instance, he cites a precedent in which Greece vanquished its enemy. Hector threatens to have Busiris killed if he does not find an equally convincing argument to stop the battle. Busiris quickly complies. Priam asks Hector to give a speech in honor of the war-gate closing. Hector refuses to glorify the dead: "War seems to me to be the most sordid and the most hypocritical means of equalizing humans, and I will not allow for death to be a punishment or expiation for the cowardly or a recompense for the living." The gates are closed, as Hecuba (who earlier had said that war looked like Helen) declares that the war resembles a monkey's behind.

Andromaque sends little Polyxene to talk to Helen, but the child confuses her message. Andromaque confronts Helen and asks her whether or not she loves Paris. When Helen replies that she does not, Andromaque laments the pointlessness of the war: "To think that we are going to suffer, to die, for an official couple . . . that's the horror." Helen calmly asserts that humanity is made up of both martyrs and stars. If Andromaque insists on a perfect couple to make the war worthwhile, let the love of Hector and herself serve this purpose.

The Greeks arrive. A drunken warrior, Oiax, precedes Ulysses and insults Hector, who ignores him. Demokes taunts Hector and is slapped. Ulysses, who arrives to declare war, is surprised to learn that Helen will be returned. He insists that Paris must have violated Helen during the voyage to Troy, but Hector denies this. Two Trojan sailors, feeling their national pride has been insulted, describe their captain's amorous conquest. The divine messenger, Iris, interrupts the argument to bring contradictory messages from Aphrodite and Pallas and from Zeus, who suggests that Hector and Ulysses settle the argument.

The two great leaders begin by weighing their respective worth, and both men quickly see that Ulysses is stronger. Ulysses, who knows that Helen is merely Fate's object, agrees to try to overcome destiny, take Helen back to Greece, and avoid war. As he leaves, he confesses he was won over because "Andromaque blinks her eyes just like Penelope."

As Hector and Andromaque watch Ulysses descend toward his ship, Oiax rushes forward and insults Hector by vulgarly embracing Andromaque. Hector overcomes his urge to stab the sailor, and when Demokes denounces his cowardice, calling for war, Hector stabs him: "The war will not take place." Moments before he dies, Demokes says he has been murdered by Oiax, who must be punished. Hector sorrowfully whispers: "It will take place." And the war gates are opened to reveal Helen kissing young Troilus. "The Trojan poet is dead," Cassandra declares: "the word is for the Greek poet."

Critical Opinion

The Trojan War Will Not Take Place is a drama in which word-play, metaphor, and argument are more important than the dramatic situations themselves. Instead of developing psychological personalities, Giraudoux makes the characters vehicles for their speeches. This juxtaposition of linguistic and philosophical assertions provides a unique type of dramatic conflict.

The ironic first line and title of the play derives its force from the audience's knowledge of Greek mythology. Giraudoux plays on this contradiction of history through constant reiteration by different characters. In the final line of the drama, when Cassandra, who can foresee the future, declares: "The Trojan poet is dead. . . . The word is for the Greek poet," Giraudoux is saying that "the word" has been his protagonist.

The play's action centers upon Hector's effort to avoid

war by sending Helen back to Greece. Although everyone
acquiesces, all await the inevitable battle. Hector repeatedly
says: "Listen to that negative block which says 'yes'! Everyone has given in to me. Paris has given in to me, Priam
has given in to me, Helen has given in to me. And in each
one of these apparent victories I feel on the contrary that
I have lost."

The road to battle is an accumulation of definitions,
metaphors, and verbal conflicts. When Andromaque asks
Cassandra if destiny could be interested in their disasters,
the prophetess replies that destiny is "simply the accelerated
form of time." She elaborates with a metaphor: destiny is
like a tiger, sleeping at the gates of Troy, who is jolted out
of innocent slumber, opens one eye, stretches, licks himself,
and starts to move. Andromaque confuses the image with
her husband. And Hector *is* the tiger, an instrument of
destiny, who despite his effort to the contrary starts the war.

Helen is the incarnation of beauty, voluptuousness, and
creative inspiration. She awakens sexual lust in the old men
of Troy and is a symbol of national pride. It does not matter
that she is indifferent to Paris, or even unfaithful to him.
Like Hector, she is an instrument of destiny: "She is one of
those rare creatures that destiny puts in circulation on earth
for personal use," observes Ulysses, pinpointing the essential
problem of the play. "The difficulty of life is to distinguish
between objects. Which is destiny's hostage?" The war is
inevitable because too many instruments of destiny are
present in Troy.

If Act I can be described as a series of definitions, Act
II consists of philosophical confrontations. The debates
between Helen and Andromaque summarize the playwright's
view of the universe. Andromaque is concerned with order.
Man, beast, and plants must be in harmony. In the first
act, when Hector and Andromaque talk about war in terms
of discord ("Everything rings false"), they point to the
disorder in Troy, which Andromaque attributes to Helen.
The world is made up of "true" and "false" couples. Andromaque does not want people to suffer and die merely because
of the superficial, frivolous activity of an "official" couple:
"To think that we are going to suffer, to die, for an official
couple, that the splendor or the misfortune of the ages, that
the habits of thinking for centuries is going to be based on

the adventure of two beings who didn't love each other, there's the horror." If Helen does not love Paris, then war, preserving nothing, becomes an injustice. Less romantic than her adversary, Helen separates people into two categories: "Those who are . . . the flesh of human life, and those who are the spark, the rhythm. The first have the laughter, the tears, and all you might wish in secretions. The others have the gesture, the pose, the look. If you force them to belong to only one race, that will not work at all. Humanity owes as much to her stars as to her martyrs."

Andromaque is an idealist who believes that universal accord and happiness are attainable, while the pragmatic Helen, indifferent to events, recognizes that the world is composed of disparate elements whose conflicts account for universal complexity and discord. Couples like Andromaque and Hector fulfill mankind's need for ideals. Helen and Paris are the arbitrary and often empty face of reality.

Hector's speech for the dead supports the view that mankind is composed of individuals, some more desirable than others. Ironically, Troy's hero and general is her most ardent pacifist. When Hector defines war as "the most sordid and the most hypocritical means of equalizing humans," and declares that he "will not allow for death to be a punishment or expiation for the cowardly or a recompense for the living," he expresses a universal condemnation of all wars.

In the confrontation between Hector and Ulysses, Hector epitomizes the young, conscientious, life-loving leader who is devoted to his agricultural peoples. Ulysses, the world-weary general, however, wins the test of strength. He is distrustful of life, circumspect before gods, men, and things, and aware of the hardships of work and man's victimization by the elements. Maturity brings caution and a consciousness of man's precarious position in the universe. Although Ulysses believes that the war is inevitable because he has seen the workings of destiny, he will try to help Hector avoid the conflict which his weaknesses seem certain to bring about. But ironically, human idosyncrasy, which encourages the fight against destiny, is the cause of the ultimate outbreak of war. Despite man's rational efforts to overcome Fate, war is precipitated by accident.

While Giraudoux recognizes the dramaturgical necessities,

he maintains that poetic language must have a dramatic expression in order to move the audience:

> The theater is not an algebraic formula but a show; not arithmetic but magic. It should appeal to the imagination and the senses, not the intellect. For this reason the playwright must have literary ability, for it is his style that shines into the minds and hearts of the audience. Its poetry need not be understood any more than sunlight need be understood to be enjoyed.

Giraudoux uses metaphor to fire the imagination of his audience.

Written in 1935, *The Trojan War Will Not Take Place* anticipates the disaster that was to precipitate France into war with Germany four years later. Like Troy and Greece in the play, France and Germany at the time of Giraudoux's drama both seemed geared for a prosperous future, but they were headed for inevitable disaster.

The play was first performed at the Théâtre Athénée on November 21, 1935, under the direction of Louis Jouvet, who also took the role of Hector. Nearly twenty years later, Sir Michael Redgrave starred in Christopher Frye's adaptation, *Tiger at the Gates,* for audiences in London and New York.

The Madwoman of Chaillot

by

JEAN GIRAUDOUX (1882–1944)

The Characters

Countess Aurelia, the Madwoman of Chaillot—a loquacious and eccentric client of the Café Chez Francis in the Chaillot section of Paris; the guardian angel of lovers, vagabonds, and madwomen. Good-humored, compassionate, and optimistic, she saves the Chaillot district from oil prospectors by galvanizing the population into action.

Constance, the Madwoman of Passy—long-time friend of Countess Aurelia, and owner of an invisible dog.

Gabrielle, the Madwoman of Saint-Sulpice—she chatters with an imaginary companion, but can put her fantasy aside to prevent the destruction of Paris.

Josephine, the Madwoman of the Concord—instigates the mock trial of the exploiters to justify their death sentence.

The Prospector—shrewd, enterprising, and callous, he mobilizes the president, baron, and stockbroker to form a corporation to drill for oil in the Chaillot section of Paris.

The Baron, President, and *Stockbroker*—three unscrupulous businessmen, prototypes of capitalistic exploiters.

Irma—a servant at the Café Chez Francis; beautiful, sensitive, romantic, and conventional, Irma believes in God, beauty, and goodness, and hates evil. She falls in love with Pierre.

Pierre—in order to escape blackmail by the prospector, he tries to commit suicide.

The Ragpicker—spokesman for the people, he alerts Countess Aurelia to the plot to take over Chaillot and later serves as ironic spokesman for the businessmen at their mock trial.

The Deaf-Mute—amiable and generous; the indefatigable messenger of the people in their fight against exploitation.

The Story

Two unscrupulous businessmen, the president and the baron, meet on a café terrace in the Chaillot quarter of Paris to discuss a corporation they have just formed. Each brags about his corruption. Their talk is constantly interrupted by a procession of poor people: a singer, a doorman, a ragpicker, a deaf-mute, a merchant, a juggler, and a professor. The singer chants the opening of "The Beautiful Polish Girl": "Do you hear the signal/Of the infernal orchestra." The president and baron are joined by a stockbroker who, like his associates, owes his success to devious manipulations.

Suddenly, an eavesdropper proposes a name for the new corporation: "Bankers' Union of the Paris Underground." The stranger is recognized as the prospector, the only man who "smells in the bowels of the earth those deposits of liquid or metal on which are founded the only human unit which our age can tolerate . . . the corporation." He tells them that there is a rich source of petroleum in Chaillot. The three listeners divulge their infamous records and the stranger begins to reveal his plan, when the Countess Aurelia, dressed as a *grande dame* of 1885, enters to demand her meal of bones, gizzard, and giblets. As soon as she leaves, the prospector explains the first stage of his program: At noon, a young man will plant a bomb in the engineer's house in order to eliminate the one man who has thwarted prospecting operations in Paris.

A lifeguard appears carrying Pierre, whom he found on the Alma Bridge about to plunge into the Seine. Irma enters and admires Pierre's unconscious form. When Pierre regains consciousness, the countess tries to comfort him and calls the police sergeant. Because the policeman is a civil servant, he feels he must convince the young man to live. When he fails, the countess tells Pierre, whom she addresses as Fabrice, that she knows he tried to commit suicide because the prospector wanted him to commit a crime. She arouses his desire to live by describing her day: After consulting her schedule, she dresses, prepares her makeup, reads the 7 October 1896 newspaper, takes a walk, and goes to confession. Her recitation is continually interrupted by Pierre's exclamation: "How beautiful!"

A crowd gathers to listen, but the tale is halted by the prospector's vain attempts to lead Pierre off. Pierre confesses that he is at the prospector's mercy because he passed a rubber check. When the countess asks what the four charlatans want with Chaillot, she is told that they seek oil to make "misery, war, ugliness and a miserable world." The ragpicker tells the countess: "The world is no longer beautiful or happy." She lives in a dream world. Reality is populated by exploiters, speculators, and pimps. It is the end of the free world. The countess formulates a plan. She asks Irma for a flask of crude oil, tells the singer to get Constance (the Madwoman of Passy) and Gabrielle (the Madwoman of Saint-Sulpice), and dictates an invitation to the deaf-mute to invite the prospectors of Paris to her house. She leaves, accompanied by Pierre, whom she now addresses as Valentine because it is one o'clock and "at one, all men are named Valentine." Alone, Irma reveals that she hates ugliness, evil, the devil, and slavery. She adores beauty, goodness, God, and liberty. She has been saving herself for one special man and suspects his arrival is at hand.

In the cellar of the countess's house, which is furnished like an apartment, the Madwoman of Chaillot asks the sewerman to open the secret door in the ground. He tells her what to do. Whoever enters and descends the steps will find himself trapped and unable to ascend. When the sewerman leaves, Constance and Gabrielle enter dressed in outlandish, old-fashioned clothing. Constance reprimands her invisible dog for barking, and Gabrielle chats with an invisible companion. The two ladies argue about each others' mannerisms, but Countess Aurelia insists they stop their make-believe and listen to her serious business. She will reveal the world's plight as soon as Josephine, the Madwoman of the Concord, arrives. But when she learns that

Josephine is waiting for Carnot, who was assassinated in 1893, the countess makes her announcement. Bandits wish to destroy Paris: "Humanity's occupation is nothing more than a universal demolition enterprise." Men are culprits—no better than the basest animals.

The countess asks if she has the right to condemn these men. Her inquiry is interrupted by Josephine's arrival. The countess of the Concord immediately approves of mass-killing, but stipulates that the malefactors must be given a trial. The ragpicker is called to plead in behalf of the rich. Speaking for his clients, he denies loving money and defends his unscrupulous dealings on the stock market as a means of buying mansions, women, and luxuries. The tribunal of four madwomen condemns him when the ragpicker, acting as a rich man, cannot identify a camellia. The three guests are escorted out, singing the missing verses to "The Beautiful Polish Girl." The song that began as a warning of infernal activity ends as a love ballad in which the lovers dance the mazurka.

Alone with Irma, the countess is resting when Pierre arrives with her missing boa. With her eyes shut, the countess addresses the young man as Adolphe Bertaut, the lover who deserted her. When he swears eternal love, Aurelia dismisses him, calls out for Pierre, accepts her boa, and prepares to meet her guests. As the troop of exploiters enters, Irma tells each group to yell because the old woman is deaf. The countess opens the secret door and entreats the evil men to enter and examine the oil. Presidents, prospectors, directors, secretaries, and newsmen descend into the infernal passage. The trap is temporarily closed, but it is reopened for the descent of a dirty old man who insults the countess by calling her and her friends "crazy."

Irma, Pierre, the ragpicker, and all the café people re-enter. The countess hears her praises sung by a cortège of smiling men who are visible only to her. When a group representing all the Adolphe Bertauts of the world says they are returning to ask for her hand in marriage, the countess cries: "Too late." The vision disappears and the countess instructs Pierre and Irma to embrace before it is too late. They love each other. She declares: "The business is over. You see how simple it was. It took one sensible woman to break the folly of the world." The curtain falls as the countess leads her friends upstairs: "Now let us be concerned with worthy people."

Critical Opinion

The Madwoman of Chaillot is a lyrical fantasy about the poetic spirit's triumph over society. Written in 1944, shortly before the playwright's death, this drama is perhaps Giraudoux's whimsical assessment of world problems: the insane astutely discern reality and the sane are only doomed opportunists. Strongly influenced by Pirandello, Giraudoux takes the position that "madness" may well be the ultimate form of sanity when "reality" has become a monstrous perversion of man's soul and intellect.

Like Pirandello's characters, the countess is devastatingly sane. She can distinguish between frivolous escapism and the true world of feelings and ideas. She knows that the objective world is ugly, brutal, and inhuman, and that the human imagination can eradicate the machine-made terrors of modern civilization.

In Giraudoux's scheme of things, men are rational, unimaginative, and materialistic. They make wars, destroy beauty, and exploit people for money; the male force seeks unity with the bestial or inanimate. Women, who are more sensitive than men, are closer to angels. They can save the world by uniting it with the heavenly (emotional, intuitive, beautiful, loving) elements. Salvation and harmony may be achieved by uniting the male and female forces.

The countess intuitively understands the growing love between Irma and Pierre and brings about their union. Giving hope to Pierre and encouragement to Irma, Aurelia finds new meaning in her life and is inspired to save the world for lovers. The pathos of Aurelia's imaginary rejection of her lover, Adolphe Bertaut, underlines her intuitive knowledge that love must be nurtured at the right moment; if it is neglected, it will die.

Aurelia is an aristocrat of refined sensibility. Although she eats chicken bones, gizzards, and giblets, she insists that they be elegantly prepared and served. She relishes them as if they were the most expensive delicacies. Aurelia is unconcerned about material possessions. She is oblivious of the passage of time, and reluctant to distinguish between intuitive insight and scientific fact. She dresses in the style of *La Belle Époque* (1885–1914), when France's cultural life and art flourished in unprecedented magnificence. She reads old newspapers. Her life is an embodiment of the effervescence and graciousness of pre-World War I European civilization, when the upper classes indulged in a wild pursuit of love and pleasure. To her, time has stopped. The values of her youth and of France's cultural splendor epitomize the ideal world.

Like Aurelia, the three other madwomen people their world with imaginary companions: Constance, the Madwoman of Passy, has an invisible dog; Gabrielle, the Madwoman of Saint-Sulpice, chats with an imaginary friend; Josephine, the Madwoman of the Concord, is waiting for Carnot, who was assassinated in 1893. Yet when a crisis arises and action becomes imperative, the three friends abandon their fantasies and conquer their enemies by implementing Aurelia's plan to condemn the entrepreneurs.

The philistine president, baron, stockbroker, and prospector, however, reject humanity. They care nothing for beauty, love, the past, or even the future. They are completely absorbed in satisfying their virtually insatiable greed. They are condemned not merely because they are unscrupulous and evil. It is their ignorance of beauty, as symbolized by the camellia, that seals their fate.

The Madwoman of Chaillot is a festive procession. Humanity parades across the stage in a colorful series of tableaux. In the opening scene, the poor, life-loving people (the singer, doorman, ragpicker, deaf-mute, juggler, and professor) stand in contrast against the affluent, destructive businessmen who plot the sack of Paris. Finally, when the guilty are condemned, presidents, prospectors, directors, secretaries, and newsmen descend into the infernal passage while the countess and her friends, joining in a celebration of life, climb the stairs out of the cellar into the sunshine.

The Madwoman of Chaillot is not a sophisticated polemic advocating the overthrow of capitalism. Although Giraudoux attacks the vices of the rich, he is neither a democrat nor a Marxist. He caricatures the perversions of avarice, materialism, and insensitivity, but he does not propose to cure these vices by economic revolution. He would, instead, reawaken his audience to a new sensibility. Giraudoux employs the procession for dramatic contrast—almost as if the characters were puppets or clowns in a popular theater. The garish variety of speech, costume, and behavior glorifies the diversity and emotional richness of humanity as against the somber, rational, and conformist appearance of the industrial and bureaucratic world. Giraudoux sentimentalizes poverty, eccentricity, and madness in order to exalt the artistic personality. Like the artist, the characters are outcasts from society; they get no security and recognition, but are rich in their knowledge of joy and love.

Giraudoux's literary style is marked by its wit, sophistication, and evocative imagery. It illuminates the spirit and stimulates the imagination. Giraudoux's plays have richly been praised for their elegant, melodious, and poetic language, rich in irony, whimsy, and charm. Like Pirandello, Giraudoux believed that the imaginary world of the stage could be the ultimate reality.

The Madwoman of Chaillot has enjoyed continuous success since its initial Paris production under Louis Jouvet in 1945–46. Jouvet revised the manuscript that Giraudoux left upon his death and prepared the play for production. It has been frequently revived in New York and other theater capitals. In 1965, Georges Wilson mounted a new production for the Théâtre National Populaire in Paris and played the ragpicker opposite Edwige Feuillère as the countess. Most recently, a film of Maurice Valency's English adaptation was produced, starring Katharine Hepburn and Danny Kaye.

The Author

Born in a provincial town in central France, Giraudoux prepared for a diplomatic career at the Sorbonne. After a year in Germany (1905–06), he entered the foreign ministry and began to publish novels that reflected national and political concerns. He received the greatest recognition, however, for his dramatic works.

His first play, *Siegfried* (1928), was an adaptation of a novel he had published seven years earlier. *Amphitryon 38* (1929), *Judith* (1931), *The Trojan War Will Not Take*

Place (1935), *Electra* (1937), and *Sodom and Gomorrah* (1943), are deft and provocative interpretations of mythological subjects. *Intermezzo* (1933), *Ondine* (1939), and *The Madwoman of Chaillot* (1944) continue to explore the themes of imagination, love, and war. *Pour Lucrèce,* incomplete at his death, is a witty satire based on the legend of the rape of Lucretia.

In his plays, Giraudoux eschews set formulas to create, by turns, philosophical, political, and romantic works of extraordinary sophistication and theatricality. He is clearly indebted to Pirandello. The seriousness and optimism of even his darkest visions of mankind's folly and cruelty are characteristically Gallic.

Giraudoux was a theatrical technician, a master of an elegant prose style, and the versatile creator of light comedy, fantasy, contemporary drama based on history or legend, poetic drama, and moral drama. Whether or not all of his cool, intellectual plays will survive remains a matter of conjecture, but his masterpiece, *The Trojan War Will Not Take Place,* is considered by many to be the final comment in our day on the superfluity of war.

R.U.R.

by

KAREL ČAPEK (1890–1938)

The Characters

Harry Domin—general manager of Rossum's Universal
Robots. A dynamic and aggressive administrator motivated
by a dream of freeing the human race from poverty and
work, he ruthlessly pursues his objectives while ignoring
the human values he would exalt. Domin's obsession with
changing the world through science and technology violates fundamental human values and concerns.

Helena Glory—Domin's wife, who originally came to the
island as an agent of the Humanity League, is easily
dominated by her husband, but retains the desire to make
the robots equal to man. Her dedication to this ideal
prompts her to induce Dr. Gall to make robots with a
soul.

Dr. Gall—head of the Physiological and Experimental Department. The only true scientist on the island, Dr. Gall
has dreams of fulfilling Old Rossum's original scheme: to
create real human beings. He realizes that the robots are
a destructive force in the world, but continues to assist
manufacturers in their development. Dr. Gall is the
scientist without a conscience, amoral, insular, and vain.

Mr. Fabry—Technical Controller, a colorless and unimaginative man, totally enslaved by Domin.

Dr. Hallemeier—Head of the Institute for Psychological
Training of Robots. Simplistic, conventional, and naively

optimistic, Dr. Hallemeier believes that the external mechanisms of human society, such as laws and conventions, assure the steady and inevitable progress of mankind.

Mr. Alquist—architect, the only executive who places a value on human individuality. His belief in manual labor spares his destruction by the robots, while his humanity and skepticism closely ally him to Helena.

Consul Busman—business manager. Shallow, cowardly, and sentimental, he continues to work on account ledgers during the robot attack and is destroyed when he naively attempts to buy off the robots with the company's assets.

Radius—one of the first of the new breed of robots developed by Dr. Gall. A sense of pain, anxiety, and individuality destines Radius for leadership of the rebellion on the island.

Helena—a robot with a soul and finally with a capacity for love.

Primus—Helena's robot lover, the Adam of the new world.

The Story

On a vast island, some time in the future, Harry Domin dictates letters acknowledging enormous orders for robots. Addressed to corporations and governments around the world, these letters are typed by Sulla, a highly advanced robot in the form of a woman. Domin is interrupted by the entrance of Helena Glory, daughter of the president. She is given permission to visit the secret factory that makes robots, but first Domin briefs her on the history of the venture: In 1920, Old Rossum, a physiologist, "discovered a substance which behaved exactly like living matter although its chemical composition was different." His son, an engineer, developed robots by simplifying the organs of the human body and eliminating the necessity for emotions, will power, or other "nonessential" qualities. The perfect worker was thus manufactured.

When Helena asks if the robots have souls, Domin mocks her. Nevertheless, she is horrified at the idea of "human" creatures being coldly sold and "used." Domin insists that they are merely machines that cannot be hurt or killed.

Helena interviews Marius, a robot, that tells her it knows no pain, emotion, or fear of death. Helena refuses to see the factory where the robots are made and is overcome with shock and loathing when she is told that Sulla is also a robot.

Domin offers to change the subject and introduces her to Fabry, Gall, Hallemeier, Busman, and Alquist, some of the only other human beings on the island. Helena at first thinks that they, too, are robots, and before discovering her error reveals that she has come from the Humanity League, an organization devoted to the humane and equal treatment of robots. The men accept her announcement with equanimity and show themselves to be pragmatic engineers. Fabry exclaims: "From a technical point of view, the whole of childhood is a sheer waste. So much time lost," and the others show the same blind confidence in technology.

Helena says that the Humanity League wants to liberate the robots and "make them happier." But she is reminded that robots must have no will, passion, or soul if they are to be efficient workers. Some robots occasionally go berserk and are returned to the stamping mill, but a sensitive nervous system that will make them fearful of pain is being developed as a deterrent: Suffering must be introduced. However, a soul would increase the cost of production and would not be in the manufacturer's interest. A Utopia is at hand, for although men are unemployed, the price of consumer goods is quickly dropping and "there will be no poverty," "everyone will live only to perfect himself," and through machines man will be "the Lord of creation." After the others leave, Domin suddenly makes violent love to Helena and demands that she marry him. Her will is quickly broken and she consents.

Exactly ten years later, in celebration of the anniversary of Helena's arrival on the island, flowers and jewels are presented to her. But the scientists are disquieted by ominous news from the outside world. Nana, Helena's maid, repeats pietistic and superstitious misgivings about the new order of robots, and Domin points to the harbor where a yacht (really a gunship) lies at anchor. Helena's anniversary present has an ominous meaning: There are wars everywhere, robots are used by battling nations to decimate human populations, and now the robots have issued a manifesto of revolt against human rule. The birthrate has dropped to zero, and universal slaughter is imminent. Domin scoffs at these portents of disaster, but Alquist shows his understanding of Helena's fears when he reflects that he, too, is afraid of "all this progress." He has prayed for Domin's enlightenment and the destruction of the robots.

Suddenly, Radius, a highly intelligent robot that works in the library, runs amok and is restrained. Helena's questions elicit hate: "I want to be master over people." Helena is thunderstruck, but pleads for Radius' preservation. Dr. Gall reluctantly agrees, but confides to her that Radius has alarmingly human characteristics, maybe even emotions: "I don't believe the rascal is a robot any longer." Dr. Gall then tells Helena that the human race has stopped breeding because it is now superfluous. Although all the universities are sending in petitions for restricting production: "The R.U.R. shareholders, of course, won't hear of it. All the governments, on the other hand, are clamoring for an increase in production to raise the standards of their armies." The scientists know the end of mankind is at hand, but the force of technological progress makes them powerless to change the course of events.

After Dr. Gall leaves, Helena burns Rossum's secret manuscript containing the formula for the manufacture of robots. As the flames consume the paper, Domin enters with the news that they must flee from the island to escape the insurrection. On the mainland, where the robots outnumber man by a thousand to one, they have seized all weapons and communications facilities.

Despite the immense disaster, Domin announces a plan to "make robots of different color, a different language. They'll be complete strangers to each other . . . then we'll egg them on a little in the manner of understanding, and the result will be that for ages to come every robot will hate every other robot of a different factory mark." Increased robot production at any price is the scientist's aim. Helena's entreaties to close the factories are answered by Domin's boast that they are just beginning on a bigger scale than ever. But the long-awaited rescue boat, too, is controlled by robots demanding their surrender. The men draw pistols and close the shutters as the robots sound the signal for the attack.

Later that afternoon, the scientists again assemble in one of the drawing rooms and are appalled by the "hundred thousand expressionless bubbles," faces of humanlike robots surrounding them. A high-tension wire is connected to the metal fence surrounding Domin's house. Busman obsessively balances his account ledgers. When Alquist says it was a crime to make robots, Domin answers: "Not even today, the last day of civilization. It was a colossal achievement." Domin's musings are interrupted when Hallemeier tells Fabry to switch the current into the fence: Four robots are electrocuted, but countless thousands remain.

Suddenly, Dr. Gall confesses that he secretly altered the manufacturing process and gave robots a soul, a will, and emotions. He has transformed them into human beings because Helena begged him to. In great panic, Busman says he can purchase their escape for the secret to the making of robots. The machines cannot refuse, for in twenty years they will all run down, and they do not know how to reproduce.

Domin says: "There are over thirty of us on this island. Are we to sell the secret and save that many human souls, at the risk of enslaving mankind . . . ?" Busman retorts that they should sell only part of the manuscript. While they are bickering and feeding upon their illusions, it is discovered that the manuscript is missing. Helena confesses that she has destroyed it and Busman decides to bribe the robots with the company's assets. But in his excitement, the accountant touches the electrified wire and is killed. A few moments later, the robots, led by Radius, invade the house and murder everyone except Alquist, whom they decide to save because "He works with his hands like robots."

One year later, in the laboratory, Alquist vainly tries to reconstruct Rossum's formula so that life on the planet will not cease. Radius tells him that the machines in the factory produce only shapeless clods and that eight million robots have died in a year; none will be left in twenty years. No human beings can be found. Soon all life will be extinct. Alquist tells the dismayed robots that the secret of their manufacture was destroyed. Radius asks Alquist to dissect robots—even Radius himself—until the secret is discovered, but the old man is incapable and falls into a troubled sleep. Two robots, Primus and Helena, enter and express human sympathies and affection for each other. Alquist awakens, realizes that finally mutations have allowed the robots to love and reproduce, and blesses them: "Go, Adam. Go, Eve. The world is yours."

Critical Opinion

Karel Čapek's science fantasy is a startlingly contemporary satire on man's dehumanization. First performed immediately after World War I (1920), the play became one of the modern theater's first protests against the perversion of scientific and social values. Like two other outstanding fantasies about the future, Aldous Huxley's *Brave New World* and George Orwell's *1984*, *R.U.R.* has achieved an almost prophetic insight into twentieth-century society. Its fame added the word "robot," derived from the Czech *"robota"* (work), to our modern vocabulary.

Harry Domin's name reminds the audience of the words Dominus (Lord) and domination. As general manager of Rossum's Universal Robots, he assumes the role of God the Creator, manufacturing millions of robots out of artificial protoplasm. The robots proliferate into human institutions—industry, agriculture, and the armed forces—Domin's supremacy becomes complete. But when governments totally depend on his ability to produce robots in great quantities, Domin's role of creator is ironically twisted into that of annihilator. The nations employ robots for destruction, and Domin, a slave to the idea of the consumer market, can only increase production in response to demand. When his creations suddenly attain the human lust for power, his great ambition to free mankind from the onus of manual labor is smashed.

Čapek sees the robots as a multiple symbol. They are the absurd and monstrous results of man's blind faith in science, technology, progress, profit, and the consumer market. Originally creations of the egotistical and atheistic genius of Old Rossum and the cruelly practical and immoral technological wizardry of his engineer son, the robots symbolize man's intellectual vanity and fatal curiosity. Young Rossum's modern ambition to make something useful regardless of its moral or human value is exemplified by his ingenious application of his father's intellectually and scientifically motivated discoveries.

Harry Domin believes in a Utopia where "things will be practically without price. There will be no poverty. All work will be done by living machines. Everybody will be free from worry and liberated from the degradation of labor. Everybody will live only to perfect himself." When human beings are made obsolete and the birthrate drops to zero, Domin continues to insist on the importance of technological progress at any cost, even at the price of mankind's extinction. As the robots proclaim their intention to destroy human life, Domin spins an intricate web of plans to increase production, and when his dream is blighted by the imminent holocaust of the robot revolution, he madly insists that the robots were a brilliant invention.

Like the modern arms manufacturer who claims that he is merely producing what the government needs, Domin does not consider the human misery that will flow from his diabolical plans and processes. His gang can think only of greater production and more profits, even at the moment of doom when their own products are about to destroy mankind.

The governments of the world swamp the factory with orders for soldier robots who are instructed to decimate mankind as a matter of national policy. Factories and other industrial enterprises use robots to produce staggering quantities of consumer goods while the consumers languish for lack of purpose in their lives and then perish because they are superfluous. Production, profit margin, and material abundance are the only criteria in a world where destruction and dehumanization take precedence over morality and love.

Domin's life is devoid of human sentiment. He wins Helena by an act of brutal will power, reducing her with his eyes and his mechanical insistence upon her capitulation to his lust. Only Hallemeier and Alquist are capable of feeling. The former proclaims, moments before his death: "It was a great thing to be a man. There was something immense about it." Alquist, although incapable of teaching robots how to produce, survives their domination and tearfully recognizes the rebirth of humanity in Primus and Helena.

Busman, the accountant, continues his bookkeeping as

the robots invade his office and dies while trying to bribe
the mechanical monsters to spare him. Like Domin, Busman is no more than a robot made of human flesh. Dr.
Gall possesses the same mad desires as Old Rossum and
the immoral technical proficiency of Young Rossum: he
imbues the robots with souls in his perverted desire to create
life. But the human soul can be an instrument of hate and
destruction when love and compassion are absent.

Čapek dramatizes the dehumanization of society by cleverly making his characters unable to distinguish between
robot and human. Modern man is the horrible result of a
technologically oriented society: a mechanical, soulless robot.
Rossum's Universal Robots are the ultimate perversion of
man's passion for creation and progress.

The play is imbued with dreamlike qualities. The setting
is claustrophobic: an isolated island far away from reality.
Only a handful of human beings inhabit a vast wasteland of
gigantic factories manned and managed by thousands of
expressionless, soulless machines. The human characters,
possessed by inhuman passions, act with absurd but consistent logic to realize monstrous fantasies of domination.
Remotely familiar yet grotesquely frightening images pre-
dominate: inhuman human beings, gunships in harbors,
savage yet mechanical violence, sexual passion without
tenderness.

Čapek's dramatic logic is impeccable, from the opening
exposition that introduces the bizarrely mechanical universe,
through the shootings and stabbings and the final rather
sentimental rediscovery of human feeling. The juxtaposition
of dreamlike fantasy and scrupulously logical structure
creates a tension that is at once emotionally unsettling and
esthetically correct.

In a civilization dominated by think tanks, computerized
systems, blind devotion to progress, science, profits, and
ideals that are irrelevant to the welfare of mankind, *R.U.R.*
is still a pertinent indictment of contemporary society. Since
its United States premiere in 1922 and a revival in 1937,
R.U.R. has been more widely appreciated by readers rather
than by theater audiences. The expressionistic elements of
R.U.R., the repetitive and mechanical dialogue, the possibilities for exaggerated, stark, and primevally violent action,
as well as the dreamlike quality of this modern nightmare

fantasy, have discouraged recent productions of this uniquely powerful play.

The science fantasy of *R.U.R.* is so commonplace today that Čapek suffers the fate of Wells and Verne: he is respectfully relegated to the reference shelf. Yet anyone who looks closely at the films of Stanley Kubrick, *2001: A Space Odyssey* and particularly *A Clockwork Orange,* is looking at a cinematic development of Čapek's plays. With Toller and Kaiser, his fellow Expressionists, Čapek inspired many American playwrights, including Elmer Rice in *The Adding Machine* (1923) and Paul Green in *Johnny Johnson* (1936), as well as Thornton Wilder in *The Skin of Our Teeth* (1942). These authors are indebted to Čapek's use of novel devices to make their themes more powerful. Čapek's highly individual approach to theatrical form has earned him a firm place in world drama, although his ideas are no longer startling.

The Author

Born in eastern Bohemia (modern Czechoslovakia) in 1890, Karel Čapek studied in Berlin, Paris, and Prague, where he received his Ph.D. degree at the age of twenty-seven. During the final year of World War I, he wrote stories, newspaper articles, and miscellaneous pieces and entered the theater as a stage manager in a provincial Czech playhouse. The national renaissance inspired by Czech independence from the Austro-Hungarian Empire drew Čapek to the Prague National Theater, for which he wrote a series of experimental dramas bginning with *The Robbers* and *R.U.R.* (1920), *The Insect Comedy* (1921), *The Makropoulos Affair* (1923), and *Adam the Creator* (1927). In collaboration with his brother, Josef, Karel created a distinctive and imaginative theater that gained international fame. Josef's literary assistance and bold experimental staging revolutionized European dramatic styles during the two decades following the war. The subjective vision, imaginative use of lighting, and exaggerated, intense external depiction of internal experience characterized the expressionistic theater as developed by the Čapek brothers.

As the Nazis surged across Europe, Čapek turned from

imaginative and speculative fantasies to social protest: *The White Plague* (1937) and *The Mother* (1938) were anti-fascist dramas, and the stories *War with the Newts* (1936) and *The First Rescue Party* (1937) were, respectively, a satire in the vein of *R.U.R.* and an exposé of mine conditions.

When Čapek died in 1938, practically on the eve of Hitler's invasion of his native land, his dramas, novels, and stories had won international acclaim.

Corruption in the Palace of Justice

by

UGO BETTI (1892–1953)

The Characters

Vanan—president of the court, Elena's father. A proud, distinguished-looking gentleman, Vanan has allowed years of duty to dull his humanity and self-knowledge. When accused of dealings with a gangster, Vanan crumbles under the pressure of criticism, self-doubt, and fear.

Elena—Vanan's daughter, the embodiment of total innocence and devotion. Although she is the only character not directly employed by the palace of justice, her loss of innocence gives her wisdom. She cannot withstand the horror of seeing destroyed her illusions about her father, herself, and life.

Erzi—the investigating counselor who is in charge of discovering which judge betrayed the ideals of justice by dealing with the gangster Ludvi-Pol.

Croz—chief justice and archrival of Cust to succeed Vanan. Croz is very cynical about human attempts to emulate divine justice. Having no ideals and professing no faith in man's goodness and nobility, he attempts to undermine the whole structure of human justice by offering a false deathbed confession.

Cust—the most intellectual and corrupt of the judges, who tries to sidetrack Erzi in his search for Ludvi-Pol's associate. His great subtlety of mind and daring guile

291

enable him to destroy Elena and Vanan and elude detection. Faced with his own guilt, he cannot endure his perverted and corrupt life.

Bata
Persius } sycophantic, craven, and insecure judges in the palace.
Maveri

The Story

When a stranger ominously appears in the palace of justice and asks for the chief justice, everyone is first suspicious and then terrified. Their unnamed guilt prompts them to defend their imagined and real transgressions. Judge Bata acknowledges that "The place is just a dung heap. . . . In fact, the magistrates' crime . . . is simply that they're a little too like the man in the street." The city's king of vice, Ludvi-Pol, has corrupted innumerable government officials and has just killed himself in a chamber of the palace of justice.

When the stranger identifies himself as Erzi, a deputy of the government who will conduct an investigation, the judges are terrified of exposure. Each affects confidence and promises to cooperate. They do not feel guilty for Ludvi-Pol's death, but they fear exposure of their other transgressions against the code of judicial conduct. In self-defense, they threaten to become less tolerant of defendants brought into their courts, and implicitly blame each other, creating an atmosphere of petty intrigue, sycophantism, and mistrust. They decide that Vanan, the absent president of the court, must certainly be the guilty one. Croz and Cust, two rivals to succeed Vanan, bitterly carp at each other. When it is revealed that Ludvi-Pol's corpse was found in Vanan's office, they decide to turn on him.

Vanan enters and is greeted with respect. Erzi, the investigating counselor, questions him. But the president seems disoriented and evasive about his relationship with Ludvi-Pol. Vanan unconvincingly says that Ludvi-Pol was in debt to his family, but refuses to elaborate when Erzi presses the point. It seems obvious to the other judges that Vanan is guilty of corruption, but Vanan imperiously denies any transgression. Cust advises him to go home and examine his conscience, after sending Erzi a note that he will be withdrawing from the palace of justice for several days. Just as Elena, his beautiful daughter, enters the courtroom, Vanan reluctantly agrees. Vanan finishes the note to Erzi and hands it to Cust as he guides his daughter out of the palace of justice.

Several days later, Cust and Erzi have a long discussion about Vanan's guilt. Cust has come to the president's defense and has convinced Erzi that the culprit is elsewhere in the palace. Cust himself breaks into a clammy sweat when Erzi reconstructs the final interview between Ludvi-Pol and the party they seek. Cust warns Erzi that the guilty man will be diabolically clever in covering his traces and will feign innocence: "I believe the real dangers are inside himself. . . . He is at the end of his tether. He longs to run away . . . to run away . . . to be dead and buried. That's the most complete flight of all." Cust finally tells Erzi that by examining the decisions of every judge in the court: "the insistent recurrence of such-and-such an ambiguity or quibble: the flavor of corruption . . . that will be the flavor that will distinguish that judge's words from those of all the others."

Vanan, greatly aged and wasted, enters with Elena and delivers a cryptic speech that implies his guilt but asserts his innocence. Cust asks for Vanan's written statement, but the president denies he has one; the soul-searching of the last days has made Vanan doubt his whole existence. He blames his daughter for wanting him to appease somebody, but after he has left, Elena hands Cust the statement that Vanan wrote. She says: "Sir, I have read that even people condemned to death—even when they've been innocent— at the last moment, they've begged forgiveness just as though they were guilty. I know that can happen. My father is a very tired man; but he is innocent."

Left alone with Elena, Cust begins to seduce her, telling her she reminds him of a beautiful girl he knew when he was a boy but had to renounce for his career. In an impassioned, strangled speech during which he contradicts himself in a welter of sexual passion and twisted logic, Cust turns upon Elena and proclaims her father's guilt. He destroys her innocent vision of Vanan. She tries to retrieve her father's statement, but Cust retains it and blurts out the story of how he lost his innocence when he saw his parents having intercourse: "There always comes a day when a door opens a little way and we look through. And that day has come for you, too, now, my dear. Look! Look at your father, for God's sake, look at him for the first time." Elena rushes out, repelled by the vision of moral and sexual contamination Cust has created.

Erzi enters to tell Cust that the documents in the archives pertaining to Ludvi-Pol have been removed. Cust says that they must have been purposely misfiled by the criminal. They are suddenly interrupted by a noise: Elena has thrown herself down the elevator shaft and is being carried into Cust's chamber.

That evening, Cust confronts Croz at the archives. Croz thinks he has trapped his hated rival meddling with the archives, and they exchange vitriolic accusations. Croz admits to a modicum of corruption and urges Cust to confess. Cust denies everything. Suddenly, Croz is seized with horrible spasms and falls to the floor. Cust confesses to his dying colleague that he is the man they have been looking for; he is a leper, steeped in corruption and filth. Croz rises and shouts for Counselor Erzi so he can expose Cust. Although he was not totally faking his seizure, Croz has enough time to live so that he may accuse Cust on his deathbed. Such a confession has always been deemed irrefutable, and Cust believes he is doomed. Erzi arrives and takes the dying Croz into another chamber.

Meanwhile, Vanan is brought in by a nurse. He has been totally broken by his daughter's death. Cust is overwhelmed by remorse when Malgai, the court clerk, announces that the criminal's name has been revealed by Croz, who died at the end of his confession. Vanan has been exonerated. Croz admitted his guilt. Cust will now be the new president of the court. Erzi tells Cust: "Administration: that is a human fact, its task is to smooth things out, not to dig things up, and turn them upside down! Nature: she heals her wounds so rapidly that perhaps the real truth is something else: that she is unaware of them."

Cust is left alone to think about these truths and ask God's forgiveness. He exclaims: "There is no argument on earth that would let me shut my eyes in peace tonight. I shall have to wake the Lord High Chancellor; I must confess the truth to him." He throws open the door to the chancellor's office and slowly begins to ascend a long staircase as the curtain falls.

Critical Opinion

Like the novels of Franz Kafka, *Corruption in the Palace of Justice* is both a realistic and symbolic depiction of the human condition. The behavior of the judges, the physical setting, and the initial situation are credible and realistic. The "large severe room in the palace of justice," the locale of the entire play, is adorned with the bookcases, filing cabinets, desks, and chairs common to any courtroom. Although the play has its melodramatic moments, the action is rational and psychologically valid. Yet there are ambiguities and mysteries in the archetypal drama of men confronting the temporal and divine imperatives for justice. Betti has written an allegorical drama that touches upon the eternal moral, philosophical, and religious issue: What is justice?

The darkness, obscurity, and universality of the drama are reinforced by the characters' names, which evoke the Central European settings usually associated with the works of Kafka. Ludvi-Pol, Cust, Malgai, and Vanan are names that suggest the psychological underground that has a prominent place in non-Italian literature. Betti may have had political reasons for having the action take place in "a foreign city" and giving non-Italian names to the judges, for *Corruption in the Palace of Justice* was written during World War II, when Italy was under the pall of fascism.

Man's obsession with guilt is explored by Betti's exposure of corruption on three different levels: Vanan, the president of the court, succumbs to the inevitable doubts and compromises that follow a long career of meting out imperfect human justice. Finally obliged to judge himself, he crumples at the spectacle of his own moral decay. Although innocent of collusion with Ludvi-Pol, Vanan recognizes his complicity. He asks Cust: "Have you ever been bathing in a river, and suddenly seen the water all running the other way? You stand there, still, alone, by yourself, in the middle of the flowing water." Worldly success can suddenly appear worthless, for the human toll it exacts is beyond measure. Vanan's introspection leads him to believe that he is indeed a guilty man and that his complicity is greater because he has been a judge of other men. The destruction of his illusion is accompanied by the death of Elena, the one element in his life untainted by worldly ambition.

As Croz gasps out his final confession to Erzi, the audience understands the self-devouring malevolence of total cynicism. Fully believing that Cust, whom he deeply hates, is guilty of commerce with Ludvi-Pol, Croz destroys the institution to which he has devoted his life: He falsely confesses his own guilt and exonerates his enemy. At this climactic moment, Betti exposes the overwhelming pride of a man who hates so inveterately that he must destroy everything as he goes to his end.

Cust sees himself simultaneously as the leper and the quarantine officer. He baits Erzi as he draws him down the path that will ultimately lead to his own exposure. Cust's destruction of Elena is a double revenge against Vanan and his own thwarted emotional life. He destroys her illusions about her father's saintliness to even the score for his own parents' accidental revelation of their carnal acts and desires. Cust sees in Elena the symbol of ingenuous youth and desirable beauty, both unattainable for him. He is the most corrupt judge in the palace, not only because of his dealings with Ludvi-Pol but because of his intellectual superiority and the choice of his victim—Elena, who is outside the palace of justice. Her innocence is perfect; her father's is questionable. But Cust destroys both through his arrogance and his desire to revenge himself on the world.

Betti felt that no matter how cruelly or unjustly man may act, he will ultimately cry for justice and mercy. Human justice for Betti is a reflection of divine perfection: unattainable in this world, yet a necessary human goal. In a sense, *Corruption in the Palace of Justice* is a theological play. At the end, Cust realizes: "There is no one who can help me." Betti's stage directions evoke the image of a man ascending a stairway in a final attempt to obtain freedom through divine justice and mercy.

Written in 1944, during one of the bleakest periods in European history, Betti's drama was a positive moral document for men of his generation. Its central question, "What is justice?" was on the lips of every man during the final holocaust of fascism. The terrible implications in the play about the imperfection of human justice became stunningly apparent in the closing days of the war. Today, the same questions persist and continue to be central to our society. What qualities of human nature pervert justice and yet depend upon it as the rationale for crimes? What forces compel men of power to ignore moral imperatives and twist laws to their own ends? Is there not something about human justice that is ultimately above man? Betti's scrupulous attention to psychological detail and his awareness of the complexity of human motivation create an allegorical drama of immediate and compelling force.

The Author

Ugo Betti was born in Camerino, Italy, in 1892. After receiving a law degree in 1914, he served in World War I. For his distinguished conduct as a judge between the two world wars, he was rewarded with an appointment as chief justice of the Italian courts, an office he retained while embarking on an important literary career.

Betti's prolific output includes three volumes of short stories, dozens of plays, and several books of poetry. Outside of Italy, *Corruption in the Palace of Justice* (1944) is his best-known drama. His preoccupation with human and divine justice is reflected in Betti's life and work. He was a great humanist who believed that all men, no matter how corrupt, yearn for mercy, trust, and love. Betti died in 1953, one of the most honored figures in modern Italian letters. A revival of interest in his drama has prompted the recent publication of English translations of *Goat Island* and *The Gambler*.

Pantagleize

by

MICHEL DE GHELDERODE (1898–1962)

The Characters

Pantagleize—naive, idealistic, and oblivious of the world around him, a poetic and charming man incapable of grasping the difference between dreams and reality.

Bamboola—a flamboyant, crude stereotype of the black savage, both obsequious and arrogant with his master and the rest of the white world.

Rachel Silberschatz—a young Jewish revolutionary, the typical Marxist zealot of the time (1929).

Creep—a secret police agent and spy who undermines the revolution and is devoted to the government's concept of law and order.

Innocenti—a café waiter, an idealistic revolutionary who despises his fellow-conspirators, but accepts responsibility for their acts.

Blank—an effeminate, foppish poet, coarse and avaricious.

Banger—a grizzly, maimed veteran revolutionary.

General MacBoom—boorish, obtuse, and cowardly, a caricature of the blundering general.

The Story

Somewhere in Europe, "on the morrow of one war and the eve of another," Pantagleize is awakened by Bamboola, his black servant. It is the first of May and Pantagleize's birthday. When Pantagleize declares that it will be a lovely day, Bamboola goes into paroxysms of ecstasy, dancing, and gesticulating.

In a café, Innocenti complains about his life as a waiter. Blank appears and demands a drink. The men discuss "a huge and delicate plan" that will be realized that day. They are awaiting the signal. Bamboola comes in, dancing wildly and talking excitedly about the revolution. Creep, a secret agent, overhears their conversation, and Banger, carrying a machine gun under a cloth, joins the group and tells everyone to prepare for the uprising. Pantagleize arrives, confused about the activity in the streets. An eclipse of the sun is imminent, and it will coincide with the revolution. He remarks: "What a lovely day!" and pandemonium erupts; everybody rushes out. Creep telephones his report and is attacked by Rachel Silberschatz, a young revolutionary.

The sun is in eclipse and the revolution has begun, but Pantagleize, lost in his own dreams, is oblivious of the tumult. Bamboola and Creep each set up telescopes and vie for business. Rachel enters, hears Pantagleize give the signal ("What a lovely day!"), and rushes out. Later, in her room, Pantagleize tries to make love to her, but is ordered to steal the treasure from the bank. He goes out; Creep enters and shoots Rachel.

At the state bank, the pompous and cowardly General MacBoom tries to organize the defenses against the insurgents. He rants against civilians and reveals his stupidity and incompetence. Pantagleize stumbles through the ranks of sentries, inadvertently giving the password ("Go to the devil!") when asked to identify himself. He takes the treasure and leaves.

The revolutionary council, consisting of Innocenti, Bamboola, and Blank, bickers and debates. Pantagleize is applauded when he delivers the treasure. News of the counter-revolution throws everyone but Pantagleize into panic. He rhapsodizes on various subjects, escapes Creep, and goes to Rachel's apartment, where he finds her corpse.

The streets are littered with corpses and debris, and Pantagleize, in a daze, laments the shooting, chaos, and destruction. He plays dead when MacBoom and his soldiers enter. After they leave, Creep, who had also been feigning death, strikes him on the head, confiscates the treasure, and arrests him.

The counterrevolutionary court convenes. MacBoom is acquitted of incompetence because the treasure is fake. Blank, Bamboola, Banger, and Innocenti are sentenced and executed. Pantagleize, still unaware that he has been the leader of the abortive uprising, amazes the tribunal by his naive demeanor. He is taken into a yard and, while still rhapsodizing about his fate and his lost youth, is shot. However, it is necessary for an officer to administer the *coup de grace*. With his dying breath, Pantagleize exclaims: "What a lovely day!"

Critical Opinion

A forerunner of Giraudoux, Ghelderode shares the latter's ability to delineate the chasm between real and imaginary worlds. Using slapstick and farce, reveling in extravagant rhetoric, Ghelderode creates a world of dreamers who poignantly capture the pathos of modern existence. Pantagleize is Everyman. Unassuming and full of dreams about the world, in one day he travels through a lifetime of experiences, until he is killed by forces that he neither perceives nor understands. His fortieth birthday marks both his first and last day on earth, the birth and death of a misconceived proletariat revolution, and a solar eclipse.

The story of Pantagleize is the ironic and touching tale of all men. Unknowingly, he triggers cataclysmic events yet insists that his exclamation, "What a lovely day!" is "not striking, but it's safe enough." The tool of forces beyond his ken, he only seems to be in control of his actions. He gives the signal for the revolution, stumbles upon the password that enables him to filch the nation's treasure, and maintains an innocence that is as incriminating as genuine guilt. The judges do not believe that Pantagleize can be ignorant of his powerful role in the uprising. At the end, the bullet-riddled hero doggedly asserts his faith: "What a lovely day!" A Candide who does not learn from his adventures, Pantagleize is a symbol of the childlike, innocent, and naive artist destroyed by a crass world. The name of Ghelderode's hero is reminiscent of Voltaire's optimistic philosopher, Pangloss, who despite adversity always believes that "This is the best of all possible worlds." Pantagleize overlooks the bestiality of his surroundings, hopes for a state of ideal bliss, and dies reaffirming the beauty of the day.

But Pantagleize is not a hero in the classical sense, for he remains oblivious to the forces that destroy him. If he suffers, it is from confusion, not from spiritual doubt. By maintaining his innocence, Pantagleize first becomes the world's dupe and then triumphs over those who would use him for their base ends. Even the military tribunal that executes him cannot believe his profession of innocence. By condemning him, it fails to fulfill its counterrevolutionary mission. Pantagleize addresses this tribunal and is asked if he is feigning stupidity:

> What is the issue? Being stupid, or acting as though stupid? Everything is relative. You can't see yourself, and you can't make yourself either. I am Pantagleize. What is Pantagleize? According to some, a qualified imbecile, according to others, a superman. And what do I think of myself? Philosopher, journalist, lover, rioter, robber, minister, multimillionaire? I am what? An imbecile? No. A failure—because love is missing!

Pantagleize is like Giraudoux's heroes. If love is missing, then universal harmony is impossible and questions of guilt, innocence, baseness, and nobility are meaningless. After Rachel's death, Pantagleize wants to leave society and live on the fortune he has stolen. But the fortune is counterfeit and Rachel loved only the revolution, not Pantagleize. His failure to achieve worldly fulfillment is insignificant, however, because Pantagleize is indestructible. He embodies the spirit of innocence and creativity. His rebellion transcends the political tactics of conspirators and counterrevolutionaries, because it takes place beyond the limitations of space and time. Pantagleize is striving to reaffirm the verities of life ("a lovely day") in a world that systematically destroys fantasy and creativity. His rebellion is the artist's struggle to maintain his integrity in a milieu of Philistines and clods.

When imaginatively staged, this picaresque drama is a fanciful epic in which the protagonist is born, commits great acts, descends into the underworld, emerges, and dies, amid a variety of scenes enlivened by the constant presence, whether physical or poetic, of Pantagleize the picaro. The two-dimensional characters are achetypes who attempt to pervert Pantagleize's pure spirit. Bamboola is a crude clown whose ridiculous speech mannerisms, shuffling and dancing antics, and outlandish costumes give motion and variety to the dramatic scene. The episodes in the café and at the state bank deal with generalities and types rather than with contemporary issues and individual human beings. The false poet, Blank, is foppish, effeminate, and self-indulgent; Innocenti is a surly waiter whose capacity for action is as ignoble as his scrounging for tips from customers; MacBoom is a cowardly blusterer. Creep is everything his name implies, and Rachel Silberschatz is the type of obtuse and fervent revolutionary who can be found in any society. The theatrical brilliance of the war council scene, in which the costumes are absurdly elaborate and the members of the tribunal are "seen from the waist upward" and wear identical masks, is enhanced by imaginative lighting effects (including blackouts), off-stage sounds, and onstage gongs and trumpets. Songs, dances, and recitations create a festive atmosphere. Many of these devices were adapted by Bertolt Brecht, whose "epic theater" certainly owes much to Ghelderode.

In an *Epitaph* for his hero, written for a 1957 production of *Pantagleize,* the playwright said that the protagonist is "the Poet, the incarnation of the poet unfit for anything except love, friendship, and ardor—a failure, therefore, in our utilitarian age." *Pantagleize* is a protest, but not a political one. It is an attack on what Ghelderode has called "our atomic and autodisintegrated age, this age from which dreams and dreamers are banished . . . this fellow Pantagleize remains an archetype . . . who has nothing to do with that dangerous thing, intelligence, and a great deal to do with that savior, instinct."

Pantagleize was born in a short story in 1925; the play was completed four years later and first produced in 1930. Since then, the play (originally in French) has been translated into several languages. It was produced in England in 1957 and enjoyed a great success in New York in 1968 when it was given an elaborate and imaginative production by a distinguished company.

The Author

Born in Brussels in 1898, Michel de Ghelderode was until recently a relatively unknown dramatist. His life has given rise to much speculation and some fantastic stories. Because Ghelderode preferred to be discussed solely in relation to his work, he disclosed little about his personal life, except that he has always been interested in writing. His father, a clerk in the Brussels Archives, instilled in his son a respect for the past. The young Michel experimented with various artistic media, including painting, music, and theater. Although he was in poor health, he was able to attend the popular marionette theaters in his native Belgium. In 1918, he began writing plays (in French) for puppets.

Saint Francis of Assisi, Ghelderode's first drama, was performed by the Flemish Popular Theater in 1927, the same group that later produced *Barabbas* and *Pantagleize.* When his friend (and the first Pantagleize) twenty-six-year-old actor Renaat Verheyen died suddenly in 1930, Ghelderode wrote *The Actor Makes His Exit* for him and suddenly withdrew from the theater. After that, Ghelderode continued to write plays, but these works have not been performed.

Ghelderode's most popular plays were written in the late 1920s and early 1930s. They include *The Women at the Tomb* and *Barabbas* (1928), *Pantagleize* and *The Chroniclers of Hell* (1929), *The Blind Man* (1933), and *Lord Halewyn* (1934).

After being relatively obscure, Ghelderode is now recognized as one of Belgium's greatest artists. He has been the subject of numerous critical studies in his own country and abroad.

Blood Wedding

by

FEDERICO GARCÍA LORCA (1898–1936)

The Characters

The Mother—an embittered and passionate old woman who has seen the men in her life destroyed by the Felíx family. Understandably protective of her only surviving son, she is devoted to life but engulfed by death—the deaths of her husband and eldest son and her unborn children and grandchildren.

The Bride—Impulsive, moody, dissatisfied, she is overcome by passion and allows herself to be abducted at her own wedding. Nevertheless, her sense of honor survives even in the arms of Leonardo and after the death of the bridegroom.

The Mother-in-Law—a conventional and loyal woman who witnesses her son's mysterious nocturnal activities, but is subjugated by his bullying attitude.

Leonardo's Wife—a conventional and loyal woman who is aware of her husband's uncontrollable lust for his former love.

Leonardo—tormented by an old passion, a truculent, cruel man.

The Bridegroom—manly, gentle, and honorable, he is deeply in love with his bride. Love and honor draw him inexorably to his death.

The Bride's Father—proud, stern, and wise, he understands the worldly importance of love and property.

The Story

The play opens in rural Spain. The mother tries to dissuade her son from going to the vineyard with a knife. She fears the continued slaughter of her family. She has already lost her husband and eldest son in a blood feud. The bridegroom insists that he will be safe and reassures his mother that his fiancée is chaste and had nothing to do with Leonardo Felíx, son of the family's inveterate enemy.

In Leonardo's home, his wife and mother sing a lullaby to his son. The lyrics describe an agonized horse that is destroyed at a poisoned river. After the child falls asleep, the two women gossip about how Leonardo's steed is often covered with sweat and nearly dead of exhaustion. Leonardo enters and becomes violent when a girl tells of the finery purchased for the wedding of the bridegroom and bride.

The bride's home is a cave in a desolate region. The bridegroom and mother enter to discuss the marriage contract with the bride's father. The wedding day is set, and the bride coolly receives her new relatives. Later, alone with her servant, the bride learns that Leonardo has been seen in the vicinity; hoofbeats signal the return of the former suitor.

On the day of the wedding, the bride is disconsolate as the servant dresses her for the ceremony. Leonardo appears and offers a bouquet of orange blossoms, the traditional gift of the bridegroom. The servant tries to eject the fiery lover, but Leonardo is importunate and leaves only upon the arrival of the wedding party. Leonardo reluctantly agrees to ride to the church in a cart with his wife. After the ceremony, outside the bride's house, the festivities begin. The ecstatic bridegroom and morose bride receive the guests. Leonardo strides around in the background. The bride withdraws. When she is sought by the others, they discover that she has fled with Leonardo.

Three woodcutters discuss the calamity, sympathizing with both the bridegroom and the fugitive lovers. They remark that when the moon appears Leonardo and the bride will be found and slaughtered. The moon, "a young woodcutter with a white face," intones a violent and lyrical poem, pleading that his white face should be covered with the blood of the lovers. A beggar woman, death incarnate, admonishes the moon to shine brightly, encounters the bridegroom, begs alms, and ominously invites him to join her. In another part of the forest, the bride and Leonardo, fleeing from their pursuers, exchange recriminations about their impetuous act, confessing total submission to the passion that consumes them. They pledge to stay together until death. The search party approaches. Two violins and shrieks are heard as the beggar woman, like a gigantic bat, spreads her cloak on the darkened stage.

In an arched, white, churchlike construction, the townspeople gossip about the catastrophe. Leonardo and the bridegroom have slain each other. The mother utters an impassioned lament. The bride allows the mother to beat her and offers her throat to the mother, swearing that she is still a virgin. Leonardo's wife enters in despair and the women chant mournfully about the cruelty of fate.

Critical Opinion

Blood Wedding, a poetic tragedy, depicts the Spanish peasant's pride, passion, and enslavement to tradition. Lorca tempered the stark events of his play with surrealism and poetic symbolism. The play's lyricism bridges the worlds of realism and symbolism. An integral element of the play, the poetry introduces themes and images that give the action a rhythmical continuity. The lullaby sung to Leonardo's son picturing a dying horse, with bleeding hooves, frozen mane, and dagger-pinioned eyeballs, drinking at the stream of death, anticipates the horrific imagery of Picasso's painting, *"Guernica,"* one of the most astounding depictions of death and suffering in twentieth-century art.

Lorca's surrealistic portrait of Leonardo's steed, and by extension his passion and hate, is a paradigm of the savage lusts suffered by all the characters in this drama. The playwright's stylized settings include a room painted yellow (the bridegroom's house), one painted rose (Leonardo's home), a cave (the bride's prisonlike abode), a forest with "great moist tree trunks" (the refuge of Leonardo and the bride), and "a white dwelling with arches and thick walls" giving "the monumental feeling of a church" (the final scene of ritualistic lamentation). Violin and guitar music, native dances, lighting, and off-stage sounds, as well as imaginative makeup, heighten the atmosphere of this drama. The ghastly white face of the woodcutter who represents the moon, the two violins of death, off-stage shrieks, and the horrifying beggar woman, who is death, are incarnations of the mood and imagery implicit in the characters and explicit in the verse. These surrealistic techniques augment the poetry of the play's essentially classic form, with a "chorus" of townspeople commenting upon the stark melodrama.

Combining surrealism with the realism of authentic peasant customs and dances, Lorca provides a ritualistic contrast that gives the action of this tragedy an air of inexorability. The inevitability of the tragedy is forecast in nearly every incident: the vendetta, Leonardo's uncontrollable lust, the bride's suicidal passion. The denouement is suggested and symbolically reenacted by the lighting effects and the gestures of the beggar woman and the moon. In the last scene, ritual and naturalism give way to symbolic lamentation.

The characters in *Blood Wedding* are archetypes. The story is one of elemental passion in conflict with tradition and honor. The mother, an archetypal figure of bereavement, yearns for the marriage of her son and the continuance of her nearly extinguished family line; the bridegroom respects his mother, is sexually attracted to the bride, and is conscious of the wealth his marriage will bring to future generations. The bride's father, a dignified peasant, laments the early death of his wife and hopes for grandchildren to keep the land. Leonardo is soured by passion. After courting the bride, he marries her cousin and has a child by her. But lust turns him against life. He tortures his horse by riding it to the bride's home, mistreats his wife, dishonors his mother, and ignores his son. His wife is a long-suffering, suppressed woman, expecting another child, yet unable to hold her husband's love. These traditional characters emerge as monumental and elemental as the characters in a Greek tragedy.

The triumph of death is celebrated by the mother's final incantation to the symbolic knife that she feared so much in the first scene:

And it barely fits the hand
but it slides in clean
through the astonished flesh
and stops there, at the place
where trembles enmeshed
the dark root of a scream.

The rivals have slain each other; yet through her suffering
the mother has triumphed over death by reaffirming the
elemental truth of life and refusing to kill the bride: "What
does your death matter to me? What does anything about
anything matter to me? Blessed be the wheat stalks, because
my sons are under them; blessed be the rain because it wets
the face of the dead. Blessed be God, who stretches us out
together to rest." Weeping and lamentation are the lot of
Spain's women. Lorca here dramatizes the violent, sensuous
nature of his people, the Spaniards, who are capable of
terrible deeds, great suffering, and incredible endurance.

Lorca was deeply committed to Spain and believed that
the theater should be an important part of the national life:

A nation which does not help and does not encourage
its theater is, if not dead, dying; just as the theater
which does not feel the social pulse, the historical pulse,
the drama of its people, and catch the genuine color
of its landscape and of its spirit, with laughter, or with
tears, has no right to call itself a theater.

Federico García Lorca attained his greatest fame as a
poet. He is especially known for his *Gypsy Ballads*. Lorca's
plays appear occasionally in repertory companies or in
university theaters and are frequently produced in Spanish-
speaking countries.

Lorca's audience has grown in recent years; the Andalu-
sian blend of naked violence, mysticism, and poetry is universal despite the political myth that now surrounds the
poet's life. Responsible during his brief lifetime for a national
revival of poetic drama in Spain, Lorca filled several volumes
with verse dramas that are remarkable, even in translation,
for their stagecraft and for their lyricism. *Blood Wedding*,
his first major play, is a savage piece with enough feuding,

illicit love, and foul play to satisfy the most sanguinary audience, but it is the magnificent poetry that sustains it today.

The Author

A native of Granada, the Spanish poet and dramatist Federico García Lorca went to study in Madrid in 1919. The following year *The Butterfly's Evil Spell*, his first play, a one-act symbolic fantasy, was successfully produced, and Lorca entered into the mainstream of Spanish creative life. Muchado, Unamuno, and other members of the "Generation of '98" deeply influenced the young poet. He entered into collaboration with the composer Manuel de Falla and struck up friendships with the painters Juan Gris and Salvador Dali. In 1927, Dali contributed sets to the production of *Mariana Pineda*, Lorca's first full-length drama, a "popular ballad" about a revolutionary heroine.

Now admired principally for his poetry, Lorca produced theater pieces that encompassed burlesque, puppet shows, surrealist plays, comedies, and tragedies. *Chimara, The Lass, The Soldier and the Student*, and *Buster Keaton's Constitutional* were all completed in 1928. *The Puppet Farce of Don Cristóbal, The Shoemaker's Prodigious Wife, The Love of Don Perlimplín and Belisa in His Garden*, the surrealistic *If Five Years Pass* and *The Public* were written during 1930–31, while Lorca explored every aspect of the Spanish personality.

In 1932, the young poet organized an itinerant group that toured the provinces. It was not until the following year, however, that the first of Lorca's great plays appeared in his mature style—peasant tragedy poetically presented. Beginning with *Blood Wedding* (1933) and continuing with *Yerma* (1934) and *The House of Bernarda Alba* (1936), Lorca created a poetic mythology depicting the Spanish soul. Essentially a nonpolitical artist, Lorca at the age of thirty-eight, was executed by a Franco firing squad in 1936.

Mother Courage and Her Children

by

BERTOLT BRECHT (1898–1956)

The Characters

Mother Courage—an earthy, shrewd woman determined to survive in a chaotic social and political milieu. She profiteers from the war that destroys all her children. She will sacrifice everything in order to endure.

Eilif—Mother Courage's eldest son. He joins the army and becomes a hero because of his unscrupulous exploitation of the weak.

Swiss Cheese—the youngest son; his honesty and plain-dealing lead to his martyrdom.

Kattrin—the mute teen-age daughter who has been promised a husband at the end of the war. An extremely sensitive and magnanimous person, she joins her brother in martyrdom.

Sergeant—basically very superstitious, he is terrified when Mother Courage informs him he will not live out the war.

Yvette Pottier—a camp follower who adroitly exploits her suitors in the Swedish regiment.

Chaplain—an opportunist who changes from Protestantism to Catholicism as easily as he changes his clerical garb for civilian clothes.

Cook—an aggressive, outspoken man who unsuccessfully courts Mother Courage.

The Story

In the spring of 1624, during the Thirty Years' War, two Swedish army officers are recruiting for a campaign in Poland when Mother Courage and her three children arrive with their canteen wagon. The recruiting officer and sergeant have been discussing the benefits of war: it orders existence, and it accounts for provisions, crops, and men. Mother Courage calls the soldiers to buy: "Boots they will march in till they die!" She explains that she is called "Courage" because "I was afraid I'd be ruined, so I drove through the bombardment of Riga like a madwoman, with fifty loaves of bread in my cart." Her real name is Anna Fierling, but each of the children, Eilif, Swiss Cheese, and Kattrin, bears the name of a different man.

The recruiting officer wants to enlist Eilif, but is driven off with a knife by Mother Courage. The sergeant accuses her of living off the war but being frightened of it. Mother Courage takes the sergeant's helmet, throws lots into it, and starts to tell his fortune and her children's. All will die before the end of the war. Mother Courage sells a belt to the sergeant and the recruiting officer leaves with Eilif.

Two years later, Mother Courage is concluding a deal with the regiment cook when she discovers her son Eilif. He is the commander's guest because he has bravely robbed the peasants of two oxen. Eilif sings a song he learned as a child about a soldier who died because he went to war against the advice of a wise woman.

Three years go by, and Mother Courage continues to follow the Swedish army. Swiss Cheese has become regimental paymaster. His mother advises him to be honest. The army prostitute, Yvette, confesses that business is bad and sings a ballad, "The Fraternization Song," to warn Kattrin against the dangers of mixing with soldiers. Her mother seconds this and Yvette leaves.

The chaplain talks to Mother Courage, and Kattrin puts on Yvette's red boots and struts about imitating the whore's sexy walk. Suddenly gunfire is heard. The Polish Catholic army has invaded. The chaplain throws off his Protestant garb and takes cover with Mother Courage. They are joined by Swiss Cheese. Later, spies find Swiss Cheese, who has hidden the regimental paybox. Mother Courage plans to pawn her wagon and bribe the spies in order to save her son. But she haggles too long over the price and Swiss Cheese is shot. When his body is brought in, she denies knowing him in order to maintain her credit with the army.

Mother Courage must pay a fine for the right to keep her wagon-store open. While waiting to see the captain, she meets an angry young soldier. In "The Song of the Great Capitulation," Mother Courage tells of the necessity of submitting to attain success. She decides not to complain to the captain and leaves.

Three years pass; Mother Courage and Kattrin arrive in Bavaria for the commander's funeral. His death provokes serious discussion between Mother Courage and the chaplain about the duration of the war. The chaplain proposes an intimate relationship, but Mother Courage is not interested. She sends Kattrin off for supplies. Kattrin returns with the goods, but she has been wounded above the eye. Mother Courage curses the war. Business prosperity is momentarily interrupted when peace is announced. The cook and Yvette return to say hello. Upon the cook's advice, Mother Courage goes off to sell her supplies. In her absence, Eilif returns. Once again he has robbed peasants. His wartime heroism, however, is now considered a crime and he is marched off. Unaware of her son's fate, Mother Courage enters with news that the war has been resumed. She moves on, accompanied by the cook and Kattrin.

After a hard winter, the three travelers arrive in a poor village. The cook says his mother has died and he has inherited a small inn. While Kattrin is behind the wagon, he asks Mother Courage to join him, but stipulates that her daughter may not come. He sings "The Song of Great Souls of This Earth," a ballad about Solomon, Caesar, Socrates, and Saint Martin that proves that the virtues of wisdom, bravery, honesty, and unselfishness are useless in this world. Meanwhile, Kattrin, who has overheard the cook, climbs out of the wagon ready to leave. But Mother Courage refuses to join the cook and stops Kattrin just in time. The two women drive off.

In January 1636, Mother Courage has left Kattrin with some peasants while she is in the village selling supplies.

Soldiers arrive and start to pillage the farm. The old peasant woman begins to pray for their lives while Kattrin sneaks off and returns with a drum under her clothes. She climbs to the roof and beats the drum to warn the villagers of the soldiers' presence. Despite threats to burn the canteen wagon and shoot her, Kattrin continues. She is shot, but too late; cannon fire is heard in the distance. The villagers have heard the warning.

Mother Courage returns and finds Kattrin's body. She sings a lullaby mourning the death of two of her children and pondering the fate of the third. The peasants offer to bury the girl for a fee, and Mother Courage leaves to follow the army, saying: "I must get back into business."

Critical Opinion

Mother Courage and Her Children depicts the indomitability of the human spirit viewed from Brecht's Marxist approach to the human dilemma. Mother Courage, an antiheroine, is a businesswoman; her relationship to all society is affected by her economic condition. As an economic animal impelled to continue her life, she gains strength—courage—to endure unspeakable hardships and bereavements. The traditional Marxist interpretation of war as the result of a capitalistic system that thrives upon human suffering colors Brecht's highly didactic and philosophical play.

Mother Courage and Her Children is about the business of war. One of the basic elements in life, war orders existence but destroys it. The emphasis on business dealings rather than on war itself is evident throughout *Mother Courage*. In the opening scene, the sergeant underlines the uselessness of peace: "Peace is one big waste of equipment." He declares that only war organizes life: "In a war, everyone registers, everyone's name on a list. . . . That's the story: no organization, no war!" Mother Courage exploits the business opportunities of war. She is continually engaged in some transaction: selling a belt, a capon, bullets, or shirts; buying supplies, or, as in the last scene, concluding funeral arrangements. Yet she does not ignore the atrocities of war, but uses them as part of her inducement to buy. Her *leitmotif* calls the

soldiers to buy and die: "It's to death they're marching for
you/And so they need good boots to wear!"

The character of Mother Courage unifies this episodic
drama. She is a figure full of contradictions. Her nickname
points to the basic paradox of her character:

> They call me Mother Courage 'cause I was afraid I'd
> be ruined, so I drove through the bombardment of Riga
> like a madwoman, with fifty loaves of bread in my cart.
> They were moldy, what else could I do?

The archetypal human being, she courageously endures despite suffering. Yet her courage, neither heroic nor laudable,
is motivated by avarice and fear. She is a proud woman who
cannot be beaten by adversity.

From the beginning, Mother Courage predicts the family's
destiny. As she tears a piece of parchment to draw lots, she
comments: "So shall we all be torn in two if we let ourselves
get too deep into this war!" And she correctly predicts that
all three children will die. Her prophecy is repeated in the
"Song of the Wise Woman and the Soldier," which Eilif has
been taught from childhood: "Woe to him who defies the
advice of the wise!/If you wade in the water, it will drown
you!"

Finally, in the form of a parable, "The Song of the
Great Souls of This Earth," the cook recapitulates the fate
of Mother Courage and her three children. Each person
embodies a virtue that contains the seeds of his destruction.
Eilif, whom the commander praised for his heroism as a
new Julius Caesar, follows Caesar's fate. Swiss Cheese
perishes for his scrupulous honesty when he tries to hide
the strongbox, and thus, like Socrates, receives death instead
of thanks. Finally, the dumb Kattrin, who has been described
by her mother as suffering "from sheer pity," will repeat
the fate of Martin, who "could not bear/His fellow creatures'
woe" and died a martyr's death.

Necessity makes Mother Courage a cynic. She recognizes
the futility of struggle and in her "Song of the Great
Capitulation" preaches the death of idealism and the wisdom
of submission for the attainment of success. Pragmatic by
nature, she does not care whether she sells to the Swedes
or the Poles, and like the chaplain can change flags and

religions according to the times. Yet for a moment, in the sixth scene, she achieves an insight into the human dilemma and recognizes her own plight. Her children are the helpless victims of a merciless existence, and she bitterly curses the war. But her cynicism and business sense prevail, and Mother Courage strikes this moment of truth from her memory, ignores destiny, and continues her occupation.

The other characters in the play are foils for Mother Courage. All three children are lost because of their mother's business deals. Eilif is led off to war as Mother Courage sells a belt; Swiss Cheese is shot because his mother haggles too long over the price of his ransom; finally, Mother Courage goes off to investigate business prospects as Kattrin is left unattended and dies trying to save the villagers.

The prostitute, Yvette, the chaplain, and the cook second Mother Courage's pragmatic view of life. They often substitute for Mother Courage and present views similar to hers. Yvette warns the innocent Kattrin against men in the "Fraternization Song"; the chaplain expresses Mother Courage's cynicism in "The Song of the Great Souls of This Earth" when he concludes: "For virtues bring no reward, only vices. Such is the world, need it be so?" All the characters point to the rottenness of the existing order of things, yet at the same time reveal the necessity of continuing to play the game in order to exist.

Bertolt Brecht is a revolutionary playwright. He deliberately sought to change the Aristotelian conception of drama and to create a theater of anti-illusion. In his essay "On the Experimental Theater," Brecht explained that the audience should be jolted out of the illusion that it is watching "real" people. The playwright should always announce the philosophical purpose of his work:

> The theater no longer seeks to intoxicate him, supply him with illusions, make him forget the world, to reconcile him with his fate. The theater now spreads the world in front of him to take hold of and use for his own good.

Brecht, therefore, deliberately strove to show the artifice of drama and make it as unrealistic as possible. The episodic structure of *Mother Courage and Her Children* and the frequent songs that comment on the action emphasize that the drama is a performance and not a photograph of "real" life.

The twelve episodes are unified by the constant presence of the principal character. Other characters double in parts to further discourage the audience's tendency to identify with an actor. In addition, almost every scene contains at least one ballad that momentarily stops the action.

Stage business is a very important element in a Brecht play. The use of screens, slides, backdrops, and props of various kinds underscores the artificiality of the situation. *Mother Courage and Her Children* is frequently presented in the round or on a moving stage. The moving circle intensifies the play's message and adds to the audience's awareness of the cyclical nature of existence.

The story of *Mother Courage and Her Children,* like that of many of Brecht's other successful works, is derived from another literary creation: Grimmelshausen's seventeenth-century novel set during the Thirty Years' War. The play first appeared in English translation before it was staged in German. It opened in 1941 at the Zurich Schauspielhaus, with music by Paul Burkhard. *Mother Courage and Her Children* did not become well known until the 1949 Berliner Ensemble production in which Brecht's wife, Helene Weigel, played the title role. But because the Nazi press in 1941 emphasized the material qualities of *Mother Courage,* Brecht modified several scenes in the 1949 version in order to make his central character appear less pleasing. She is in the modern antiheroic tradition. Since 1949, *Mother Courage and Her Children* has been staged in London, Dublin, and many cities in the United States, Canada, and Europe. Anne Bancroft recently starred in a New York production. Darius Milhaud, the French composer, created music for Eric Bentley's English lyrics, but his score was never used. Paul Dessau's music is generally presented in modern productions.

The Caucasian Chalk Circle

by

BERTOLT BRECHT (1898–1956)

The Characters

Georgi Abashwill, the Governor—arrogant, cruel, and selfish, he is concerned only with his glory and power.

Natella, the Governor's Wife—a vain and overbearing woman, a snob who cares more for her wardrobe than for her son, and never learns humility or love.

Arsen Kazbeki, the Fat Prince—a Machiavellian nobleman who can congratulate the governor on the christening of his son while plotting to murder them.

Grusha—a kitchen maid of great kindness and humanity who risks her life and happiness for the governor's son. Deeply in love with Simon, she is torn between her devotion to Michael and her passion for Simon. She is rewarded when she is freed of her tyrant husband, given Michael, and awarded a fabulous fortune.

Simon—a good-hearted, affectionate soldier who remembers his pledge to Grusha after the war and returns to marry her. He patiently waits until she is granted a divorce.

Lavrenti—Grusha's loyal brother who shelters her from the pursuing soldiers and arranges for her marriage. He has a tyrannical wife.

Peasant Woman (Grusha's mother-in-law)—a schemer who overcomes the suspicions of the townspeople and priest to marry her son to Grusha.

317

Jussup—Grusha's husband, who beats his wife and mistreats his mother. At first he appears to be on his deathbed, but miraculously recovers when the war is over.

Azdak—a wily, earthy, and unscrupulous village scribe who sees the paradoxes of humanity. As a judge, he metes out unusual sentences full of common sense and moral perception.

The Grand Duke—disguised as a beggar, he is unmasked and his trial serves as a contest of merit between the fat prince's nephew and Azdak.

Arkadi Tscheidse—a professional storyteller who has been brought to the peasants by the central government.

The Story

Immediately after the expulsion of the Germans following World War II, peasants from two villages argue over the repartition of land. The group on the right wants the restitution of old boundaries and the resumption of traditional agricultural techniques; the group on the left has developed a plan for the drawing of new boundaries and for the scientific use of the land. After some bitter arguments, the delegate from the central government decides in favor of the left group and introduces Arkadi Tscheidse, a professional storyteller, who recites "The Chalk Circle." He begins the tale in verse, and slowly the characters he describes emerge on the scene.

The wealthy governor and his family are attending the christening of a newborn son. The milling crowds are shabby and starving, but the ruler is sumptuously dressed and well fed. A rival, the fat prince, congratulates the governor and his vain and selfish wife, but a few moments later rallies his forces to begin a bloody revolution. Meanwhile, at the governor's palace, Grusha, a servant, flirts with Simon, a soldier. They are in love, but as the noise of slaughter moves toward the palace, they are forced to separate, pledging to be faithful and meet at the end of the war. The governor's wife rushes into the courtyard and supervises the packing of her household. But she is more concerned with her dresses and other finery than her infant son, who is abandoned in the confusion. Grusha discovers the baby and, when warned that she will be killed if he is found with her, exclaims: "He looks at me! He's human." She flees with the child, pursued by the rebel forces.

Nearly fainting with starvation, Grusha and the child arrive at a peasant's cottage where she leaves the baby in care of an old woman. On the road, Grusha encounters ironshirts searching for the governor's son, returns to the cottage, rescues the child, and strikes one of the soldiers. Later, after traversing a rotten bridge at great risk, Grusha narrowly escapes the pursuing ironshirts and arrives at her brother's. Although her priggish sister-in-law is unsympathetic because she thinks Grusha has an illegitimate child, she is allowed to stay because of her desperate condition. Lavrenti, Grusha's brother, arranges for her marriage with a dying peasant who suddenly recovers when peace is declared and he knows he cannot be conscripted.

Grusha's husband is a tyrant who mistreats his wife. Simon arrives and Grusha is in despair because she had married thinking that her husband would soon die. She confesses that she is married and at first does not tell Simon that Michael, the governor's son, is not her own. In the moment when she is overwhelmed by love for Simon and reveals the truth, the ironshirts seize the boy and arrest Grusha.

In a nearby city, Azdak befriends an old beggar. Shauwa, a policeman, enters and demands that Azdak stop killing the nobility's rabbits. Azdak replies: "Man is made in God's image. Not so a rabbit, you know that. I'm a rabbit eater, but you're a man eater, Shauwa." After the policeman leaves, Azdak discovers that the beggar is the grand duke who is in hiding from the people who deposed him. He denounces himself and orders "the policeman to take him . . . to court to be judged."

In the courtroom, Azdak confesses sheltering the duke and predicts a new age when the guilty will give themselves up because the people will be the final judges. The ironshirts have just hanged the judge. Azdak entertains them with the story of how in Persia a peasant ruled the people, a soldier commanded the army, and a dyer paid the wages. Meanwhile, another revolution is occurring. The ironshirts unchain Azdak just as the fat prince arrives and demands that his nephew be the new judge. The ironshirts stage a contest between Azdak and the nephew, with the grand duke on trial. Azdak's wit and humanity triumph over the nephew's dry legalities, and he is appointed judge.

Now firmly established, Azdak hears a succession of cases and rules with peasant cunning, meting out unconventional justice. He often tries several cases at a time, adjudicating disputes between an invalid and a doctor, a blackmailer and his victim, a father and his adulterous daughter-in-law, and farmers and a bandit. Grusha and the governor's wife appear before him and demand that he decide who is the rightful mother of the child. The attorneys for the governor's wife disclose that the governor's estate, now restored, has been bestowed on the son, and whoever possesses him will become rich. Grusha recounts the hardships she has endured with the child and insists the child is hers. The governor's wife, still an arrogant snob, makes her claim. Finally, Azdak decrees that a chalk circle be drawn on the floor. The child will stand in the center, and on either side the governor's wife and Grusha will hold his hand and try to pull him out of the circle. The woman who succeeds will be declared the mother. The governor's wife pulls violently and Grusha lets go, declaring: "I brought him up! Shall I tear him to pieces? I can't." Azdak awards the child to Grusha, and gives her a divorce from her tyrant husband so she can marry Simon. A general dance closes the play.

Critical Opinion

The Caucasian Chalk Circle, first published in German in 1949, was written during World War II and widely circulated in a manuscript dated 1946. In a very real sense, this is a war play. Like many Brechtian dramas, it describes the embattled human condition in terms of war. Grusha, like Mother Courage, moves through a world of betrayal, negation, and destruction. Motivated by powerful human instincts, she suffers physical, emotional, and spiritual agonies to reaffirm the life principle in a war-torn universe.

Although she is exploited by the social system, Grusha rescues the son of her oppressor. Her maternal feeling and humanity have not been corrupted by society. Her constant refrain, "He's mine!" indicates her absolute devotion to humanity. Only once does she falter; when Simon reproaches her for marrying while he was at war, she momentarily denies her motherhood. This classical conflict between love and honor is resolved when Grusha redeems herself in the test of the Caucasian chalk circle. Oblivious of law, wealth, and force, her motherhood is triumphant. Physical hardship, social penalties, and even sexual passion do not vitiate the instinctive strength of moral responsibility.

Some critics have noted that *The Caucasian Chalk Circle* is typical of Brecht's later works in its fervent expression of faith in humanity. Unlike the pessimistic *In the Jungle of Cities* or *The Threepenny Opera,* it celebrates man's capacity to rise above greed, war, and oppression, and to triumph through goodness. The women in Brecht's later works embody his belief in survival through instinctive behavior and even love.

Grusha's loyalty to Michael is perhaps more dramatic because the child is not hers. Had Simon been the father, Michael would have been merely a physical token of Grusha's love. But an adopted child becomes all children, and Grusha's devotion becomes the passion of all mothers. She refuses to deny the accusation that Michael is her illegitimate offspring not only because she fears the iron-shirts but because the child is, metaphorically, from her loins. If she may be said to weaken in Simon's presence, Brecht is dramatically reassuring us that Grusha has successfully met the trial of love and honor. Michael may be regarded as the child of their love.

In *The Caucasian Chalk Circle,* we sense a softening of Brecht's earlier didacticism. Yet Brecht does not entirely abandon the idea embodied in *The Threepenny Opera* (1928), where he expresses his purpose as "two pronged, instruction and entertainment stand together in open hostility." The opening scenes vividly project the conflict between traditional and revolutionary social and economic attitudes, and the triumph of the peasants on the "left" and the government administrators clearly demonstrates Marxist principles in operation. The storyteller remarks: "We hope you will find that the voice of the old poet also sounds well in the shadow of Soviet tractors." Brecht simplistically draws the parallel between the debate over land usage and the struggle for the custody of a child; the storyteller concludes: "That what there is shall go to those who are good for it,/Children to the motherly, that they prosper,/Carts to good drivers, that they be driven well,/The valley to the waterers, that it yield fruit." Even in this play, Brecht has demonstrated that "the two constituent elements of the drama and theater, entertainment and instruction, have come more and more into sharp conflict."

The obvious and sometime crude sermonizing in *The Caucasian Chalk Circle* is augmented by songs and poems recited throughout the play. These interludes, often introduced in an arbitrary fashion, refer to events outside the play's action, but are infused with a folkloric quality.

Azdak's unconventional wisdom, iconoclastic procedures, and peasant cunning complement Grusha's emotional, direct, and innocent responses. But they are both aspects of the "new" personality that can be galvanized into a creative force by Marxism. The play's conclusion does not seem consistent with Marxist principles, however. Of course the nobility are despoiled of their wealth while Simon and Grusha receive the governor's estates. But although a soldier and a domestic servant receive wealth that has been taken from their oppressors, there is little in the play to suggest that this kind of justice will bring into being a new and better society or that wealth will not turn the couple into a new generation of *bourgeoisie*.

Brecht's lapses and inconsistencies are not emphasized enough by critics. They are impressed and distracted by his undeniable wizardry, his mercurial change of mood and perspective, and his inventive and surprising (alienating) twists in character and plot that provide such stimulating intellectual and theatrical fare.

The alienation effect that he had been developing for more than two decades is still apparent in this late drama. Brecht will not let his audience forget that they are witnessing a play. The storyteller controls time and place, manipulates action, and introduces themes by reciting poetry. He reminds the audience of the play's significance by interrupting the action to avoid prolixity and pure emotional intensity. Lyrical interludes, summaries of off-stage action, manipulations of time and place are really comments on the drama's significance. Like the chorus in Greek tragedy,

Arkadi Tscheidse brings the action into intellectual perspective.

The Caucasian Chalk Circle is regarded as one of Brecht's late masterpieces. The play has been widely performed throughout the world. In 1970, it was produced at Lincoln Center in New York City.

The Author

Born in 1898 in Augsburg, Bavaria, of well-to-do parents, Bertolt Brecht interrupted his study of medicine at Munich University because of World War I. He served as a medical orderly in the war, and wrote "The Legend of the Dead Soldier," a strongly antiwar poem that circulated in the German army and later became famous. In 1918, *Baal,* Brecht's first play, explored man's ruthless instincts, and in 1922, the first production of *Drums in the Night,* about postwar uprisings in Berlin, brought him the Kleist Prize. Brecht moved to Berlin soon after.

Germany in the twenties was the turbulent scene of social revolution and economic and social upheavals. The cynicism and despair of young artists found sympathetic reception, and Brecht's sensibility developed a scathing and mordant quality. To Lion Feuchtwanger, Brecht had "an unmistakable odor of revolution" about him.

After working with Max Reinhardt and Irwin Piscator, Brecht evolved a theory that he called Epic Realism. Rejecting the Aristotelian ideal of catharsis, Brecht developed a dramatic technique that refused to allow the audience to become emotionally involved in the play. Ballads, dance, motion picture projections, direct addresses to the audience, and sparse or nonexistent stage props constantly jar the spectator into awareness that he is a witness or a judge, not a participant in the spectacle. A series of plays in the 1920s, including *In the Jungle of Cities* (1921–23), *A Man's a Man* (1926), *Mahoganny* (1927), *St. Joan of the Stockyards* (1929), and perhaps his most famous work, *The Threepenny Opera* (1928), written in collaboration with Kurt Weill, brought Brecht world fame In association with musicians and scenic designers, he wrote oratorios, operas, and plays that strengthened his convictions concerning the dramatic possibilities of multi- and mixed-media presentations.

The social and political turmoil in Germany between the wars supported Brecht's Marxist beliefs. With the coming of Hitler, he fled to Denmark, Sweden, Finland, Russia, and finally, the United States. These years of exile (1933–45) saw the creation of *The Good Woman of Setzuan* (1938), *Mother Courage and Her Children* (1939), *The Life of Galileo* (1937–39; 1947), and *The Caucasian Chalk Circle* (1944–45). After hostile and humiliating confrontations with the House Un-American Activities Committee in 1947, Brecht departed for Switzerland, and then finally, in 1948, he went to East Berlin, where as head of the famed Berliner Ensemble, with his wife, Helene Weigel, he staged his own and others' plays that followed the epic theater techniques. Brecht died in 1956, one of the most highly regarded modern playwrights and dramatic theorists.

No Exit

by

JEAN-PAUL SARTRE (1905–   )

The Characters

Garcin—a middle-aged journalist whose sexual duplicity, hypocrisy, and cowardice render him incapable of recognizing the truth about his life. Cruel, sadistic, and selfish, Garcin is obsessed with his glory and worries because he will be remembered on earth as a coward.

Inez—strong, cold, and remorselessly truthful, she acknowledges the cruelty of her acts. She is in "Hell" because her sexual perversion has driven her to cruelty.

Estelle—vain, mindless, and without compassion, she is absorbed with the details of social convention.

The Story

Garcin, accompanied by the valet, enters a sumptuous drawing room done in Second Empire style. He is surprised because he finds no instruments of torture. Calmly remarking on the absence of windows, mirrors, and breakable objects, Garcin flies into a sudden rage because he has been deprived of his toothbrush. He soon realizes the absurdity of his anger, for here he has no need for a toothbrush, mirror, or even a bed. His fate will be "life without a break." When Garcin asks if it is daytime, the valet replies: "The lights are on," and goes out after explaining that the call bell does not always operate. Alone, Garcin explores the room, tries to open the door, and in a fit of anger pounds on it.

Just as Garcin regains his composure and sits down, the valet returns with Inez. She inspects the room and asks where Florence is. When the valet replies that he does not know, she comments: "Ah, that's the way it works, is it? Torture by separation." She assumes Garcin is her torturer and is surprised when he introduces himself as a journalist. Garcin suggests that living together will be easier if they both try to be extremely polite, but Inez gruffly refuses.

The door opens and Estelle enters and screams when she notices Garcin, who has covered his face with his hands: "Don't look up. . . . I know you've no face left." Again Garcin explains that he is not the torturer. Regaining her composure, Estelle objects to the hideous sofas and comments that the one left for her clashes with her clothing. When Inez' offer to switch is refused, Inez rudely suggests Garcin surrender his, and he complies.

The three inmates begin to talk of their deaths, and Inez mentions she was gassed the previous week. Estelle starts to describe her burial service, which is still going on, and explains that she died of pneumonia yesterday. Garcin was a victim of "twelve bullets through the chest" some time ago. As he starts to talk about himself, he seems to see his wife in Rio. She doesn't yet know about her husband's death. Estelle comments on the absurdity of putting the three of them together. Inez rejects Garcin's suggestion that it is mere chance: "I tell you they've thought it all out. . . . Nothing was left to chance." They decide to tell their life stories in order to discover why they have been grouped together.

Estelle tells how she was orphaned at an early age and had to bring up her six-year-old brother. In order to escape poverty, she married a wealthy old man with whom she lived happily until two years ago, when she fell in love with a young man. Yet she refused his offer to run away, caught pneumonia, and died.

In turn, Garcin reveals that he was a pacifist journalist who had rescued his wife from the "gutter." But Inez scoffs at these two attempts to depict angels and exclaims:

"We are criminals—murderers—all three of us. We're in hell, my pets; they never make mistakes and people aren't damned for nothing." She points out the absence of the torturer and concludes: "Each of us will act as torturer of the two others." Garcin rejects this suggestion but to avoid its realization asks that they keep away from each other and remain silent.

While Inez sings a vulgar song about execution, Estelle applies powder and lipstick. She asks for a mirror, commenting that in life she always made sure she was next to a mirror so that she could watch herself. Inez offers to serve as Estelle's looking glass and notices a pimple on her cheek. She inquires what would happen if the mirror lied, or even worse, if she refused to look at Estelle? Inez soon admits that she is too attracted to Estelle not to look, but Estelle cares only for Garcin. Because he cannot be left in peace, Garcin turns to Estelle and starts fondling her. When Estelle objects, Garcin insists they all must tell the truth about themselves, and he begins by confessing his mistreatment of his wife during their five years of marriage. He made love to a half-caste girl while his wife heard everything from her bedroom, and in the morning, she served the lovers coffee in bed.

Inez describes her Lesbian affair with Florence. She lived with her cousin, Florence, and her husband, planted the seeds of hatred between the couple, and moved away to live with Florence in a rented room. Soon after, the husband was run over by a streetcar. Inez cruelly made her lover suffer until one night Florence turned on the gas while Inez slept and killed both of them.

Estelle denies having anything to confess, but when asked about the man she expected to see without a face, she reluctantly reveals that he was her lover. She had a daughter by him, and one day while he watched, she tied the baby to a big stone and threw her from the balcony into the lake below. Estelle returned to Paris to her unsuspecting husband, and the young man shot himself.

The confessions completed, Garcin remarks: "None of us can save himself or herself; we're linked together inextricably." Estelle implores Garcin to hold her, but he gestures toward Inez and backs away. Estelle retorts: "But she doesn't count, she's a woman." She spits in Inez' face as Garcin goes to take her in his arms. They start to make love, when Garcin insists that Estelle respect him and admits he was shot for defecting from the army. She refuses to decide whether or not he was a coward. Garcin laments that his comrades will talk about him as a coward and starts to sob when he relates how his wife died of grief two months ago. He begs Estelle to have faith in him, but she laughingly replies that she cannot love a coward; yet because she likes men, she loves him.

Garcin frantically tries to open the door, and it unexpectedly opens. He refuses to leave and Inez closes the door again, proclaiming they are "inseparable." Garcin realizes he can only gain peace if he convinces Inez he is no coward; Estelle does not count. When Inez reproaches him for his deeds, he replies: "I died too soon." She retorts that it's always too soon: "You are—your life, and nothing else." She proclaims he is at her mercy, but Estelle reminds him of his weapon—he can kiss her before Inez' pained eyes. There is no need for a torturer, Garcin concludes: "Hell is —other people." Estelle rushes at Inez with the paper knife, but her act is met with laughter. Inez is already dead. All three break into laughter as they realize they are together forever. They regain their sofas and Garcin says: "Well, well, let's get on with it. . . ."

Critical Opinion

No Exit is a philosophical inquiry into man's responsibility in the modern world. As a philosopher-poet, Jean-Paul Sartre is interested in man's recognition of the consequence of his acts and his affirmation of existence through conscious choice of action. This existentialist viewpoint is a criticism of people like Garcin who see their lives as a formless process that can be set in order at any arbitrary moment. But no one is entitled to say, "I am not ready." Each person is responsible for his acts and must be conscious of his choice, whether it be voluntary or involuntary. Once this awareness is achieved, the individual *exists*. He must suffer or enjoy the consequences of his behavior. Even if the modern world is unjust and absurd, the individual must hold to a course of action dictated by his inner world and continue to act with a cognizance of the existence he has forged by his existential course.

No Exit is a philosophical rather than a psychological drama. The characters, situations, and events are vehicles for Sartre's philosophy. Inez, Estelle, and Garcin are modern archetypes rather than individuals. The archetype of homosexuality in Inez is vivid and arresting because she is a woman who has denied her femininity. Estelle, the essential female, is sensual, conventional, vain, and hypocritical.

Sartre chose to depict the antihero in his male character, Garcin. Masculinity usually connotes physical strength, bravery, and moral courage. But Garcin is a physical and moral coward, lustful and passionless. Although by conventional standards Inez is considered perverted, she is the only character who takes responsibility for her acts and has an existential authenticity. She is in hell because she has lived as though her existence were predetermined during her lifetime; she never chose her life: "I was already a damned woman."

In the course of the drama, Garcin achieves consciousness by confronting the choices in his past action and realizing that he does not live in a moral world. When he observes that "Hell is—other people," Garcin acknowledges that he lives in a world of people, that he cannot forget them, and that he must assume responsibility. In Garcin's own words, Estelle "doesn't count," for she cannot illuminate the human drama of responsibility. She is a frivolous product of a hypocritical society and ultimately has no moral meaning.

Hell in *No Exit* is not depicted in the Christian sense. There is no Christ balancing evil and good and no St. Peter or Satan awaiting the verdict. Hell is earthly existence. The characters are condemned to a room without egress because as murderers they have violated conventional morality. But the real source of their damnation and torment is their abdication of responsibility in a moral world (essentially nonsocial). Sartre is condemning the mode of existence and the process of arriving at actions in modern society rather than female homosexuality or fornication. There is "no exit" from life or hell, or from the necessity for moral action. Man cannot escape from his responsibility to society, to other individuals, or to himself. In their self-contained hell, the characters are on a merry-go-round. There is no beginning and no end to their damnation and, therefore, at the end of the play Garcin can only say: "Well, well, let's get on with it."

No Exit exemplifies Sartre's theory that French drama written during the German Occupation must be direct, succinct, and single-purposed. Although presenting a philosophical thesis, Sartre does not neglect traditional theatrical devices. At the beginning, the comic dialogue temporarily stays the austere and remorseless unfolding of the play. Garcin is foolishly enraged at the absence of his toothbrush, an irrelevant social convention. To him, this is the worst possibility hell can offer. The tastelessly elaborate nineteenth-century decor provides comic relief through social satire.

The play opens on a comic note as the characters refer ambiguously to hell. There are no doors or windows and the room is perpetually lit. The characters comment on the claustrophobic atmosphere. Like people in a crowded elevator, they coldly try to ignore their neighbors. Everyone expresses a nearly childlike disappointment at the absence of torturers and the other traditional accoutrements of hell. But once the occupants are ready to admit they are dead, the drama darkens and each person begins to evaluate his life. As the lies and illusions are stripped away, guilt emerges. Although acts motivated by sex dominate the catalogue of sins, Sartre clearly implies that society has made the modern individual a murderer. The statement "Hell is—other people" means that hell is life, life is hell. But whether it is life or hell, the individual must act and be responsible to himself and other people.

First produced in 1944 during the German Occupation of France, *No Exit* has become one of the most often produced one-act plays in modern drama. During the 1950s, when Existentialism was exerting a profound influence on the younger generation, it was often presented in small theaters and on college campuses. In 1962, an Argentine-American film starring Viveca Lindfors as Inez and Rita Gam as Estelle received international acclaim. In 1970, a Paris revival once again demonstrated the play's enduring popularity and relevance.

The Author

Jean-Paul Sartre was born in Paris and educated at the illustrious École Normale Supérieure. Teaching posts in the provinces and extensive travels in Europe and the Near East, as well as philosophical studies with Husserl and Heidegger in Germany, prepared him for the development of his revolutionary thinking. Returning to Paris in 1935, Sartre popularized Hemingway, Dos Passos, Steinbeck, and Faulkner in a series of articles on American literature.

During the next four years, Sartre wrote three psychological studies entitled *Imagination* (1936), *Emotions* (1939), and *The Psychology of Imagination* (1940), but his most noteworthy creations were the novel *Nausea* (1938) and a collection of short stories, *The Wall* (1939). With the appearance of *Nausea,* Sartre was acclaimed as a philosophical novelist. His hero's discovery of the meaninglessness of life anticipates Existentialism.

In 1939, Sartre was drafted into the French army. He was taken prisoner by the Germans, released after nine months, and upon his return to Paris joined the French Resistance, working on the underground paper *Combat.*

The Flies (1943), a full-length drama, depicted the necessity for moral responsibility during adversity and delineated the idea of *engagement*—engaging in shaping one's life. A long philosophical volume, *Being and Nothingness* (1943), was followed by the one-act play, *No Exit* (1944).

After the war, Sartre became the center of the influential philosophical movement know as Existentialism and in 1946 organized the review *Les Temps Modernes.* With Simone de Beauvoir, Albert Camus, and other leading intellectuals, Sartre developed his unique ideas. *Dirty Hands* (1948), a play that dramatized Sartre's and Camus's philosophical differences, reveals Sartre's sympathy with communism, which he renounced in 1956 after the Soviet intervention in Hungary.

Sartre's works include film scenarios, novels, plays, and philosophical treatises. In his essays *Existentialism Is a Humanism* (1945), *What Is Literature?* (1947), and *Situa-*

tions (1947–65), Sartre defined his view of Existentialism. The novel trilogy *The Roads to Freedom* (1946–49) illustrates this philosophy, as do numerous dramatic works, including, *The Respectful Prostitute* (1946), *The Devil and the Good Lord* (1951), and *The Condemned of Altona* (1959). In 1952, Sartre wrote a controversial biography of the playwright Jean Genet *(Saint Genet)* and in 1963, with Roger Garaudy, he examined *Marxism and Existentialism*.

Demonstrating his contempt for established institutions, Sartre declined the Nobel Prize for Literature in 1964. He continues to live according to his precepts, has publicly opposed the Vietnam war and all colonialism, and actively supports protest movements, often subjecting himself to arrest. At present, he resides in Paris with Simone de Beauvoir, an existentialist writer with whom he has lived since World War II.

Waiting for Godot

by

SAMUEL BECKETT (1906–   )

The Characters

Estragon (Gogo)—a scruffy tramp whose innocence belies his life of frustration. Childishly dependent upon Didi for food, solace, and companionship, Gogo is emotional and self-pitying. He used to be a poet.

Vladimir (Didi)—parent, professor, and friend to Gogo. Although his memory is unsure and his perception is cloudy, he never doubts the importance of waiting for Godot.

Pozzo—violent, sadistic, and tyrannical. His cruel and cowardly acts are elaborately rationalized. At first, he dominates Lucky, his slave, but then, blinded, he becomes a whimpering, impotent wreck.

Lucky—lives with a noose around his neck. His body and willpower have been destroyed by his enslavement to Pozzo. When commanded, however, he dances and thinks, revealing the world's "wisdom."

A Young Boy—Godot's messenger.

The Story

Seated next to a barren tree in the center of an empty stage, Gogo struggles to take off his shoe. "There's nothing to do,"

he declares when Didi enters. Didi is happy to find his
friend again and inquires where he spent the night. Fortu-
nately they have found each other, for Gogo would be lost
without him. But Gogo listens distractedly and continues to
pull on his shoe until he finally wrestles it off. Didi reflects
on the two thieves who were hanged with Christ: Was one
saved and one damned? But his metaphysical musings are
halted by Gogo, who wants to leave. They cannot, Didi
explains: They are waiting for Godot, who told them he
would come. Both tramps question the correctness of the
spot, the day, the hour.

When Gogo falls asleep, Didi awakens him because he is
lonely. In order to pass the time, they decide to hang themselves from the tree. Gogo insists that Didi must be the
first because he is heavier. If Gogo went first and the branch
broke, Didi would be left alone. However, they decide to
wait for Godot to hear what he will say. Gogo complains
of hunger, and Didi gives him a carrot. While munching,
Gogo asks if they are "tied" to Godot, but his inquiry is
interrupted by the entrance of Pozzo and Lucky.

Lucky, wearing a noose around his neck, carries a heavy
suitcase, a folding chair, and a picnic basket. Pozzo yanks
his servant's rope, cracks a whip, and demands the chair
and basket. Watching in amazement, the two tramps ask
if the master is Godot. They wonder why Lucky does not
put down his burden. Pozzo, who continually forgets what
he is going to say, finally says that Lucky is trying to impress his master so he will keep him. When Lucky cries,
Gogo wipes his tears, but is kicked in the shins. A little
later, after eating and feeding Gogo the bones, Pozzo
stands up and asks Gogo to invite him to sit down again.
Once seated, Pozzo decides to repay the tramps' politeness
by letting Lucky entertain them. Lucky pathetically hobbles
on to his toes for "The Dance of the Rope." Moments later,
when his bowler hat is placed on his head, Lucky begins a
long monologue filled with nonsequiturs and puns. His
cosmic diatribe seems to encompass all human activity:
research, anthropology, science, nutrition, physics, aviation,
sports, metaphysics, excretion. Pozzo, driven mad by the
speech, tugs frantically at his servant's rope and orders
Didi to remove Lucky's hat. Once Lucky is silenced, Pozzo

beats him, and then, with the help of the two tramps, he reloads the drooping figure. The couple departs.

Soon Godot's messenger, a young boy, arrives and asks for "Mr. Albert." He tells Didi that Godot will not come today. When questioned about his master, the boy reveals that Godot beats his brother, the shepherd, but feeds them both well. The messenger does not know whether he is unhappy. Alone again, Didi and Gogo contemplate separation. They resolve to leave, but do not move.

The following day, the two tramps are in the same place, but the tree is now covered with leaves. The barefoot Gogo examines a pair of shoes while Didi tries to recite a poem. Once again they argue about separating, but conclude that they might be happier together. Didi reminds Gogo that they were in the same spot yesterday, but Gogo denies it. Reconciling their argument, Gogo sighs: "We always find something, eh, Didi, to give us the impression of living." They discover Lucky's hat and are momentarily occupied trying it on. In order to pass the time, they pretend to be Pozzo and Lucky, then argue again and even call to God for mercy. Their prayers are interrupted by the entrance of Pozzo and Lucky. Pozzo, now blind, is led by Lucky. When they both collapse before the tramps, Gogo suggests assistance while Didi philosophizes about humanity. Gogo calls to Pozzo to learn his identity and is surprised when he answers to the names Abel and Cain. The tramps help Pozzo, who explains that one day he awoke blind and one day Lucky became a deaf-mute. "The blind have no notion of time." The strange pair go off, again leaving Gogo and Didi alone to discuss their futile existence. While Didi paces, a messenger announces once again that Godot will not come. Despite his appearance, he is not the same boy who came yesterday. He tells Didi that Godot's beard is white and leaves. As the moon rises, the two tramps decide to commit suicide. They will hang themselves with Gogo's belt. But when they test its strength, the belt breaks. They resolve to hang themselves tomorrow if Godot does not arrive. "Let's go," they announce; they do not move, they remain standing as the curtain falls.

Critical Opinion

First produced in Paris in 1953, *Waiting for Godot* seemed to fit into the catchall category of Theater of the Absurd. But it went beyond Ionesco's surrealistic drama by sounding the metaphysical depths of existential absurdity. The theatrical scene in Paris since World War II was marked by the revolt of Genet, Camus, Sartre, and Ionesco against traditional assumptions about man. These playwrights, and Brecht in Germany, developed new kinds of dramatic dialectic that, although differing from each other, posed fundamental questions about man's metaphysical existence. Through Marxism, Existentialism, surrealism, and erotic ritualism, Brecht, Sartre, Camus, Ionesco, and Genet had reoriented the audience's consciousness.

The Theater of the Absurd encompasses different philosophical orientations. Its two most famous exponents, Ionesco and Beckett, both obsessed with the destruction of the individual, envision different patterns of disintegration. Ionesco is concerned principally with the mechanical breakdown of values, language, and objects. In *The Bald Soprano,* words and feelings become meaningless and fragmented; in *The Chairs* and *Amédée, or How to Get Rid of It,* the material world—objects and the body—destroys the individual through its mere physical presence. Language, objects, and conventions clutter modern existence. Beckett, however, still gives meaning to language and physical reality when he emphasizes the metaphysical void of modern existence. While Ionesco believes that as a tool of communication language has broken down, Beckett insists that although words are valid, there is nothing to communicate. The barren clutter in his plays (garbage cans, sand piles, tape recorders) indicates the emptiness of man's soul.

In *Waiting for Godot,* the futile act of waiting epitomizes the empty and helpless course of modern life. The two tramps' mission in life is to wait for Godot, a mysterious, ominous Godlike figure who obsesses their consciousnesses, sends messengers, but never appears. His existence is doubted, and Didi and Gogo are afraid of missing their rendezvous. The audience learns that the white-bearded Godot owns lambs and goats, treats his shepherds with capricious justice (he beats one and not the other), and only communicates through messengers. Didi and Gogo never consider going to see Godot, but blindly await his arrival.

But is Godot really God, as his name suggests, or is he a figment of the fear and imagination of two outcasts? The tramps ponder theological questions, but remain confused about the reality of grace (was one thief really saved on the cross?). Gogo mistakes Pozzo for Godot and later addresses him as Cain and Abel, implying that Pozzo is man (evil and good), not God. The existential absurdity of modern life resides in man's need for God and his belief in His existence.

If the tramps are dependent on Godot, they are also tied to each other in their misery and confusion. They keep expressing their desire to separate but are incapable of action. Gogo tries to leave Didi but is reminded of his dependency when Didi tells how he thwarted Gogo's suicide. Only during the night, when they go their separate ways, do the tramps have private lives. Gogo describes how he is beaten each night and returns to Didi for comfort and reassurance.

The two tramps, although dependent, are not identical. Gogo, a former poet, is childlike, inquisitive, and compassionate; Didi, protective and rational, comforts Gogo when he is beaten and thwarts his desire for independence from him and Godot. Didi receives Godot's messengers and poses rational questions in an attempt to ascertain the nature of their awaited visitor. Gogo, however, never reflects upon Godot's identity and prefers to sleep, dream, and play games to pass the time. Compassionate and vulnerable, he is solicitous of Lucky's misery, but is kicked when he tries to console Pozzo's slave. When Pozzo collapses in Act II, Gogo rushes to his aid while Didi philosophizes. A child of the senses, Gogo is conscious of sore feet, hunger, and cold; he is a poet whose senses and dreams distinguish him from Didi. He feels overwhelmed by their oppressive condition and wants to escape through suicide, but loyalty prevents him; in his youth, he was rescued by Didi; two subsequent attempts are thwarted because of inertia and circumstance (his belt breaks).

Dependency is universal. Gogo and Didi are emotionally

inseparable, but Pozzo and Lucky are physically tied to each other. They elaborate upon the ramifications of the tramps' dependency. Pozzo and Lucky appear at the moment when Gogo asks Didi if they are "tied" to Godot. The second couple is literally bound together. Tyrannical and brutal, Pozzo exploits Lucky, forcing him to carry his paraphernalia, give him food, set up his chair. Pozzo wants to sell Lucky, but says he keeps him out of compassion and tolerates Lucky's efforts to prove his worth. In Act I, Pozzo admits that without Lucky he would never have known about beauty, grace, or truth. Lucky represents the artistic and poetic side of human nature. His speech is a phantasmagorical summary of human endeavor and knowledge: he rants about Watt-man (Everyman), God, science, food, and unsuccessful enterprise. His garbled message indicates that even excre-ment, man's greatest accomplishment, has failed to arrest the despair, horror, and futility of existence. Despite his suffering, he can create art: he dances with a noose around his neck. In "The Dance of the Rope" Lucky draws on his bondage for poetic inspiration. In Act II, Pozzo has lost his sight and Lucky is a deaf-mute. Their bondage is complete.

The pathetic dependence of the characters suggests both man's reliance on all facets of his spirit and on some higher being. Godot's identity and existence are irrelevant; man's search for something to direct him gives the unknown a reality that must be acknowledged. Bondage to a new entity points to the ultimate futility of an existence where man is shackled to a philosophical concept (God) that, in Beckett's view, is empty.

The nonappearance of Godot is unimportant because the waiting in life and the process of living, not the final rendezvous with God or death, are most significant. For Beckett, living is nothing—it is merely waiting, questioning, and passing time. Time, place, and events are fluid and meaningless. Pozzo exclaims: "One day we were born, one day we shall die, the same day, the same second." The crucial and perhaps insane quest for Godot keeps life form-less and provides the illusion of purpose to a futile existence in an empty universe. Gogo reminds Didi: "We always find something, eh, Didi, to give us the impression of living." Their waiting becomes a ritual. They debate whether or not to remain near the tree, whether or not they should separate, whether or not they should return the next day. Their conclusions are always final but not acted upon; at the end of each act, they agree to leave and do not move. Their static, impotent existences are touchingly dramatized as the lights dim, leaving them immobile in a barren landscape.

Much of the laughter in *Waiting for Godot* arises out of simple and natural vulgarities and obscenities. Didi urinates, both tramps scratch for bugs, and Gogo picks at his feet. Their vaudevillian antics add an element of theatricality to the spectacle. Poorly fitting shoes, exchanged hats, tripping and falling, and grotesque suffering *seem* to remove the clowns' world from our own. The barren stage, the twisted tree, and the mechanical moon are cheap music-hall trappings. But they, nevertheless, project an image of the tawdry landscape of the soul.

Waiting for Godot, written in French, was first produced in Paris in 1953. The American premiere took place in 1955, starred Bert Lahr, and had a successful Broadway run. Subsequently, the drama has been translated into more than twenty languages. A television version with Zero Mostel and a 1971 revival received high critical acclaim in the United States. *Waiting for Godot* is a staple of contemporary university and regional theater.

The worldwide influence of Beckett, chiefly through his dramatic masterpiece, *Waiting for Godot,* has no counterpart in modern drama. In awarding the Nobel Prize for Literature to Beckett, the secretary of the Swedish Academy spoke of his "combination of paradox and mystery, containing a love of mankind that grows in understanding as it plumbs farther into the depths of abhorrence, a courage of despair, a compassion that has to reach the utmost of suffering to discover that there are no bounds of charity."

Happy Days

by

SAMUEL BECKETT (1906–   )

The Characters

Winnie—a bespectacled lady, about sixty, who is buried up
to her waist in dirt. By the end of the play she is nearly
engulfed, but her loquacity, optimism, and will to live are
undiminished. Winnie continually reaffirms her humanity
while revealing the pathetic emptiness of her life.

Willie—slightly younger than Winnie, he spends his time
reading the newspaper, masturbating, ogling filthy pictures,
and crawling around the mound. Willie's responses to his
wife's badinage are laconic and often cryptic.

The Story

On a barren, scorched piece of land, Winnie sleeps, buried
up to her waist in a mound of dirt. A piercing bell finally
wakes her, and she exclaims upon the beauty of the day.
Rummaging through a black bag within arm's reach, she
extracts various objects and calls her husband, Willie, who
apparently is hidden behind the mound. As she examines the
various objects in the bag (spectacles, toothpaste, toothbrush, handkerchief, magnifying glass, pistol), she scolds
him for his lack of interest in life. Even her thrusts with a
parasol fail to rouse him as she admonishes him to cover

himself from the sun. Finally, Willie half-emerges, reading a newspaper and reciting an obituary. Winnie reminisces about the dead man's life as Willie reads from the classified section: "Opening for smart youth."

As Winnie tries to decipher the writing on a toothbrush handle ("Fully guaranteed genuine pure hog's setae"), she remarks that hardly a day goes by "without some addition to one's knowledge however trifling." Willie shows her a pornographic postcard, which Winnie examines and tosses away in disgust. Still pondering the meaning of the legend on the toothbrush ("What exactly is a hog? . . . Oh well what does it matter, that is what I always say, it will come back, that is what I find so wonderful, it all comes back"), Winnie attempts to start a conversation. She cannot bear to be alone and is compelled to talk even though she is ignored: "What *could* I do, all day long, between the bell for waking and the bell for sleep?"

As habit, memories, and picayune grammatical points arise, Winnie continues her monologue, spouts formulas, and prepares for visitors. Willie's monosyllabic responses to her questions elicit both joy and annoyance from her as she harangues and cajoles him. Winnie discusses her dependence, isolation, and happy memories, frequently veering from one emotion to another. She spies an ant carrying a white object that Willie identifies as an egg. Winnie is thankful that nothing is growing on the plain and that time is passing. The parasol bursts into flames, and she tosses it away, exclaiming: "Ah, earth, you old extinguisher." Winnie describes a couple who came upon them and were astonished at Winnie's plight and Willie's indifference. As she prepares for the night bell, Winnie reminds herself to pray.

Some time later, Winnie is buried up to her neck. In another long soliloquy, she recounts fragments of her past romances. Winnie, falling asleep, is reawakened several times by a bell. Her total immobility forces her to look at her own nose, pouting lips, tongue, and distended cheeks, and she recalls the days when she was beautiful and admired by Willie. Memories and fantasies obsess her about a child named Mildred who had a wax doll and was attacked by a mouse. She wonders if she should sing an evening song, but fears that if she ends it before the sleep bell rings she will become depressed.

Finally, Willie emerges in formal attire and climbs the mound, but rolls off just before reaching Winnie. She is ecstatic and sings a long song.

Critical Opinion

After *Waiting for Godot,* Samuel Beckett continued to refine his vision of human existence as a static, empty, and absurd charade. The futile stage business of *Godot* is reduced to people imprisoned in garbage cans and empty rooms in *Endgame* and memory mechanically encoded upon magnetic tape in *Krapp's Last Tape.* This paralysis of body and spirit is extended through the imagery and poetry of *Happy Days.*

The mound of earth that entraps Winnie is a physical manifestation of man's spiritual incarceration. At first buried only up to her waist, Winnie is able to rely on the material paraphernalia of everyday life. Her black satchel contains the props of a living death: toothbrush, toothpaste, mirror, handkerchief, spectacles, and revolver. Objects without meaning, they are playthings whose only real significance is to remind the owner of her existence and help her organize her day into an empty routine. Winnie's pathetic attempt to decipher the legend on the toothbrush and her belief in the significance of its message epitomize man's blind faith in the importance of knowledge. She is an archeologist of the modern soul, surrounded by artifacts and pondering meaningless legends on useless objects. Only the revolver presents a real course of action; yet she warns herself: "Take it away, Winnie, take it away before I put myself out of my misery." She places the revolver on the ground in front of her but fails to use it before she is buried up to her neck in the mound of earth.

Winnie's greatest consolation is her certainty that Willie, although often invisible and silent, is attentive and loyal. She fears the time "when I must learn to talk to myself a thing I could never bear to do." Willie's monosyllabic verbal responses, though often symbolic in their allusions to Shakespeare and other poets, are as empty as his companion's. Her faith in speech is, in fact, a devotion to emptiness.

> Words fail, there are times when even they fail. . . .
> What is one to do then, until they come again? Brush
> and comb the hair, if it has not been done, or if there
> is some doubt, trim the nails if they are in need of
> trimming, these things tide one over.

In his stage directions, Beckett indicates long pauses, showing his belief that human speech is a mechanical means
of filling a void and not a mode of communication. But
silence is also death, and Winnie's compulsive banter becomes her only hold on life as her body sinks into immobility. She speaks to herself and often calls her name merely
to keep the horrible void of her soul from overwhelming
her.

Man's reliance on the inaccurately remembered past, the
sound of his own voice, and the solidity of material objects,
is spiritual death. Winnie observes that if she were to
smash her glasses they would somehow become whole again
and find their way back into her bag the next day. She is
consoled in the knowledge that objects will outlast human
beings; yet she realizes her enslavement to them when,
holding a parasol, she exclaims: "I am weary, holding it up,
and I cannot put it down. I am worse with it up than with
it down and I cannot put it down."

Willie passes his time sleeping, reading the newspaper,
masturbating, gazing at obscene pictures, and crawling on
all fours. Obituaries and classified ads, symbols of death
and replacement, are his major literary interest. Winnie
waxes sentimental about the deceased. Arrayed in formal attire
Willie fails to reach the top of the mound in which Winnie
is buried and is last seen lying face down on the ground. The
emptiness and despair of his life are nonverbal, and his
"actions" include being invisible or half-hidden. His responses
to Winnie's loquaciousness are laconic and infrequent. He
represents the mute degradation that man endures while he
waits for death.

The passage of time is indicated by Winnie's sinking into
the earth. Physically immobile, she must contort her face
to gaze upon protruding lips, nose, and cheeks. As she
becomes more aware of time (and death), Winnie is
obsessed with her past and the inevitable sleep bell that will
signal the end of another "happy day." Her song acknowl-

edges the futility of speech ("Though I say not/What I may not/Let you hear") and ironically indicates that the "Dance" (of life—or death) expresses her love. Willie rises to his hands and knees and gazes at her, and the play ends.

The absurdity of Winnie's insistence upon the joy of life is reinforced by the inane formulas she repeats. She smirks and nods her head and announces that her conversation was in the old style. Then she unsmilingly continues her discourse, implying that the new style, although it includes the same clichés, is more brutal. Her constant refrain, "O Happy Days," is a formula response that is both heartfelt and ironic. As long as Winnie goes through the routine of living—delving in her satchel or talking to Willie—she believes she is happy. Yet ironically, the trivia of her existence point to the meaninglessness of her happiness. "Happy Days" is but another effort to fill a void.

The world premiere of *Happy Days* took place in 1961 in New York, starring Ruth White. A subsequent American production in 1970 (in French) starred Madeleine Renaud and Jean-Louis Barrault, who repeated their triumph in Paris, during an engagement that included productions of Beckett's dramatic works.

The Author

Samuel Beckett was born in Dublin in 1906. His well-to-do Protestant Anglo-Irish parents sent him to Trinity College. In 1927, he went to Paris to teach at the École Normale Supérieure. Before he returned to Dublin in 1931, he published a poem entitled *Whorescope*. Although he began work on a master's degree at Trinity, he abandoned the academic profession and traveled in England, France, and Germany. His friendship with James Joyce and other writers in Paris during the 1930s persuaded him to live in France, where he settled permanently in 1937.

Critical studies of Proust and Joyce and a collection of stories *(More Pricks than Kicks)* and poems *(Echo's Bones and Other Precipitates)* preceded two novels, *Murphy* (1938) and *Watt* (1953). After the war, Beckett began to write in French and published three novels, *Molloy* (1951), *Malone Dies* (1951), and *The Unnamable* (1953). *Waiting for*

Godot (1952), his first published play (his *Eleutheria* [1946] remains unpublished and unperformed), was followed by radio dramas, mimes, one-act and full-length plays. *Endgame* (1958), *Krapp's Last Tape* (1960), and *Happy Days* (1961) are among his most famous theatrical pieces. Beckett's most recent dramatic experiments have become increasingly cryptic and elliptical; he has also written a film, *Buster*, starring Buster Keaton. In 1969, Beckett received the Nobel Prize for Literature. In 1970, Jean-Louis Barrault and Madeleine Renaud presented a festival of Samuel Beckett's dramas in Paris.

Antigone

by

JEAN ANOUILH (1910–   )

The Characters

Antigone—Oedipus' impulsive young daughter, engaged to Haemon. Although she loves Haemon and dreams of the life they might have had together, she is determined to disobey the royal edict and bury her brother, even if it means her death.

Creon—Oedipus' brother-in-law, the present king of Thebes, who orders a ceremonious burial for Eteocles and condemns Polynices to rot in the desert. He is conscientious, pragmatic, and follows the path of expediency.

Haemon—Creon's son. When everyone expected him to choose the beautiful Ismene for a bride, he asked the wallflower Antigone to marry him. Having worshipped his father all his life, Haemon is disillusioned to discover a tired, compromising monarch who condemns people to death.

Ismene—Antigone's beautiful and vivacious older sister. She wants to help Antigone bury Polynices but is afraid to break the law.

The Nurse—a loyal, loving woman who raised Antigone and Ismene.

The Story

Dressed in elegant evening clothes, the characters are assembled on the palace steps in separate clusters, waiting to be introduced. The chorus declares that Antigone "will have to play her part through to the end." Haemon is talking to Ismene. One night at a ball, to everyone's surprise, he asked Antigone to marry him. But "His princely title will only give him the right to die." Antigone and Ismene are Oedipus' daughters. His sons, Eteocles and Polynices, waged war for possession of the throne, but when the brothers killed each other, Creon, their uncle, declared that Eteocles would have a state funeral; Polynices would be left to rot, and anyone who tried to bury him would be executed. The assembly disperses and the dimming lights indicate the approach of dawn.

After searching the palace, the nurse finds Antigone barefoot in the garden. She reprimands her charge for a clandestine meeting with her lover. When the nurse begins to cry, Antigone sends her off, reassuring her that she has been virtuous. Ismene appears and abruptly informs Antigone that she cannot proceed with their plan to bury Polynices; she does not want to die. Although Antigone rejects death, she declares she is not afraid of Creon's laws and sends her sister back to bed. After the nurse returns, Antigone wistfully asks her to care for her little dog if something should happen to her, but such thoughts are interrupted by Haemon's arrival. As soon as they are alone, Antigone apologizes for her previous night's quarrel, swears her love, and talks about the little boy they would have had together. She tells Haemon that she will never marry him and asks him to leave.

One of the guards informs Creon that someone has tried to bury Polynices. A child's shovel was found near the body. Creon swears the guard to secrecy and sends him back to uncover the body and watch over it. "Now the spring is wound," declares the chorus: ". . . the rest is automatic. For the first time, little Antigone is going to be able to be herself."

Two guards drag Antigone across the stage. She has been

caught trying to bury her brother again. Confronted by
Creon, she admits her guilt. Creon dismisses the guards,
again swearing them to secrecy. Creon berates Antigone for
having inherited her father's pride: she thinks it is her fate
and duty to die. But he rejects fatality. Antigone is young,
she must grow up, marry Haemon, have a son, and be happy.
Antigone says nothing and goes out in the direction of the
desert to attempt the burial once more. Furious, Creon
denounces the hypocrisy of religious burial; it is only an
empty ritual. Yet Antigone insists that she will bury Polynices and die. Creon brutally seizes his niece, confessing
that he did not want to be king. But it is his job. Antigone,
however, refuses to say "yes." Creon insists someone must
steer the ship; saying "no" is easy. He decides to tell Antigone the truth about her brothers. When the two men were
found, their bodies were so disfigured that it was impossible
to identify them. One was arbitrarily given a burial and the
other condemned. Antigone must find Haemon and happiness.

Quietly agreeing, Antigone is about to retreat when Creon
tells her: "Life is perhaps nothing more than the happiness
you find." This reminder of her happiness changes Antigone's
mind. She refuses to commit little sins for happiness. Like
her father, she asks questions to the end. Antigone insults
Creon, but is interrupted by Ismene, who asks to be killed
with her sister. But Antigone claims the act for herself
as she goads Creon into action. She is imprisoned.

Haemon runs to his father to plead for Antigone's life.
When Creon refuses to alter his edict, Haemon reveals his
disappointment in his father and leaves, declaring he will not
live without Antigone.

In her prison cell, Antigone chats quietly with the guard,
questioning him about life. She asks him to write a letter
for her, but when he seems incapable of understanding her
message, she merely says: "Forgive me." Before she can
give the address, the guards march in and take her to a
cave to be buried alive.

A messenger enters, describing how Antigone hanged herself by the cord of her dress. Haemon, kneeling at her feet,
refusing to listen to his father's calls, suddenly drew his
sword and killed himself. In the palace, the queen calmly

committed suicide. Alone with his page, Creon looks at his agenda for the day and goes off to a cabinet meeting.

Critical Opinion

Antigone is a drama about freedom—about man's struggle for dignity, heroic action, and self-liberation. Written during the German occupation of France, *Antigone* emphasizes a new consciousness: the refusal to submit to tyrannical authority. While many Frenchmen toadied to the Nazis, Anouilh subtly encouraged his compatriots to rebel.

Anouilh's adaptation of the classical myth was not innovative for French twentieth-century theater. Cocteau (*Orpheus*, 1926), Gide (*Oedipus*, 1930), and Giraudoux (*Amphitryon 38*, 1929) had already employed Greek legends to present new philosophies and esthetic ideas. The wartime mythological parallels of Sartre (*The Flies*, 1943) and Camus (*Caligula*, written in 1938) had already been conceived. However, while the subject matter of *Antigone* was not revolutionary, Anouilh's use of a female heroine was unique.

Antigone is a symbolic play. From the beginning, the chorus eliminates all elements of surprise, foretelling the disaster and all its consequences. Antigone represents the theme of freedom. She will "rise up alone in front of everyone." Creon, who "plays the difficult game of leading men," embodies the principle of authority. Both characters are completely isolated. As two uncompromising forces, they have only to be pitted against each other for the tragedy to begin. Anouilh underlines the inexorable nature of tragedy as well as his dramatic intention when the chorus declares:

In tragedy everyone is tranquil. First, you're at home. Everyone is innocent! It's not because there's someone who kills and someone else who is killed. It's all a matter of the part you are playing. And then, above all, tragedy is restful because you know there is no more hope, foul hope. . . . In drama, you fight because you hope to escape. It's unworthy, it's practical. There [in tragedy] it's gratuitous. It's for kings.

Through the chorus, Anouilh emphasizes the inevitability of tragedy and frees the drama from its traditional reliance on plot. The philosophical arguments are the most important aspect of the play; the story serves merely as a vehicle for their presentation.

Antigone is a product of her heritage but also a self-made rebel. Like her father, Oedipus, she is not afraid to meet her fate and willingly seeks truth even if it brings death. She refuses to bow to Creon's counsel of expediency.

Antigone believes in a moral code: if happiness means that she must commit petty sins, then the price is too high. "Like my father, yes," she tells Creon, "we're those who ask questions to the end." Moments before her death, Antigone murmurs: "Only now do I understand how simple it is to live. . . ." She dies heroically, not a victim of fate but a molder of her own destiny.

In a sense, Antigone is an existential hero. Like Camus's Meursault (*The Stranger,* 1942), and Sartre's Oreste (*The Flies,* 1943), she refuses to play the game and will not conform to society's will if it means compromising her individuality. She recognizes the absurdity of existence because the defilement of Polynices' corpse is purely arbitrary. Identification of the two brothers was impossible; one corpse received an honorable burial and the other was left to rot on the battlefield. Despite this absurdity, Antigone acts. She buries her brother and accepts responsibility for her action.

Antigone's liberation from tyranny might be interpreted in terms of a new female consciousness. She refuses to "understand" the way of the world. She rejects the idea that a woman must not come in contact with the dirt and rottenness of life, and that she must be beautiful and passive, like her sister, to attract a husband. When Ismene advises her to forget her brother because she is only a little girl, Antigone confesses that she has already acted.

Creon summarizes the hopelessness of the conflict with Antigone when he tells her: "It's agreed that I have the bad role and you the good." Creon is a sympathetic figure who because of circumstances is obliged to assume the difficult role of leadership. Someone must stand at the helm and think of the ship, not of himself: "In order to say yes, you must sweat, roll up your sleeves, plunge both hands into life up to the elbow. It's easy to say no, even if it means dying." Putting the case for law and order, Creon argues in abstractions, failing to recognize the difference between people, ships, or animals, for when he suggests to Antigone that animals never reject their responsibilities, Antigone astutely comments: "What a dream, a king for animals! It would be so simple." For her, man is not passive like an animal; he acts of his own will.

Creon nearly convinces Antigone that her death would be in vain. Fighting for religious burial is pointless; it is merely a hypocritical ceremony. Dying to restore Polynices' honor is equally futile. Antigone is not even sure that he, and not Eteocles, is the defiled corpse. However, Creon loses his case when he declares: "Perhaps life is nothing more than happiness."

Like all tyrants, Creon thinks in absolutes. People must be happy and kings must rule. Young girls should marry and have children. Morality is simply a device to be used by the ruling class when expedient. Despite Antigone's death and the suicides of his son and wife, Creon is virtually unaffected. As the king, he goes off to a cabinet meeting.

In Anouilh's theater, there is a symbolic contrast between adulthood and childhood. Maturity means compromise, and therefore the playwright's heroes are always childlike, refusing to accept the arbitrary standards of society. Haemon reluctantly acknowledges that his father is no longer "this giant god who held me in his arms and saved me from monsters and shadows." When he pleads that he is naked and alone if he cannot admire his father, Creon pragmatically asserts: "Look at me, that's what becoming a man is, one day to look directly into your father's face." Antigone also refuses to grow up and acquiesce. Even Creon acknowledges the tragedy of adulthood when he tells his page: "You must never grow up." The child retains his sense of the absurd and preserves a human perspective.

Anouilh's *Antigone* is based on the drama by Sophocles that was written about 442 B.C. While the basic story of the two plays is similar, the philosophy has been modernized. In Sophocles' tragedy, Creon has sinned against the gods and religion. In Anouilh's, Creon has betrayed humanity, and his conflict with Antigone concerns a question of *per-*

sonal morality. Although the French drama is patterned after Greek dramaturgy, with a chorus and a sense of fatality, it is unquestionably a modernization of the classic tragedy. The characters are in evening dress, and there are other anachronistic elements—from the coarse and stupid guards who discuss their wives and card games to the motherly nurse who chides Antigone for her flirtations and the heroine's little dog who soils the carpet.

Antigone is one of Anouilh's "black dramas." The hero is in revolt against tyranny. In spite of its implicit criticism of the German regime in France, the play was highly successful when it opened in Paris on February 4, 1944. In the fifteen months that saw the retreat of German forces and the Allied liberation, the play was presented 475 times. Perhaps the sympathetic portrait of Creon encouraged the Nazis to overlook the revolutionary material in the drama. Yet *Antigone* is more than a play about the liberation of France. It is a universal statement about individual freedom and human dignity. *Antigone* has been especially popular with repertory theaters. In recent years, it has been widely performed on college stages.

Becket or The Honor of God

by

JEAN ANOUILH (1910–   )

The Characters

Henry II—loutish, passionate, and sensitive, he is deeply devoted to Becket, almost as much as to his kingship of England.

Thomas Becket—the epitome of intellectual man searching for a mode of existence that will give him self-esteem in a chaotic world. A Saxon in a land dominated by Normans, he yearns for a life free of political and racial problems.

Gwendolen—Becket's mistress, appropriated by Henry II. She commits suicide when she is forced to leave Becket.

Four English Barons—brutish followers of Henry II, who typify mindless feudal loyalty. They reflect the coarse, pragmatic side of Henry's character.

Queen Mother—cold, insolent, and domineering, she tries to control her son even after he becomes king.

The Queen—a nagging and unattractive shrew who remonstrates with her husband over his mistresses and his love for Becket.

Louis, King of France—an intelligent, cynical monarch whose humanity is aroused by Becket's dilemma.

Gilbert Folliot—a "thin-lipped, venomous man," Bishop of London. He becomes Henry's ally in overthrowing Becket.

The Pope—a stereotype of the Machiavellian, Italian politician; he is unscrupulous and self-seeking.

The Story

Henry II, kneeling at the tomb of Becket, prepares to be whipped in penance for his destruction of the former archbishop of Canterbury. He addresses his dead friend. The subsequent scenes are extended flashbacks. As Henry laments the end of his friendship with Becket, the dead man emerges into a scene that took place years earlier. Becket tells Henry how his father, a Saxon, collaborated with the Norman invaders and avoided ruin.

At a council meeting, the king demands taxes from the Church; Becket, who has been designated chancellor of England, effectively argues in favor of the state. The clergy are scandalized at Becket's opposition, for he is a deacon of the Church and they considered him their man. Later, Becket and the king are hunting and seek shelter in a peasant's cottage during a rainstorm. The king bullies the peasant and is astonished to find his people living in wretchedness. When a young girl is discovered, the king decides to make her a palace whore and gives her to Becket, who has just defended his life against the girl's brother. Henry, however, demands "Favor for favor," not stipulating what Becket will have to give in return.

At the palace, Gwendolen declares her love for Becket, but he seems reticent. The king and the barons enter, listen to Gwendolen sing about Becket's Saracen mother, and mock Becket's feelings. Henry then demands that his friend give him Gwendolen; she leaves reluctantly and the peasant girl is delivered to Becket's bed. Henry rushes in; Gwendolen has killed herself in his arms. The peasant girl is dismissed and the terrified king crawls into bed with Becket and falls asleep. Becket asks himself: "But where is Becket's honor?"

In Henry's military camp in France, the barons ponder Becket's character. Becket enters and declares that the captured cities must not be sacked. He then goes to wake the king, summarizes the preceding day's battle, and reminds Henry that he must govern his captured provinces with wisdom. Guards bring in a young monk who had been lurking near the king's tent with a knife hidden under his habit. Becket immediately identifies with the youth and has the would-be assassin sent back to Hastings.

During the triumphal march through a captured city, Henry is impressed by the tumultuous reception accorded him. Becket dampens his spirit, however, by telling Henry that the people have been bribed to demonstrate their affection for their conqueror. Later, in the town's cathedral, rumors of an assassination plot cause momentary panic, but Becket is master of the situation. News of the archbishop's death in England is received. The king plans to designate Becket as archbishop, thus ending the State-Church dispute in his kingdom. Some time later, in the archbishop's palace, Becket sells all his worldly possessions for the benefit of the poor and invites the beggars to a sumptuous banquet. Communing with God, Becket murmurs: "Lord, are You sure You are not tempting me? It all seems far too easy."

At the royal palace, the queen mother and the queen berate Henry for having given Becket power. The king, in an agony of remorse, cries: "He is my friend!" He violently insults the women and learns that Becket has ignored his summons and has returned the lord chancellor's seal, indicating his change of allegiance from the king to the Church. The king demands that Folliot destroy Becket's power; Henry plays upon Folliot's prejudice against the Saxon archbishop and impresses him with the political wisdom of turning against Becket. Folliot confronts Becket and tells him that the king, deeply resenting the archbishop's excommunication of his three most trusted advisors, has accused Becket of embezzling state funds. The battle lines are drawn.

Becket defies the royal tribunal and flees to France, where he takes refuge in the court of King Louis. The French monarch refuses to extradite the fugitive archbishop, and in an interview with Becket, he expresses his admiration and sympathy and grants Becket safe conduct to Rome. In the papal palace, the pope confers with a cardinal, revealing that Henry has offered a bribe for Becket's return to England. In a comic scene, the churchmen decide to accept the bribe and send Becket to a monastery in France.

At the French court, Louis tells Becket that he will be sent back to England. A meeting with Henry is arranged on a desolate plain, and Henry tells Becket: "I will help you defend your God, since that is your new vocation, in memory of the companion you once were to me—in all save the honor of the Realm." But Henry decides to have the archbishop of York crown his young son as King Henry III, thus insulting Becket by ignoring his prerogative.

The queen and queen mother predict rebellion if there are two kings and lament Henry's obsession with Becket. In a fury of despair, Henry dismisses the women and asks his four barons: "Will no one rid me of him?" The barons gird on their swords and rush out.

In Canterbury Cathedral, Becket dresses in his most sumptuous clerical garb. The young monk, now a close companion, warns him of impending doom. The barons rush in and slay Becket and the monk, and the stage becomes dark. As the lights come up, we see Henry being flogged next to Becket's tomb. When his punishment is over, he gloats that now all England—Saxons as well as Normans— will acknowledge him as sole ruler because of his penance. He will suppress his son's rebellion.

Critical Opinion

Ostensibly an historical drama, *Becket* is really an imaginative reinterpretation of a crisis that has timeless significance. Like *The Lark* and *Antigone,* this play presents crucial moments in an individual's struggle for integrity. Themes of martyrdom, innocence, and idealism, which recur in all of Anouilh's works, are restated and elaborated upon in *Becket.*

Anouilh plays upon the ironies implicit in historical or mythological situations, intellectual tension, and comic release, by juxtaposing modern attitudes and manners with archetypal problems. The action takes place in the twelfth century, when Henry Plantagenet was consolidating the Norman conquest of the Saxons in England. But the essential drama deals with the universal dilemmas of friendship and authority, feeling and duty.

Thomas à Becket is a Saxon whose quest for order and meaning in the world obliges him to pledge his allegiance to King Henry. The love Henry feels for his young companion is a luxury that only a man in power can afford. Becket's fealty to Henry is both a political and intellectual necessity that supersedes affection for Gwendolen, loyalty to the banished Saxon race and, before his designation as archbishop of Canterbury, loyalty to the Church. Although this play is subtitled *The Honor of God,* Becket is really concerned with self-respect and honor. As a faithful servant to his king, he successfully opposes the Church; as archbishop of Canterbury, he defies his former master. But Becket's love for king and God is formal and unfeeling; it is without meaning in human terms. In his loyalties, Becket fulfills his office according to his sense of duty and honor. Because he is intellectually involved, he can mechanically switch roles without letting a former allegiance influence his purpose.

The turning point of the play occurs when Henry designates Becket archbishop in the mistaken belief that his young companion in arms will be a tool of his will. Failing to understand the complex, intellectual nature of his friend, and unwilling to recognize that Becket does not return his love on a human level, Henry creates his own enemy. Becket explains:

> I felt for the first time that I was being entrusted with something, that's all—there in that empty cathedral, somewhere in France, that day when you ordered me to take up this burden. I was a man without honor. And suddenly I found it—one I never imagined would ever become mine—the honor of God.

Becket's sense of honor is essentially a medieval or French classical ideal; it is something external to the individual and his personal feelings, signifying duty and allegiance to an established order. Becket reiterates this point several times in the play. While hunting with the king, he is asked: "Why do you put labels onto everything to justify your feelings?" Becket replies: "Because without labels, the world would have no shape, my prince . . . otherwise we can't know what we're doing." And in his last interview with Henry, Becket declares that although he cannot say that he loves God, he has "started to love the Honor of God." He likes the idea of duty because it gives him identity. His martyrdom occurs when, as he goes to celebrate vespers in the great cathedral, he declines to take refuge behind the choir gates. Becket calmly announces: "It is time for vespers. Does one close the choir gates during vespers? I never heard of such a thing. . . . Everything must be as it should be." The archbishop's insistence on formality as a way of giving shape to a world fraught with passion, intrigue, and disorder is a final definition of his concept of honor.

Henry frequently asks if Becket loves him, but human love has no meaning for the young man. When his first duty is to the king, he is loyal. He does not reciprocate Gwendolen's love and expresses himself only through lust. Although Becket knows that their separation will bring about her destruction, he relinquishes Gwendolen because of his duty to the king. He is incapable of placing human feelings above legal considerations. Only the memory of his Saracen mother moves him to a display of feeling when he asks that her song not be sung in front of the king and his barons. But he succumbs to the king's insistence.

The young monk who Becket saves from execution and later befriends is, like Becket, a Saxon from Hastings who is intent upon avenging the humiliation of his race. Becket's mercy is merely an expression of self-love: "It's pure selfishness, you know. Your life hasn't any sort of importance for me, obviously. But it's very rare for Fate to bring one face to face with one's own ghost when young." Anouilh confirms the significance of their identity by depicting their simultaneous deaths.

The martyrdom of Anouilh's Becket is different from that of T. S. Eliot's hero in *Murder in the Cathedral*. Questions of holiness and self-abnegation do not concern the French dramatist. Eliot's protagonist is torn by doubts and misgivings: if a man seeks martyrdom, can he be a true martyr? Anouilh's Becket never doubts his actions because they are based on intellectual, not emotional or spiritual, considerations.

Vulnerable, passionate, and self-pitying, Henry must accept the duty of kingship and ignore his true feelings. Anouilh's shrewd understanding of political motivation illuminates Henry's struggle to accept the lonely eminence of kingship. After being whipped by the monks, the king rises, dons his royal cloak, and proceeds with the business of consolidating his realms and crushing his son's rebellion. Like Creon in *Antigone*, he has learned how to manipulate power and is willing to compromise his love and humanity for its preservation.

Henry's love for Becket is not a homosexual passion but an expression of his loneliness and insecurity. Because Henry is proud of his indifference to intellectual, moral, and esthetic problems, he regards Becket as fulfilling a deficiency in his character. Henry is moved to admiration for his young companion and drawn to his wit and loyalty because of his total isolation in a world of nagging women and bestial men. The flogging at the tomb is both a sincere personal act of repentance and a shrewd political maneuver. In the course of the drama, Henry learns that a king cannot have a companion; he must guard the honor of the realm alone.

The historical fact of Becket's death is essential for the dramatic structure of Anouilh's play. The opening scene underlines the finality of the story, and the drama depicts Becket going to fulfill his destiny. The play derives its central impact through the juxtaposition of the present and the past. Anouilh's dramaturgy is brilliantly effective in communicating the fluidity of time and memory. An epic quality is established through the rapid succession of tableaux. By eliminating static scenes, Anouilh gives the drama momentum and flamboyance. The New York production included false horses, removable backdrops and scrims, portable thrones and props.

The scene between the pope and his cardinal achieves a comic mood when their two thrones are rolled out from opposite ends of the stage to the accompaniment of Italian baroque music. Henry, too, has comic elements in his character. He rails at his wife and mother, ignores decorum, and revels in lust and boorishness. When he criticizes the esthetic taste of his wife, Eleanor of Aquitaine, the audience is amused, because in historical fact she was one of the most learned, cultured, and artistic women of the Middle Ages. But the comedy is always tempered by the deadly seriousness of the psychological and political drama, which (thanks to the adroit manipulation of sets, props, and lighting) moves with inexorable speed to its preordained conclusion.

Becket or The Honor of God was completed in 1958 and that year received its premiere in Paris. A London production was followed by a widely acclaimed New York opening that starred Anthony Quinn as Henry and Sir Laurence

Olivier as Becket. An elaborate film (1964), featuring Peter
O'Toole and Richard Burton, vitiated the wit and compression of Anouilh's masterpiece, but brought worldwide attention to one of the finest dramas written since World War II.

The Author

When asked to write his autobiography, Jean Anouilh
once said, "I have no biography, and I'm very happy about
it." Born in Bordeaux, France, the son of a tailor and
violinist, the young Anouilh moved to Paris where, after
attending both grammar school and high school, he entered
the Faculty of Law. However, this career was brief. After a
year and a half, Anouilh quit to work for an advertising
company. During these years, Anouilh began writing. By the
age of nineteen, he completed two plays, *Humulus the Dumb*
and *Mandarine* (1929). Although he worked briefly as secretary to Louis Jouvet, the famous French actor-director-pro-
ducer, Anouilh suffered great poverty, and even after his
marriage had to struggle for mere survival.

Anouilh says he decided to devote himself to the theater
after writing *Hermine* (1931). Since that time, he has written a new play practically every year, including *Thieves'
Carnival* (1932), *Traveler Without Baggage* (1936), *Antigone* (1942), *Waltz of the Toreadors* (1952), *The Lark*
(1953), *Poor Bitos* (1956), and *Becket* (1958).

Grouping his works into four categories, black, rose, brilliant, and grating, Anouilh tried to distinguish them by
their mood and tone. The four groupings, however, are
fairly fluid, and seriousness and wit inform all his dramas.
Themes of liberation, self-discovery, conflict between youth
and age, and the quest for mutual understanding are common in Anouilh's early and late plays. Today, Jean Anouilh
continues to write. He is considered one of France's foremost dramatists.

The Maids

by

JEAN GENET (1910–   )

The Characters

Solange—a thirty-five-year-old spinster who has always lived with her sister, Claire. She is masculine and domineering but fundamentally cowardly. Solange is sensitive to the physical beauties of Madame and Claire, and in matters of the imagination, she reacts to others' stimulation. Claire's harangues send her into a frenzy and her letters arouse her passion. Although she seems to direct the masquerade, she is incapable of carrying it through.

Claire—five years younger and more feminine than her sister, she is imaginative, strong-willed, and ultimately ruthless enough to bring about the symbolic deaths of her sister and Madame by her own suicide.

The Madame—a twenty-five-year-old beauty, emotionally extravagant, self-dramatizing, and scatter-brained.

The Story

In a sumptuously furnished Louis XV bedroom, Claire and Solange, two maids, enact a ritualistic scene in which Claire pretends to be their mistress and Solange plays the part of Claire, her sister. As the mistress, Claire is haughty, cruel, and demanding. Dresses, jewels, and other apparel are prepared for Claire. Solange obsequiously polishes patent-leather shoes while being reprimanded for her laziness. During this scene, Claire drops a comment to her sister about their failure to seduce a milkman, but she quickly resumes her role. Claire (once again playing the mistress) confesses that she sent her lover to prison by writing an anonymous letter to the police. She haughtily says she will follow him to Siberia or to Devil's Island, where she will share his criminal glory. Solange suddenly exclaims: "I'll follow you everywhere. I love you."

Claire condescendingly describes the sisters' garret, where they fall asleep "dreaming of one another." The conversation increases in intensity and Claire kicks Solange in the head. Solange bursts into a tirade: "I'm tired of being an object of disgust. I hate you, too. I despise you. I hate your scented bosom. Your . . . *ivory* bosom! Your . . . *golden* thighs. Your . . . *amber* feet! I hate you!" There is a momentary break in the masquerade as Solange addresses her sister as Claire, but Claire, as the mistress, reminds her sister of their roles. Just as the two women are reaching a frenzy of sexual, murderous passion, an alarm clock warns them of the imminent return of the real Madame.

Disappointed, like two people whose lovemaking has been interrupted, they rush to straighten up the bedroom, but are overwhelmed by exhaustion. The sisters discuss their hate for Madame's lover, Monsieur, and describe the expression on his face when he was arrested as a result of their anonymous letter to the police. Solange then reveals that she has seen Claire playing Marie Antoinette and strolling about the apartment at night. Again the maids engage in vituperation, this time without playing roles. Solange exclaims that they cannot love each other, for "filth . . . doesn't love filth . . . and if I have to stop spitting on someone who calls me Claire, I'll simply choke! My spirit of saliva is my spray of diamonds!" They refer to former masquerades, when Solange played the role of Madame and Claire that of the maid Solange. Apparently they have invented imaginary lives with lovers who are criminals.

The sisters continue their recriminations as Solange reveals that just as she was about to kill the real Madame one night, the woman turned over in bed and was so beautiful that Solange became powerless. The phone rings and Monsieur leaves a message that he has been released by the police and will meet Madame in a bar. The sisters realize that they soon will be discovered and plan to poison Madame's tea upon her return.

A few moments later, the mistress enters in an emotional flurry. She extravagantly gives her dresses and furs to the sisters as presents and refuses to look at the day's accounts. She renounces life without her lover. But when she receives his telephone message, she reprimands her maids for not telling her of Monsieur's release and forgets about the gifts she has made. She checks over the accounts and prepares to meet her lover. Solange is sent to find a taxi while Claire attempts to offer Madame the cup of poisoned tea. But Madame's excitement is too intense. She neglects to drink it and rushes out to the taxi.

Alone once again, the sisters argue about their failure to kill Madame and anticipate their exposure as Monsieur's accusers. This time, Solange starts to play Madame, but Claire insists that it is her role. The masquerade resumes with greater intensity, and Solange proclaims: "It's God who's listening to us. We know that it's for Him that the last act is to be performed, but we mustn't forewarn Him. We'll play it to the hilt."

Claire puts on a long white dress over her own black dress whose black sleeves show. Claire (as Madame) insults the servant, when suddenly Solange (as Claire) threatens her with a riding whip and makes her crawl. Madame cannot follow her lover to prison, for the maid, who is "both the thief and his slavish shadow," is the only worthy one. Claire, overwhelmed with emotion, tries to break the masquerade, saying "We're out of our depth. We must go to bed." But Solange brutally continues: "We're both beyond the pale." Claire collapses and is helped off the stage by Solange, who first in her own voice and then in Madame's delivers a monstrous monologue full of guilt and hate.

Claire returns, still wearing the white dress, and resumes Madame's part. She demands the poisoned cup of tea. This time, it is Solange who tries to stop the masquerade. But Claire is relentless and forces Solange to serve her the poison. As Claire drinks, Solange proclaims: "Madame is dead. Her two maids are alive: They've just risen up, free, from Madame's icy form."

Critical Opinion

In *The Maids,* Jean Genet has constructed an elaborate masquerade in which characters can play any number of roles. They are always play-acting, even when they think that they are themselves. By exploring the unconscious forces that control men, Genet has gone beyond Pirandello's idea that illusion and reality are not distinguishable.

According to Jean-Paul Sartre, Claire and Solange are "Pure products of artifice, their minds are inside out, and they are always other than themselves." The play opens with the two sisters in a complex rearrangement of their life roles. Claire, who seems more sensitive and passive, plays the role of Madame, the sisters' twenty-five-year-old employer. Solange, who is about thirty-five years old and seems more masculine and assertive than her sister, has taken the role of Claire. Claire's interpretation of Madame's personality is totally unrealistic: It is a stereotype of a servant's resentment of her employer. She bullies and berates Solange, calling her Claire (herself).

The real Madame and Claire's interpretation of her differ radically. Yet there is a mythical and elemental truth in the idea that the mistress should dominate the servant and the servant should hate the mistress. Claire, in the role of Madame, is also expressing self-hatred as she attacks Solange, who is playing the part of Claire. Yet Claire dramatizes *both* her own and Madame's hatred for Solange.

The two sisters have engaged in this ceremony of masquerading for a long time. Sometimes Solange plays Madame and addresses Claire as Solange. The dimensions of the masquerade are expanded when the real Madame enters and the two sisters masquerade as attentive, loving servants. The maids' private fantasies, stimulated by the religious and erotic tales they read, their fantasies about Mario the milkman and their failure to seduce him, add depth to their complex masquerade. Letters written by Claire, strewn around their garret, imply fantasies about an exciting and adventurous life. And finally, their anonymous letter of accusation that has put Monsieur in prison is the ultimate extension of their love-hate for this masculine figure, their desire for revenge against Madame, and their identification with her. In various speeches, they vow to follow their lovers (or each other) to penal institutions and revel in their criminality. Claire says:

> . . . if I have to leave for Devil's Island, you'll come with me. You'll board the boat. The flight you are planning for him can be used for me. We shall be that eternal couple, Solange, the two of us, of the criminal and the saint. We'll be saved, saved, I swear to you!

Throwing herself on Madame's bed at the end of this speech, Claire reveals her identification with her mistress and her attachment to Monsieur and Mario. Yet in both identities the male is rejected and replaced by a couple consisting of two women—Claire (as Madame) and her maid Solange; Claire as Claire with Solange. Claire refuses her two identities: she is both the innocent mistress (a saint) and the criminal servant whose false accusation of her mistress's lover has put him in prison. Yet in her appeal to Solange while she is playing the mistress, Claire imagines herself as the saint; her sister (the maid) is the criminal. The eternal couple, consisting of the antithetical saint and criminal, parallels the union of the more passive sister Claire with her domineering sister Solange.

This situation illuminates the play's conclusion in which Solange, the masculine and criminal personality, reveals that her "real" existence is as false as her assumed role. She is incapable of murdering Madame in bed because she is aroused by her mistress's physical beauty, just as later, when Claire appears in Madame's white robe, Solange is momentarily unable to continue the masquerade because "You're beautiful." As Claire (in the role of Madame) begins her insults, Solange gasps "Go on. Go on! I'm getting there, I'm getting there!" In the frenzied climax, Solange is incapable of completing the ritual and killing Madame (Claire). It is the seemingly passive and more feminine Claire who assumes Solange's previous personality and kills both the mistress and herself by drinking the poison. Solange must then become two personalities. Deprived of her sister, she is aware of her isolation, but exalts the perfect union of the two sisters into one flesh: Solange is Solange and she is Solange pretending to be Claire. Now, because the Claire who played the role of Madame no longer exists, both sisters are free from Madame's real and imaginary dominance and they are united. "We are beautiful, joyous, drunk and free!"

The Maids is a homosexual and homicidal ritual. Each evening Solange and Claire enact the confrontation between the mistress and the servant, alternating their roles, with neither ever playing herself. This ceremony is an expression of jealousy, love, and hate. The sisters despise each other because they know each other so well. Solange knows that Claire poses as Marie Antoinette and wanders through the apartment receiving imaginary guests and greeting crowds from the balcony. Claire knows that Solange has taken her letters: "I invented the most fantastic stories and you used them for your own purposes. You frittered away my frenzy. Yesterday when you were Madame I could see how delighted you were at the chance they gave you to stow away on the *Lamartinière,* to flee France in the company of your lover." These letters apparently describe Claire's fantasies about following her criminal lover to remote penal colonies and prostituting herself for him. As Claire must pretend to be Madame or Marie Antoinette (who, like Madame, is young, beautiful, and fated), Solange can only live as being Claire, Madame, or the imaginary Claire as conceived in Claire's fictional letters. Reality recedes into the infinite distance.

Critics have remarked that the maids' ceremony is a Black Mass with the murder always being interrupted. Genet's own admiration for the Mass is evident in nearly all his works, most notably his novel *Our Lady of the Flowers,* and the dramas *The Blacks* and *Deathwatch.* A symbolic ceremony in which things represent other mysterious realities, the Mass appeals to Genet because it suggests the mystery of identity (Christ as wine and wafer in the Catholic liturgy) and because it unites the spectators as participants in a religious ceremony. The ideas of repetition and incompletion are central to Genet's vision of humanity's tragic condition.

The connections between death and life, murder and sexual intercourse, and love and hate, are fully explored in *The Maids.* The attraction and revulsion Solange and Claire feel for each other combine homosexual lust with homicidal jealousy. The most violent scenes are sado-masochistic.

Solange is aroused when Claire (playing Madame) hurls insults at her. She approaches sexual climax, clutches her genitals, and then beats her sister with a whip. The sisters are humiliated because they have been rejected by the young milkman by whom they desire to become pregnant. Even in their sexual fantasies about men, they depend upon each other and must be in each other's presence.

Images of criminals, saints, water, exile, and flowers abound in this play, as they do in all of Genet's works. The sisters see themselves as criminals and saints. The union of these two types, achieved by Claire's death, is the ultimate reality for Genet. The criminal is an outcast from society, just as the servant, homosexual, and artist are. Water is both a symbol of the physical and psychological. The sisters describe their involvement in the masquerade in terms of submersion ("I'm sinking"). Images of voyages, boats, and prison islands proliferate. Flowers are in the boudoir, and at the imaginary funeral of Madame. The servants lend a decadent note to this play about voluptuousness and death.

The story of *The Maids* has a basis in history. One of the most famous crimes of the 1920s occurred in a French provincial town where the Papin sisters murdered their master's household and meticulously and gruesomely dissected their bodies into small pieces.

Genet's first play, *The Maids,* was produced in Paris in 1947. Immediately it was recognized as a savage and unusual artistic vision. In the tradition of Antonin Artaud's Theater of Cruelty, Genet's play frees the stage from the restrictions of society and reveals the elemental nature of human experience. The undiluted savagery and perversion strip away the facades imposed by moral and theatrical conventions. By indicating that he wanted young men to play Solange, Claire, and Madame, Genet extended the artifices to another dimension while fulfilling his homosexual fantasy. Louis Jouvet, the play's director, insisted that women play the parts, and Genet reluctantly agreed. Since that production, actresses have always taken these roles. The play has been widely performed throughout Europe and the United States.

The Balcony

by

JEAN GENET (1910–   )

The Characters

The Bishop—a self-pitying, guilt-ridden man, perhaps the
most intellectual of the masqueraders; he becomes en-
tranced by his own ecclesiastical regalia. The garish
makeup, elevated shoes, and padded shoulders contribute
to his fantasies of grandeur and moral superiority that he
later transforms into ambitious plans for his bishopric.

The Judge—more dependent upon temporal and social relationships than the bishop, he acknowledges the importance
of the thief, whom he must persecute, and the executioner,
whom he must use as a complement to his existence. He
does not lose contact with reality as completely as the
bishop or the general and acknowledges that his judgments
would result in his death if they were known outside the
studio.

The General—he is the only masquerader we see out of costume. "A timid-looking gentleman," he wears a bowler
hat and gloves in his public life. The general's fantasies
demand sexual mastery of a beautiful woman.

Irma (The Queen)—a masculine-looking woman of about
forty who wears a tailored suit and moves with brisk
efficiency. She is the madame of the Grand Balcony, a
brothel equipped with studios. Through a special device
in her office, she watches the performances of her clients
and employees. Although the chief of police and Arthur

368

are her lovers, she is attracted to her assistant, Carmen. Irma's practical materialism is balanced by a passionate nature and a bold imagination.

Carmen—After having played the Virgin Mary in Irma's studios, she has been removed to the office, where she does accounts. Carmen longs to see her illegitimate daughter before the insurrection destroys everything, and yearns for her return to a life of dreams and illusions as a prostitute in the brothel.

Arthur (The Executioner)—a gigantic, muscular man, Irma's pimp and lover; he acts as the sadistic executioner in the judge's drama.

The Chief of Police—an aggressive, bullying figure who yearns for immortality through the dreams of Irma's clients. His obsession with death and destruction causes him to ignore Irma, his former mistress.

Chantal—a prostitute who has left the house of illusion to join the insurrection. She becomes the symbol of the revolution and is assassinated upon the order of Queen Irma.

Roger—Chantal's former lover, the first man to dream of impersonating the chief of police. He revolts, however, by leading the character to the limit of his destiny and by castrating himself.

The Court Envoy—Genet's *raisonneur*, an intruder from outside the brothel and the revolution. He recruits the bishop, judge, general, and Irma to replace the murdered government and reaffirms the continuity of civilized institutions.

The Story

The room of a brothel has been transformed into a sacristy in which an actor, wearing grotesquely elevated shoes and exaggerated shoulder-padding, is adorned as a bishop. Irma, the madame, argues with the bishop about the money he owes her. She warns him that a revolution has spread to the environs of the whorehouse and that he must quickly leave. But the bishop is reluctant and insists upon reviewing the evening's activities with a whore who played his penitent.

As he is being divested of his costume, the bishop makes the
whore reaffirm the gravity of her confessed sins and the
efficacy of his pardon. After the women leave, the man
delivers a soliloquy in front of a mirror. He disavows his
ambitions in the Church and then, kissing the flap of his
surplice, revels in the pomp and glory of his ecclesiastical position: "Mitres, laces, gold-cloth and glass trinkets,
genuflexions. . . ." Irma enters and reminds him that the
rebels are drawing near, and the scene ends as the bishop
again turns to the mirror and rants about the voluptuousness
and symbolic power of his ecclesiastical trappings.

In another nook of the brothel, a judge, an executioner,
and a thief enact a violent scene. The judge, like the bishop,
is mounted on elevated shoes and wears an elaborate costume to indicate his profession. He crawls toward the out-
stretched foot of the thief and is about to lick it when he
rises and begins questioning her. The executioner threatens
the young woman and the judge warns her: "Look here:
you've got to be a model thief, if I'm to be a model judge.
If you're a fake thief, I become a fake judge." He explains
that the executioner must whip the thief so that as judge he
can exercise his power by restraining him. When the thief
coyly threatens to stop her confession, the judge panics. The
executioner commands him to crawl, and the judge pros-
trates himself again and cries to the thief: "Madame, please,
I beg of you. I'm willing to lick your shoes, but tell me you're
a thief. . . ."

A timid-looking gentleman prepares to attire himself as a
general in another room. When Irma tells him of the revolution, he recoils at the thought of being shot outside the
brothel, but his thoughts return to his masquerade, and he
demands boots and spurs for his uniform. A magnificent
girl with bare bosom, black corset and stockings, and high-
heeled shoes enters, tossing her long hair like a mane. She
is the general's horse. The general commands her to remove
his street clothes and dress him. The girl delivers lyrical
speeches about battles and death as the gigantically padded
man struts grotesquely. Drunk with his joy as he envisions
his suffering and dying troops, he is about to reach a climax
when he shifts out of his role and inquires about the revolution raging outside of the brothel. Again he tries to regain
the illusion by looking into mirrors and exclaiming that he

is really dead and that "What is now speaking, and so beautifully, is Example. I am now only the image of my former self." He tries to dismiss his horse as she describes the general's funeral procession while singing Chopin's "Funeral March." An off-stage orchestra augments the music, which is counterpointed by the firing of machine guns in the streets.

The next scene is a dumb show in which a little old man dressed as a tramp prepares to have intercourse with a beautiful girl. He undresses in front of a mirror, and Genet indicates that three actors are needed to play the roles of the reflections. Irma hands a filthy lice-ridden wig to the girl, who puts it on the man's head as she is offered a bouquet of artificial flowers. The girl whips the man and strikes the bouquet from his hands while his face lights up with tenderness. Again machine-gun fire intrudes upon the scene as the man hopefully asks if there are lice in the wig.

In Irma's private room, she spies on the various activities of her clients and addresses Carmen, who is doing the day's acounts. Carmen resents having been removed from her role as the Virgin Mary and expresses a desire to see her illegitimate child. But Irma discusses her studios and her great role in helping men realize their fantasies, and laments the absence of the chief of police, who has been her lover. The two women talk about various masquerades being performed, and Irma reaffirms that "The Grand Balcony has a worldwide reputation. It's the most artful, yet the most decent house of illusion. . . ." The illusions of life are consummated through fake details that make them even more real.

Suddenly, the two women approach each other, and there is a moment of unspoken sexual attraction between them. But it passes as Irma deliriously recites a list of the studios she has constructed: the Hay Studio, the Rustic Scene, the Studio of the Hangman, the Throne Room, the Studio of Mirrors, the Studio of State, the Studio of Perfumed Foundations, the Urinal Studio, and so on. Her masterpiece is the Studio of Solemn Death: "Studios, girls, crystals, laces, balconies, everything . . . rises up and carries me off!" After this lyrical flight, the two women again face each other in an erotic daze, and Carmen longs for her role as the Virgin Mary. But death in the form of rebellion is everywhere:

"Death—the real thing—is at my door, it's beneath my window. . . ."

Although destruction is imminent, Irma knows that men will always need illusions, and that her studios, if destroyed, will be rebuilt. Even if they are betrayed by Chantal, a former whore who has disappeared from the brothel, they will ultimately triumph. Carmen dresses Irma in her jewels and laces to receive the chief of police. Arthur, who played the role of the Executioner in the judge's pageant, enters dressed in a "classical pimp's outfit." His light gray suit, silk shirt, and felt hat bring a glint of reality into the room, but this too is his attempt to realize fantastic illusions. Arthur wants to stay and look at himself in the mirrors so Irma can see him dressed as a pimp, but she sends him out in search of the chief of police. He crawls out on his knees.

The chief enters in a state of great excitement, for the royal palace has been surrounded and death is everywhere. He inquires if anyone has asked to impersonate him in the brothel, but Irma replies that his "function is not noble enough to offer dreamers an image that would console them." A chief of police is full of hatred and love, but no glory. Through death and killing, however, he hopes to impose his image on the popular imagination.

The chief says that the rebellion is a game and that he will master the reality of it. He no longer has any love for Irma and does not resent her sleeping with Arthur. He strikes Irma just as Arthur, with torn clothes, stumbles in the door. The whole city is in ruins. A shot is heard and a mirror near the bed is shattered. Arthur falls dead with a bullet in his forehead; the rebels have reached the brothel.

In a public square, Chantal is appointed the symbolic leader of the insurrection. Although she is slatternly and impure, her *image* will appear on posters, insignias, and flags. Roger, her companion, wants to keep her as his private symbol of desire and unfulfillment. But the rebels ignore him. In a lyrical parting, Chantal and Roger each declares: "You envelop me and I contain you." As she departs, Chantal exclaims: "At least the brothel has been of some use to me: it's taught me the art of pretense, of acting. I've had to play so many roles that I know almost all of them."

In the funeral studio of Irma's establishment, desolation reigns. Everything has been wrecked and explosions rock the city outside. An envoy from the court implies that the palace has been destroyed, the queen killed, and the bishop, general, and judge assassinated. Everyone understands that in order to avoid total chaos, Irma must assume the role of the queen, and her clients in the brothel must masquerade as the bishop, general, and judge. When Irma objects, the envoy asserts that she is needed to counteract the image of Chantal. Irma demands that her mirrors should be smashed or veiled and says to the chief of police: "George . . . this is our last minute together! From now on, we'll no longer be us. . . ." The envoy promises the chief of police an enormous red marble mausoleum with a tiny diamond sentry box: "He who gets it will be there—dead— for eternity."

On the balcony, the bishop, general, and judge, gigantically enlarged by shoulder-padding and elevated shoes, survey the populace. The queen (Irma) joins them; only the chief of police, dressed as the hero, is of normal size. A beggar screams "Long live the Queen," and Chantal appears. A shot is fired, she falls, the general and queen remove the corpse.

In Irma's room, which is in great disarray, three photographers pose the judge, general, and bishop for official portraits. They are instructed to appear in stereotyped attitudes and postures. Meanwhile, they comment upon the success of their triumphal procession through the city and their grandiose project to perpetuate their historical images. The men and Irma are enveloped by their roles, and a battle for power emerges. The chief of police is desolate because no one has chosen to emulate him, and he proposes to appear as a giant phallus to establish his place in the people's imagination. The archbishop laments his withdrawal from the fantasy world of the brothel, but is determined to live up to his public image. The general complains: "I'm rigged . . . for all eternity. By Jove, I no longer dream." Appearance has given way to reality and their arguments about their prerogatives become violent. Carmen enters to announce that someone has requested to masquerade as the chief of police in the mock mausoleum that has been constructed in the brothel, and the characters assemble to spy upon the new client.

In the Mausoleum Studio, Roger and Carmen begin the

enactment of their scenario. Dressed as the chief of police, Roger asks to see the slave whose moans have been overheard from the depths of the tomb. This slave is the man who formerly masqueraded as a tramp. He places Roger's foot on his own back. The slave sings the praises of the chief of police and begins crawling into the depths of the mausoleum. Carmen tells her client: "You're dead, or rather you don't stop dying and your image, like your name, reverberates into infinity." The session ends and Roger complains: "If the brothel exists and I have a right to go there, then I have a right to lead the character I've chosen to the very limit of his destiny . . . no, of mine . . . of merging his destiny with mine." Roger castrates himself with a knife and the real chief of police proclaims: "Though my image be castrated in every brothel in the world I remain intact." The chief moves toward his tomb and is photographed as he disappears into its depths. Machine-gun fire is heard outside, indicating another insurrection, and Irma prepares to close her brothel until dreams once again are possible.

Critical Opinion

The theme of reality and illusion becomes political in *The Balcony*. Madame Irma's brothel is, in her own words, a house of illusion where men can realize their most secret fantasies. As in all of Genet's writings, the sexual perversions and fantasies of repressed individuals are translated into masquerades. The pageantry and cruelty of political institutions are extensions of secret hallucinations that are acted out in the privacy of the elaborate studios.

In *The Balcony,* as in *The Maids* and *The Blacks,* Genet is preoccupied with ritual and the Mass. The clients of the Grand Balcony repeat the same drama each time they enter the studio constructed for them. The chief of police draws the parallel between the ceremonies and the powerful symbolic association implicit in the Roman Catholic Mass when he asks: "—so tell me: in this sumptuous theater where every moment a drama is performed—in the sense that the outside world says a Mass is celebrated—what have you observed?" Ritual and ceremony enable man to objectify his personal obsessions. In their everyday lives, the bishop, judge, and general are upper-class family men whose normal existences do not fulfill their terrible secret loves: "Entering a brothel means rejecting the world," Carmen observes. Each client has prepared a scenario to exorcise his secret lusts, and every night he repeats it with the same props and characters. The forces that Genet believes dominate everyone are set free in the Grand Balcony, whose private theaters are cluttered with bishop's mitre, judge's wig and robe, and general's bloody spurs. "In real life they're props of a display that they have to drag in the mud of the real and commonplace. Here, Comedy and Appearance remain pure and the Revels intact." The organized entertainments allow the individual to externalize his fantasies. But this must have some limits: "They all want everything to be as true as possible. . . . Minus something indefinable so that it won't be true." The constant awareness that life's dreams can never be fully realized is the psychological and philosophical basis of *The Balcony*. When illusions become real, as they do in our political institutions, there is no life-giving fiction for existence and the Grand Balcony must close its doors and have its mirrors draped or smashed until someone can dream again.

The Balcony, the play's central symbol, is by nature a place removed from the common world. Its occupants may be pathetic habitués of a brothel, clad in filthy and tattered costumes, but from below they appear to be gigantic embodiments of man's deepest fears and desires. Genet's symbol for reality is the insurrection that rages around the brothel. It intrudes upon the fantastic world of the studios despite elaborate soundproofing and shutters on the windows. The noise of machine-gun fire is the gruesome counterpoint to the orgiastic revels. The brothel's clients are constantly reminded of the ultimate reality of flux and death.

At the beginning of the drama, illusion and reality are effectively separated. Bishop, judge, and general can perform their masturbatory rituals in the privacy of their own imaginations. Outside of the brothel, reality is embodied in wanton slaughter, destruction, and chaos. The bishop's attempt to formalize the mechanics of guilt and repentance is effective only so long as he can function within his own concep-

tion of the outside moral world. The imagined sins he listens
to in confession are more horrible than his real transgressions. The judge, who reminds the reader of Camus's Judge
Penitent in *The Fall,* can impose justice on his prisoner
because he controls the executioner and can manipulate the
rules that demand punishment. By establishing spurious
moral standards and forcing the persecuted victim to confess
her sins (or thievery), bishop and judge negate the efficacy
of divine and temporal justice and free themselves from their
own masochistic guilt. Both bishop and judge pathetically
insist upon their victim's reaffirmation and self-accusations.

The bishop's soliloquy in front of the mirror is the masturbatory climax to the frenzy he has attained during his
encounter with the penitent. But doubts occur when the
prostitute coyly asks: "And what if my sins were real?" His
facade breaks and in his normal voice he exclaims: "You're
mad! I hope you really didn't do all that." Left alone, he
explains to himself the impossibility of true virtue and
humility, and succumbs to the erotic stimulation of his orna-
ments, laces, and religious paraphernalia. Reality has no
function in his erotic fantasies.

The sexual climax of the judge's drama arrives as he
licks the thief's boot when she refuses to affirm her identity
as thief: "You won't refuse to be a thief? That would be
wicked. It would be criminal. You'd deprive me of being!"
The judge says: "If there were no judge, what would become
of us, but what if there were no thieves?"

The judge's homosexual identification with the muscular
and sadistic executioner is a necessary link in the dynamic
chain of action. He pretends to look at himself in the executioner: "Mirror that glorifies me! Image that I can touch, I
love you. Never would I have the strength or skill to leave
streaks of fire on her back. . . . You're all there, my huge
arm, too heavy for me, too big, too fat for my shoulder,
walking at my side or by yourself!" The executioner and
thief complement the judge and give him being. Both rein-
force his sense of personal guilt, but from opposite directions. The executioner reminds him of his brutality, while
the thief recalls the harsh sentences he has rendered in the
past and his present severe judgment. This sense of guilt is
related to the judge's awareness of his mortality and free-

dom. Like the sisters in *The Maids*, the judge pushes his masquerade to the farthest extreme and imagines himself as the ultimate judge—God or Satan. His verdicts are outrageous and vile: "If every judgment were delivered seriously, each one would cost me my life. That's why I'm dead. I inhabit that region of exact freedom, I, King of Hell, weigh those who are dead like me." By aligning himself with Hell, he judges his own culpability; yet by declaring himself dead, he escapes responsibility. Like the devil, he can sin no more, and he inhabits a region of total degradation and nihilism. The criminal, for Genet, is the freest of all. If all men are criminals in their own hearts, they contain within their secret lives the will to freedom—and hopeless damnation.

The general elaborates upon the theme of death with bloody spurs and leather boots. He masters his rebellious and beautiful steed (a whore dressed in black corset and stockings and high heels) and hears a description of his own funeral. Death is the final reality that freezes the image or idea of the general for eternity.

At the end of the play when the envoy suggests to Irma and her clients that the inevitable process of history requires them to transform into reality their secret lives as queen, bishop, judge, and general, illusion becomes reality. They appear before a crowd on the balcony, order the assassination of Chantal, ride a regal caravan, and have their portraits taken. The photographers' sinister black hoods symbolize the process that creates a true image from a false spectacle. The photographers (historians) transform frightened men who are dressed in elevated shoes and padded shoulders into bulwarks of civilization. Chantal, an ugly whore, becomes a symbol of freedom, purity, and justice, and depraved and craven individuals are unrecognizable to their neighbors when they are enshrouded in the vestments of their public functions. The bishop's fruit and vegetable man kisses the sacred ring without recognizing him, proving that people ignore the decayed reality of their myths.

When the envoy explains that "everything beautiful on earth you owe to masks," he is voicing Genet's idea that the continuity of existence is sustained by illusion. The costumes, props, and mirrors of the Grand Balcony allow man to objectify forces that emerge as paradigms of the nature of society.

Hidden neuroses and perversions are transformed into recognizable forms in the privacy of Irma's studios as the individual nearly achieves fulfillment in the secret dramas he enacts with prostitutes, costumes, and stage props. These ritualistic ceremonies reaffirm the individual's creative ability. Each client can formulate a new identity for himself without suffering the relentless chastisement of the outside world. But with the appearance of external necessity in the person of the envoy, the clients lose their privacy, imagination, and freedom. By assuming the public role, they relinquish individuality. They can no longer dream, for like Pirandello's Henry IV, they are thrust into an unyielding mold that demands strict adherence to public forms of behavior. When the photographers disappear under the black hoods of their cameras and freeze the stereotyped images of bishop, judge, and general, they complete the annihilation of individuality that, Genet posits, is part of the life process. The grandiose schemes of the now institutionalized figures must conform to what the "real" world demands, and the cycle of insurrection and destruction begins anew. The forces of continuity and flux clash and a new rebellion is spawned.

The chief of police attains a kind of freedom by plunging into the chaos and slaughter of rebellion. He becomes frozen in time and space when Roger has dreamed him. Yet Roger's fantasy culminates in castration and entombment in a mausoleum. The real chief orders food for two thousand years and withdraws into an eternal image. The significance of Roger's act of self-mutilation while playing the chief of police reveals his idol's impotence and sterility. Formerly a brutal and dynamic individual who could not be mythologized, he has succumbed to the allurements of the Establishment by accepting an enormous mausoleum called Valley of the Fallen. Perhaps Genet is alluding to Franco's mausoleum of the same name, which also is an attempt to immortalize and institutionalize a rebellion. But Genet's political satire is more universal. Irma seems to pass the final judgment against society: "Distribute roles again. . . . prepare yours . . . judges, generals, bishops, chamberlains, rebels who allowed the revolt to congeal." The flux, chaos, and freedom of the insurrection was literally prostituted when Chantal became its figurehead and the chief of police achieved deification in a house of illusions (a brothel). The machine-gun fire at the end of the play indicates that society and its rebels are symbolic—so complementary that their interaction is the only means of exposing the reality of human existence. The rebels are characterized by Irma as Workers. Without imagination. Prudish and maybe chaste." But Carmen replies: "It won't take them long to get used to debauchery. Just wait till they get a little bored. . . ." Human history is the process of creating illusions and destroying them in favor of new illusions.

Genet has touched upon the wellspring of human civilization. He has shown that the necessity to escape from conventional identity is a natural result of social restraint. In the most conventional terms, a house of prostitution is an unrealistic arena for unbridled lusts. As defined by Madame Irma, the Grand Balcony is a house of illusions replete with scenarios, props, and mirrors that allow the most private and onanistic fantasies to approach realization. If society, as we know it, is no more than an orgiastic embodiment of compulsive psychoses, Genet's vision is both startling and revelatory.

The sex in the brothel is of a special kind. The unfulfillment between Irma and her three lovers—the chief, Arthur, and Carmen—parallels the incomplete relationship of Chantal and Roger and the sterile sexuality in the studios. Irma concedes that Carmen is an orgy of her *heart,* and the prostitutes are "my big, long, sterile girls," whose lovers' seeds never ripen in their wombs. The tousled beds and mirrors are reminders of impossible sexual consummation.

The stagecraft employed in *The Balcony* is one of the most imaginative aspects of the play. The grotesquely exaggerated padding and elevated shoes underline the bombastic and illusory nature of each client's fantasy. A chandelier suspended from the ceiling serves as a unifying object in a multi-chambered arrangement that allows scenes to fade into each other. Highly mobile props require a revolving stage, intricate machinery, or an arena stage without the conventional proscenium. The arena stage was employed in the successful New York production of 1960, which was directed by José Quintero.

The Balcony was first produced in English. The 1957 controversial London production led to restaging in Paris by

Peter Brook in 1960, the same year it was played in New York. In 1962, Genet revised the drama, shortening it considerably, and a year later it was adapted for the screen with music by Igor Stravinsky.

The Blacks

by

JEAN GENET (1910–   )

The Characters

Archibald Absalom Wellington—the *raisonneur* of this play,
   who officiates over the ceremony and constantly reminds
   the actors that they are performing a ritual and not expressing their personal sentiments.
Deodatus Village—the appointed murderer of the "white
   victim," who is in love with Virtue and represents the
   energy and fecundity of the black race.
Edgar Alas Newport News—one of the blacks who takes
   part in the ritual murder; he brings in the handcuffed
   victim who will be slaughtered in a sacrificial rite.
Stephanie Virtue Secret-rose Diop—Archibald's female counterpart and Village's beloved, who exhorts the blacks to
   assert their freedom.
Diouf—wearing a mask, wig, and costume, he plays the
   white female victim who will be murdered.
Felicity Trollop Pardon—an archetypal black woman who
   defiantly confronts the queen's symbolic whiteness.
The Court (blacks in white masks):
Missionary—he represents the white colonial religious con-
   science in his overbearing righteousness and hypocrisy.
Judge—his interest in the law extends only to the protection
   of the white colonial establishment.
Governor—the stereotyped image of a cruel but weak tyrant.

Queen—symbolizing white womanhood and the hegemony
of the white race in Africa; emotional, cruel, and insecure.
Valet—the clownlike servant of the court. Uncouth and
comic, he embodies the whites' impotence.

The Story

A tiered stage embellished with black velvet curtains,
screens, and a flower-bedecked tomb that is bathed in garish
neon light. Seven formally dressed blacks and one in casual
clothes dance around a coffin and cast flowers from their
bodices and lapels. The court, consisting of the queen, her
valet, the governor, the judge, and the missionary—black
men wearing white masks—enters and takes its place on the
platform above the dancers. The dancers are introduced and
announce the beginning of a performance. The queen expresses fear that the blacks are about to kill someone. The
governor threatens retaliation.

After the audience is reassured that everything is merely
a play, the governor acknowledges: "We've come to attend
our own funeral rites." The blacks announce that they have
killed a white woman and that they will be judged by the
court. This rite of murder, mourning, and judgment is a
repetition of an eternal ceremony. A character called Snow
accuses the black men of desiring and hating their victim;
black women have pure hatred for the whites. When Village
promises to reveal something new in his account of the
murder, Archibald replies: "You've no right to change anything in the ceremonial, unless, of course, you hit upon a
cruel detail that heightens it." As the court discusses the
value of colonial commodities on the stock exchange, the
blacks below them discuss their color, odors, and the rich
putrescence of the African soil. Village describes the search
for fresh white corpses needed for each night's ceremonial
and the murder of a female bum on a former night. Although the woman reeked of wine, urine, and vermin, she
symbolized the purity of white women.

Newport News says that he has brought a handcuffed
victim to be murdered in a sacrificial rite. He procures a
revolver and leaves, despite Diouf's entreaties for mercy.
Archibald replies: "But we're bent on being unreasonable,

on being hostile. You'll speak of love. Go right ahead, since our speeches are set down in the script." Diouf wants to come to some kind of agreement with the whites, but the others insist upon assuming the archetypal role of savages. When the missionary suggests adapting Christian mythology for the blacks, he is rebuked by his peers, and both blacks and whites are committed to enacting a ceremony that excludes reconciliation.

Village delivers a speech to white-masked Virtue in which he exclaims that she (as a white woman) has made him detest his blackness. The governor orders Virtue to the whorehouse and as the ceremony proceeds, Archibald warns the actors: "Don't allude to your life." Village complains of the painfulness of the ceremony and Archibald agrees, but says that the theater (play-acting) is all that is left to them. The theme of sexual domination expands when Archibald says blacks have been deprived of love and "On this stage, we're like guilty prisoners who play at being guilty."

A character called Bobo lists the whites who have been murdered for the nightly ceremony and insists that any corpse will be sufficiently symbolic for their purposes. A passionate love scene between Virtue and Village almost intrudes upon the play-acting. Only the dozing queen is unaffected by love and passion. Virtue, "as if in a state of somnambulism," proclaims herself "the lily-white Queen of the West." Now awakened, the queen, on the platform, answers Virtue's lyrical outpouring and identifies with her. They both proclaim their love for Village, but the queen suddenly realizes her crime.

After invoking more artifacts of white culture, the queen hears the missionary admit that white people have "only just begun the long death struggle, which gives them such pleasure." Everyone's attention returns to the catafalque where the murdered white woman reclines. Village says that it was only his murderous gesture that he loved, but the others insist that he loved his white victim. The murder was a sexual and homicidal act—inseparable in motive. Village insists that his motive was pure hatred, and Archibald exhorts blacks to "negrify themselves. Let them persist to the point of madness in what they're condemned to be."

The murder of the white person is recounted in a ritualistic manner as Village threatens: "I'm going through with the whole thing. This evening, I'm giving a farewell performance." Diouf plays the part of the white woman, donning wig, mask, makeup, and gloves. Village is blackened with shoe polish to intensify his color, and the ceremony begins with a parody of the litany to the Blessed Virgin. Village tells how he intruded into the garden of white people and lay in wait for his victim. After some cruel parodies of white manners and speech, the drama of the murder unfolds, only to be interrupted by unruly intrusions into the ceremonial order of the event. Village follows the white woman to her bedroom. The queen praises the soon-to-be-martyred white woman, and the court becomes impatient for the denouement. The white woman gives birth to dolls representing members of the court, and Village takes her behind the screen for the slaughter. The queen weeps and the blacks break into ecstatic cries about Africa and blackness. The Dies Irae is chanted and a parody of the Requiem Mass is recited. The court listens to the governor describe the murder ritual that includes fornication.

The blacks discuss the fate of the murderer and Archibald observes: "It's no longer a matter of staging and performance: the man we're holding and for whom we're responsible is a real man." All the blacks are guilty of the crime. The governor rouses support for revenge.

The black actors relax as Village, who played the murderer, says that the ceremony of the murder went off well, with Diouf (who played the white woman) even offering him his seat when they retired behind the screen. The court resumes its cries for revenge and the missionary promises to beatify the slain woman. Archibald reminds the blacks that the white man's judgment and revenge "is only play-acting." The court disappears from the stage as it sets out on a crusade to avenge the murdered woman. The blacks ask Diouf what it was like to be a white woman. Diouf puts his mask on just as the drunken valet and the rest of the court come on stage, marching backward. They are weary from their trip and scourged with fever. As they rest, the court sits in judgment on the blacks, who tremble with obsequiousness.

The judge slyly proclaims: "No, one can't hold all of Africa responsible for the death of a white woman." Yet the killer acted out of hatred for the white race, and "That was tantamount to killing our entire race and killing us until Doomsday." Although the corpse and the catafalque were imaginary, the crime has a metaphysical reality. In a frenzy of rage, the court devises diabolical punishments for the criminal. But when threatened by the blacks, the queen piously exclaims: "In exchange for a crime, we were bringing the criminal pardon and absolution."

The queen and Felicity, as symbols of the two races, confront each other and exchange accusations. The queen says she is death, and Felicity replies: "I shall have the corpse of your corpse's ghost." They reveal their profound hatred for each other, and the queen orders a slaughter of the blacks. But Felicity reminds her that whites cannot exist without blacks and "For this evening until the end of the drama let us therefore remain alive."

Village is executed by the blacks themselves, and the members of the court remove their masks to reveal their black faces. The ceremony's purpose was to inspire the blacks to continue their fight against their white oppressors. The performance must be finished; it is decided that the court must be executed. When Village asks: "Will we have to slit your throats in order to get rid of you?" the black actress who played the queen replies: "There's no need to. We're actors, our massacre will be lyrical." The members of the court don their masks again, and now taking on the pious, martyred attitudes of outnumbered whites, they face death. As each member of the court is executed, he delivers a speech expressing his pride and sense of superiority. The queen summons her court to hell, and Archibald thanks everyone for a good performance, for "The time has not yet come for presenting the dramas about normal matters. . . . We are what they want us to be. We shall therefore be it to the very end, absurdly." As she marches to hell, the queen wishes the blacks good luck and warns that some day she and her court will rise again. Only Virtue and Village remain on the stage and proclaim their love for each other.

Critical Opinion

An exorcism of the reality of colonialism over illusion, *The Blacks* is a ritualistic elaboration of themes introduced in Genet's *The Maids* and *The Balcony*. Once again the masquerade is of central importance to the argument of Genet's drama. But where men play women who assume the roles of other women in *The Maids,* and habitués of a brothel are forced to realize their fantasies in the actual world in *The Balcony,* Genet's characters in *The Blacks* switch roles with even greater virtuosity. Here all the actors are blacks, but they also play at being blacks, their white oppressors, and their victims.

The piling of masquerade upon masquerade does not obscure the basic and startling metaphoric contrast of black and white, reality and appearance, art and artifice, injustice and revenge. The entire spectrum of the playwright's obsession with dramatic contrast is deployed with a scenic variety that includes masks, balconies, dolls, costumes, and above all, the assumption of physical and mental attitudes that are at once false and true.

The subtitle of the play, "A Clown Show," emphasizes the false appearances, attitudes, and emotions the audience must sort out in order to get at the truth embedded in a matrix of contradictory gestures. The reverse of the American minstrel show, where whites masquerade as blacks, Genet's spectacle calls upon stock responses to black and white from an audience that may be predominately black and that *must* include at least one white man. Genet prefaces the text of his play with instructions that a white person must be in the audience ("preferably in the front row of the orchestra") with a spotlight on this *symbolic* white. The playwright insists upon the vital connection between audience and players when he specifies that in the absence of a white spectator a black should be given a white mask: "And if the blacks refuse the masks, then let a [white] dummy be used."

The problem of the play, as Genet states it, is "What exactly is a black? First of all, what's his color?" In order to delineate the difference between black and white, Genet portrays the black image of himself and his white oppressor. The court, played by black actors wearing white masks, whines, cajoles, threatens, and bullies in a stereotyped re-enactment of Western white colonial victimization of the black race.

Archibald, the master of ceremonies and Genet's *raisonneur,* insists that the rite to be performed in front of the court must be done in perfect ceremonial fashion. This echo of Solange and Claire and the denizens of the Grand Balcony reminds the audience that the archetypal crime—here, the violation and murder of a white woman by a black man— must not be particular or personal in order to retain its power. He reminds the players: "You're a Negro and a performer. . . . On this stage, we're like guilty prisoners who play at being guilty." Thus guilt is an attitude that must be assumed in order to attain identity. Genet believes that the need for guilt and self-hate is the operative force in man's life, and the accoutrements required to achieve these feelings are ultimately irrelevant: "And if we can't find a kid [to murder], then an old horse will do, or a dog or a doll."

The court is also fixed in an inflexible posture. The missionary acknowledges the ceremonial aspect of the play when he admonishes the queen: "Have patience. We've only just begun the long death struggle, which gives them such pleasure. Let's put a good face on it. It's in order to please them that we're going to die. . . ." But for Genet, whiteness represents repulsive virtue, sterile self-righteousness, power, and the artifacts of a dead civilization ("Heroic couplets, poppies, sunflowers, a touch of coquetry, vicarage gardens"); blackness represents all the mysterious and creative possibilities of mankind. Archibald calls upon blacks to "negrify themselves. Let them persist to the point of madness in what they're condemned to be, in their ebony, in their odor, in their yellow eyes, in their cannibal tastes. . . . Let them invent a criminal painting and dancing." The criminal is more heavenly than the saint; the *Black* Mass is better than the real Mass; sensual expression is superior to sterile civilization. Village and Virtue, the two black lovers whose union is an affirmation of the creative vitality of blackness, symbolize Genet's belief in the regenerative force of blackness.

When the queen acknowledges that the court masked its black faces "in order to live the loathesome life of the whites and at the same time to help you sink into shame," she insists upon the unreality and criminality of make-believe. After having avenged the murder of a white woman, the inevitable dramatic action must include the court's massacre. But the queen rejects knives, guns, gallows, rivers, and bayonets and proclaims: "We're actors, our massacre will be lyrical."

The violence of Genet's theater is deceptive in its lyricism. His insistence, through Archibald, that "This is the theater not the street. The theater and drama, and crime," accounts for the flamboyant trappings of neon lights, luxuriant flowers, velvet curtains, galleries, balconies, extravagant costumes, and obscene, comic, and violent language.

Ritual and ceremony shape the action of this festive and macabre drama. The queen explains: "In exchange for a crime we were bringing the criminal pardon and absolution"—the corrosive and meaningless dialect (ritual) of white civilization. The massacre of the queen and her court is accepted as an historical inevitability that in itself is futile; "and if I'm dead, why do you go on killing me, murdering me over and over in my color? . . . Do you need the corpse of the corpse?" Everything here is a ritual even more ancient than the rites of the Roman Catholic Church that Genet invokes as a metaphor of eternal pattern. The melody of the *Dies Irae* accompanies the death of the white woman, and Archibald continually warns the actors to refrain from letting their private lives influence the inexorable unfolding of events. He urges them to adhere to the formal ritual that is the essence of drama. Like Solange, Claire, and the characters in *The Balcony,* Archibald fears that the intrusion of capricious and unstructured reality into the artificiality of illusion will destroy the ultimate reality.

Published in 1958 and first performed a year later in Paris, *The Blacks* had its American premiere in 1961 at New York's Saint Mark's Playhouse. James Earl Jones and Godfrey Cambridge played the parts of Village and Diouf and the cast included many actors who were later to become members of the prestigious Negro Ensemble Company. The production employed an extravagant style that complemented the imaginative masks, costumes, sets, and musical numbers. More recently, in the United States, a production of *The Blacks* sponsored by *The New York Review of Books* made the play available to many communities.

The Author

Jean Genet, the illegitimate child of an unknown father and Gabrielle Genet, was abandoned at birth. He spent his childhood in an orphanage and with foster parents in the peasant village of Morvan. Docile, pious, and industrious, the ten-year-old Genet was unjustly accused of theft and imprisoned in a house of correction for six years. This episode, which Jean-Paul Sartre has called the central drama of Genet's life, marked his determination to become the criminal that society labeled him.

The betrayed, abandoned, and falsely accused orphan became a thief and a homosexual prostitute. Genet describes this life in *The Thief's Journal* (1949). In France, Spain, Italy, Yugoslavia, Austria, Czechoslovakia, and Poland, he was imprisoned for various crimes. Using his homosexuality as a passport to the underworld, Genet wandered throughout Europe. In Germany, he became fascinated by Hitler, the greatest criminal and thief of all times; but believing that he himself was no longer unique in Germany, a nation of criminals, Genet set out for Antwerp, Marseilles, Brest, and Barcelona. He continued in the life of a thief and prostitute.

During one of his numerous imprisonments, Genet wrote *The Condemned* (1942), a long poetic elegy in classical Alexandrines, dedicated to the memory of a friend, Maurice Pilorge, who had been executed in 1939. This volume marked the appearance of themes central to Genet's work: death, the beauty of criminality, homosexual eroticism, and the lyricism of love. Circulated clandestinely while Genet was still in prison, *The Condemned* was followed by *Our Lady of the Flowers* (1944), *Miracle of the Rose* (1946), *Funeral Rites* (1947), and *The Quarrel of Brest* (1947). In 1948, *The Maids* won him the support of Jean-Paul Sartre and Jean Cocteau, who successfully obtained his release from prison.

Genet embarked on a life of travel and writing. He followed the success of *The Maids* with *Deathwatch* (1949), *The Balcony* (1956), *The Blacks* (1958), and *The Screens* (1961). During his travels in the United States, Genet wrote about the 1968 Chicago riots and has been much interested in black militancy.

Perhaps the most powerful influence on Genet's reputation has been Sartre's 600-page study: *Saint Genet: Actor and Martyr* (1952), still considered a fundamental document about the author and his works. No less effective is Genet's autobiography, *The Thief's Journal,* an eloquent celebration of theft, treason, and homosexuality. Genet has been a catalytic and liberating force on younger playwrights.

The Bald Soprano

by

EUGÈNE IONESCO (1912–   )

The Characters

Mr. and Mrs. Smith—a typical middle-aged, middle-class English couple who live in a tastelessly decorated, comfortable London suburban home and speak the type of English to be found in English primers intended for foreign students. They are emotionally, physically, and intellectually dead. Contented, slightly bored, and totally unimaginative, the Smiths (a common Anglo-Saxon name) really have no desires, fears, ambitions—or thoughts.

Mr. and Mrs. Martin—they are precisely the same as the Smiths.

Mary—the Smiths' maid. She is, like the other characters in the play, not really a human being. She goes to the cinema, gossips, drinks milk and brandy, and, like Mr. Smith, reads the newspapers.

The Fire Chief—officious, bureaucratic, and intensely stupid, he differentiates between duty and pleasure until he is enticed into telling stories and parables—and until he has his fiery passion quenched by Mary, his "little firehose."

The Story

In their middle-class suburban London home, Mr. and Mrs. Smith discuss their dinner. Their conversation is mo-

ronic, cliché-ridden, and filled with *non sequiturs*. When the
subject of Bobby Watson is brought up, a great confusion
arises because everyone in the Watson family—men, women,
adults, and children—is named Bobby.

Mary enters and delivers a short speech in the form of
an exposition used in conventional drama. She recounts her
day: "After the cinema, we went to drink some brandy and
milk and then read the newspaper." The bell rings and the
Smiths retire to prepare for their guests, Mr. and Mrs.
Martin. Alone, the Martins start an elaborate recognition
scene, at the end of which they discover that they are married. (They sleep in the same bed and have the same child
who has a white eye and a red eye.) Mary enters and tells
the audience that the Martins have come to a false conclusion because Mrs. Martin's child had a red *right* eye and a
white *left* eye, while Mr. Martin's child's eyes are the reverse.
But Mary allows the confusion to remain undiscovered and
concludes: "My real name is Sherlock Holmes."

When the Smiths reappear, they exchange *non sequiturs*
with their guests, recite pointless anecdotes and banalities,
and comment on the ringing doorbell. But each time Mrs.
Smith answers the bell, she finds no one there. On the third
ring, she fights with her husband who insists that she answer
it. The fire chief enters and apologizes for not being able to
stay long because he is very busy. He is on official business
and is disappointed that there are no fires in the Smiths'
house. The conversation again deteriorates into nonsense as
the chief agrees to recite some "experimental fables." Then
Mr. Smith recounts a story that contains a nonsensical and
confusing genealogy and history. The chief asks the time and
is informed that the clock "runs badly. It is contradictory,
and always indicates the opposite of what the hour is." Mary
enters and is forbidden to tell her story, but she is finally
granted permission when she embraces the chief as an old
lover and says to him: "I'm your little firehose." She recites
a poem, dedicated to the chief:

> The polyploids were burning in the wood
>> A stone caught fire
>> The castle caught fire
>> The forest caught fire
>> etc. . . .

The chief then excuses himself: He must leave because "in exactly three-quarters of an hour and sixteen minutes I'm having a fire at the other end of town."

The Martins and Smiths resume their conversation, which explodes into a wildly illogical frenzy. Suddenly, the clock violently strikes. The stage directions read: "The speeches which follow must be said, at first, in glacial, hostile tones. The hostility and the nervousness increase. At the end of the scene, the four characters must be standing very close to each other, screaming their speeches, raising their fists, ready to throw themselves upon each other."

The dialogue completely disintegrates into a recitation of vowels, consonants, and meaningless sounds, until the characters chant in an increasingly rapid rhythm: "It's not that way, it's over there, it's not that way, it's over there," and so on. The stage lights are extinguished, and when the chant abruptly ceases, the opening scene is repeated with the Martins replacing the Smiths. The curtain falls as soon as the original pattern is reestablished.

Critical Opinion

Ionesco originally entitled his play *Learning English Without Pain* because he was inspired by the Assimile guide to English conversation for Frenchmen. The meaningless phrases and strings of clichés signified to him the breakdown of language, reason, and communication in the modern world. It was not until the play was in rehearsal at the Huchette Theater in Paris during the spring of 1950 that the present title was suggested. An actor carelessly substituted *"cantatrice chauve"* (bald soprano) for *"institutrice blonde"* (blonde schoolmistress).

Language plays an important role in Ionesco's drama. Its perversion through everyday usage and misusage is a symbol of the moral degeneracy of modern civilization. The playwright, reacting to his English language primer in a violent way, observed that words began to "become corrupt, unnatural, unruly, and degenerate. Truths became madness, language was incommunicable, characters became disintegrated; the word was absurd and meaningless."

The drama's subtitle, "Anti-play," is a key to Ionesco's

disenchantment with literature. As a poet and essayist who lived in two countries, he had become aware of the degeneration of both European literature and conversational rhetoric. His revolt against the decline of modern letters included a rejection of Brecht's didactic Epic Theater, for Ionesco believes that political and social themes should be treated on a metaphorical, subjective plane. In *L'Impromptu de l'Alma* (1956), he said:

> . . . for me, theater is the projection of my interior world onto the stage; it is in my dreams, in my agonies, in my obscure desires, in my internal contradictions . . . I reserve the right to make this material for the theater.

Unlike conventional drama, *The Bald Soprano* has no true dialogue, story, plot development, exposition, or climax. Ibsen's carefully wrought rational structures are rejected and parodied when Mary enters and delivers a patently absurd exposition of characters and situations. Ionesco mocks ordinary character development in his intentional failure to differentiate between the Martins and the Smiths. Exchanging roles, the two families are precisely the same at the play's end.

Realistic perception of time is destroyed by the frequent, haphazard, and comic striking of the clock. All verbal references to time ignore "reality," for time is not measured by feeling and intellect. The chief says he has been standing outside the door for forty-five minutes when the audience has observed that Mrs. Smith has answered the doorbell in two or three minutes. But to the chief, it has been a long wait. He also says he must extinguish a fire in three-quarters of an hour and sixteen minutes, meaning that he cannot tolerate the conversation, feels very rushed in his official duties, and, like the others, has no conception of time. Similarly, the Smiths claim to have been waiting for the Martins for several hours and admit that their clock strikes the "opposite" time, indicating that they also have no idea of what time is. All the characters move in a timeless void of ennui and mindlessness.

Ionesco parodies traditional stage conventions at the beginning of *The Bald Soprano* when he indicates the place and time of the nonaction: "A middle-class English interior, with English armchairs. An English evening. . . . A long moment of English silence. The English clock strikes seventeen English strokes." At this moment, Mrs. Smith says: "Seven o'clock." All the characters live in a time-space continuum (and a moral world) that bears no relationship to intelligence or reason.

Even the most fundamental personal relationships are confused and meaningless. The Smiths discuss the "Bobby Watsons" and the Martins, recapitulating the absurdity of dramatic time, place, action, dialogue, and character, fail to recognize each other, except by the most circumstantial evidence that is proved fallacious by Mary. This antiplay is a refutation of nearly all conventional dramaturgical techniques.

Ionesco was surprised when people laughed at his play because, as he later commented, he had thought of it as a nihilistic vision of modern man's absurd and futile existence. But *The Bald Soprano* has been interpreted as a satire on bourgeois insensitivity and the monotony of contemporary life. The Martins and Smiths spout inane formulas and discuss subjects without realizing the connection between words and meaning. They are anesthetized into the automatic behavior that reflects modern society. The failure of language is not only an index of the present dissociation of reality and convention. This total absence of emotional communication is a gruesomely comic symbol of man's alienation from himself and from his fellow beings. Glib verbal formulas eliminate the need to think or feel; unimaginative verbal and mental procedures blind man to his relationship with other men and to the material world he can draw spiritual strength from. The meaninglessness of language is emphasized at the end of the drama as communication totally breaks down and the characters recite vowels, consonants, and idiotic sounds. Like the nonsense rhymes and stories of Edward Lear and Lewis Carroll, the text of *The Bald Soprano* contains words that have arbitrary relationships and meanings—or none at all. These sounds reveal the absurdity of modern language as it has been perverted.

Critics have zealously pointed out that Ionesco is an eclectic writer, subject to many influences. The Surrealists and Dadaists have contributed to his artistic vision. Jarry's *King*

Ubu and Huysmans' *A Rebours,* in their presentation of the absurd and insane, have undoubtedly influenced certain aspects of Ionesco's theater. Apollinaire and even Gertrude Stein, whose exploitation of the sounds (rather than the meaning) of language was well known, also have contributed to the evolution of the Theater of the Absurd. Ionesco himself acknowledges Kafka as a prime influence, but although he has been called an avant-garde artist and founder of the Theater of the Absurd, Ionesco has rejected these appellations.

Absurdity is an important ingredient in Ionesco's writing, but it is absurdity based on the "meaningless" accumulation, expansion, and transformation of objects (men become rhinoceroses, corpses grow, chairs and furniture multiply), the lack of communication and feeling in human relations, and the irrelevancy of formulas and institutions. Ionesco's world is different from the absurd world of Sartre or Camus, for his vision does not force the individual to take a position. The playwright recognizes the complete futility of action in a world of computers, television, and habit. He is a pessimist, believing that man is without redemption.

Ionesco is the playwright of the vulnerable man who is vulnerable because he sees himself threatened from both outside and inside. Existence is without a goal and therefore absurd; at his own center, there is nothing but a pit of meaninglessness. Ionesco, in a frenzy of the tragicomic, dramatizes the madness underneath banality.

Since its first performance in Paris in 1950, *The Bald Soprano* has been presented innumerable times in more than thirty languages. It is one of the most arresting and popular plays to have been written since World War II.

The Chairs

by

EUGÈNE IONESCO (1912–   )

The Characters

Old Man—ninety-five, senile, self-pitying, and inarticulate.
Old Woman—ninety-four; is sometimes maternal and dutiful; sometimes imagines herself a young beauty.
The Orator—forty-five to fifty, a younger version of the old man, with the elder man's inarticulateness. "He's a typical painter or poet of the nineteenth century; he wears a large black felt hat with a wide brim, loosely tied bow tie, artist's blouse, mustache, and goatee," and is "very histrionic in manner, conceited."

The Story

In a crescent-shaped room of a building on a remote island, the old man and old woman argue. Like two quarreling children, they scold and play games, the old man consents to "imitate the month of February" and recite a story he has been telling for seventy-five years. The tale is ominous but nonsensical, and the man collapses into a fit of senile laughter and tears before he concludes. Weeping bitterly, he cries for his mother and is consoled by the old woman. They lament his alienation from his friends and his failure in the world despite his great potential. But soon he

397

will reveal his "message" to the world: the accumulated wisdom of nearly a century of life.

The couple has invited the world—intellectuals, scientists, kings, and workers—to hear a hired orator expound this message. The sound of an approaching boat is followed by the doorbell's ring. The old man goes to a door (hidden from the audience) and welcomes the guest. But this person, like all the subsequent visitors, is invisible. After an elaborate conversation with this invisible lady, the old man and old woman welcome a colonel, who joins the couple and the first guest. Only the old couple speaks, making conversation with the invisible visitors.

Soon others arrive and, in confusion, the old woman hastily brings in chairs to set before a dais and a blackboard. The couple is in a frenzy of activity, seating the company, conversing, and revealing contradictory "facts" about their past.

On a stage cluttered with chairs, the old people dash around, mollifying their restless guests when, suddenly, through the main door, accompanied by a cold white light, the emperor arrives. The old man and old woman are seized by paroxysms of adulation; the room is too crowded to allow them to approach the emperor, and they shout their grateful praises from opposite ends of the stage. Continuing an elaborate apology for his failure in life, the old man again promises clarification and vindication through the orator, who will shortly appear.

The orator enters, and Ionesco specifies that "he is a real person. . . . Just as the invisible people must be as real as possible, the orator must appear unreal." Dressed as a nineteenth-century painter or poet, he moves with stylized motions, signs autographs, and sits impassively on the dais.

After giving a long, hysterical, and contradictory introduction to the "message," which at times seems like a funeral oration, the old man and his wife fling themselves out of windows, committing suicide. The orator, apparently deaf and mute, utters incomprehensible sounds and finally turns to the blackboard and writes: "ANGELFOOD" and "NNAA NNM NWNWNW." Apparently reacting to the disapproval of his invisible audience, he then erases the board and writes more letters and signs. Still offended by the lack of favorable response, the orator descends from the dais, bows to the emperor, and leaves. Soon human voices are heard: "Bursts of laughter, murmurs, shh's, ironical coughs." The sound builds to a crescendo and then fades, "long enough for the audience—the real and the invisible audience—to leave with this ending firmly impressed on its mind."

Critical Opinion

The Chairs (1952) is a tragedy in which the absurdity of the human condition appears comic. The couple's age, decrepitude, and senility evoke sympathy and laughter. Ionesco has explained his intentions in an essay entitled "Experience of the Theater" (in *Notes and Counter Notes*):

> I have called my comedies "antiplays" or "comic dramas" . . . for it seems to me that the comic is tragic and that the tragedy of man is pure derision. . . . In *The Chairs* I tried to submerge tragedy and comedy or, if you like, to confront comedy and tragedy in order to link them in a new dramatic synthesis.

Isolated, impoverished, and vanquished, the old man and the old woman revert to childish pastimes. Their lives have disintegrated so that past and present have only an idiotic significance. They embody the dilemma of the common man at the end of a fruitless life, remembering pointless anecdotes and unable to articulate the wisdom accumulated in nearly a century of life. The old man sadly justifies himself when he apologizes:

> I am not like other people, I have an ideal in life. I am perhaps gifted, as you say, I have some talent, but things aren't easy for me. I have served well in my capacity as general factotum, I have always been in command of the situation, honorably, that should be enough.

Although no more than a handyman, he believes that the world is ignorant of his potential, and he has hired the orator to explain his plan to save humanity. Like most people, the old man justifies his failures by claiming that the world has persecuted him and that powerful men have been in collusion to drive him into oblivion.

The audience is invited to laugh at the ludicrous behavior of the couple as they comfort each other at the end of life. Ionesco is not sentimental about people in the twilight of their years. He draws a picture of their mindlessness, senility, obsequiousness, and childish dependency. The old woman is the old man's wife and mother. He sits in her lap and laments being an orphan, argues about petty things, and enjoys her slavish agreement. The couple is contradictory about their family life, for within a few minutes they say that they are childless, that they have lost a son through cruelty or neglect, and that they have been devoted parents. Of course to Ionesco it does not matter whether they are parents or whether their children have been loyal or well-treated; their predicament and fate would remain the same; they are his prototypes of humanity.

Ionesco has attempted to write farce that is "the extreme exaggeration of parody. Humor . . . using the methods of burlesque . . . everything raised to paroxysm, where the source of tragedy lies. A theater of violence: violently comic, violently dramatic."

Slapstick is one of the principal means of evoking laughter in *The Chairs*. It is violent, grotesque, and absurd. Like a French theater usher, the old woman rushes back and forth trying to seat the audience, sell programs and refreshments, and maintain order. The couple barks violently to dramatize their abject and obsequious homage to the emperor. The abrupt double suicide is a brutal surprise that parodies death. Vivid slapstick and farce coupled with pantomime, conversations with the invisible guests, and the couples' difficulty in moving about on a stage that is crowded with nonexistent people brings this play into the tradition of the most primitive popular theater.

When the old woman behaves lasciviously toward the invisible photographer, she reveals her hidden personality. Her actions are tragic and pathetic, uncovering a woman's lost dreams of sexual happiness. She sidles up to the empty chair:

Simpering grotesquely . . . she shows her red stockings, raises her many petticoats, shows an underskirt full of holes, exposes her old breast; then, her hands on her hips, throws her head back, makes little erotic cries, projects her pelvis, her legs spread apart: she laughs like an old prostitute.

Aside from arousing the pity of the audience, this stage business is, in Ionesco's words, "violently comic, violently dramatic."

Although the audience hears boats, doorbells, trumpets, and sees lights announcing the emperor's arrival, the invisibility of the guests provokes conjecture about the "reality" of the *dramatis personae*. Are the old man and old woman, who have lived empty, meaningless lives, real? Or is the world that they have tried to please the only reality? In his stage direction, Ionesco stipulates that the orator must seem less real than the invisible characters. As the old man's alter ego, perhaps this inarticulate figure symbolizes the unreality of the visible characters.

The couple lives outside of time, space, and reality. Observing that darkness has fallen at six o'clock, the old man asks his wife: "Surely you remember, there was still daylight at nine o'clock in the evening, at ten o'clock, at midnight. . . . things have certainly changed." Prefiguring his suicide, this image of premature twilight symbolizes withdrawal from the world. Later, the old man remarks that Paris "has been extinguished, extinguished for four hundred thousand years."

The island the couple lives on has "water under the windows stretching as far as the horizon," and when the invisible visitors arrive, it becomes apparent that the two characters exist in limbo. They have never lived, or they have always lived, and their double suicide is a physical realization of their spiritual state. As they rush about in frantic and rhythmic circles, loading the stage with chairs and invisible visitors, they are overwhelmed by the material and social worlds that have defeated them.

The orator's romantically bohemian costume symbolizes the impossible yearnings of his clients, and his message, "Angelfood," is a pathetic indication of the old man's emptiness. Man cannot escape oblivion. His message is absurdity and death.

First performed in Paris in 1952 and often given in conjunction with *The Lesson* or *The Bald Soprano, The Chairs* has been frequently produced in nearly every country of the world.

The Author

Born in Slatina, Rumania, to a French mother and Rumanian father, Eugène Ionesco spent his early life in France; his first language was French. He returned to Bucharest in 1925 at the age of thirteen, completed his preliminary schooling, entered the university, and became a professor of French literature, an essayist, and a poet. In 1938, two years after his marriage, he returned to Paris, having won a grant to write a thesis on sin and death in modern French poetry. The rise of fascism in Rumania caused him to remain in Paris, where he worked in the production department of a publishing house.

It was not until he was thirty-six years old that Ionesco, in 1948, turned to the theater and wrote the one-act play *The Bald Soprano,* first produced in 1950. *The Lesson* (1951), *The Chairs* (1952), *Victims of Duty* (1953) are other one-act plays that brought him subsequent fame. In 1954, *Amedée, Or How to Get Rid of It* was the first in a series of full-length dramas, of which *Rhinoceros* (1960) became the most famous.

Exit the King (1962) drew mixed reactions from New York and Paris critics after its initial productions and revivals, but the play has nevertheless become the most popular of Ionesco's full-length "late" dramas. In the summer of 1969, Ionesco came to the United States to supervise the production of *Hunger and Thirst,* a piece he had been working on for some years. It is an ambitious inquiry into man's deepest fears and desires. In 1970, Ionesco was elected to the Académie Française, France's most prestigious academic institution.

Caligula

by

ALBERT CAMUS (1913–1960)

The Characters

Caligula—an intellectual and ultrarational young tyrant with a deep-seated philosophical concept of kingship and the world.

Young Scipion—a compassionate young poet who identifies with Caligula and stoically accepts his destruction by Caligula.

Cherea—a passionate advocate for humanity and truth who opposes Caligula and leads the conspiracy to assassinate him.

Helicon—a faithful servant who dies defending his master.

Caesonia—Caligula's pliant and devoted mistress, who allows the emperor to murder her.

The Story

Roman patricians gather in a palace chamber to discuss the strange absence of their emperor, Caligula. Since the death of Drusilla, his sister and mistress, Caligula has been roaming the countryside. When the patricians leave, Caligula timidly appears. He is no longer satisfied with his existence: "This world, such as it is made, is no longer bearable. Therefore I need the moon, or happiness, or immortality, some-

403

thing that might be crazy perhaps, but which is not of this world." Caligula wants to teach the world how to live.

When the royal attendant tells Caligula that the treasury needs attention, the emperor promulgates new legislation: All the patricians must bequeath their fortunes to the state and, when it is necessary, Caligula will have them arbitrarily executed. He justifies this act by declaring: "If the treasury is important, then human life isn't." To all censure, Caligula retorts that he will make the impossible possible, and he dismisses his two best friends, Cherea and Scipion, declaring that friendship is meaningless.

Alone with his former mistress Caesonia, Caligula confesses that he is suffering, but if the impossible exists, men will not die and they will be happy. Frenetically ringing a gong to assemble the entire palace, Caligula smashes his mirror, declaring: "No more memories," and asks Caesonia what remains in the world. She fearfully replies: "Caligula!"

Three years later, the patricians assemble at Cherea's home to plot Caligula's assassination. The tyrant has confiscated their possessions, killed the elder Scipion, stolen Octavius' wife, and murdered Lepidus' son. Cherea enters to support the conspiracy: Caligula must be eliminated because he is destroying the reason for existence by negating man and the world. Caligula suddenly appears with his assistants Helicon and Caesonia. During a banquet with the patricians, Caligula deliberately insults his guests by laughing at their grief. Later, he announces the closing of the granaries in order to starve his people. When he notices Mereia, an old patrician, secretly swallowing some liquid, Caligula accuses him of taking an antidote and violently murders the old man by ramming a flask down his throat. He is indifferent upon learning that the old man's flask contained medicine.

As the young Scipion waits to see Caligula, Helicon says that the emperor would not be unhappy to die. Alone with Caligula, young Scipion discusses the nature of his poetry. Caligula is able to anticipate every thought because "we love the same truths." He reveals his true nature, however, when he remarks that Scipion's verse "lacks blood," and the poet makes Caligula confess his immeasurable loneliness.

Later, Caligula dons female garb and pretends to be Venus. When Scipion accuses him of blaspheming, Caligula retorts: "There is only one means of equaling the gods: it's sufficient to be as cruel as they are."

In private, Helicon tries to warn Caligula of a plot against him and gives Caligula Cherea's list of conspirators. An old patrician warns him of the conspiracy, but Caligula again refuses to listen. Cherea enters and Caligula asks whether or not it is possible for two men to reveal their hearts to each other. Although Cherea agrees it is possible, he declares Caligula is incapable of such honesty. Nevertheless, they talk openly and Cherea confesses he wants to kill Caligula because he is destructive. One cannot live in a universe where the absurd is pushed to the limits of reality. But Caligula believes that all acts have the same value. Both men realize they have just done what Cherea declared impossible: spoken the truth to each other. But when Cherea asks for his punishment, Caligula realizes that the frankness was simulated. He destroys the list of conspirators and sends Cherea off, declaring: "Your emperor awaits his rest. It's his way to live and to be happy."

In a dimly lit room, Scipion tells Cherea he can no longer go along with the conspiracy; he understands Caligula too well to kill him. But Cherea says this is only another reason for Caligula's death; he has robbed a young poet of hope. The patricians assemble to watch Caligula dance. At a poetry competition, only Scipion successfully writes a poem about death. He bids Caligula goodbye, saying that he knows the emperor's choice.

Later, Caligula tells Caesonia that he is comfortable only with the dead, not the living. He says that love is not enough for him, because nothing, not even remorse, lasts. In a violent frenzy, Caligula strangles his mistress. Standing alone in front of his mirror, he accuses himself, acknowledges defeat, and awaits his assassins. Suddenly, Helicon calls out a warning. The conspirators rush in and stab Caligula. Laughing and gasping, Caligula screams: "I am still alive!"

Critical Opinion

When Albert Camus was asked to write a preface to the American edition of his plays in 1955, he contended that *Caligula* was not a philosophical drama. The only philosophy present, he insisted, is Caligula's assertion: "Men die and they are not happy." Nevertheless, if Camus's novel *The Stranger* (1942) can be said to be an existential discovery of freedom, *Caligula* presents an exploration of the abuse of freedom.

In his quest for the impossible, Caligula exercises total liberty by going beyond human morality and divine laws. The death of Drusilla, his mistress and sister, brings him to the realization that men are not happy. Caligula's longing for the moon symbolizes his search for the impossible: the ability to transcend the human condition. He muses that when the impossible can be achieved:

> all will be leveled, at last the impossible will be on earth, the moon will be in my hands, then, perhaps, I myself will be transformed and the world with me, then, at last men will not die and they will be happy.

Caligula rebels against fate through tyranny, murder, and the perversion of all values. While his strength lies in his absurd power to impose his will on the universe, Caligula's failure lies in his negation of the meaning of human life. The patricians he robs, humiliates, and murders are ultimately meaningless because Caligula's rebellion is essentially intellectual. Only Scipion and Cherea, who are not shackled by petty affairs, confront Caligula on his own level.

The four acts of the play follow Caligula's progression from his discovery of truth and power to his acceptance of death. By striving for the impossible, Caligula hopes to escape human limitations and teach others how to transcend the human condition. He, therefore, rejects his former values, morality, and sense of justice in order to carry reason to its absurd conclusion. If the treasury is important, human life is meaningless and thus expendable. In Act II, Caligula exercises his liberty through the humiliation, theft, and murder of his subjects. But despite these acts of violence, Caligula and his two opponents recognize that his true weapon is intelligence. In the third act, the tyrant debates the meaning of life with Cherea, who also seeks to live according to truth, but who refuses to negate life. Finally, in Act IV, Caligula seeks death, preparing for his own assassination.

In his preface, Camus wrote that *"Caligula* is the story of a superior suicide." The hero is an extremely sensitive, creative individual who attempts to change the universe through power by negating everything that previously existed. But in the course of his destructiveness, Caligula realizes that he cannot escape the human condition at the expense of others. From his earliest discovery of the new being in him, Caligula suffers a feeling vaguely similar to Roquentin's early discovery of nausea in Sartre's *Nausea*. He tells Caesonia:

> I feel unnamed beings stirring in me . . . I knew that one could be without hope, but I did not know what that word meant. Like everyone else I thought it was a disease of the soul. But no, it's the body which suffers. My skin hurts me, my chest, my limbs.

Later, when Scipion angrily recognizes Caligula's solitude, Caligula distinguishes between the poetic ecstasy of being alone with nature and silence and this solitude, populated by memories of the past, visions of the future, and ghosts of murdered people. When Scipion insists that all men have something that makes the continuation of life possible, Caligula replies that his consolation is scorn. He considers himself to be superior to the trivialities that occupy ordinary men and seeks only the impossible. Twice he had almost reached this goal. The moon seemed to come into his room, and he and Cherea were able to bare their thoughts to each other. But both instances were illusions. At dawn, the moonlight left and Cherea did not speak freely because he knew Caligula was aware of the conspiracy.

Caligula eventually recognizes that his quest for the impossible is futile: "Even if the dead trembled again under the sun, the murders couldn't go back underground." Although his objective is unworthy, Caligula pursues this logic to the end, even preparing for his own death. In his rebellion against fate, he is still the creator of his destiny. At the poetry competition, he announces that every day he has written about death: "I am the only artist Rome has known, the only one . . . who puts his thoughts in harmony with his acts." And choosing to ignore the conspiracy, he tells Cherea that he needs rest.

Waiting for his assassins, Caligula comes to terms with his failure. He tells Caesonia that love is not the answer to living; it is merely agreeing to grow old with someone; grief is equally futile, because it does not last. His freedom consists rather in the ability to transcend time, memory, and illusions by engineering events. Caligula has become the supreme murderer:

> This is happiness, this unbearable deliverance, this universal scorn, the blood, the hate surrounding me, this unequalled isolation of a man who all his life nurses the incomparable joy of the unpunished murderer.

But after strangling Caesonia, Caligula realizes: "Killing is not the answer." His search for the impossible has been fruitless. "I have not taken the right path, I've arrived at nothing. My liberty is not the right one." The only way to transcend human suffering is to die. Yet Caligula's death, like his life, is not a consolation, but a prolonged agony. Caligula dies, screaming: "I am still alive!"

In the course of Caligula's futile exercise of freedom, he confronts two hurdles: Cherea and young Scipion. Cherea recognizes the true menace Caligula presents. Caligula's limitless use of power goes beyond human morality to negate man and the world. He tells the conspirators: "To lose your life is nothing and I would have this courage when it's necessary. But to see the sense of life dissipated, to see our reason for living disappear, that is what is unbearable. One can't live without a reason." Like Caligula, Cherea wants to live according to truth, but unlike his emperor, he will not allow logic to destroy humanity. Confronted by Caligula in Act III, he openly says Caligula must be destroyed because man cannot live and be happy if he pursues the absurd. Cherea denounces Caligula, but admits his undeniable influence: "He forces thought. He forces everyone to think. Insecurity is what makes people think." Cherea understands Caligula, but refuses to accept his morality. Unlike Scipion, who is too compassionate, Cherea can act.

Young Scipion confronts Caligula twice, first to discover an unknown (the poetic side of Caligula's soul), and then to predict the reason for Caligula's death wish. In Act II, Caligula anticipates Scipion's thoughts until both young men simultaneously create a lyrical paean to nature. When Caligula explains their mutual vision ("Perhaps because we love the same truths"), Scipion is ready to embrace his father's murderer with love. Yet Caligula cannot accept the old morality in which nature and art are benevolent. "You are pure in goodness," he tells Scipion, "like I am pure in evil." In order to prove his malevolence, Caligula must criticize Scipion's poetry for lacking blood.

Scipion later tells Cherea that he cannot kill Caligula because he understands him. His poem on death is an expression of this compassion. For Scipion, as for Caligula, death is the only possible happiness, "a delirium without hope." Scipion bids Caligula farewell because he realizes Caligula has already looked to death as the only way of attaining peace. Although Scipion does not defeat Caligula, like Cherea he has partially vanquished him by showing Caligula that he cannot destroy everything without destroying himself.

Helicon and Caesonia think they understand Caligula, but unlike Cherea and Scipion, they are not moved by reason. Both act merely on feeling, and encourage Caligula's absurd schemes. A freed slave, Helicon is forever grateful and devoted to his liberator. Caesonia, although once rejected as a mistress, loves Caligula so completely that she gives up her life for him.

Written in 1938, *Caligula* precedes Camus's and Sartre's Existentialist works. Like later Existentialist heroes, Caligula discovers the absurdity of the universe ("Men die and they are not happy"), but unlike Meursault (*The Stranger,* 1942) or Orestes (Sartre, *The Flies,* 1944), Caligula misuses freedom and does not accept the responsibility that must accompany the exercise of liberty. Rather than helping mankind, he destroys the meaning of human existence. Man does not learn to transcend his condition merely by recognizing human absurdity. Caligula is destroyed by his knowledge of absurdity and his failure to act responsibly. Death for Caligula is not a supreme triumph and exaltation of individual freedom, as it is for Meursault. Caligula's death is merely an escape from failure and a hope for solace.

Camus wrote *Caligula* in Algiers when he was twenty-five, hoping to use the drama for his own theater group. But

Caligula was not performed until 1945, at the Théâtre-Hébertot in Paris, with Gérard Philippe in the title role.

Subsequent productions have not been well received. To many critics, Camus's dramas are little more than intellectual equations into which no life has been breathed, and it is often said that the weaknesses of Camus's plays bring into relief the strengths of his novels. *The Stranger* and *The Plague* are such superior examples of the art of narration that we do not feel we are reading pamphlets of ideas, while *Caligula* is the work of a man superbly endowed to be almost anything except a craftsman of theater; it reveals too many discrepancies between style and theme. To Kenneth Tynan, it seems "a bad great play." Enjoying it remains a matter of taste.

The Author

Born to European parents in Algeria on November 7, 1913, Albert Camus struggled with poverty and grew up among the working class of Algiers. Camus's father died when he was an infant, and he was brought up by his mother and grandparents. As a youth, Camus wandered the shores of the Mediterranean, close to the Arab population and the sun, sand, and sea that were to play so large a role in his works.

Although Camus's early teachers were impressed by his intelligence and sensitivity, he was prevented by tuberculosis in 1930 from pursuing a vigorous physical or scholastic life. A brief flirtation with communism ended in 1935; his marriage in 1933 had lasted only one year. Always interested in the theater, he organized an amateur group that gained some prominence in Algeria.

By 1937, Camus had begun to publish: *The Two Sides of the Coin* (1937), *Nuptials* (1938), and *Caligula* (written in 1938, performed in 1945), appeared while he was doing newspaper work. Journalism intensified Camus's interest in political action, and from 1939 to 1941 he worked on a newspaper in Paris.

After two years in Paris, Camus remarried and returned to Algeria, where he wrote for the underground newspaper *Combat* and created his novel *The Stranger* (1942) and his philosophical essay, *The Myth of Sisyphus* (1942). In Paris again, Camus became engaged in dangerous underground activities against the German Occupation and received the Medal of Liberation in 1944.

Algeria's struggle for independence from France is reflected in *The Plague* (1947) and *The Rebel* (1951) and his other writings of the period. Camus's works for the theater include *The Misunderstanding* (1944), *State of Siege* (1948), and *The Just Assassins* (1949).

In 1957, Camus received the Nobel Prize for Literature, and three years later he died in an automobile accident.

Appendix

50 European Plays, arranged chronologically

MANDRAGOLA   1524
LE CID   1637
TARTUFFE   1664
THE MISANTHROPE   1666
THE MISER   1668
THE BOURGEOIS GENTLEMAN   1670
PHÈDRE   1677
MARY STUART   1800
FAUST   1831
THE INSPECTOR GENERAL   1836
WOYZECK   1837
A MONTH IN THE COUNTRY   1854
PEER GYNT   1867
GHOSTS   1881
THE POWER OF DARKNESS   1886
THE FATHER   1887
MISS JULIE   1888
HEDDA GABLER   1890
THE WEAVERS   1891
EARTH SPIRIT   1894
KING UBU   1896
THE SEA GULL   1896
LA RONDE   1897
CYRANO DE BERGERAC   1897
THE THREE SISTERS   1901
THE LOWER DEPTHS   1902
THE CHERRY ORCHARD   1904
LILIOM   1909
HE WHO GETS SLAPPED   1915
R.U.R.   1920

SIX CHARACTERS IN SEARCH
OF AN AUTHOR   1921
HENRY IV   1922
PANTAGLEIZE   1929
BLOOD WEDDING   1933
THE TROJAN WAR
WILL NOT TAKE PLACE   1935
CALIGULA   1938
MOTHER COURAGE AND HER CHILDREN   1939
ANTIGONE   1944
NO EXIT   1944
CORRUPTION IN THE PALACE OF JUSTICE   1944
THE MADWOMAN OF CHAILLOT   1944
THE CAUCASIAN CHALK CIRCLE   1944
THE MAIDS   1947
THE BALD SOPRANO   1950
THE CHAIRS   1952
WAITING FOR GODOT   1953
THE BALCONY   1956
THE BLACKS   1958
BECKET   1958
HAPPY DAYS   1961

Recommended Bibliography

Bentley, Eric. *The Playwright as Thinker*. New York: Reynal and Hitchcock, 1946.

Brustein, Robert. *The Theatre of Revolt*. Boston: Little, Brown, and Co., 1964.

Esslin, Martin. *The Theatre of the Absurd*. Garden City, N.Y.: Doubleday Anchor, rev. ed., 1969.

Fergusson, Francis. *The Idea of the Theater*. Garden City, N.Y.: Doubleday Anchor, 1953.

Fernandez, Ramon. *Molière: The Man Seen Through the Plays*. Translated by Wilson Follet. New York: Hill and Wang, 1958.

Fowlie, Wallace. *Dionysus: A Guide to Contemporary French Theatre*. New York: Meridian Books, 1960.

Garten, H. F. *Modern German Drama*. New York: Grove Press, 1962.

Gassner, John. *Masters of the Drama*. New York: Dover Publications, 1954.

Grossvogel, David I. *Twentieth Century French Drama*. New York: Columbia University Press, 1961.

Guicharnaud, Jacques. *Modern French Theatre from Giraudoux to Beckett*. New Haven: Yale University Press, 1961.

Meyer, Michael. *Ibsen: A Biography*. Garden City, N.Y.: Doubleday Anchor, 1971.

Moore, W. G. *Molière: A New Criticism*. Garden City, N.Y.: Doubleday Anchor, 1962.

Mortensen, Brita M. E. and Bryan W. Downs. *Strindberg: An Introduction to His Life and Work*. Cambridge, England: University of Cambridge Press, 1965.

Peacock, Ronald. *The Poet in the Theatre*. New York: Hill and Wang, 1960.

Simmons, Ernest. *Chekhov: A Biography*. London: Jonathan Cape, 1963.

Slonim, Marc. *Russian Theater: From the Empire to the Soviet.* New York: Collier, 1962.

Taylor, John Russell. *The Penguin Dictionary of the Theatre.* London: Penguin, 1966.

Wellwarth, George E. *The Theater of Protest and Paradox.* New York: New York University Press, 1964.

Index